HELPING
THE
SEXUALLY OPPRESSED

HELPING
THE
SEXUALLY OPPRESSED

Harvey L. Gochros
Jean S. Gochros
Joel Fischer

EDITORS

PRENTICE-HALL, INC., *Englewood Cliffs, New Jersey 07632*

Library of Congress Cataloging-in-Publication Data
Main entry under title:

Helping the sexually oppressed.

Includes bibliographies and index.
1. Discrimination—United States. 2. Sex discrimination—United States. 3. Sexual harassment. 4. Social
service—United States. I. Gochros, Harvey L.
II. Gochros, Jean S. III. Fischer, Joel.
HN57.H46   1986   305.3   85-16687
ISBN 0-13-386129-5

Editorial/production supervision: *Edith Riker*
Cover design: *Lundgren Graphics Ltd.*
Manufacturing buyer: *John Hall*

Printed in the United States of America

10 9 8 7 6 5 4 3 2

ISBN   0-13-386129-5   01

Prentice-Hall International (UK) Limited, *London*
Prentice-Hall of Australia Pty. Limited, *Sydney*
Prentice-Hall Canada Inc., *Toronto*
Prentice-Hall Hispanoamericana, S.A., *Mexico*
Prentice-Hall of India Private Limited, *New Delhi*
Prentice-Hall of Japan, Inc., *Tokyo*
Prentice-Hall of Southeast Asia Pte. Ltd., *Singapore*
Editora Prentice-Hall do Brasil, Ltda., *Rio de Janeiro*
Whitehall Books Limited, *Wellington, New Zealand*

We have found it impossible to give our support to conventional morality or to approve highly of the means by which society attempts to arrange the practical problems of sexuality in life. We can demonstrate with ease that what the world calls its code of morals demands more sacrifice than it is worth, and that its behavior is neither dictated by honesty nor instituted with wisdom.

SIGMUND FREUD
A General Introduction to Psychoanalysis
(1920, pp. 376–377)

This book is dedicated to
the sexually oppressed who assert their humanness,
and to those who help them do so.

CONTENTS

CONTRIBUTORS

Linda Perlin Alperstein, LCSW
Private Practice
Formerly, Co-Director of Clinical
    Training, Human Sexuality Program,
    University of California, San Francisco

Raymond M. Berger, PhD
Associate Professor
University of Illinois
School of Social Work
Urbana, Illinois

Janne Dooley, MSW, CSW
Private Practice
West Babylon, New York

Joel Fischer, DSW
Professor
University of Hawaii
School of Social Work
Honolulu, Hawaii

Charles A. Glisson, PhD
Associate Professor
University of Hawaii
School of Social Work
Honolulu, Hawaii

Harvey L. Gochros, DSW
Professor
University of Hawaii
School of Social Work
Honolulu, Hawaii

Jean S. Gochros, PhD
Private Practice
Honolulu, Hawaii

Diane F. Harrison, PhD
Associate Professor
Florida State University
School of Social Work
Tallahassee, Florida

Elaine Hatfield, PhD
Professor
University of Hawaii
Department of Psychology
Honolulu, Hawaii

Lois Jaffee, MSW
Formerly Associate Professor
University of Pittsburgh
Graduate School of Social Work
Pittsburgh, Pennsylvania

James J. Kelly, PhD
Associate Professor
California State University, Long Beach
Department of Social Work
Consultant, Department of Psychiatry,
   UCLA School of Medicine
   and Sepulveda Veterans' Hospital

Winifred Kempton, MSS
Consultant for Education and Training
Planned Parenthood of Southeastern
   Pennsylvania
Private Practice
Philadelphia, Pennsylvania

Susan E. Knight, LCSW
Private Practice
Formerly Director of Sex and Disability
   Unit,
University of California, San Francisco

H. Lawrence Lister, DSW
Associate Professor
University of Hawaii
School of Social Work
Honolulu, Hawaii

Noreen Mokuau, PhD
Assistant Professor
University of Hawaii
School of Social Work
Honolulu, Hawaii

Susan Rice, DSW
Assistant Professor
Michigan State University
School of Social Work
East Lansing, Michigan

Wendell Ricketts
MSW Student
University of Hawaii
School of Social Work
Honolulu, Hawaii

Virginia M. Satir, MSW
Consultant, Author, Lecturer
Anterra, Inc.
Menlo Park, California

LeRoy G. Schultz
Professor
West Virginia University
School of Social Work
Morgantown, West Virginia

Arthur Schwartz, PhD
Professor
University of Maryland
School of Social Work and Community
   Planning
Baltimore, Maryland

PREFACE

"Sexual oppression." The term conjures up myriad images for the helping professional: the rape victim who encounters insensitive law enforcement and rejection from her family, the resident of the mental hospital who is denied any outlet for his sexuality, the experienced worker who loses out on promotions and raises because of her gender, the gay man and the lesbian who are prevented from renting an apartment because of their sexual orientation, the child who is reprimanded for exploring his or her sexuality but given none of the information he or she hungers for, the physically disabled person who is given help in nearly all aspects of life *except* the sexual, the mentally disabled person whose sexual desires are viewed with horror, and socioeconomic populations whose sexual needs are either overlooked or suppressed by those who have power over them.

Sexual oppression can take many forms. People may be deprived of their right to give and receive sexual satisfaction in accordance with their needs and capabilities. Their general well-being may be unjustly diminished because of their gender, sexual orientation, or lifestyle. People in the helping professions may ignore the sexual needs and concerns of those they work with. In such situations, whether the oppression is inadvertent or deliberate, we believe that those people are indeed "sexually oppressed."

This book is our attempt to explore the issues involved in sexual oppression and, even more importantly, to offer specific ideas about how professional helpers—and even friends and relatives—might go about being helpful.

Our concern about the problems of those populations we collectively refer to as the *sexually oppressed* goes back to the late 1960s. We noted the profound effect that the so-called "sexual revolution" was having on the lives of many Americans by providing them with more sexual options. At the same time we were also aware that there were considerable disparities in the degree to which people belonging to such groups as the aged, disabled, and the homosexually oriented were able to share in the benefits of that "revolution." Their needs were often still being either ignored or suppressed by the general public and even by many professional helpers.

We realized, of course, that these groups were not equally oppressed and that individuals within such groups encountered varying degrees of oppression. Indeed, there were many members of such groups who did not *feel* oppressed at all. Still it seemed to us that, to varying degrees, many people had been bypassed in the general progress toward greater sexual choices.

We also came to realize that the oppression of diverse populations was not a random process but was clearly related to social attitudes about the perceived purposes of sex. Those people whose attributes and sexual behaviors approximated those necessary to create a socially approved pregnancy were recognized as legitimate sexual beings. Their sexual behaviors were sanctioned by significant social institutions, such as the law, the church, and the helping professions. We decided to call these people the *sexual elite.*

The sexual elite are certainly not without their problems. Our reproductive bias limits not only who may engage in sexual behavior but also suggests what gender-assigned roles and sexual behaviors are acceptable. Thus the elite (especially the men) are taught that sexuality is essentially equivalent to "doing it." "It" involves getting a willing partner, achieving and maintaining an erection, inserting it into her vagina, and, after an appropriate interval, ejaculating. That *is* what it takes to create a pregnancy. Thus, if one is lucky enough to be in the elite and to have sanctioned sexual opportunities, one had better want "it" and be good at "it."

At a relatively young age the adolescent is set on the quest of seeking "it" and doing "it." Even in marriage, sex is generally equated with "it." Alternatives to "it" (for example, stroking, fondling, oral or manual contact, self-stimulation, and so on) are often seen as either cumbersome, effete, or sick, and, at best, merely a prelude ("foreplay") to the "real thing." Masturbation, as either a supplement or an alternative to intercourse, still provokes anxiety among many of the elite. It clearly violates the reproductive bias in that one can neither become nor make anyone else become pregnant through masturbation. And many teenagers have been led to believe that while intercourse without marriage may sometimes be acceptable, contraception, which involves "premeditated sex," isn't. Such a paradox can be hazardous.

Even for those we call the sexual elite, then, the reproductive bias limits the range of potential sexual expressions and joys and may even interfere with some of the responsible behaviors that society expects to accompany sexual behavior.

There are, however, large numbers of people whose sexual behavior, for one reason or another, cannot lead to a socially approved pregnancy. At best, their needs, therefore, have been ignored or, at worst, deliberately suppressed.

To a greater or lesser degree we (that is, significant segments of society) have considered it unlikely, undesirable, or impossible for members of these diverse groups to enjoy their sexuality. Such groups include, among others, adolescents, whose biological sexual urges are perhaps strongest, and whose range of acceptable sexual behaviors are circumscribed but increasingly vague; the old, who are exhorted to "act their age," which means to be sexless; the imprisoned, who are expected to relinquish their sexuality as a punishment for their crimes; the homosexually oriented, who cannot make each other pregnant and who therefore are seen as having no "healthy" or "moral" right to enjoy each others' bodies; the disabled, whose physical condition may prevent them from assuming the traditional roles considered essential for being sexual; the developmentally disabled, who go through life supposedly not smart enough to qualify for intimate relationships; unmarried adults whose sexual fulfillment is often illusive despite the *Playboy* and *Playgirl* image of the happy swinger; women, who have "come a long way" but still suffer from sexism and sexual ambivalence; and the poor, who have everything against them as far as sex goes, from poor nutrition to crowded housing to restrictive welfare laws.

In 1972, one of the present authors published an article and coined the phrase "the sexually oppressed" to describe the situation of these people.[1] Over the next few years, we became increasingly concerned that workshops, classes, and books for professional helpers on the subject of human sexuality often gave only minimal attention, if any, to the unique needs, problems, and concerns of sexually oppressed groups. Perhaps more important, they offered no useful direction for professional helpers or others who wanted to work with these populations.

At the same time, we began to place more and more emphasis on these groups in our own practice and teaching of professional helpers, despite the fact that many of our students seemed much more interested in the sexuality of healthy, intelligent, verbal, attractive, heterosexual, pair-bonded young adults. We noted with pleasure that students exposed to the concerns of the often neglected groups showed increasing interest, concern, and commitment to work with them.

On the other hand, however, we noted that many practitioners still went along with the restrictions on the sexual expression of the sexually oppressed. Those working with the aged, the homosexual, the disabled, the adolescent, and so on rarely perceived the legitimacy of their sexual needs and wishes or assertively supported them. All too often the sex-related needs of such groups were considered frivolous luxuries or even as psychopathology to be suppressed or "cured."

As we ourselves continued to learn more about the problems faced by sexually oppressed groups, we wanted to reach more people. As a result, two of the present authors published a book entitled *The Sexually Oppressed*,[2] dealing with the sources of sexual oppression and the broad range of problems encountered by the sexually oppressed. We also included what we considered to be some innovative interventive strategies being developed around the country to help these groups as well as some suggestions for further efforts.

Much has happened since then. American society has slowly and unevenly accepted the idea that reproduction and sexual expression need not necessarily be bound together, and that they may be treated, accepted, and enjoyed separately. Thus, the social factors which contributed to sexual oppression have

---

[1]H. Gochros, "The sexually oppressed." *Social Work*, 1972, *17*(2), 16–23.
[2]H. Gochros and J. Gochros (eds.). *The Sexually Oppressed*. New York: Association Press, 1977.

somewhat diminished (despite some resurgence recently) and the needs and concerns of sexually oppressed people are better understood and better accepted by the general public as well as by the helping professions.

At the same time, new and more effective interventive strategies have emerged to back up the growing recognition that the helping professions have responsibilities in this area that cannot be ignored.

We also began to reevaluate some of our ideas about sexual oppression. We believe that there are two major categories into which sexual oppression falls. The first is oppression directed at people whose characteristics are incompatible with those associated with reproductive potential; their sexual options are severely limited. The aged, the disabled, and children, among others, would fall into this category.

The second category is comprised of those whose sexual characteristics such as gender or erotic orientation result in limitations on their *nonsexual* options, such as social and vocational opportunities and even civil rights. Women and homosexuals would be included in this category.

Given all the ramifications of sexual oppression, one might argue that *everyone*—women and men, gays and straights, young and old—is, in various degrees, sexually oppressed. We subscribe to that argument. Holding such a global view of sexual oppression, however, presents us with some apparent contradictions. If *everybody* is oppressed to some extent, does the term "the sexually oppressed" become meaningless? If everybody is oppressed, why focus on particular groups? How can we include people who do not consider themselves oppressed?

We would suggest the following responses: First, one can *be* oppressed without being aware of either the degree or the nature of one's oppression. Many individuals within historically oppressed groups—slaves, child laborers, non-unionized workers—did not recognize their oppression. One of the major tasks of the initiators in any civil rights movement, for example, is consciousness raising.

Second, just as "some people are more equal than others," so some people and groups are more oppressed than others.

Third, we are not dealing with separate, discrete, mutually exclusive categories. Any given group contains many individuals who also fit one or more other categories of sexual oppression (for example, black widows, aging gays, disabled women). One set of oppressive factors interacts with others, forming complex networks and interrelationships between individuals, groups, and social institutions.

With these observations in mind, the three editors of this book decided to produce a new work which could both describe and illuminate the categories of sexual oppression and show how they affect specific groups.

We were also eager to do more than just raise conceptual issues; we saw a need to transfer general knowledge into everyday practice. Hence we decided to emphasize emerging effective interventive strategies on behalf of sexually oppressed groups in general, with specific approaches to the unique problems of certain specific sexually oppressed groups.

We very much regret that space did not permit our including all the oppressed groups we would have liked to include. There can be no question, for example, that transsexuals are oppressed or that the blind have significant problems to overcome in order to achieve a rewarding sex life. However, the groups we have selected for inclusion—some of the largest and most oppressed—represent the problems encountered by all sexually oppressed groups.

We also recognize that in the ambitious attempt to suggest practical interventions within the framework of broad issues, there will be times when the discussion may seem superficial. Nevertheless, by providing an overview of problems and some suggestions for change, it is our hope that this book will be useful to helping professionals in such disciplines as social work, clergy, medicine, law, psychology, psychiatry, and education.

We further hope that this book may be of interest and help to sexually oppressed individuals, their families and friends, and to the general public as well.

Selecting our contributors was only slightly less difficult than selecting our topics. We limited ourselves to original material written especially for this book by knowledgeable people, those who have had first-hand experience in working with, understanding, and helping the populations about whom they write.

Wherever possible, we chose authors who were themselves members of these groups and who might thus be able to speak from personal experience. Over the years we have had the opportunity to meet many people who have taken the initiative to develop clinical, community-service, and educational programs for particular oppressed groups. We have been fortunate in being able to convince many of them to join us in producing this book.

We have made only two exceptions to our rule of including only newly written material for this book. The late Lois Jaffe's chapter on the terminally ill patient was, we believe, a unique contribution to our previous book, *The Sexually Oppressed*. We are including it in this work by the kind permission of Lois's husband. We are also reprinting Virginia Satir's epilogue "The Fable of the Restored Left Arm" from an earlier work by one of the authors. Although it was written a decade ago, it still carries a valid message today. It seemed an appropriate way to end this book.

The reader will also note that most of our contributors, like the editors, are social workers. This is not by accident. The social work profession has long concerned itself with problems of oppression in general, and sexual oppression (although not always defined in these terms) in particular. Experts in many professional disciplines share this concern and are quite knowledgeable. We feel, however, that social workers bring a perspective to social problems that combines conviction about the dignity and worth of all people, an understanding and appreciation of psychological, cultural, and socioeconomic influences, and an array of effective interventive strategies on a number of levels.

Finally, given the concerns that many people share in the "backlash" period of the so-called sexual revolution, a few comments about our own values would seem in order. We believe—and this belief will be evident throughout the book—that society must go beyond the reproductive bias. The assumptions that were held about sexuality and male-female roles and relationships were understandable and even necessary under different social and economic situations. Today, however, our society is more complex and its needs are different. Our individual problems are likewise more complex, yet there are now more solutions to those problems. The simplistic solutions of yesteryear no longer suffice.

This belief must not be misinterpreted as willingness to change values to suit one's convenience (an attitude that many people *incorrectly* call "situation ethics"), a lack of regard for the institutions of marriage and family, or a suggestion that "anything goes as long as it feels good and doesn't hurt." Quite the contrary. Our values insist on respect for the integrity and worth of the individual, responsibility for one's actions, the need to use one's sexuality to bring happiness rather than unhappiness. We see committed relationships, marriage and family, or at least the commitments that those institutions seek to provide, as sound options for bringing into harmony the satisfaction of individual and societal needs.

We also believe, however, that, to remain true to those values, the ways in which they are translated into attitudes, policies, laws, and behaviors must be continually reevaluated in the light of new knowledge, changing socioeconomic realities, and differences in individual needs, capabilities, and spiritual beliefs.

ACKNOWLEDGMENTS

We thank all our contributors for the generous gifts of their time, effort, experience, and competence to this project. We also thank our research assistants, David Wynde and Daryl Carson, for their help. And we thank Wendell Ricketts for once again tidying up our grammar, syntax, punctuation, and thinking.

ORGANIZATION OF THE BOOK

This book is divided into two parts. Part I presents an overview of our perspective on human sexuality and sexual oppression. Chapter 1 examines the social control of sexual expression and the relationship between various mechanisms of social control and the development of sexual oppression. Chapter 2 describes the components of sexual expression. We present our view that the understanding of sexuality involves more than the science and art of intercourse. Rather it involves a complex set of interacting attitudes, behaviors, and feelings. We describe the core components of sexual expression and suggest that we must appreciate the role of each of these components in our sexual lives if we want to understand and be helpful to members of sexually oppressed populations.

The last two chapters of Part I offer interventive strategies that human service practitioners will find useful in working with the sexually oppressed and those people significant in their environment. It is these specific interventive strategies and techniques that distinguish professional helpers from well-intentioned observers. Chapter 3 presents some basic counseling strategies, ways of helping people cope effectively with their sexual needs in the context of their social environment. It also suggests ways in which families may be affected by sexual oppression, and methods of helping such families.

Chapter 4 describes a number of strategies that practitioners can use to change large, social systems within which the sexually oppressed live. In many situations it is these systems which may be responsible for creating the stress and stigma experienced by members of the sexually oppressed. Too often, strategies for changing social environments—organizations, agency and institutional policies, public attitudes—are overlooked by professional helpers. It is our intention to highlight the importance of such interventions.

Part II of this book examines a number of specific oppressed groups and ways of helping them deal with a range of problems typically encountered in their lives. We recognize that there are many obvious similarities in the problems encountered by various oppressed groups, as well as in the approaches to these problems. All suffer from social stigma, a sense of powerlessness, social controls limiting their options, and often lack of information about their particular sexuality. On the other hand, there are many differences among the sexually oppressed groups. Likewise, there are obviously many differences in the life experiences, characteristics, goals, and concerns of the individuals within each group. It is our intention both to augment the limited literature on each of the groups we have selected and to offer specific methods which may be applied across the board in all situations of sexual oppression.

Each chapter in Part II addresses the nature of sexual oppression commonly encountered by a particular sexually oppressed population and how that oppression is typically manifested, and then describes a range of interventive strategies.

The book concludes with a brief fable that reflects our ideas and values about sexual oppression.

It is our hope, and the hope of all the contributors to the book, that the ideas we have presented will heighten the reader's awareness about the common problems and concerns of the sexually oppressed. We also hope that the suggestions and interventive strategies described here will provide a framework that practitioners can use to overcome some of the problems associated with sexual oppression.

It is also our hope that this book will help the reader see people as total human beings rather than as walking sets of symptoms of either biological, psychological, or societal pathology. And that it will call attention to sex-related problems, raise questions, suggest effective interventions, and stimulate further comment and research. If it does that, then perhaps it will serve as another step toward reducing sexual oppression and creating a climate in which people with diverse backgrounds, characteristics, and needs can find greater personal fulfillment.

Honolulu, Hawaii
February 12, 1985

Harvey L. Gochros
Jean Schaar Gochros
Joel Fischer

HELPING
THE
SEXUALLY OPPRESSED

PART I
A Perspective on Human Sexuality and Sexual Oppression

CHAPTER

1

SOCIAL CONTROL AND THE SEXUALLY OPPRESSED

People are disturbed not by things, but by the views they take of them.

Epictetus. A.D. 60

The understanding of sex is essentially the understanding of sexual attitudes. Most of the sex-related problems that confront professional helpers are products of the ideas people have about the feelings, thoughts, and behaviors that tend to be classified as "sexual." Whether the reaction of an individual to the brief moment during which he or she fantasizes a sexual activity, or the "climate of opinion" about the purposes of sexuality shared by generations of people, it is the *beliefs* we have about sex that determine the way people play out their roles as sexual beings. An awareness of the power of sexual attitudes and an acceptance of a range of viable sexual belief systems are the basic ingredients for being helpful with people experiencing sexual problems.

An understanding of the ways in which societies exercise control over sexual expression, as well as the reasons for this control, is a prerequisite for appreciating the stresses on those populations whose sexuality is either ignored or explicitly oppressed. The purpose of this book is to explore the problems of these people—the sexually oppressed—and to offer specific suggestions for ways in which helping professionals can reduce oppression and can enhance the positive expression of sexuality. We start this exploration by discussing the ways in which control over sexuality is exercised.

WHO CONTROLS SEX?

To illustrate these points, one of the authors usually begins his lectures with a "warning" to his listeners. Perhaps this book should begin with a similar caveat: *Warning: The people*

1

who have selected and organized the material for this book are white, middle-aged, well-educated, comparatively comfortable financially, and two also are male.

Each of these attributes—being white, middle-aged, male, well-educated and financially comfortable—can have a powerful influence on how one views sexual phenomena. Let's consider a few examples:

White. Every culture develops concepts of acceptable sexual behavior. Those values are communicated throughout the culture by way of custom, folk tales, laws, and even language. Concepts about relationships also vary from culture to culture. At the start of a recent class on intimacy taught by one of the authors, he asked his students to think about what the word "intimacy" conjured up in their imagination. The class was about evenly divided between students of European ancestry on one hand and students of Polynesian or Asian ancestry on the other. When the students reported on their fantasies about intimacy, the "whites" described basically romantic fantasies about themselves being alone and in love with a real or ideal partner. The Polynesian and Japanese students, however, reported very different scenes in which they were with large groups of close friends and family. Their primary partners, real or fantasied, might be there, but the emphasis was placed on the joy of being close to a large group of people who were important to them.

Another classroom example illustrates the sometimes very subtle power of culture on sexual values, attitudes, and beliefs. The class was discussing sexual fantasies. Several of the participants in the discussion were married women. Another student, an unmarried woman from Thailand, gently interrupted the discussion and asked, "Do you mean that in your country women sometimes think about private things with men besides their husbands?" Some of the other women giggled and one replied that this was known to happen. The woman from Thailand was shocked and replied "Ohhh, in my country they would not allow that!"

Cultural differences are not limited, of course, to other countries. Within the United States there are many divergent cultural views on what is good and bad in sex. There are numerous ethnic, religious, and socioeconomic subgroup differences among "whites," each subscribing to somewhat different viewpoints on what is desirable sexual behavior.

Middle-aged. As one ages there are not only changes in sexual anatomy and physiology, but in sexual attitudes as well (see our chapter on aging). Someone once said that in politics, at least, if you are not a radical in your twenties you have no guts, but if you are not a conservative in your thirties you have no brains. A common reaction of middle-aged adults, for example, is to enforce the same strict sexual rules on their teenagers that they rebelled against when they were teenagers.

Some of the common physiological changes that occur in adulthood can affect the way in which people evaluate sexual behavior. Men's attitudes toward orgasm often go through a subtle evolution. When men are young, orgasms tend to be experienced as an almost blinding light at the end of every sexual tunnel. Sexual acts, whether solitary or with a partner, are often experienced as just a vehicle for "getting their rocks off." The major purpose of the activity is to relieve a powerful preorgasmic buildup of tension. As the man grows older, the light does not go out—indeed the potential for orgasm remains throughout a man's life—but the relative role of the orgasm in the complex of sexual experiences diminishes. As the light decreases in intensity, other pleasures and aspects of the sexual experience, tactile and emotional, become more "visible." Perhaps that is why some of the greatest writers of romantic poetry and literature are older men.

Women, too, go through changes regarding orgasm. As women grow older they are more likely to experience orgasms in sexual activities. The reasons may not be physiological in origin but perhaps a response to a decrease in inhibitions that allows them to attend more to their sexual responses.

Changes in orgasmic response are just one aspect of how age can affect sexual attitudes. Obviously, age also reveals during what era in a culture's sexual evolution a particular individual went through childhood and adolescence, and absorbed cultural attitudes that tend to stay with him or her for life.

Male. Men are different from women. Not opposite (as the term "opposite sex" implies), but different. The primary male sexual organs are external and easily visible, the primary sexual organs of women are not as visible. Men tend to be bigger and physically stronger than women. Thus, they are less vulnerable to physical attack. Few men, other than prisoners, have been raped, and few worry about that possibility. Men do not get pregnant, deliver babies, or nurse them. Many women don't either, of course, but the potential for as well as the social expectations about these female capabilities often affect how women see themselves, and how they are perceived by many men.

All these differences have implications for the contrasting ways in which men and women may approach certain significant sex-related phenomena. Perhaps the greatest difference in this area has been that, historically, men have had the power to impose their sexual views on women. Using the power of labeling, men have invented such terms as "frigid," "nymphomania," and "promiscuity" to maintain female sexual responses within the bounds that they found acceptable. Populations that have more power generally define the parameters of "normalcy" for populations that have less power.

Relative affluence. Wealth tends to spawn a "Joy of Sex" orientation to sex. With wealth there is leisure time, and the search for plea-

sure. Our relatively affluent middle class has evolved a perception of sex that emphasizes the need to savor it slowly and creatively in all its glorious flavors.

To many of the less affluent, this approach is ludicrous. Sex to them is "no big thing"—just one more human activity to be enjoyed but not overevaluated. How the less affluent see the elaborate advice of many sex educators and therapists might be illustrated in the following analogy. It would be like seeing someone enter a MacDonald's restaurant, spread out a linen tablecloth, set the table with fine china, crystal, and flatware, light a candle, and dine leisurely on their Big Mac, enhanced by assorted condiments and spices and a bottle of Pouilly Fuissé. Thus even our attitudes about how elaborate an experience a sexual activity should be are a product of our circumstances and accumulated learning experiences.

Wealth also allows for other sexual "luxuries." Our treasured privacy is often only possible when one can afford it. Furthermore, good nutrition and effective medical care facilitate a satisfying sex life, and both in our country generally require money.

Well-educated. Well-educated people tend to conceptualize human interactions. Common human behaviors are often pseudo-scientifically labeled and perceived as having several levels of meanings. This is especially true in sex.

Well-educated people tend to think about and analyze sexual transactions, whether in their own lives or those of others. Zorba the Greek chastised his scholarly young English friend: "You think too much. *That* is your trouble. Clever people and grocers, they weigh everything!" Even Freud admonished us all with his comment that "sometimes a cigar is just a cigar."

This is not to say that less educated people are free of sexual concerns. We know this is not true. They just don't seem to spend their time searching for their answers in the realm of abstractions. Perhaps it is only the affluent and well-educated who have the time, privacy, and sense of self-importance to expect that sex can and should be a very special, exhilarating experience, worthy of courses, self-enhancement workshops, and how-to-do-it books.

In addition to this "warning" about being male, white, middle-aged, well-educated, and relatively affluent, the lecturer in our example also introduces another caveat to his classes. He notes that there are other assumptions made about him: that he is liberal, that he attempts to be scientific and objective in his approach, that he is married and a parent, and that he is ostensibly heterosexual. Each of these attributes might also carry with it biases that can affect what the teacher teaches, what the writer writes, or what the practitioner practices.

The Influence Monopoly

However, these attributes are not what is most significant about this warning. After all, the potential biases of one speaker, teacher, workshop leader, or writer might be discarded or soon forgotten. What *is* significant is that almost everyone who has the power to influence and control the minds and behaviors of others has the same attributes: being white, male, middle-aged, well-educated, and relatively affluent. These individuals are most of our law makers, elected officials, ministers, physicians, and sex researchers. They write our laws, control our media, and give us medical care and psychotherapy. They set the standards for sexual behavior and enforce them.

Of course, there is nothing unique in these people having so much power over our sexuality. This is the group that tends to have a major role in influencing *most* aspects of our lives. It is worth noting, however, that there are few areas in which most people are more vulnerable than in the area of sexuality. People constantly seek outside guidance, direction, and reassurance about their sexual feelings and behaviors. But with their

monopoly on influence, this group of standard setters has within it the seeds of bias that can limit sexual options and, as we shall see shortly, oppress large segments of the population.

It is true that there have been some changes in the composition of this group, at least in the fields of sex education, counseling, and therapy. Now there are white, middle-aged *women* who are well-educated and relatively affluent (for example, one of the authors). However, ethnic minorities, the young, lower-income groups, and people with little formal education have had relatively little power to influence their own or other people's sexual behavior.

It is not, of course, just "sexologists" who influence peoples' sexuality. Indeed, neither of the two men who have had the greatest impact on Americans' sexuality over the last half century were trained to be sexologists. Both *were* white, middle-aged men who were well educated and relatively affluent. However, in addition to the biases inherent in those attributes, they also brought with them biases from their professional disciplines. And, again, because people were vulnerable in their sexual beliefs and attitudes, professional biases have had considerable impact on America's sexual values over the last two generations.

The first of these American sexual revolutionaries was a entymologist named Alfred Kinsey. How did an expert in wasps get to be a specialist in human sexuality? His biographer and associate, Wardell Pomeroy, explains that when Kinsey was a student a friend approached him about his anxieties over masturbation. Kinsey could offer no other aid but the suggestion that they both get on their knees and pray to God for forgiveness.

Later, when Kinsey was selected to teach an undergraduate class dealing with sexuality and had encountered a procession of students troubled with sexual concerns, he did what any good biological scientist would do: he went to the library for guidance. He found no help there, however. Although there was ample research reporting on the sex lives of wasps and other animals, there were virtually no data on the sex lives of college students or other kinds of people. Kinsey decided to rectify this ommission and undertook his now classic studies of human sexual behavior.

But this is where professional biases came in. Kinsey approached his investigations from the perspective of a biological scientist. What he considered important was to discover how many of what types of people did what how often. In essence, it was *numbers* that Kinsey felt were most important.

A generation later another white, middle-aged, affluent, and well-educated man took over the scientific investigation of sexuality. But this time it was a man who approached sex from the bias of a gynecologist/physician. William Masters, with his associate Virginia Johnson, focused his attention on the center of a physician's universe, the human body. While Kinsey focused on numbers, Masters and Johnson attended to how and why the human body works and doesn't work in "the sexual act." Certainly they attended to social and emotional factors, but primarily as they impinged on physical response.

American society, particularly its professional helpers, responded enthusiastically to Masters and Johnson's research. A generation of psychologists, physicians, social workers, and nurses memorized the four phases of the sexual response cycle as if it were the central catechism of human sexuality. The body and its sexual responses and inadequacies became the essence of sex. Thus the physician's bias became the cornerstone of the "new" understanding of sex. Sexual dysfunctions and sexual "plumbing" became synonymous.

In recent years, as more and more people became disenchanted with a physical focus in sex, this preoccupation with the workings of the sexual anatomy has begun to ebb. This trend would seem to parallel some disenchantment with recreational sex. But

changes in social attitudes about sex are often difficult to detect except in retrospect. We are too immersed in our own climate of opinion to tell what new focus will emerge to supplant the preoccupations of the past with numbers and bodies. We must admit that the authors of this book hope it will be broader than the previous conceptualizations.

Although biologists, physicians, and other professionals have prejudices and biases, we would like to think that we can transcend some of these to offer a perspective or point of view that sees "sex" as more than an accumulation of countable events (à la Kinsey) or bodily functions (à la Masters and Johnson). We see the focus of understanding sexuality as a process of accommodation between the needs and learned sexual responses of individuals in interaction with the expectations, demands, and restrictions of the social environment.

Such a perspective implies that the understanding of sexual phenomena requires an appreciation of the interplay of an individual with his or her social environment. It also makes it obvious that the prevention of sexual problems and the maintenance and restoration of satisfying sexual behavior requires not only effective interventions with those individuals experiencing difficulties, but, just as importantly, with those individuals, groups, and social institutions that affect their sexual lives. This book is written with that perspective.

SOURCES OF SOCIAL CONTROL

As a first step in considering how we might be more helpful to the groups we will later define as the sexually oppressed, we will first consider how and why sexual behavior is controlled (Haeberle, *The Sex Atlas*).

There are, of course, in each society a number of vehicles through which social control is exercised. Probably the family is the most universal avenue through which sexual values are communicated, and the vehicle by which many powerful social sanctions are exercised. Folklore and more recently, in developed countries, the "media" have also served to support the communication and maintenance of a particular culture's sexual values. But who gives direction to these channels of social control? Neither the family nor folklore usually invents new social values. Their functions are generally to maintain and broadcast the values that are promulgated by those institutions that are granted the stewardship of that society's congregate behavior.

In modern western societies there have been three social institutions that have had the most influence in controlling sexual behavior. Certainly these institutions have been supported by public opinion, folkways, and in the modern era by the media. But the power behind this social control has largely emanated from these three social institutions:

Religion

In virtually all cultures, religions have served more than a spiritual function. They have shaped and controlled those behaviors that were seen to have significance for the preservation of the societies they served, as well as for their own continuation.

Few behaviors have as much significance for a culture as the patterns in which people express their sexuality. The Judeo-Christian religions have long stressed the importance of living a sexual life governed by god-given mandates. Indeed it often seemed that sex was at the top of the morality agenda for much of the recent history of western churches. If one word were to be chosen to reflect the power of western religions to control sexual conduct it would be "sin." Generally one could avoid the labeling of "sinful" by self and others by limiting one's sexual activity, and even sexual desires, to the marital bed.

Many western churches have been actively redefining sexual sin in recent years. Some Protestant denominations have, for exam-

ple, reexamined some long-held bans on such diverse sexual and gender issues as masturbation, homosexuality, intercourse outside of marriage, and even the ordination of women. Indeed, the religious rules for sexual conduct have become increasingly unclear, and perhaps as a result, if not as a cause, the power of churches to control sexual conduct has diminished. The word "sin" increasingly sounds archaic and seems to have lost much of its power to control sexual behavior.

The Law

Over the last few centuries, as secular law began to replace the control of day-to-day behavior previously exercised by the church, it began to assume some of the responsibilities for limiting sexual conduct. Although the Napoleonic legal reforms in Europe reduced the role of secular law in sexual control, no such reforms occurred in the United States until approximately thirty years ago. Indeed, when our pilgrim forebears left Europe to resettle in America, seeking the blessings of religious freedom, it was with the belief that their religions should be free not only to guide but also to legislate acceptable sexual behavior.

Thus the sexual "sins" of the Bible became the sexual "crimes" of the United States. Indeed, the various labels for these crimes such as adultery, fornication, and sodomy came directly from the pages of the Bible.

In 1957, as a part of a general penal code revision, the state of Illinois removed those sections of its state laws that regulated consensual adult sexual behavior carried out in private. There was considerable support for such penal code revisions by law makers and law enforcement organizations throughout the country. Many felt that the states' overcrowded courts and law enforcement programs could put their limited resources to better use if they were not burdened with the enforcement of private adult morality.

Since 1957, approximately half of the remaining states have followed Illinois in removing private consensual sexual behavior from the domain of state law.[1]

The Helping Professions

Societies abhor a vacuum in the social control of sexual expression. As both religion and the law have begun to lose the power they once had to regulate sexual behavior, society has turned more and more to the mental health professions for guidance regarding acceptable sexuality. In the last few decades it has been psychiatrists, psychologists, and other mental health workers who have become the arbiters of sex.

While law and religion have had only a few key words such as "sin" and "crime" to define unacceptable sexual behavior, the mental health professions produced volumes of value-laden words. Among the more powerful are "sick," "diseased," "perverted," "pathological," and perhaps the most devastating and meaningless label of all, "abnormal." These labels have had the authentic ring of scientific wisdom behind them.

But labels carry with them no guarantee of accuracy, relevance, or even helpfulness. It has been said that many of the labels used to describe sexual patterns, such as "frigidity," "impotence," and "premature ejaculation," are more insults than they are diagnoses. Each one of these, and the many other such labels, reflect the biases—often destructive biases—of the user. They lack specificity, imply a desired "normal" standard of sexual behavior, and give a negative connotation to patterns of behavior that depart from that standard. Further they tend to create a dysfunctional reification of the label. People

described by these labels *become* the label. A person *is* impotent, frigid, homosexual, and so on. The condition permeates their very being.

Further, the biases inherent in these labels reflect the power relationship of the labeler to the labeled. For example, the primary mental health labelers in the past have tended to be, as previously noted, men. Generally it has been men who have told women how they are supposed to experience their sexuality—and not just mental health personnel, but physicians, husbands, and lovers as well.

Because women seem to display a wider range of sexual responses than do men, it is not surprising that men have attempted to limit women's sexual response to a range that is comfortable and nonthreatening to them. Thus the "professional" control labels of "frigid" (not sexual enough) on one hand, and "promiscuous" and "nymphomaniac" (too sexual) on the other, have become part of the language of the social control of women's sexuality. No woman invented these labels.

Perhaps it may seem that we dwell too much on what sexual behaviors are called. However, as W. I. Thomas stated, "If men define situations as real, they are real in their consequences." The biases inherent in the words we use have a profound effect on the way we view and react to those behaviors. Indeed, words are often the vehicle through which sexual oppression is communicated and exercised. Encouraging people to rethink the ways in which they describe themselves and others can be one of the most helpful things we do for them.

A case in point is the word most commonly used to describe one of the most universal and frequently practiced form of sexual behavior: masturbation. The words we use to describe our everyday activities tend to be short, usually one syllable. Thus, we talk, walk, run, laugh, cry, live and die . . . and we masturbate. Obviously "masturbate" doesn't sound like it belongs in this list. "Masturbate" seems more at home in a list that includes meningitis, diphtheria, mononucleosis, and

---

[1]General exceptions to these revisions have been to maintain legal restrictions against prostitution and incest. Forced sexual activities, public acts, access to pornography, and sexual acts involving children are of course still legislated against. In addition, there are many places in this country today (including virtually every state south of the Mason-Dixon line) in which biblical law is still the law of the land. Despite this fact, it would appear that the law is increasingly removing itself from the regulation of private sexual activities among consenting adults.

Herpes Simplex II. This is not a semantic accident. The word "masturbation" did not evolve from centuries of common usage but was manufactured only about a century ago, to describe a disease that was thought even to cause other diseases. The word masturbation is not just a description of a sexual act but a warning. It literally means "to defile oneself with one's hand," hardly an inviting description.[2]

A more recent illustration of the helping professions' efforts to make their moral judgments sound scientific is the definition of the perjorative term "promiscuous" provided by the American Psychiatric Association in the latest edition of *Diagnostic and Statistical Manual of Mental Disorders.* The arbitrary criterion for promiscuity is "ten or more sexual partners within a year" (p. 321). By implication, then, to have eleven partners—even if one loves them—would be pathological, while nine partners would be all right—even if one doesn't love them.

Thus the helping professions have carried on an often subliminal campaign through their words to cast an aura of distaste on common and often very pleasant sexual activities. As a result, the socially acceptable "scientific" words we use reveal a basic discomfort with and subtle distancing from sexuality. Only recently have any substantial segments of the helping professions begun to sanction a range of sexual options that departs from their previous model of "normalcy."

In summary, then, the three major social institutions of religion, law, and, most recently, the helping professions have actively defined and enforced a standard for acceptable sexual behavior. But why, and toward what end? Is there some worthwhile function to the social control exercised through the argot of these institutions, whether it be the "sins" of religion, the "crimes" of the law, or the "abnormalcies" of the mental health pro-

fessions? After all, isn't there some need to control the expression of sexual feelings? Could any society survive sexual anarchy? Doesn't *someone* have to define limits?

Certainly. But before we can decide the direction control might take, let us first consider the underlying assumptions that have generally determined what forms of sexual expressions are to be supported and endorsed, and which are to be prevented and punished. In the authors' opinion there is a single common denominator in the control of sex as it is exercised, until comparatively recently, by religion, the law, and the helping professions. Sexual oppression is largely the product of one powerful belief system: the reproductive bias.

THE REPRODUCTIVE BIAS AND SEXUAL OPPRESSION

Until recently the strength of any family, social institution, religion, and country could be measured in large part by the number of children born into that group, and by the quality of care given to those children. A country could be best defended if it had bred a full complement of healthy, well-fed men. And a family could best endure the hardships imposed by nature and its neighbors by producing as many children as humanly possible. Children could not only assist with the myriad household chores, they could form marital connections with other families and also provide the parents with financial security as they got older. They were therefore a significant economic and defensive essential for families and for societies as well.

Children can, of course, be conceived in or out of marriage, but most societies have found that the family unit is the best vehicle for the care and socialization of children. With these objectives in mind—the channeling of sexual impulses into the creation of as many children as possible in situations in which they would be well cared for—the reproductive bias emerged and until recently flourished. It is this bias that has underlain most of our sexual values, beliefs and laws.

---

[2]"Fellatio," "cunnilingus," and "homosexual" are other relatively new words that were invented in similar fashion.

Stated simply, the reproductive bias asserts that the only sexual acts that are normal, free from sin, healthy, legal, beautiful, and approved by the Boy Scout and Girl Scout Manuals are those acts that could conceivably lead to socially approved pregnancies (pun intended). Similarly, the only *people* who should be involved in sexual acts (as long as they are the "right" kind of acts) are those whose sexual activities could conceivably lead to socially approved pregnancies.

Conversely, the further a person's significant characteristics are from those of someone who could conceivably have a socially approved pregnancy, the more that person will be discouraged or prevented by the agents of social control from being sexually active. And the less that a given sexual act approximates that which is necessary to bring about a socially approved pregnancy, the more that act will be considered immoral, illegal, or abnormal.

The Sexual Elite

We refer to those who comply with the rules of the reproductive bias as the *sexual elite*. Their sexual lives, as long as they confine themselves to the mandates of the reproductive bias, are supported and legitimized by a number of social institutions. In a previous book, we described the ideal of the sexual elite as follows:

The sexual elite is best exemplified by the idealized hero and heroine of the [novel and] film *Love Story*. In that film the hero is a young and handsome law student and the heroine is a young and beautiful music student. They fall in love immediately, engage in premarital intercourse primarily as an expression of their love, and subsequently marry. She uses four-letter words, but underneath it all, is a nice girl who would not dream of marital infidelity. They have a great deal of fun and never stop loving each other until she dies an elegant death. Neither seems to feel much love or even affection for anyone else except her father, who is sweet but passive. One is led to speculate that the hero is always potent, the heroine always achieves multiple orgasms, and that they never need Kleenex. They would probably consider genital-to-genital intercourse in the missionary position culminating in simultaneous orgasms the logical and normal conclusion to every sexual activity that occurs 2.7 times a week immediately following Johnny Carson. (Gochros and Gochros, *The Sexually Oppressed*, 1977, pp. xx–xxi.

Those who comply with this image of the sexual elite, however, are not without their sex-related problems. If one is among the sexually chosen people, one had better live up to the expectations for that group. Heterosexual intercourse leading to penetration and intravaginal ejaculation, ideally in the missionary position (one of the positions most likely to lead to conception) is the preferred sexual act. The preferred sexual actors are married, loving (predictive of sustained parenting relationships), heterosexual, young, healthy, intelligent, attractive, well educated, affluent, and members of the ethnic racial majority.

To comply with the bias, a woman had better be able to attract and hold on to the right man and submit sexually only to him. She must have and maintain those attributes that sexually entice her partner and which hold his interest indefinitely. She must also be responsive to his sexual desires.

As for the man, he had better be sexually robust and competent. He must not only be continually ready for sex, and specifically interested in sexual intercourse as the primary sexual outlet, but he must be physically able to carry out the act correctly. That is, he must be able to achieve erections, and insert them in the right place, ejaculating in the right place at the right time. In doing so, he must make his partner satisfied that he has done his job well. Again, his primary goal should be ejaculation through intercourse. Other erotic activities must be viewed only as foreplay, mere preparation for the main event. Masturbation can only be an outlet of last resort, when a suitable partner is not available.

The elite do have problems, often referred to as sexual dysfunctions—erectile, ejaculatory, and orgasmic dysfunctions, not to mention problems in desire and inability to attract and maintain relationships. Very few people are free of some form of sexual oppression.

However, it is the contention of the authors that the problems of the sexual elite have been extensively explored in the literature and that there is no shortage of well-trained and not so well-trained helping professionals willingly and, perhaps knowledgeably, offering services to the elite. The technology and motivation of the helping professions to deal with the sex-related problems of those who are *not* in this group are less developed.

The Sexually Oppressed

The further an individual and his or her sexual activities are from the expectations of the reproductive bias, the more likely it is that the acts and the actors will be ridiculed, condemned, or persecuted by others, and perhaps by themselves. Social institutions either ignore or, more likely, try to prevent such sexual expression.

Those people whose sexual behavior cannot conceivably lead to a socially approved pregnancy we call the *sexually oppressed.* They include those who are too young or too old to have a socially approved pregnancy; the disabled who are not considered physically or mentally equipped to care for offspring adequately; the institutionalized who cannot care for their young; the homosexually oriented who cannot conceive through their sexual acts no matter what they insert in or rub against what; those who appear physically unattractive; and those who belong to the "wrong" race, ethnic group, or socioeconomic class. In other words, the sexually oppressed are those who cannot produce socially approved additions to their number as determined by those with more social influence than they. The sexual needs and behaviors of these populations have generally been either ignored or suppressed by the helping professions.

There is little question that the reproduc-

TABLE 1-1   Membership in the Sexual Elite and the Sexually Oppressed as Determined by Compliance and Noncompliance with the Reproductive Bias

Sexual Elite:	Sexually Oppressed:
Characteristics Comply with the Reproductive Bias	*Characteristics Do Not Comply with the Reproductive Bias*
Married	Single, divorced, widowed
Young adult	Youth and aged
Sex in loving relationship	Recreational sex
Heterosexual	Homosexual
Physically healthy	Chronically ill
Ablebodied	Disabled
Mentally healthy	Mentally ill
Intelligent	Mentally retarded
Financially comfortable	Poor
Dominant ethnic group(s)	Minority ethnic group(s)
Attractive	Unattractive

tive bias is breaking down. As economic, social, and military realities have changed, societies and families have seen that reproduction is no longer an unmitigated blessing. As a result, the pressure to funnel sexual energies exclusively into reproductive enterprises is dissipating. There *is* a growing acceptance of sexual relationships and living together outside of marriage, masturbation, same-sex intimacy, and sex among the aged.

Overpopulation and the loss of the economic benefits of large families have served to alter our sexual landscape slowly. Both the women's movement (you don't have to be a mother to be a worthwhile female human being) and the gay and lesbian movement (your sexual acts don't have to be potentially reproductive to merit acceptance) bear witness to the reduction of the bias.

However, universally entrenched values die slowly, and residues of the reproductive bias linger in many aspects of daily life. "Sex" education of children still begins with reproduction and the assumption that all sex stems from its reproductive origins. We still call the sex organs "genitals," and teach that the penis and the vagina (rather than the clitoris) are analogous. It is their conjunction that is the essence of reproduction, therefore they "go" together. We still equate sex with intercourse. The basic *reproductive* act is almost universally assumed to be the ultimate *sexual* act. Every other activity is at best foreplay.

It is not enough just to have intercourse, but men *must* want it as often as possible, must be capable of sustained penetration and be able to delay their ejaculation until their sperm can be deposited at the right time and in the right place. Women must be responsive—to the right men and under the right circumstances. The reproductive bias has its impact on the sexual elite as well as the sexually oppressed.

Implications of the Reproductive Bias

The ideal characteristics imposed by the reproductive bias are relative, and the sanctions a matter of degree. They vary from time to time and from place to place. The sanctions can also be increased by compounding the oppressed characteristics. For example, an institutionalized paraplegic living on welfare will encounter more oppression than a rich one living at home. An attractive lesbian might encounter less oppression than an unattractive one.

Also, an individual can compensate for some characteristics that impede his or her capacity to generate a socially approved pregnancy if the individual excels in most of the other characteristics. We call this process the Sidney Poitier syndrome. Some of our readers may remember a "revolutionary" motion picture entitled *Guess Who's Coming to Dinner?* That film postulated that a black man could be acceptable as a sexual partner for a white woman *if* he were Sidney Poitier and *if* he were to have just about all the *other* attributes of the sexual elite: good looks, wealth, intelligence, and success.

The same Sidney Poitier syndrome was seen in another popular film, *Coming Home*,

in which the hero was an acceptable sexual partner despite the fact that he was a paraplegic because he had so many other virtues to compensate for his disability. Similar compensations were shown for lesbians in *Personal Best* and gay men in *Making Love*. American society seems more able to accept the sexuality of those with characteristics that violate the reproductive bias if they are meritorious in all other regards.

CONCLUSION

Even those in the helping professions who have recognized the need to attend to sex-related problems have largely focused on the problems of the sexual elite. The volumes of work on erectile difficulties and orgasmic dysfunctions of the elite far outweigh the literature on intervening strategies for the much wider range and complexity of problems encountered by the sexually oppressed.

This book will attempt to explore the problems of the diverse populations whose sexual behaviors cannot conform to the reproductive bias and offer extensive suggestions for interventions that might not only diminish their problems, but might even enhance their sexuality. We believe that the major challenge to human service professionals in the area of human sexuality is to minimize the effects of sexual oppression so that all people, whether members of the sexual elite or oppressed, can express their sexuality in nonexploitive ways that provide the maximum in personal satisfaction and self-fulfillment.

REFERENCES

American Psychiatric Association. *Diagnostic and statistical manual of mental disorders*, 3rd ed. Washington, D.C., 1980.

Haeberle, E. *The sex atlas*. N.Y.: Continuum Publishing Co., 1983. (Originally published, 1981.)

Thomas, W. I. *Social behavior and personality*. N.Y.: Social Science Research Council, 1951.

CHAPTER
2
THE COMPONENTS OF SEXUALITY

In the previous chapter we explored the roots of sexual oppression. In this chapter we will go back a step and consider what is meant by "sex." By so doing, perhaps we can gain a better perspective on the range of sex-related problems that may be encountered by the sexually oppressed.

First of all, let's be clear that "sex" and "intercourse" are not synonymous, although in many people's minds they are. Books or discussions about sex are frequently interpreted as being books or discussions about intercourse. Indeed, the two terms are often used interchangeably: "At what age should one begin having sex?" "When was the last time you had intercourse?" We even use the therapeutic euphemism "sexual dysfunction" to mean, generally, problems in "successfully" carrying out intercourse.

Even when the terms are not used synonymously, it is often assumed that intercourse is the only logical, desirable, or nor-

mal culmination of a sexual encounter. As Zilbergeld has pointed out (Zilbergeld, 1978), many men feel obligated to carry any sexual encounter through to "completion," and completion means coitus. ("A man never begins something he can't finish!")

The origins of this value can, of course, be traced to the reproductive bias. Penis-in-vagina intercourse *is* the most effective pathway to conception (excepting perhaps artificial insemination). A woman cannot get pregnant through any orifice but the vagina, and no other appendage but the penis can do the job. In fact, the missionary position (man on top), considered by many Americans to be the only normal position for intercourse, is also one of the positions most likely to facilitate conception.

Intercourse can be a very pleasurable act. It is not, however, the *only* pleasurable sexual activity, and other sexual behaviors need not be considered only as second-best, warming-up activities. The benign sounding term "foreplay" reinforces the concept that any other sexual contact is merely an appetizer for the entrée of intercourse.

Coital primacy has a myriad of implications for the sexual values and behavior of those who subscribe to it. Overcoming it may be a first step to a richer, less demanding sexual adaptation. Having decreased the pressure to "perform," both men and women can be more spontaneous within a range of sexual options. Men need not be devastated by occasional or even frequent inability to complete *the* sex act. Erections are not essential for enjoyable sex. (After all, soft penises have feelings too.) Women need not feel that their sexual self-worth hinges on their ability to turn on and lubricate "on demand." The primary focus on intercourse, therefore, creates unnecessary difficulties for the sexual elite.

Coital primacy is also associated with many of the difficulties encountered by the sexually oppressed. Unwanted adolescent pregnancies can, of course, be a product of the peer expectation that adequate adolescents should engage in intercourse. Aging people often have not developed a repertoire of or comfort with other sexual activities to meet their sexual/intimacy needs as physiological processes make intercourse more difficult. Likewise the sexual freedom and enjoyment of many other groups of the oppressed who will be discussed in this book are impaired by their belief, or the belief of others, that coitus is "where it's at."

DEFINING SEX

If sex is not synonymous with intercourse (or, for that matter, with any specific act) then what is it? Defining sex is more than an academic exercise. If we want to help people with sex-related problems, we have to understand the topography of their sexuality. We have to know what we are looking for before we can find it.

Sex is the combination of a number of components that interact in certain ways at particular points in time to make people feel, think, and behave uniquely. Sex cannot be fully understood through any single dimension, whether it be the differences of the genders, the emotions of attraction and intimacy, or the physical expression of eroticism. Thus, in order to describe a person's sexuality accurately at a given time we must take into account the manifestations of sexuality in the context of personal experiences, cognitions, and environment. In this way, we can understand a person's sexual "fingerprint" and communicate the empathy essential to help anyone who is oppressed.

The Gestalt of Sex

A large number of factors within and around an individual influence the ways in which sexuality is expressed. Collectively, these factors form the gestalt of sex. The following are among the more significant variables that influence how a person manifests his or her sexuality.

Climate of opinion. Economic, political, and religious conditions influence the climate of opinion that helps shape sexual beliefs and behaviors. These conditions can influence a population so subtly that they are scarcely noticed except, perhaps, in retrospect. In America, for example, the 1940s was a decade of sexual inhibitions and conservatism; the 1960s was a time of preoccupation with sexual "emancipation," interest in the mechanics of sexual plumbing, and increased acceptance of sexual diversity (sex for sex's sake); and the 1980s may come to be seen as a period of concern about sexual crimes and diseases, a return to romantic values and to concerns about the relationships within which sexuality is manifested.

Again, it should be noted that a climate of opinion is so broadly accepted by so many people in one's world that it is scarcely noticed as a variable influencing individual opinions, feelings, and behaviors. A Zen saying suggests that "one cannot explain water to a fish." However, the helping professional who gains as complete a perspective as possible on the shifting climate of opinion will be able not only to detect how conducive it is to achieving fulfillment in sexual functioning, but also to evaluate the extent to which a particular client is in step with that value system or *wants* to be in step with it.

In contrast to the effects of the climate of opinion, some of the following influences can more easily be perceived because they involve factors that differentiate people from each other within their environment.

Religion. What is loosely referred to as religion plays a major role in shaping the sexual thoughts and behaviors of many people. There are several elements related to religion that can affect how a person manifests sexuality. To which organized religion does one belong? How invested is one in the belief systems of that religion? What are the tenets of that religion regarding the expression of sexuality? How accurately does the individual understand and to what extent does he or she accept the current positions of that religion? It should be noted that it sometimes takes considerable time for the current stands on sexual matters of a religious denomination, which are often in flux, to filter down to the individual members of particular churches. For this reason, it is desirable for helping professionals to keep abreast of changing doctrines in the major denominations.

Beyond the effects of organized religion, there is a broader sense of "religion." That is the way in which an individual perceives himself or herself in the context of other people and, perhaps, the universe. This might loosely be defined as a person's spiritual self and may go beyond the tenets of any particular religion. What does this person see as his or her obligation to family, tradition, society, humanity, or even God? Is the self seen as the center of the universe, or as part of a broader plan? Although some professional helpers experience discomfort

with such philosophical-existential explorations, they might be central to an individual's conflicts and concerns.

Culture. As we noted in the previous chapter, culture plays a large part in shaping not only our sexual behaviors, but our sexual beliefs and values as well. People (including professional helpers) tend to be chauvinistic regarding their sexual beliefs. It is therefore important to transcend one's own cultural biases to ascertain how well or poorly individuals fit into their cultural environment, and to what extent they are comfortable with getting their needs met through their culture's belief system.

Geographical location. The geographical area in which a person spent formative years can influence sexual development. Contrast the learning experiences one encounters in such large but varied cities as New York, Chicago, or San Francisco. Furthermore, any of these cities may provide significantly different learning experiences from those in, say, a rural area of Alabama or North Dakota.

Family and friends. Much of a person's sexual beliefs, feelings, and behaviors are a product of past and current family life and friendships. The family molds a person's sexuality both by what is said and not said about sexuality, and also by what is demonstrated. Was sex an acceptable topic of conversation among family members and friends? What was said about both the dangers *and* the joys of sex? How was masturbation, nudity, homosexuality, and sex outside of marriage dealt with? Were these attitudes compatible with those in the family's reference group? What experiences or attributes of members of the immediate and extended family and friends—marriages, divorces, incest, rape, homosexuality—were known to the individual? How were the factors dealt with by family members and friends?

Equally important, how were warm affectionate feelings (if there were such feelings) communicated within the family and among friends? Were they consistent with cultural norms? Did parents openly express affectionate, even erotic feelings to each other? Was the individual shown physical affection, and how did she or he react to it? How is affection currently expressed within the network of family and friends? To what extent is the person satisfied with this pattern?

Other socioeconomic variables. There are, of course, a number of other environmental factors that can have an effect on the foundation of one's sexuality. Both poverty and wealth can influence sense of self and the opportunities for a range of sexual experiences. Education can determine one's information level about factors related to sexual expression. The state of the nation's general economy, as well as the country's involvement in international conflicts, can have an indirect or direct bearing on one's sexual beliefs and behavior.

Health. It has been said that health involves more than the absence of disease; health includes the capacity to enjoy fully all of one's physical and mental being. It may be difficult for someone to enjoy the pleasures of physical sexuality, or even intimate relationships, when one is experiencing the pain of arthritis, the threat of heart attack, the disfigurement of colostomy, the fear of cancer, or the side effects of medication. None of these conditions, not even the proverbial headache, need necessarily preclude sexual desires or the capacity for sexual fulfillment, but their impact on any particular client must be sensitively explored and, perhaps, modified.

Age. As noted in the previous chapter, age is one of the major variables that has an impact on the way we express our sexuality. Age alters our physiological responses to sexual stimuli. It can also have an impact on our approach to the meanings of relationships, especially as people begin to increasingly deal with their own mortality.

Age also determines the "climate of opinion" prevalent during our formative years.

To a considerable extent people reflect the social-sexual ideas they encountered in their adolescence, not necessarily from their parents, but from peers and the models within their environment. Contrast, for example the weekly watching of "Ozzie and Harriet" and "Father Knows Best" in the 1950s with a weekly exposure to "Three's Company" and "Charlie's Angels" in the 1970s. The programs of the 1950s modeled family values and understated if not denied sex, while the programs of the 1970s modeled the joys of sex outside of the context of "meaningful" relationships.

Gender. We have also previously reviewed the powerful impact of gender on the way we express our sexuality and the kinds of sexual concerns and difficulties we might encounter. Some of these are products of the many physiological and anatomical differences between women and men. It is likely, however, that a more substantial element is the socially ascribed and learned differences characteristic of most cultures, and of the differences in personality, ability, and emotionality attributed by others to individuals on the basis of biological sex. We'll get into this more later.

THE COMPONENTS OF SEXUAL EXPRESSION

Each person, whether a member of the sexual elite or of one of the sexually oppressed groups, is unique in the ways in which the configuration of sexuality is shaped by the above factors. Indeed, it is essential to remember that members of the sexually oppressed are unique individuals. There is as much variation among aging people as there is among young adults, among the homosexually oriented as among the heterosexually oriented, and among the disabled as among the able-bodied. People do not lose their individuality simply because they are oppressed.

Sexual expression in human beings involves a complicated interplay of anatomical characteristics, physiological functioning, cultural and class values, religious and moral beliefs, age, health, personality, as well as the accumulation of learning experiences. Because this constellation of interacting components of sexuality changes over time—often subtly and sometimes dramatically—sexual functioning must be viewed in relation to the specific context in which it exists, an individual's sexual gestalt.

Understanding this backdrop against which we play out our sexual lives is not a simple matter, and it is difficult to define precisely all the dimensions of "human sexuality" that have combined to form the totality of a particular individual's sexuality. The collective and individual manifestations of sexuality might be broadly described in six separate but interrelated areas.

All of the six manifestations discussed here are probably equally important in the expression of sexuality in general, but they may also take on various degrees of significance for the sexuality of any particular individual at any particular point in time. Because these manifestations overlap, and because they extend into considerations that may not seem obviously "sexual," it becomes virtually impossible to describe where the sexual component ends and other aspects of human life begin. These then, are the components of sexuality.

Sensuality

Sensuality is the psychological and physiological enjoyment of one's body, and often a partner's body. It includes the release of tension associated with orgasms. It can also satisfy the hunger for physical contact ("skin hunger") that most people experience and which many of the sexually oppressed frequently find unsatisfied. It involves those behaviors and partners that one perceives as potentially sexually satisfying. For most people, the sexual partners and forms of sexual expression selected are chosen on the basis of psychological and sociocultural criteria.

In many societies, sensuality is enhanced if it is shared with someone who is loved. For perhaps most people in America today, affection is considered a major prerequisite for sexual relationships if they are to be perceived as healthy, satisfying, or moral. Indeed, for many Americans at least, love is the only true aphrodisiac (Hunt, 1974; Kaplan, 1975).

Although most cultures consider coitus the ultimate erotic-sensual expression, research suggests that self-stimulation is the most common source of orgasms for both men and women and produces the most intense (physiologically if not emotionally) orgasms (Kinsey et al., 1948, 1953; Hunt, 1974; and Masters and Johnson, 1966). There are many paths to sensual enjoyment.

Professional helpers should attempt to understand the range of sensual/affectionate behaviors a particular individual feels comfortable engaging in, as well as the meanings he or she ascribes to them. Performance pressure and other anxieties may be reduced if acts of physical touching—even those experienced as sensually gratifying—are not automatically considered part of the arousal process to the end of sexual intercourse. Likewise, people may find that clarifying the meaning of sensual touching may help them focus on pleasurable feelings without worrying that a request for a specific sexual activity is being made or construed by a partner.

Intimacy

Intimacy is the capacity for, and expression of, the pleasure of openness and interdependence with another person; it includes the desire for closeness or merger with that person. It tends to reduce if not eliminate feelings of loneliness which plague many sexually oppressed individuals. Indeed, it can be argued that loneliness is pandemic for all people in contemporary urban transient societies.

Among most Americans, the need for intimacy is met primarily through the nuclear family or a single lover, rather than through the network of family and friends often available to those in more settled societies, such as in rural Asia, Europe, and Africa. This tends to put a considerable burden on primary partners to meet all of each other's intimacy needs. This might also suggest why American marriages seem to be such fragile arrangements.

In much of middle-class American society the concepts of intimacy and genital sexual expression are closely bound together. Genital sex is sometimes perceived as the only avenue to intimacy, and "real" intimacy without genital contact is considered, at the least, awkward. Thus one is taught to love deeply only those nonrelated adults with whom one has the possibility of genital contact, and to have genital contact only with those one loves deeply. Recreational sex—as well as sex engaged in to express affectionate feelings, the closeness of friendship, or perhaps to assuage feelings of loneliness—is not widely accepted in contemporary America, although it is in some other societies.

Intimacy has only recently undergone the scrutiny of serious and extensive psychological and sociological research (Hatfield, 1978; Duck, 1981). It is difficult to identify and measure. Therefore researchers have found it more productive to study the manifestations more than the phenomena of love and intimacy.

In most close relationships, intimacy seems to be expressed more or less by the same repertoire of behaviors. These usually include verbal expressions of affection, appreciation, support, concern, interest, and encouragement; self-disclosure; physical expressions of intimacy (hugging, kissing, stroking, and perhaps genital contact); and willingness to tolerate the more unpleasant attributes of the loved person (Swenson, 1972; Duck, 1981). Although any number of these manifestations are found in varying degrees in all intimate relationships, intense passionate love (which is generally short lived) is characterized by the presence of a relatively high level of all these manifesta-

tions along with a strong desire for union or merging with the person who is loved (Hatfield).

Practitioners may be able to help their clients by asking them to describe the components of relationships the individuals consider intimate. They can also help their clients understand the ways in which relationships may change based on their or the partner's perception of a relationship as a "sexual" one or not. Perhaps of greatest importance, however, practitioners working with the sexually oppressed may be able to help them find opportunities and develop skills to achieve intimate relationships of various levels of intensity which may or may not include various forms of physical intimacy. In Chapter 3 we will discuss some procedures helping professionals might use to bring this about.

Sexual Identity

"There are three dimensions to sexual identity that are frequently confused with each other and with erotic preferences as well. They concern biological sex, gender identity and social sex role."

Biological sex. This dimension of sexual identity is manifested in the genetically determined sexual anatomy of an individual, and by hormonal factors. Generally speaking, it is this dimension that commonly identifies individuals as male or female based on aspects of sexual anatomy and physiology. In rare cases the physical characteristics of an individual (for example, genital ambiguity at birth) or chromosomal anomalies do not permit ready classification as either male or female. Such situations can create immediate dilemmas for parents and medical staff, and obvious difficulties for such individuals later on.

Gender identity. The distinctive element in this dimension of sexual identity is the subjective feeling of being a female or a male. Some individuals perceive themselves as being members of the sex other than the one their sexual anatomy would suggest. For example, an individual whose anatomy, biochemistry, and genetic structure identify him as a male may nonetheless think of himself as a female.

Individuals whose subjective perception of their gender identity differs from their physical characteristics are often labeled "transsexuals." An increasing trend until the late 1970s was the procedure known as sexual reassignment, in which interventions including surgery, hormonal therapy, voice training, and counseling were used to modify physical as well as behavioral characteristics, conforming them to the gender identity experienced as natural by the individual. Recently, these medical procedures have been viewed less favorably by medical authorities. They have expressed some doubt about the long-range effectiveness of this complex and irreversible process in terms of the recipient's subsequent life satisfaction.

Several issues arise in regard to surgery that is profound in its physical effects, expensive, and that may or may not bring about the desired emotional goal. Given the uncertainties about the satisfaction it may bring, candidates for surgery need to be properly informed about the possible consequences of such procedures in order to make a decision.

Social sex role. Social sex role includes that cluster of feelings, beliefs, and attitudes people have about their biological sex: What they learn to expect of themselves as a result of their being born male or female, what they have learned to expect of people of the other biological sex, and what they believe others expect of them as girls and boys, women, and men. Such expectations, which we often refer to as "masculinity" and "femininity," vary from culture to culture, and over time. Individuals and cultures that deemphasize differences in social sex roles are referred to as androgynous. This orientation probably tends to decrease tensions between the sexes and resultant oppression.

There has been a trend recently to conceive of both social sex role (masculinity and femininity) and sexual object choice (heterosexuality and homosexuality) as continua rather than as polarities. Gender identity, however, has continued to be perceived as an exclusively dimorphic biological phenomenon. Our language still describes the two genders as "opposite" sexes rather than "different" sexes. "Men are men and women are women." Future research may show that some people *feel* more or less male or female at different points in their lives, without having the desire to change the unequivocal physiological and anatomical characteristics that mark them as one biological sex or the other.

Erotic Preferences

This variable is defined by the characteristics of those with whom an individual would prefer to be involved in erotic or romantic relationships. As far as we can tell, it is rare for anyone to be erotically attracted to everyone. Most people develop over the years a set of criteria for those who will at least attract their attention, and thus be candidates for their erotic and romantic interest. To a large extent, these attributes are socially determined and are related to the dictates of the reproductive bias. Many if not most people are attracted to those with whom they could most conceivably produce socially approved pregnancies. For example, such characteristics as similar age, ethnicity, attractiveness, outward appearances of fecundity, virility, and similar socioeconomic and interest levels often determine one's erotic and romantic choices.

However, many people will make their choices by criteria which may be difficult to explain or of which they are only dimly aware. There are people who can only "turn on" to people with a particular level of intelligence, sense of humor, ethnicity, stature, hair or eye color, or other anatomical characteristic. When there are many such requisite characteristics, one's range of options may be severely narrowed. (As Woody Allen once quipped, "There is this to say about bisexuality: it doubles your chances on Saturday night.")

Most often, when erotic choice is discussed, it refers to the biological sex(es) of the people to whom one tends to be erotically and/or romantically attracted. Those individuals who prefer involvements (real or fantasied) with others of their own biological sex are often labeled "gay" (generally referring to men), "lesbian" (referring to women), or "homosexual" (referring to either). Individuals who prefer involvement with those of the other biological sex are labeled "straight" or "heterosexual." And individuals whose erotic and/or romantic choices include both men and women may carry the labels "bisexual" or "ambisexual."

It is important to note that the defining characteristic of all these orientations is the preference for whom to *love* as well as to whom one is erotically attracted. No sexual orientation has a monopoly on love, affection, or romance, nor is any limited to only erotic interests.

Despite the helping professions' penchant for labeling sexual preferences, in practice an individual's erotic and romantic choices may vary over time. At a given moment, an individual's choice may range from exclusively homosexual to exclusively heterosexual or at any number of points on a continuum between these two extremes.

Kinsey (1948, 1953) and subsequent sexual researchers found that a large percentage of individuals have desires and sexual contacts with people of both biological sexes. Despite popular stereotypes, no significant differences have been found in the emotional adjustment or life satisfaction of homosexually, ambisexually, and heterosexually oriented individuals in the general population (Kinsey, 1948, 1953; Siegelman, 1972). Most of the stresses encountered by homosexually and ambisexually oriented individuals are products of the prejudices and oppression of those people within their environment.

These four dimensions of sexual identi-ty—biological sex, social sex role, gender identity, and erotic preference—may be considered as discrete components of sexual identity as a whole. Although separate, they are intimately interrelated and interact among themselves, with the other manifestations described in this chapter, and with ongoing external realities.

Reproduction

Most human sexual activities do not result in reproduction. Unlike any other mammal, human beings generally display sexual interest which has little to do directly with the oestral cycle or the reproductive potential of a sexual act. Obviously, sex serves many important functions for humans besides reproduction. Yet, as we have shown, attitudes about reproduction greatly affect sexual behavior and the traditional sanctions toward such behavior. Generally, sexual behaviors are perceived as acceptable only if they could conceivably result in socially acceptable conceptions, or approximate such acts.

In many cultures, adequacy within one's sexual identity is closely linked to reproduction, and a person's worth is measured by the number of children one has mothered or fathered. Even in many segments of American society, people tend to feel that sex without the possibility or the desirability of conception is unacceptable or at least "unnatural" and so reject contraceptives and terminate sexual activities (which they see as synonymous with coitus) at menopause.

As with other manifestations of sexuality, reproduction affects and is affected by other factors within one's sexual gestalt. For example, someone who doesn't want to create a pregnancy, and who understands and has access to contraceptives may *still* not use them, because of their effect on their or their partner's sensual experiences. Some clients may also view the planned use of contraceptives as "premeditated sex," and therefore find them unacceptable within their particular moral code.

With the growing concern about over-population and the decreasing economic utility of children for the majority of families, the pressure for individuals to prove their "worth" by reproducing is diminishing. Supported by improved technology and accessibility of contraception and abortion, the other functions of sex are increasingly being separated from their reproductive consequences.

Sexualization

This term refers to the use of sexual behaviors, beliefs, or thoughts to influence the feelings, attitudes, or behaviors of others, or to prove something to one's self. Although such sexual activities may lead to sexual stimulation and even gratification, the original intent or motivation for the sexual behavior is to accomplish nonsexual ends.

It is likely that many sexual behaviors—including sexually implicit ones such as seductiveness—fall into this category. Many sex-related problems arise from the use of sex to influence others and/or prove something to oneself.

For example, coitus and other sexual acts are widely used—or withheld—to dominate, punish, humiliate, or barter with a partner. People frequently build up their self-esteem, avoid boredom, or attempt to keep a relationship intact by the nature and frequency of their sexual encounters. Sexual partners will often engage in coitus because each believes that the other expects it or they consider it their duty. Teenagers, and often adults, may engage in sexual activities to prove to their peers that they are adequate, worthy of peer respect, as well as living up to their own sexual standards. Some wives initiate sexual contacts because their husbands pay attention to them only while they are having sexual intercourse.

Perhaps the most vivid example of sexualization is rape. As is generally acknowledged, men seldom commit rape out of desperation because they lack other sexual outlets. Rather, it is an expression of their frustrated or excessive need to dominate, or of their rage. Rape is not truly a "sexual" act.

Clearly, helping practitioners must go beyond a knowledge of client's specific "sexual acts" if they are to understand their client's real sexuality. What sex *means* to a client may be even more important than what the client does.

CONCLUSION

One of the most significant observations about sexuality is that its expression is as varied as are individuals. Not only do the words we use in describing and discussing sex have different meanings for different people, but the importance people attach to the various manifestations of sex in their lives varies tremendously.

The forces that combine to create individual sexual patterns mold each person so differently that general discussions of human sexuality can only be useful when viewed as a backdrop against which particular flesh-and-blood "real" people live out their sexual lives in patterns that are exclusively theirs.

REFERENCES

Duck, S., and Gilmour, R., eds. *Personal relationships—vol. I: Studying personal relationships.* London: Academic Press, 1981a.

———. *Personal relationships—vol. II: Developing personal relationships.* London: Academic Press, 1981b.

———. *Personal relationships—vol. III: Personal relationships in disorder.* London: Academic Press, 1981c.

Hatfield, E., and Walster, G. W. *A new look at love.* Reading, Mass.: Addison-Wesley, 1978.

Hunt, M. *Sexual behavior in the 1970s.* Chicago: Playboy Press, 1974.

Kaplan, H. S. *The illustrated manual of sex therapy.* N.Y.: Quadrangle Press, 1975.

Kinsey, A., Pomeroy, W., and Martin, C. *Sexual behavior in the human male.* Philadelphia: Saunders, 1948.

KINSEY, A., POMEROY, W., MARTIN, C., AND GEBHARD, P. *Sexual behavior in the human female.* Philadelphia: Saunders, 1953.

MASTERS, W., AND JOHNSON, V. *Human sexual response.* Boston: Little, Brown, 1966.

SIEGELMAN, M. Adjustment of male homosexuals and heterosexuals. *Archives of Sexual Behavior,* 1972a, 2:9–25.

————. Adjustment of homosexual and heterosexual women. *British Journal of Psychiatry,* 1972b, 120:477–481.

SWENSEN, C. H. The behavior of love. In H. A. Otto, ed. *Love today: A new exploration.* N.Y.: Association Press, 1972.

ZILBERGELD, B. *Male sexuality: A guide to sexual fulfillment.* Boston: Little, Brown, 1978.

CHAPTER
3

COUNSELING THE SEXUALLY OPPRESSED

There are two levels on which the concerned professional can provide services to those we have described as sexually oppressed. On one level, the helper attempts to intervene in those social systems that may have contributed to the problems of the oppressed by "sins" either of commission or omission. Examples of such targets of intervention are hospital and institutional policies, behavior patterns of health care personnel, state or local laws, and educational programs for members of oppressed groups, helping professionals, paraprofessionals, and volunteers. These approaches will be discussed in the next chapter.

The other level of intervention involves providing direct services to individual members of the oppressed groups and to those who are directly involved with these individuals. In Part II of this book, our contributing authors describe specific strategies for helping particular oppressed populations

such as children, ethnic minorities, and the aged. In this chapter we explore therapeutic and counseling principles and approaches that we believe are applicable to all oppressed groups.

ATTRIBUTES OF THE HELPING PROFESSIONAL

In recent years a mystique has developed around the quasi-profession of "sex therapy," leading many practitioners in the helping professions to believe that some extensive and perhaps mysterious training was necessary before one could provide help with sex-related problems. We do not feel that this kind of training is necessary for helping with most of the sex-related problems of either the sexual elite or the sexually oppressed that are encountered in everyday practice.

Helping the sexually oppressed *does* draw upon a wide range of skills, knowledge, and attitudes. However, the attributes most needed by practitioners are identical to those essential for any other kind of interpersonal helping. The sources for knowing what help to give are the helpers' own life experiences, professional training, and ethics and, often, just good common sense. There are, however, some special attributes and techniques that are likely to make one more useful when working directly with members of the sexually oppressed and those concerned with them.

Helper's Attitudes and Values

Giving effective help to those among the sexually oppressed means practitioners must consider carefully their personal values as they relate to professional values in the area of sexuality. Where these values conflict, a superficial commitment to the professional values can result in some unhelpful vacillation in the helper's behavior. Practitioners must therefore think carefully about their values, examine sources of bias and take steps where necessary to modify them.

Each of the major helping professions has developed a code of ethics that has clear implications for professional behavior related to sexual concerns. The following values and beliefs, however, are offered as additional guidelines the reader might consider in approaching sexual problems regardless of his or her professional affiliation. The reader will note that these values go beyond the provision of clinical services (Gochros & Schultz, 1972).

1. Sexuality is a legitimate and important area of concern for the helping professions.
2. Sexuality involves an interplay of social, behavioral, emotional, physical, and aesthetic factors that differ among individuals and cultures and over time.
3. Sexual behavior, both functional and dysfunctional, is largely learned as a product of complex social interactions.

4. Sexual fulfillment is the right of every person regardless of income, gender, sexual orientation, or age unless that fulfillment is exploitive of someone else or is prohibited by reasonable, publicly enforced laws.
5. There is a wide variety of functional sex lifestyles for those living in or out of committed pair relationships.
6. People in the helping professions have a responsibility to keep abreast of and contribute to evolving values and knowledge regarding sexual behavior and technologies for treating sexual difficulties.
7. Helping professionals have a responsibility for enhancing sexual well-being in their communities that goes beyond clinical interventions. This includes assisting in the formulation of humane, rational laws and institutional policies and practices.
8. Helping professionals are responsible for contributing to the development of relevant, rational sex education and information for all ages and statuses of people, to assist them in making responsible and rewarding sexual decisions.
9. Helping professionals should know that a wide variety of sexual problems exists, some which they themselves may have. Many of these problems are concerns of the people with whom they will be working, and professional helpers must accept the fact that they will need more than personal experience and private opinions to help these people.
10. The client's welfare is the helping professional's primary concern in offering services for sex-related problems. The helping professional must not take advantage of a client's difficulties in order to meet personal needs.

Understanding and even accepting the above values is not enough. They must be put into action to buttress professional decisions and behaviors. They must also be communicated explicitly in what one says and implicitly in what one does. If this does not happen, practitioners limit the likelihood that they will be of help to the sexually oppressed, or to anyone else for that matter.

To illustrate the importance of the subtle interplay between the helper and those he or she helps, consider what occurred in a workshop one of the authors led on aiding people with sex-related problems. At the beginning of the workshop, the instructor asked each participant to explain what he or she hoped to get out of the workshop. When it was the turn of an elderly, grey-haired man, he explained that he had been a family doctor for thirty-five years. In informal discussions with other physicians he was constantly hearing about their patients' sex-related problems. Yet, in all his years of practice no patient had ever brought a sexual problem to his attention. He wanted to find out why.

In the course of that workshop, the physician explored several possible reasons why his clients did not bring these problems to him, as well as his own discomfort in dealing with such problems. There was no question that his patients *had* these concerns. But they also had resistances to bringing them to their doctor's attention. Some of these resistances stemmed from their fear of being labeled as abnormal, chastized, or even ridiculed for their sexual concerns. His patients may not have thought it appropriate to discuss these problems with a doctor, and they might not have had the vocabulary to do so even if they had wanted to. After all, few people have had much experience in having serious, honest discussions about their sexuality with anyone, let alone an "outsider."

Practitioner Resistances

As the doctor in the workshop learned, the recipients of help are not the only people who avoid discussions of sex-related problems. Often professional helpers are reluctant to discuss sex-related problems with the people they are trying to help. This reluctance can be communicated by subtle messages, such as verbal and nonverbal responses when someone alludes to a sexual matter, discouraging them from pursuing the subject. Eye contact might be momentarily lost, the voice and choice of words may change, or the helper may suddenly become more formal. People are generally

quite sensitive to such clues and often react by promptly dropping the subject.

One of the authors taught medical students the process of taking social histories, using a general social-history outline that included several sexual items. When he listened to tape recorded interviews of these sessions, he discovered that it was usually quite clear when the student was about to plunge in and explore the sexual areas. There would be a few seconds of silence and then the student would blurt out something along the lines of "Have you ever masturbated or engaged in a homosexual activity?" The patient would respond with an immediate defensive "No!" and one could almost hear the sighs of relief from both as the student proceeded to subjects less threatening to them.

It is obvious that before one can begin to be helpful to the sexually oppressed one has to create an atmosphere in which the client is willing to talk about sexual wishes, experiences, and concerns. To do so, helpers must first overcome their *own* resistances to dealing with sexual matters.

These resistances are not significantly different from those of the people we help. Professional helpers have grown up in the same sex-negative culture as their clients, have had little experience in open discussions about sexuality, and may feel ill-equipped by their formal education to deal with the range of sexual problems encountered by their clients. Further, they may worry that their willingness to discuss clients' sexual concerns will be misinterpreted. Perhaps clients, or even co-workers, will question their motivations and suspect that if they deal frankly with this area they are doing so out of personal sexual interest in their clients, or at least out of voyeurism. The helper may even question his or her own motivations.

Finally, professional helpers, like most other people growing up in our sexually complex society, are seldom totally secure in their own sexuality. It is therefore understandable that they may withhold help out of the conviction that people who live in sexual glass houses shouldn't give advice.

Growing evidence suggests that the helping professions are doing better at preparing students to deal with some of these resistances, as well as legitimizing assertive efforts to provide help in many of the settings in which professional helpers operate (Brown, 1981). These programs first provide learning experiences that increase students' level of comfort, lessening the range of sexual expression that will shock or immobilize them, and help students separate their own sexual needs, patterns, and wishes from those whom they serve.

Once helping professionals have begun to acquire this comfort, they can move on to understand the legitimacy and importance of their assertively offering sex-related services regardless of the setting in which they work or the populations they serve. They will also understand that sex is not just the prerogative of young, healthy, married heterosexuals and that most sex-related problems go beyond coital difficulties.

But it is not easy to undo a lifetime's informal sex education with formal professional training. We can suggest some basic attitudes that we believe are essential if one wants to be helpful to the sexually oppressed. Readers can then examine these attitudes and values against their own beliefs and evaluate the extent to which they can adopt them as underpinnings for their practice.

Use a "wet" approach. First, remember the opening words in Eric Berne's book, *Sex and Human Loving.* (1971) published shortly before his death: *"Sex is wet."* Berne also said it was slippery. This phrase could well be the cornerstone of an approach to any sex-related problem. Literally, of course, sex *is* wet: it involves the secretion of a variety of body fluids. But when Berne referred to the wetness of sex, he meant more than seminal fluid, natural and artificial lubricants, perspiration, and damp sheets. He was also al-

luding to wetness in its figurative sense: feelings and emotions are "wet." Love, anger, joy, jealousy, grief, and laughter all are "wet," in that they are fluid, volatile, and spontaneous.

To understand and communicate effectively about sex, the professional helper must also act wet. Small words, for example, are wet. Long, "medical" terms for sex are dry—as are desks, straight-back chairs, laboratory coats, the color white, books, most lectures, and diplomas. Many professional helpers feel protected by their dryness: it takes the intimacy out of sex and makes sexual discussions with their clients safer. The problem is that most people do not feel or think of their own sexuality in these terms, and dryness creates an artificiality that makes discussions of sex seem remote from the "real thing."

A few years ago, one of the authors was asked to endorse a new college-level sexuality text written by a well-known sex "expert." The book was technically accurate, and even made a few attempts at lightness. The overall tone of the book, however, was "scientific," formal and remote from the quality of sexuality that the average person experiences. Perhaps the best example of its orientation was a photograph illustrating "sex therapy." (Why one was necessary, we do not know. Sex therapy is usually not visually very exciting.) In the photograph were two "therapists" dressed in starched, sanitized white laboratory coats. (Why laboratory coats, we also didn't know. Few germs are associated with discussing most sexual problems.) Opposite them, across a huge desk, was the couple seeking help. Desks separating us from those we help, not to mention starched coats, are very dry, as was probably the therapy that the intimidated couple was receiving. Our coauthor did not endorse that book.

What we do endorse is the use of simple, clear language communicated in a warm, friendly atmosphere, using appropriate humor—sex is often funny, and couples who laugh in bed often have a better time of it—

by people who do not perceive themselves as superior to the recipients of their help.

Use "invisible" language. The words we choose to use can be an important tool in helping people with sex-related concerns. Generally speaking our words should, on one hand, get our messages across to our clients while, on the other, they should not interfere with our communication. This is not always easy. One of the ways our society demonstrates its ambivalence and discomfort with most sexual activities is by providing us with two vocabularies, neither of which is very satisfactory for clear, nonbiased communication. Our choices are either a sterile, medical, multi-syllabled, pathological sounding vocabulary (for example, coitus, fellatio, cunnilingus, promiscuous, vulva, testicles) or the crude, common slang that tends to reduce sex to its erotic fundamentals (fuck, blow-job, go down on, slut, cunt, and balls).

Neither of these vocabularies is ideal for communicating comfortably with clients. Both, in their own ways, can be disruptive. One connotes a desire of the helper to distance him or herself from the subject and to "purify" it. The other tends to shock people and demean sexuality.

Of course, one could use euphemisms. Most people would understand if we used terms like "making love," "sleeping with," or "playing with yourself." These expressions neither shock nor sanitize their objects. Yet there is a problem with euphemisms. They set a tone that suggests "you and I both know what I mean, but we also know that it's an uncomfortable topic for both of us and that neither of us really wants to talk directly about it, so let's not." It is usually best to avoid euphemisms.

Then what words *are* the best to use? Actually none is ideal. Given the limitations our language imposes on us, the best we can do is try to make our language work for us. Unless we deliberately want to do otherwise, we should choose language that is invisible.

Given our knowledge of a particular client, we can find the words that would be the clearest, sound the most "natural," and convey what we want to convey. When we are speaking with a young adult, for example, we might choose to talk about either "masturbation" or "self-stimulation" depending on the comfort of the adult. Self-stimulation may sound less harsh, but is somewhat less specific than masturbation. We *might*, however, choose to say "jerk off" to adolescents we know well *if* we—and they—are comfortable with the term.

Sometimes coarse language can be used effectively. For example, some well-educated clients may choose to intellectualize their sex lives to avoid some painful feelings. Based on our understanding of clients and with a deliberate attempt to break through their intellectualizations, we might occasionally choose to use some four-letter words, if we can do so with both comfort and conviction.

Which brings us to argot, the private languages of particular subcultures. It is a valuable asset to understand the language of particular subcultures we work with. Gays, adolescents, the disabled, and many ethnic minorities use extensive vocabularies to express their unique experiences and worldviews. It may be useful to know, for example, that among some gay men the term "rice queen" refers to a man who is sexually attracted to men of Asian ancestry. However, it is also important to remember that argot differs from place to place and over time. For example, the adolescent term "making out" may mean heavy petting at one time and place, and sexual intercourse at another.

Understanding terminology doesn't necessarily mean that the helper should always use these terms in their discussions with those who usually use them. Doing so often makes the helper sound artificial and unnatural. As a result, it can distance the helper from clients rather than bringing them closer. Further, there is always the danger of inadvertently misusing the argot. One of the authors, while teaching at U. C. Berkeley during the 1960s, one day tried to prove his empathy by approving a student's observation with "straight on!"—and was hastily corrected by the class: "It's 'right on'!"

In summary, know the argot of any group you are working with, but don't use it unless you are sure it will come across as natural rather than as a phony attempt to sound like "one of the gang."

One final bit of advice regarding language: if you don't understand a word or phrase that a client uses, ask him or her to explain. It is far better to ask than to act "with it" when you actually don't know what your client is talking about. Even if you do understand the word, you may want to find out how the client is using it. There is considerable sex *mis*education in most of our lives and, as a result, many people grow up with some distorted and inaccurate ideas about sex.

Be casual. It is important to convey to clients that—with few exceptions—no sexual wishes, thoughts, or behaviors shock the helper. In essence, the helper communicates that it really doesn't matter to the helper just what clients think, feel, or do in their private sexual lives as long as it doesn't involve unwanted pain or exploitation for them or others.

This approach communicates the idea that the practitioner is there to help and not to judge. Such an attitude allows clients to be themselves and present an accurate picture of their sexual lives. It also leads clients to believe that the responses they receive from their helpers will not be colored by personal prejudices or distastes.

Open doors. The sexually oppressed are less likely to seek help for sex-related problems than are the sexual elite. The reasons are obvious. The oppressed are more likely to feel sexually alienated, to feel uncomfortable about their own sexuality. As a result they may anticipate that the professional helper will neither approve of nor under-

stand their sexual wishes, feelings, or behaviors. It is incumbent on the helper to "open the door" for the client to talk about this potentially stressful topic.

In essence, the helper encourages clients to talk about their sexual concerns by communicating these ideas:

I know that you (or someone you are close to) is a sexual human being who, despite other people's negative attitudes, may have concerns connected with sexuality. I want you to know that I understand this and will not reject or ridicule you for your sexual feelings, behaviors, or concerns. I am genuinely interested in and capable of helping you with these concerns. I will try to make it as easy and comfortable as possible for you to talk with me about these concerns. However, if you *don't* have such concerns, or don't want to talk about them if you do, that's perfectly O.K. too.

One of the best door-openers is the "many people" question. For example, the helper might avoid asking potentially threatening questions such as "Do you masturbate?" or "Are you concerned about your retarded daughter's sexual activities?" Instead, the helper may restate these questions: "Most people your age often rub their penis (clitoris/vulva) to make themselves feel good and to relieve tension. Many of them worry about this or even feel guilty about it. I wonder if sometimes you have such feelings?" or "Often parents of young people with learning disabilities are concerned about how to help their children take care of their sexual feelings and desires without getting into trouble. I wonder whether this is something you would like to talk with me about?"

Note that while introducing the questions with "many people" or similar statements, the questions were also rephrased to make it more comfortable for the respondent to answer affirmatively, the assumption being that yes might be an accurate answer.

Another technique that often makes it easier for clients to respond nondefensively to questions is the multiple-choice question. The helper provides the respondent with a range of answers that are made to sound acceptable to the questioner. For example, consider the question "How often do you desire intercourse with your partner?" Instead, you might ask, "How often do you desire intercourse with your wife: never, once a week, once a month, twice a day . . . ?" Or you might ask, "What kind of sexual activities do you like: intercourse, oral sex, stimulating yourself, sex with other men, all of those, none of those . . . ?" And so on. It is important to remember, however, that if such a technique is used, the range of possibilities must be unlimited, so as to not intimidate those clients who consider themselves asexual or who may be exceptionally frightened about revealing their thoughts or behaviors.

We often find it useful, for instance, to combine a many-people technique with an added lighthearted comment, even giving a semiridiculous category. For example, in responding to a client's anxiety or hesitation, one might say "Don't worry, you won't shock me. I know some people who *never* want intercourse and some other people who want sex every hour on the hour." This technique gives people permission to be honest. Since their real answer is usually far less extreme than the one suggested, the response is a reduction in anxiety, a more realistic perception of themselves, and an increase in self-esteem.

Accept discomfort. As we have said before, most of us have been carefully taught throughout our lives not to ask or even talk about sexual matters, and certainly not with relative strangers. This kind of learning is difficult to unlearn. It is therefore almost inevitable that professional helpers, just like their clients, will experience discomfort in open, honest discussions on sex-related topics.

However, if we accept the value that, within the limits of our abilities and responsibilities, it is important to try to help clients to deal with any sexual concerns they have,

then we have no choice but to pursue these discussions despite our discomfort. In order to do so, we must learn to be comfortable enough with our discomfort to use it rather than to be stopped by it. In so doing, we can also begin to overcome our discomfort.

Several techniques can be used to alleviate discomfort. One is to discover its sources. If the source of the discomfort is lack of knowledge, certainly the first step will be to acquire more knowledge through reading, discussion, and participating in continuing education programs. If the discomfort is a product of conflicts about values, then added education needs to include rational exploration of those values. Self-exploration, values clarification, role-playing, and rehearsal around the handling of problem issues can also be helpful.

Often, however, the discomfort is due not to our own values or experiences but to our sensitivity about the potential invasion of someone else's privacy, the potential discomfort of others, and the potential for inadvertently offending someone whose values may differ from ours or may not even be known to us. The use of such tools as door openers, empathy, honesty, and appropriate humor can help. We can also anticipate coping with discomfort-causing situations by planning tension-breaking comments such as:

Gee, we seem to be stammering a bit. That's okay—after all, sex is not something people tend to discuss easily with each other, and we're both probably afraid of shocking each other. We usually find that if we just suffer through the first embarrassment, it goes away. And I assure you, I don't shock easily.

Practice. While practice does not necessarily make perfect, it certainly helps. Beginning attempts at any kind of professional counseling are often less than perfect. We get better with experience, learning from our successes and failures. We gain those benefits, however, only if we allow ourselves to start and keep on trying.

THE FOUNDATION SKILLS

As we pointed out earlier, many, if not most, of the sex-related concerns of the people encountered by the helping professions do not require intensive sex therapy. What is required is a caring, understanding, knowledgeable person who can provide an appropriate level of skilled intervention—neither more nor less than the concern or problem requires—who knows when a referral is necessary and appropriate, and who can assist in a referral process when it is needed.

In the majority of cases, however, referral is not only unnecessary but can prevent a client from getting what he or she needs. Telling one person about your sexual concerns, doubts, and fears can be difficult; telling two people may be impossible. Referral should be based on the conviction that someone else, or some other organization, is significantly better equipped to deal with a particular problem. It should not be a product of a practitioner's reluctance to deal with a difficult topic. But how can one be helpful? Effective help seems to be a result of a number of factors. We will discuss some of them here.

Communicating Interest, Warmth, Empathy, and Genuineness

Let's assume you have developed some or most of the helpful attitudes we discussed earlier. You are able to be casual in discussing other people's sex lives. You are comfortable with your own discomfort. You have a workable sex vocabulary. And you are "wet." The next step is to develop those interpersonal skills that have been associated with successful interpersonal help (Fischer, 1978). They include the following.

1. *Interest.* Sex is difficult to talk about. Clients need to feel that they are being listened to, that their listeners are interested in them and care enough about them to remember what they have said. Active listening can be demon-strated by good eye contact, by leaning toward the client in a natural comfortable position, by comments and facial expressions that match the content of the client's presentation, and by appropriate encouraging comments with a minimum of disruptive questions.

2. *Warmth.* Because of their interactions within a society that does not fully accept their sexuality, many sexually oppressed people develop a low self-image and question their value. They may be particularly uncomfortable about how their sexual needs will be perceived by helping professionals. The helping person must communicate to them that they are seen as respected, unique human beings, not just as members of a category of "clients," "patients," or "problems." We must show that we care for and accept them, and respect their own particular nondestructive sexual choices and lifestyles. Warmth is communicated in many ways, including tone of voice, use of the client's name, recalling information clients have given us, avoiding unnecessary questions, and following clients' leads in discussions.

3. *Empathy.* Members of oppressed groups frequently wonder if others who have not shared their experiences or status can truly understand them. That concern is a reasonable one. It is essential, then, that helping professionals attempt to know what it feels like to be in the situation of the people they are trying to help, and, equally important, *show* them that they know. When working with the sexually oppressed, the helping person should be particularly aware of the feelings clients are experiencing in reference to their sexual behavior, fantasies, and wishes. Empathy is communicated by dealing directly and concretely with the client's feelings, and by our choice of words (short words usually communicate feelings more accurately than long words) as well as by facial expressions and body language.

4. *Genuineness.* If we want our clients to be honest with us, we had better be honest with them. That doesn't mean that we should share the details of our private lives with them nor report everything we are thinking. Rather it means that whatever we do choose to say is our sincere reaction to them and not a rehearsed "professional" response. The goal is to avoid sounding phony or defensive. Our professionalism should manifest itself in our compe-

tence, concern, knowledge, and ethics, not in an artificial veneer of professionalism and superiority.

The above guidelines provide the foundation for giving help. Many people among the sexually oppressed experience their sexual interests and concerns as evidence of their being sick, bad, stupid, or worthless. When a helping professional listens and communicates in a warm, empathic, and genuine manner, some of this dysfunctional self-deprecation is reduced and the individuals become able to discuss and explore their situations more openly, more honestly and completely.

These interpersonal skills are, therefore, much more than professional niceties; they, along with the other helping attributes we have discussed, are the basic building blocks of interpersonal helping with the sexually oppressed. However, as we have noted, it is not enough to listen, to feel warm, empathic, and genuine. To do any good, these attributes must be communicated to clients clearly and consistently.

LEVELS OF CLINICAL INTERVENTION

Sex-related problems can be approached by professional helpers on several levels depending on the perceived needs of the client, the setting in which the client is seen, and the helper's own level of comfort and skill. Annon (1974) has developed a useful model that suggests four graduated levels of intervention that are applicable to the range of problems and concerns encountered by the sexually oppressed. He called his approach the "PLISSIT" model, an acronym for the four levels: Permission, Limited Information, Specific Suggestion, and Intensive Therapy. We recommend this model as a basic framework for counseling members of sexually oppressed groups. The levels of PLISSIT are, in more detail:

1. *Permission-giving* for nondestructive, nonexploitive sexual expression, including permission *not* to engage in particular activities. For example, a counselor may tell an individual that it is all right to masturbate or to engage in oral intercourse—or, on the other hand, to abstain from these or other activities if the client finds them distasteful or otherwise undesirable. Such permission would naturally follow an exploration of clients' feelings and an evaluation of the options available and possible outcomes of their choices. This exploration may well involve some activities on the next level of intervention.

2. *Providing accurate information* about anatomy, physiology, laws, religious beliefs, patterns of sexual behavior, or any other information relevant to the client's situation or concerns. For example, a counselor might inform a client about sexual options and accommodations for a disability, the limits of safe sexual activity for convalescing cardiac patients, how the possibility of contracting a sexually transmitted disease can be minimized, or the various lifestyles possible for homosexual or bisexual people.

3. *Specific suggestions* for overcoming obstacles to satisfying nondestructive sexual functioning drawn from research and experience with effective clinical practice. Some examples of specific suggestions would be: suggesting that aging couples engage in sexual activities in the morning when they are less fatigued, rather than waiting until the late movie is over; that pregnant women use positions other than the "missionary" if they experience discomfort; or that gay people may want to try out their "coming out" disclosures on gay acquaintances and friends before they tell their parents or spouses.

4. *Intensive therapy* for problems that resist the previous three levels of intervention. Such intensive therapy could consist of the practitioner carrying out a specific therapeutic program with the client or possibly referring the client to someone else particularly skilled in this area. For example, a counselor might choose to refer situations involving complex sexual dysfunctions, undesired behaviors that are resistant to change, or which are potentially dangerous.

These four levels, of course, overlap and supplement each other. Each higher level usually requires more time, skill, and knowledge, and more exploration of the client's and perhaps his or her partner's sexual patterns, attitudes, and experiences than the one preceding it. The significance of this model is that a professional helper need not be trained as a skilled sex therapist to help with many, perhaps most, of the sex-related concerns they encounter in their daily practice.

ASSESSMENT

The application of the PLISSIT model we have just described, as well as any other approach to helping people with their concerns, requires an assessment appropriate to the nature of the services offered. That assessment may be as brief as a single question or as extensive as weeks of intensive exploration involving the use of tests and outside consultants.

In applying the PLISSIT model, for example, one might want to know what information, misinformation, objectives, and beliefs a client already has regarding an issue before giving permission or information. And before giving suggestions, one would want to find out what clients want to achieve, what they would be comfortable with, and what they have already tried.

Part II of this book provides useful information that can be applied to the assessment of particular sexually oppressed groups. This material sheds light on many of the problems commonly encountered by members of these populations, the lifestyles and options available to each group, environmental factors that contribute to the stresses upon them, and some common reactions (both helpful and not so helpful) of other people significant to these populations. At this point, however, we should highlight a few basic questions that help in assessing the needs of the sexually oppressed in general.

1. *Is there a problem?* It must be emphasized that just belonging to a sexually oppressed group does not mean that an individual necessarily has problems. There are countless men and women who are aged, disabled, homosexual, or members of other oppressed populations who are doing very well indeed and have no need for counseling or any other form of professional help. Uninvited "assistance" from well-meaning professional helpers may not only be unnecessary and unwelcome but potentially destructive.

2. *Is the concern or problem directly related to that person's membership in a sexually oppressed group?* A person's age, gender, disability, or sexual preference may have little or nothing to do with their budgeting problems or family disagreements. If helpers insist on focusing on their clients' sexually oppressed status, they may fail to help with their clients' real problems or issues.

3. *Who's complaining?* Who is it that feels there is a problem? Whose problem is it? Whose behavior or what circumstances will have to be changed to bring about a solution acceptable by all those concerned? If it isn't possible to satisfy everybody, on what basis should helpers decide who will get their support? Does the problem suggest interventions broader than clinical help or advice? What larger systems have a bearing on the problems experienced by the individuals who have come to the helper's attention? How might these conditions be changed? Are there basic values or conflicts in values that underlie these problems?

4. *What does the client want?* There is probably no question that is more significant, and few that are more difficult to answer, than this deceptively simple and "existential" question. It is probably true that few people know what they want from their sexuality or, for that matter, from life in general. Many people know what they *should* want, or what others have told them they *ought* to want, or what other people around them *want* them to want, but it is often more difficult to identify what they themselves want related to their sexuality. Frequently we must first assist our clients' efforts to answer this question before we can move on to helping them get what they want.

5. *To what extent does the problem reflect ethnic and cultural differences between clients and the problem-definers?* As we discussed in the previous chapter, there are few areas of life in which people tend to be more chauvinistic than in their ap-

proach to sexual expression. We have to be sure that we are not imposing our cultural values unwittingly under the guise of helpfulness. Much of our help is politically based, and we must eliminate those values from our work that preclude cultural diversity. Derald Wing Sue (1981) suggests:

For too long we have deceived ourselves into believing that the practice of counseling and the data base that underlie the profession are morally, ethically and politically neutral. The results have been a) subjugation of the culturally different, b) perpetuation of the view that minorities are inherently pathological, c) perpetuation of racist practices in counseling, and d) provision of an excuse to the profession for not taking social action to rectify inequities in the system. (p. 19)

INTERVENTIONS

In subsequent chapters our contributing authors will discuss some specific approaches that have been helpful to particular oppressed groups. Here we will review some general intervening approaches that might prove helpful to sexually oppressed people across the board.

Overcoming the Denial of Difference

No other task is as important in helping the sexually oppressed as overcoming their denial of difference: that is, helping clients accept, accommodate to, and perhaps even celebrate their uniqueness, rather than deny that they *are* different.

To paraphrase W. S. Gilbert (of Gilbert and Sullivan) in one of his operettas: "If everybody is like somebody else, then nobody is anybody." It should be clear that all of us, oppressed or not, are unique human beings, and that the attempt to deny our differences and conform to some prototype of "normalcy" leads only to frustration.

In 1970, on the occasion of his letting the United States' first abortion bill pass without his veto, the then governor of Hawaii, John

Burns, was asked how he, a Catholic, could pass such a bill. In response, Governor Burns replied with an old Hawaiian saying: "All people are brothers and sisters, brothers and sisters are all different, and difference is beautiful."

Many of those who are members of sexually oppressed groups have difficulty accepting difference, however. Often the accommodation to difference is interpreted as a submission to second-class citizenship. On occasion this is true, especially when imposed from the outside. However, denying differences can set up impossible goals and distort self-images. For example, one of the authors attended a workshop on sex and disability. One of the disabled was a handsome, intelligent, muscular, and articulate paraplegic who wheeled himself in front of the room to give a pep-talk on the ability of the disabled to have a "full sex life." He challenged the others to "get off their duffs" and get out there to find able-bodied sexual partners and show them that the disabled are just as capable as "anybody" of giving them rich, exciting sexual experiences.

As I looked around the room I saw the others, most of them severely disabled, many incapable of virtually any body movement, most unlikely to sweep many people off their feet—and they knew it. Certainly they all had the right to sexual fulfillment. Many were capable of intimate relationships and some form of sexual gratification. But to overlook their need to accommodate to their level of physical capacity was cruel and insensitive to those less well-equipped than the speaker. (I later learned that such people as the enthusiastic speaker were referred to derisively by other disabled people as "supercrips.")

Another example of the problems inherent in the denial of difference is the experience of many gay men and lesbians who try to accommodate to the heterosexual model of normalcy in their pair relationships. Although extended, monogamous pair relationships may work and be desirable for heterosexual relationships, especially for couples with children, that may not always be the most workable model for many gay men and lesbians. There may be important differences between the needs, demands, and purposes of gay and straight relationships. (See, for example, McWhirter and Mattison, *The Male Couple.*)

We are all different, and we must learn to identify and enjoy who we are, even if we cannot match some idealized model of "normalcy." If we don't help our clients identify their uniqueness, we are setting them up for failure and not for fulfillment.

There are a number of ways in which we can help sexually oppressed people accommodate to their uniqueness. Exposure to a variety of role models, each of whom has made successful and unique adjustments to their specific situations, can be helpful. The practitioner can help individuals to identify their unique strengths as well as limitations and to consider how these might affect their sexual goals. The practitioner might also challenge unrealistic or dysfunctional ideas about what the client feels he or she "should" be doing. Finally, the helper might assist the client in mapping out realistic steps he or she might take to achieve goals and support the client in efforts to do so.

Overcoming Self-defeating Self-labeling

One problem many sexually oppressed people must overcome is the internalization of the negative values they have encountered about their sexuality. Many members of oppressed ethnic minority groups harbor the stereotypes and prejudices held by the oppressing majority. It is not unusual for some gays to be homophobic, some disabled to avoid other disabled, and aging people to dislike anyone over thirty. Clients often manifest this "identification with the oppressor" through pejorative self-labeling. Terms such as "crip," "dirty old man," "queer," "sick," "over the hill" are sometimes as apt to be self-imposed as they are given by others. The practitioner must dispute these terms, help clients perceive the destructiveness of self-

labeling, and help them follow a procedure to rid themselves of these destructive cognitions.

Alternative self-statements can first be offered. The client can be helped to think of alternative positive self-statements that can be substituted for the self-destructive ones. If the client can't come up with any, the practitioner can help. Examples of positive self-statements include: "I'm O.K." "I've just begun to live." "Gay love is good love." "I am not my disability."

The practitioner then helps the client to become sensitized to the negative self-statements. When they occur, the client is instructed to stop him or herself and immediately to make one of his or her positive self-statements silently. Once the client has developed the capacity to stop the negative self-statements and substitute the positive self-statements, he or she is instructed to begin giving silent, self-congratulatory pats on the back each time this occurs. The client then practices the process in the practitioner's presence, with support from the practitioner. Then the client is urged to try the process in his or her natural environment and report back on his or her success to the practitioner. The practitioner, of course, gives considerable recognition as the client decreases negative self-labeling and begins to see him or herself in an increasingly positive light.

Overcoming Loneliness

Loneliness is probably the most common emotional problem encountered in America today. This is not surprising given the transiency of Americans, the breakdown of the extended family, and the general distrust of intimate relationships. Loneliness is probably even more common among the sexually oppressed. Many have their social contacts severely curtailed because of their oppressed status and feel isolated. They may well be avoided by members of the general population. Similarly, their sexuality may have been suppressed to the point that they avoid relationships that could conceivably lead to sexual intimacies.

Professional helpers often overlook the possibility that their clients are lonely because they are preoccupied with other more tangible problems or because their clients have either not mentioned their loneliness or have minimized it. Many clients are either not able to define the emotional deprivation and pain they experience as loneliness or would be too embarrassed to admit their loneliness to a professional helper. They may not want the practitioner to discover any perceived interpersonal inadequacies that might underlie feelings of loneliness.

Furthermore, in a society that still glorifies rugged individualism, it may be seen as a sign of personal weakness to "need" other people. It becomes necessary for professional helpers at least to consider the possibility that clients are experiencing loneliness whether or not the client brings up the problem.

To overcome loneliness Jeffrey Young (1981) suggests several sequential procedures:

Planning activities. Because many lonely people become inactive, lack energy, have lost pleasure from activities that were formerly enjoyable, and live in relatively isolated situations, the first step toward alleviating the loneliness is to get them into situations in which they are likely to meet people with whom they might develop relationships. This might be achieved by helping clients plan activities for each day in which they have some free time. These activities might include hobbies, sports, and other interests that they had enjoyed at any time in the past and could conceivably enjoy again. Priority should be given to those activities that will get them out of their homes and put them into contact with other people.

Initiating   nonintimate   relationships. Once the client has begun to initiate activities, the focus moves to helping the client begin to develop relationships that involve

companionship and self-disclosure, usually with someone for whom the client experiences no sexual attraction. Such relationships may prove difficult for clients who are still reacting to an unresolved relationship, who have only experienced a series of superficial or transient relationships, who believe they are unlovable or undesirable, or who have pronounced anxiety in social situations.

If a client encounters pronounced anxiety in social situations, the practitioner might first determine what makes him or her avoid such contacts. It might be fear of embarrassment, rejection, or loss of control. The result might be that clients engage in "spectatoring" behavior in social situations, in which they constantly observe themselves while they are in contact with other people. Of course, such self-destructive self-critical monitoring only leads to greater discomfort, decreased ability to concentrate on the other person, and diminished pleasure from the contact.

In such situations, the practitioner can be of help by teaching the client techniques to distract him or herself from the spectatoring, to discuss and role-play procedures for attending to other people without accompanying self-criticism, and to make self-statements that will give the client greater feelings of self-worth.

Self-disclosure in nonintimate relationships. Once the client has begun to have some success and confidence in initiating social contacts and derives some enjoyment from these casual relationships, the client is encouraged by the professional helper to make one of these relationships deeper by initiating the disclosure of his or her private thoughts and feelings. Once again, the client should choose a person for whom he or she has no strong sexual attraction in order to avoid the complications—and greater demands—of potential committed relationships. This is an important step in overcoming loneliness because the act of appropriate self-disclosure is a major component in intimate relationships. In this step, the practitioner encourages the client to choose a particular person with whom the client would like to develop a close friendship and then, at an appropriate time, helps the client share a personal concern, problem or feeling with that friend. The practitioner can assist the client in accomplishing these tasks by role-playing and rehearsing the process.

The helper can also discuss any resistances the client has to self-disclosure. Often people fear rejection if they reveal any evidence of personal weakness, fears, vulnerability, or other socially unacceptable thoughts. The helper can dispute this belief by pointing out that most people experience such feelings, whether they admit them or not, and that most friends welcome the opportunity to share such human emotions.

Initiating intimate relationships. Once the client has had some success in developing close relationships of a nonsexual nature, he or she may choose to move on to relationships that have a potential for sexual expression, deep emotional feelings, and commitment. First the practitioner may help clients decide where to look for such relationships, such as contacting old friends or acquaintances; asking co-workers or acquaintances to arrange a date; becoming involved in a club, church, sport, or other activity in which they are likely to meet potential partners who share their interests; approaching acquaintances in everyday situations (at work, in the neighborhood or apartment house) who seem interesting; and joining groups or going to those places that are particularly oriented to the needs and interests of single people.

The practitioner once again explores any resistances the client has to seeking out intimate relationships—such as an inordinate fear of rejection or of appearing too forward—and helps the client overcome them. Frequently the client believes that he or she is too "ugly," "stupid," or "boring" to attract any partner. These beliefs are challenged if unfounded, and the client is helped to be more attractive or interesting if this is needed.

Many clients would profit from social skills training. (See, for example, Bellack & Hersen, 1979.) Such training typically includes instructions, discussions and role playing, modeling, feedback, reinforcement, and homework. The focus of social skills training is on social interactions, how to initiate and carry on a conversation, active listening, the arts of giving and receiving, and how to say no to someone you like.

Deepening intimate relationships. The final step in helping clients overcome loneliness is for the client to be able to deepen his or her relationships. This is often a complicated procedure that might entail intensive therapy if the client experiences consistent difficulties in becoming intimate when he or she wants to do so.

There are several ways in which the practitioner can help a client achieve more intimate relationships. These include helping clients overcome dysfunctional beliefs about potential sexual partners, fears of entrapment by potential intimates, problems in sexual relationships, difficulties in making requests, adjusting expectations of partners, and consistently selecting unsatisfactory partners.

WORKING WITH FAMILIES

Members of sexually oppressed groups do not exist in vacuums. They often live in relationships with family members: parents, sisters and brothers, grandparents, aunts and uncles, spouses, and children. Often these family members, for a variety of reasons, create, maintain, or exacerbate the problems faced by the oppressed person. Often family members themselves share the oppression, and may themselves victimize or be victimized by the person they are trying to help.

Helping the individual oppressed client, then, must often—perhaps usually—include work with one or more family members, whether as counselor, educator, friend, advocate, or mediator.

The parents of a disabled person, for example, may unduly infantilize their child. Similarly, the adult children of aged parents may treat their own mothers or fathers as they were treated when they were children. Adult children may not realize the sexual needs or capabilities of their parents. Parents may fail to provide either the education or opportunities necessary for sexual fulfillment. They may be so afraid of a handicapped child's exploitation that they fail to help develop the social skills needed for even a friendship, not to mention an eventual sexual relationship.

Parents of developmentally or otherwise disabled children may so fear that their child will be rejected that they prevent him or her from taking any social risks. They may be afraid even to discuss the subject of sex for fear of building false hopes. And like other parents, they may be too uncomfortable about sex to ask for help, or too tied to traditional views of sex to consider options other than conventional intercourse for their child. Conversely, they may deny the disability completely. In many instances, the parents may have a realistic and helpful outlook, but find it difficult to deal with neighbors or other relatives who criticize their way of dealing with the situation.

Dealing with the physical and emotional problems of the disabled can be a strain on the most affectionate and sound marital or family relationship, as well as on the mental health of an individual member. It is often tempting, in the helping professions, to be acutely aware of relatives' shortcomings, without realizing the tremendous strength it takes simply to survive the many major and minor crises that occur, much less handle them as wisely as one might want.

Practitioners must be prepared to look beyond the obvious, to be sensitive to the confusing array of emotions like fear, grief, hope, frustration, love, anger, shame, and guilt that being intimately involved with sexually oppressed people can create. Moreover, they must be sensitive to the sense of stigma and isolation that accrues not just for the sexually oppressed, but to their families as well.

This is particularly true for the families of such stigmatized groups as homosexuals, the mentally ill, the developmentally disabled, or sex offenders. Although widely diverse in nature, such groups have one thing in common: their parents or spouses are apt to feel—or be made to feel—responsible for the socially unacceptable trait or behavior, and to be stereotyped as sick, neurotic, too controlling, too weak, and so on.

Spouses are in a particularly difficult dilemma. Our society is becoming more tolerant of people who depart from the norm in some way, but, because it assumes such people have little to offer the "normal" majority, it has more trouble understanding anyone who would love and marry such people. Women who marry gays (whether inadvertently or knowingly), then, are suspected of being sexless, neurotic, masculine, lesbian, or martyrs. Similar assumptions are often held about such people as women who marry physically disabled men, young people who choose older partners, white women who marry black men, and thin men who choose obese women.

It is not uncommon, then, for stigma to be transferred from sexually oppressed victims to their spouses (even by the victims themselves).

The practitioner must also be sensitive to the potential for "liberating" one family member by oppressing another. An emerging problem may be that of a "liberation ethic" (Gochros, 1982), in which oppressed victims not only assert their rights, but become insensitive to the feelings, needs, and rights of their spouses, parents, or children. True, some "blinders" must be worn during the first shaky steps toward independence. But counselors must be able to help families avoid either blaming all problems on the specific oppressed condition (for example, homosexuality or a physical handicap), on oppression in general, or using it as an excuse for inconsiderate behavior toward others.

Many families of the oppressed are in need of a support system. Professionals need to assist them in finding support from others who are or have been in situations similar to theirs, to be their allies in making the community more responsive to their needs, to help them assert their own rights and wishes, and to help them feel they are not alone.

In short, those people who are intimately involved with members of the sexually oppressed must be given the same understanding that is expected of them. Without such understanding and help, we cannot fairly expect them to be of help to the oppressed people they love.

CONCLUSION

Understanding the sources of sexual oppression, and developing the motivation to do something about it, is the first step to offering help. In this chapter we have offered suggestions for procedures to transfer that understanding and concern into useable assessments and helpful interventive strategies for members of the sexually oppressed and their families. We have stressed that there are many levels of helpful interventions. Given the basic attributes we have discussed, many of the concerns and problems encountered in the daily practice of professional helpers can be approached on several levels depending on the needs of the situation and the training and skills of the professional helper.

It is sometimes possible and often tempting to become preoccupied with clinical approaches to the problems encountered by the sexually oppressed. If that is all we do, we will have overlooked some of the persistent broadscale factors that create and maintain many of the problems experienced by sexually oppressed individuals. In the next chapter we will examine some of the approaches professional helpers might use and have used to alleviate these pressures on the sexually oppressed, and to help them realize more options and greater satisfactions in their lives.

REFERENCES

ANNON, J. S. *The behavioral treatment of sexual problems—vol. I: Brief therapy.* Honolulu: Enabling Systems, 1974.

BELLACK, A. S., AND HERSEN, M., eds. *Research and practice in social skills training.* N.Y.: Plenum Press, 1979.

BERNE, E. *Sex in human loving.* N.Y.: Pocket Books, 1971.

BLUMSTEIN, P., AND SCHWARTZ, P. *American couples.* N.Y.: William Morrow & Co., 1983.

BROWN, L., ed. *Sex education in the eighties: The challenge of healthy sexual evolution.* N.Y.: Plenum Press, 1981.

FISCHER, J. *Effective casework practice: An eclectic approach.* N.Y.: McGraw-Hill, 1978.

GOCHROS, J. Wives' reactions to learning that their husbands are homosexual or bisexual. *Journal of Homosexuality,* Spring 1985, in press.

GOCHROS, H., AND SCHULTZ, L. *Human sexuality and social work.* N.Y.: Association Press, 1972.

McWHIRTER, D. P., AND MATTISON, A. M. *The male couple.* Englewood Cliffs, N.J.: Prentice-Hall, Inc., 1984.

SUE, D. W. *Counseling the culturally different: Theory and practice.* N.Y.: John Wiley & Sons, 1981.

YOUNG, J. Cognitive therapy and loneliness. In G. Emery, S. D. Hollon, and R. C. Bedrosian, eds. *New directions in cognitive therapy.* N.Y.: The Guilford Press, 1981.

CHAPTER
4

SOCIAL SYSTEM INTERVENTIONS

Most of the professional literature on the treatment of sexual and sex-related problems has focused on direct clinical services offered to individuals, couples, or families. Often the implicit message is that the role of the helping professional is limited to that of counselor/therapist. Such a narrow focus neglects consideration of a whole array of roles and interventions available to practitioners. Moreover, many of the problems faced by the sexually oppressed cannot be treated on a clinical basis alone.

Clinical and nonclinical interventions—and work with and on behalf of people, of course—overlap. Perhaps it is splitting semantic hairs to arbitrarily separate and label particular strategies as "clinical," "psychotherapeutic," "environmental manipulation," "education," "advocacy," or "social action."

The underlying concern in this chapter, however, will be the differentiation between a "clinical" model and a general "systems" approach for helping people with their problems. At the risk of overgeneralizing, we will suggest that clinical, psychotherapeutic services tend to have an implicit medical model as their base. For the most part, interventive strategy is focused on helping individuals adjust to their environment, on the assumption that it is mainly their own maladaptive behaviors and intrapsychic processes that act as obstacles to their effective social functioning and self-fulfillment. It is individuals and their symptoms that are seen as the problem (disease) to be solved (cured), with the cure purely in the control of the individuals themselves.

A "systems" approach is more social, political, and multicausal in nature. In addition to seeing intrapsychic and interpersonal obstacles, it assumes that many problems are partially or totally outside of the individual's control, and derive from external obstacles to functioning created by the environment. That "environment" may be physical or social, and it may directly or indirectly affect the individual client. It may, for example, be the client's immediate family and the relationships within it, as well as the attitude the family has toward the individual in question. It may be a small network of people with whom the individual interacts (such as doctors, teachers, classmates). It may be a physical structure (such as a hospital or institution) and the policies and attitudes to be found within the walls of that structure. It may be a social institution (the legal system, educational system, nuclear family system, etc.) and the policies and attitudes it contains. It may be as nebulous as public attitudes toward sex or toward the particular oppressed group.

Whatever the term "environment" means—and it obviously covers numerous possibilities—interventive services are aimed at helping it to be as responsive as possible to the needs not only of specific clients, but of present and future groups of people. Individuals and the society in which they live are not seen as separate entities. Rather, individuals, social institutions, and organizations are all interrelated parts of a total organism (system). The well-being of any one part affects and is affected by the well-being of other parts and of the organism as a whole. Changes in one part affect other parts in continually reciprocal interactions. Interventive strategies hence range from resolving problems in social interactions between two people to broadscale legislation to education aimed at changing public attitudes. It is important to emphasize here that "indirect" services and "direct" services are not either-or propositions but rather serve to reinforce each other. Even in a medical model, for example, physicians are not limited to clinical treatment of individuals, but also serve as consultants, researchers, and educators to prevent the spread of disease. The remainder of this chapter will present some models of interventions "on behalf of" individuals and groups, with examples pertinent to the needs of the sexually oppressed.

MODELS OF INTERVENTION

All helping professionals must consider themselves change agents. Each profession, of course, has its own way of defining problems, categorizing levels of intervention (that is, who or what is targeted for desired change), and roles (sets of expected attitudes and behaviors) that the practitioner must fulfill to effect change.

For our purposes we need not become embroiled in the highly technical sets of professional semantics. It would seem useful, however, to provide a brief framework for the strategies to be discussed and the terms to be used in this chapter.

We would suggest three broad levels of intervention:

1. *Microlevels*—in which the targets for change are the attitudes and behaviors of individuals or small groups of individuals, with the professional role mainly that of clinician.
2. *Midlevels*—in which the targets for change are the policies and practices of community agencies or organizations, with the professional role that of a mediator trying to make the organization more helpful to individuals or specific populations.
3. *Macrolevels*—in which the target for change is society itself, including the mass attitudes of the public at large and the broad public policies of its bodies of law at local, regional, state, and national levels. The professional role at a macrolevel is more apt to be that of politician, community organizer, or social activist.

Levels of intervention and roles, however, overlap. Moreover, there are a wide variety of subroles required to effect change at any level. An analogy might be made here to that of a parent. Ostensibly, parents have only two broad roles: to provide physical care until children are old enough to survive on their own and to socialize future citizens into fulfilling the expectations of society. To fulfill those roles, however, parents must inevitably take on various aspects of a multitude of roles, acting as therapists, doctors, nurses, teachers, police enforcers, judges, friends, advocates, mediators, financiers, and so on. In the same way, professionals working mainly at one level will need to occasionally work at the other two, assuming different roles, modifying personal skills to fit different roles and levels, modifying the strategies from other roles to enhance their usual ones, and often playing several roles at the same time through a variety of behaviors.

For example, "policy" changes may be made at any of the three levels: at a microlevel, helping parents to change their "policies" toward children; at a midlevel, helping an organization to change a specific policy; or at a macrolevel, effecting changes in state or national laws.

Professionals may fill a long list of subroles: *mediators* helping to resolve conflicts between individuals or groups or between groups and legislative bodies; *educators* and *consultants* who provide new information and perspectives; *advocates* who speak or act in behalf of individuals or groups, pleading their cause to individuals in their immediate environment, to agencies and organizations, or to legislators and society at large.

Keeping that broad framework of roles in mind, there are many models for interventive strategies. One we find useful is that of Hepworth and Larsen (1982), who identify ten general strategies that practitioners can use to improve the environment and/or deal with environmental obstacles:

1. Enhancing intrafamilial relationships
2. Supplementing resources in the home environment
3. Developing and enhancing support systems
4. Moving clients to different environments
5. Increasing the responsiveness of organizations to people's needs
6. Enhancing interactions between organizations and institutions

7. Improving institutional environments
8. Enhancing agency environments
9. Developing new resources
10. Employing advocacy and social action

The following sections will examine each of these ten strategies in terms of the potential for removing environmental obstacles to both general and specifically sexual self-fulfillment for sexually oppressed groups or individuals.

Enhancing Intrafamilial Relationships

The concept of "family" has different meanings for people at various stages of their lives, varies from person to person, and is influenced by cultural values. Nevertheless, most people have one or more people important enough to them to consider "family." For our purposes, a family can be simply a partner or spouse or may include children, parents, sisters and brothers. It may be an extended family that includes aunts, uncles, cousins, nephews and nieces. In some situations, it may be a surrogate family of intimate friends, or the simulated family of a residential treatment home.

It is in enhancing family relationships that systems interventions most overlap with clinical services. Often, in fact, one or more family members may themselves be clients (or patients) receiving direct clinical services. Further, the family itself provides a microcosmic example of interventions within a system.

In engineering, when stress is placed on a structure at one point, the pressure increases existing flaws in the structure. This stress may become apparent at the weakest point and, eventually, albeit indirectly, cause the total structure to collapse. The same can be said of family relationships. Moreover, in human interactions, there are reciprocal as well as cumulative effects. The family in itself is a system or organism in which what affects one affects all, and changes in part of that system affect other parts.

A family already in conflict or suffering from such problems as poverty, illness, or death may completely collapse from the final pressure of the birth of a handicapped or retarded child. Conversely, a family that has taken such a situation in good stride may deteriorate under the cumulative effect of a series of related or unrelated problems. Given some final last straw like an unplanned pregnancy, the loss of a job, an unusual expense, sexual molestation, the family support network may collapse. Whether or not the collapse is directly related to or caused by the specific sexually oppressed client, it cannot help but affect that client and the relationship between the client and family.

Professional intervention, then, may take many forms. For example, a victim of sex abuse (whether in or outside the home) may need help in overcoming fear and guilt, particularly if the abuse has created friction between the parents. The parents, however, may need help in dealing with their own problems, their own communication and sexual relationships, and their own attitudes toward the client. The total family may need help in working out longstanding problems that have been exacerbated by the crisis situation.

A gay or lesbian client may need less help with intrapsychic problems than with the problems created by a homophobic society. A professional may need to help the client and family alike to communicate with each other empathically, to cope with conflicted feelings, and to assist each other in coping with stigma. In offering such help, the professional may need to act as educator as well as counselor. The family, for example, may simply not know enough about homosexuality to know how to react to a family member who comes out. An advocacy role may be needed to help the gay member interpret his or her feelings to other family members. Conversely, the family may be far more understanding than the gay member realizes, needing more an advocate to cope with defensiveness, paranoia, and dysfunctional behavior on the part of the gay client. The total family may need help in differentiating between problems created by the homosexuality and preexisting (often unrelated) problems that exacerbate and are exacerbated by the crisis at hand.

In addition to counseling, education, and advocacy, a family may need additional resources, extra support systems, financial help, etc. Conflict between parents and their sexually active retarded or disabled child, for instance, may be partially caused by the strain on the family pocketbook, with added worry that an unplanned pregnancy will add a further financial burden. Helping the family feel comfortable about and aiding them in obtaining financial assistance may be necessary before the parents are ready to work on their relationship with the child. Such interventions will be given further discussion in the following sections.

It could be argued that all sexually oppressed persons and their families suffer from problems imposed upon them by society, and that one of those problems is stigma. Many—perhaps most—families simply do not come equipped with the emotional, financial, or social resources needed to deal with an overload of unanticipated and unusual burdens. A systems approach, then, is aimed at enhancing the cohesiveness, empathic problem-solving capacity, and sense of mutual caring that allows each member of a family to feel both nurtured and respected, to feel supported in coping with the outside world, and to find a safe haven in times of need.

Supplementing Resources in the Home Environment

The ordinary household is not equipped to cover the needs of "extraordinary" inhabitants. It is often necessary to physically manipulate the environment, so to speak, to make it a happier fit. Such intervention may serve to increase general social and physical functioning, or may directly affect sexual functioning. Such alterations of the physical structure as wheelchair ramps, bathroom remodeling, and so on, may not only increase general functioning for a handicapped person, but may be vital to the self-esteem and self-image necessary for satisfying sexual relationships.

Modifications in home environment need not always be so drastic. The deaf, for instance, are hampered in social/sexual relationships simply by being unable to use the telephone to make a date. For those with any degree of hearing, a device attached to the phone to enhance sound may also enhance social/sexual life. Similarly, a "talking books" system (a rental library of recorded books for blind readers) may provide sex education material that might otherwise be unavailable. Some human services also enhance sexual attractiveness, indirectly aid sexual relationships, or actually provide sensual gratification. For an extremely disabled person (for instance, a patient with multiple sclerosis), it may be extremely important for physical care duties such as bathing and toilet care to be taken over by paid personnel. That does not exclude the possibility of pleasurable erotic bathing. But when physically wearing and often aesthetically unpleasant duties are completely assumed by one who is supposed to be a sex partner, the emotions engendered in both partners are less than conducive to satisfying sexual relationships.

Obviously, most of these interventions will not be made directly by the professional helper. Professional intervention may be needed, however, to help family members or a funding resource recognize the importance of such measures, to help locate resources and secure financial help if necessary, or even to help the family persuade a handicapped person to accept such services.

Developing and Enhancing Support Systems

Supportive as families and therapists or counselors may be, they are not enough. All people need some other support system— another professional service system (a medical or legal system, a church group, an activity group, or simply a circle of friends) to provide needed services, companionship, recreation, intellectual stimulation, and the "lightweight" empathic help with problem solving that comes with the sharing of common or similar experiences. The sexually oppressed, however, are often isolated from others who have experienced their problems, feel unable to find people responsive to their needs and concerns, or indeed, may actually be made to feel unwelcome, either deliberately or inadvertently.

Whether on behalf of a specific client or a defined population, then, an important social system intervention is the development of support systems. Major roles fall into four main categories of activity: (1) enhancing the responsiveness of existing support systems; (2) locating gaps in community support services; (3) creating new support systems to fill in those gaps; and (4) acting as "matchmaker," helping individuals or groups and their potential support systems find each other and get together. To fill these needs the professional helper may need to act as advocate, educator, social activist, consultant, and/or mediator.

To begin, one must know or actively take steps to learn what community systems already exist, how adequate they are, and how responsive they seem to the needs of a specific population. A gay client and his or her family or spouse, for example, may feel isolated from their church, need pastoral counseling, or may indeed need pastoral support in order to feel comfortable about homosexuality. A physically handicapped person and/or sexual partner may need pastoral support to feel comfortable about nontraditional sexual techniques. It is important for the professional to know both those members of the clergy who will be supportive and helpful and those who will not. It is also important to let clients and their families know that they can find support from a church in their community (presuming, of course, that that is the case).

One must also be aware of the wide range

of supports needed, so taken for granted by the general population that their potential for service or disservice is often overlooked. Professionals are usually alert to the need for a resource list of sensitive physicians and lawyers. They may not be alert, however—as Dulaney (1981) points out—to the need for sensitive insurance agents.

Given an existing resource, the professional may need to enhance the potential of that resource. Even when a support system is known to be available, a working relationship with the appropriate personnel may facilitate referrals and offer opportunities for cooperation, mutual reinforcement and problem solving, and coordination of services. Moreover, the professional may enable a heretofore unsympathetic system to be more responsive. Mediation and advocacy on behalf of a specific client, or education through conversations, speeches, and workshops, for example, may help an unsympathetic minister or congregation examine or even change attitudes about homosexuality and reactions to a gay client.

It is also important to assess the limitations of an existing resource and to increase its potential. Professionals might, for instance, alert a community center to the needs of a specific population, offer consultation and help in reaching out to that population, and assist with problems that may arise. In turn, they may become referral sources for that organization. They might also help hospitals, institutions, halfway houses, and so on, to offer socialization and sex education groups for handicapped patients or clientele.

If existing support systems cannot expand or modify to fill in a gap in service, new ones will need to be created. Professional intervention may be as simple as bringing to the attention of the Metropolitan Community Church (a predominantly gay church) the need for its presence in a specific community. It may, on the other hand, entail considerable social/ political action and cooperation with the gay community to bring in such a church. In some instances, the gap in service may be great enough to require the creation of a new social agency with a complete professional staff—again a project requiring community organization or social action. Often, however, a support system needs little, if any, professional staffing.

Support groups and self-help groups. To meet the needs of special groups, self-help and support groups have been gaining in popularity. Self-help groups are simply a group of people who share some common bond, experience, or problem. They gather together to offer mutual support, comfort, and help. Generally they rely purely on the members' own experiences and resources, bringing in professionals only as guest lecturers. A professional role, then, may be simply to assist in the formation of such a group and to be available as the guest lecturer. One might, at microlevel, offer one's office as an initial meeting place and provide suggestions for locating new members. At midlevel, one might suggest that an existing social agency undertake such a project.

Although self-help groups are often called support groups and do share similar structures and services, there are differences between them. Support groups, in fact, may combine elements of a self-help group, a workshop, and a therapy group, with the needs, structure, and objectives varying from group to group or changing over time within a group. The degree of help needed from a professional will depend on several factors: the severity of crisis, stress, and physical or emotional "risk" for group members; the homogeneity of membership; the ages, intelligence, knowledge, and leadership capabilities within the group; and the amount of information and help available outside the group.

The more stigmatized and closeted the group, the more professional leadership may be required to provide accurate information and help in problem solving. The group may have closed membership, be time limited, and entirely professionally led; it may have open membership, be ongoing, and simply use the professional as an advisor, trouble shooter, participant observer, facilitator, or referral source and occasional lecturer. Any combination of the above is possible. A group may change and shift focus as it and its members "mature." For example, it may become entirely a self-help group, or may form the nucleus of a social action group working to create a professionally staffed social agency and new legislation.

Whatever the combination, the role of the professional, to some degree, will be to assist in guiding discussion to make sure that it is productive, to ensure that "risk takers" find adequate support, to provide needed information, to spot individuals needing individual therapy or emergency care, and to serve as a bridge to the resources in the community. The professional, whether creating such a support system or participating in an existing one, will need to be creative in fitting the group to its members' needs and will need to have a clear contract with the members about his or her responsibilities.

Although the professional may occasionally need to protect one member from group coercion, generally, support groups and self-help groups offer only positive benefits. They provide a sense of belonging and mutual caring, validation of feelings, role models. They stimulate members to confront issues rather than avoid them and provide more realistic perspectives than might be gained in therapy alone. Alcoholics Anonymous, for instance, has demonstrated that both support and criticism may be more easily accepted when it come from someone who has "been there," and that "game playing" can be more easily recognized and challenged by fellow players. Moreover, it is important for people with unique sexual problems (like retardation, physical handicaps, stigmatized sexual lifestyles) to have access to input and sharing with people who share similar problems. A paraplegic or multiple sclerosis victim, for instance, may only be able to utilize professional information when he or she has actual role models for attaining sexual fulfillment. The potential power of such groups may be appreciated when one realizes that the women's movement was in large part started by such groups, without professional help, leadership, or structure, and with only vague personal goals in mind.

Moving Clients to Different Environments

There are times when a person's move from one environment to another is desirable, times when it is undesirable, and times when it is absolutely necessary. Whether it is a positive or negative step, however, it is one that holds profound emotional impact, particularly for the sexually oppressed and their families, often more vulnerable emotionally than others. It is not, then, an intervention to be undertaken lightly. The professional may be the initiator who proposes such a move, a client advocate who is reacting to a proposed move, or an administrator or consultant whose opinions may determine whether or not a move takes place. No matter which, the professional must be sensitive to the emotional upheaval that accompanies such changes, must carefully weigh the risks and benefits, and must help others to be equally sensitive.

For example, emotional trauma even in such temporary, positive moves as going to summer camp or going away to college is a common occurrence in the general population. No matter how "bad" the original environment or how "good" the new one may be, the old one is a known quantity and the individual has learned, to some degree, how to cope with it. For people whose self-confidence and coping skills may already be strained to the maximum, leaving familiar surroundings, important people, and stable supports may temporarily heighten anxiety, sense of loss, or fear of failure. Feelings of stigma, isolation and rejection, guilt, and poor or inadequate self-image may also surface.

Hepworth and Larsen (1982) in fact suggest that moving people from their environment is so drastic an intervention that it is appropriate only for such extreme reasons as physical or sexual abuse, unusual medical needs that cannot be met in the environment, people whose behavior is so uncontrollable that they threaten the safety of others and themselves, or when a loss of housing has already occurred because of fire or some natural disaster. Even in sex abuse and wife or child battering, they point out, the decision to remove may have more harmful effects than the original offense and should not be cut and dried. In essence they recommend such an intervention be limited to those situations in which the current environment cannot be modified enough to ensure the mental and physical safety of an individual.

Their points are well taken. Professional intervention will often be needed to discourage or even prevent an unwise or unjust move. Often in fact a move is planned as "punishment" for sexual behaviors because of agency personnel's lack of information or sex-negative attitudes. For example, some years ago one of the authors took part in court action against a public welfare agency, instituted by a family agency acting as advocate for a welfare mother. The mother was about to permanently lose custody of her four-year-old daughter, simply because while in a foster home the child had been seen masturbating. When asked by the foster mother where she had learned such behavior, the child had said quickly, "My mother taught me." Both her behavior and her automatic calling upon parental authority to defend herself had been seen as proof of "emotional abuse."

Luckily, as one last resort before going to court, a conference had been held with the welfare department to try to settle things more amiably. When misinformation about masturbation was discovered and corrected, the welfare department willingly dropped charges, and the child was eventually reunited permanently with her mother, rather than removed.

We would not go so far, however, as to insist that only "life and death" matters justify a change of environment. In fact a temporary (or in some cases, permanent) move might at times prevent such extreme crises and enhance ability to change the climate of the original environment. For example, an elderly widower might well benefit from living in a semiprotected yet independent environment, able to form social/sexual relationships and pursue his own interests without disrupting the lives of his family (or conversely, without living alone in proud and lonely independence). Yet it might take professional knowledge and skill to enable either parent or child to suggest or follow through on such a plan, to alleviate guilt, anger, hurt, and sorrow, and to build in ways to maintain and enhance the family tie if a physical separation is effected.

Professional interventions, then, may be to encourage, insist on, discourage, actively prevent, or deal with *fait-accompli* changes of environment. The interventions may be small: helping all parties concerned in the removal of a child in a sex abuse case. Or they may be broad: helping a city planning commission evaluate how its urban renewal plans will affect those dependent on a center for independent living or a halfway house, which is to be demolished. In any event, the goals of intervention must include an accurate assessment of the appropriateness of the plan, helping others to be sensitive to its impact on both the "removee" and the "removed from," and helping to achieve positive results with as little pain for people as possible along the way.

Increasing Responsiveness of Organizations to People's Needs

An important function of the helping professional is helping organizations make their policies and practices as responsive as possible to people's needs. Practitioners may act as informal educators and role models, formal educators, in-service trainers, consultants, advocates, and program planners. Some of the earlier examples would also be appropriate to this area. The range of possibilities is limitless. For example, what happens to the family of someone who has attracted public attention as a rapist or child molester? One might help an agency offer a support group for such people. One might bring to administrative attention (or as administrator, be alert to) policies that discriminate against staff or clientele because of sex or sexual orientation. One might help staff in a home for the aged accept the sexuality of its residents—for example, encourage social/sexual relationships and offer sex education programs, or designate "private" rooms in existing institutions or allow for privacy in remodeling plans. (The need for privacy, of course, is not purely to allow for sexual activity. Denying privacy to institutionalized persons, however, is in effect denying them the right to sexual relationships, or even self-gratification.)

In effecting policy changes of organizations and institutions, the professional helper will need to be sensitive to a number of factors: the fears and resistances of both agency personnel and the community; the power structure of the organization and its decision-making process; its degree of autonomy; the particular function of the organization; the professional's relationship to that agency; the potential consequences a change of policy will make; and the priorities that need to be made. Thought must be given, then, to what one wishes to achieve and how best to achieve it. Changes then, may be directed at adding policies to enhance a sex-positive climate, or decreasing oppression by eliminating sex-negative policies.

Enhancing Interactions between Institutions and Organizations

Many of the sexually oppressed are people who may need a variety of services from a multitude of people and organizations. Sometimes called "case management," the coordination of services between and within agencies is crucial to the well-being of a client. For example, it is pointless at best to enroll a mentally or physically disabled adolescent in a sex-positive education program when parents and staff members are not working together to support the program, inadvertently giving contradictory messages, or even deliberately sabotaging the program. Likewise, it is less than helpful to have three agencies which share the same concerns working independently, each feeling isolated and powerless, duplicating some efforts and often working at cross-purposes.

The case manager role, in essence, is to see that problem solving efforts are truly cooperative ventures, with agencies and practitioners working together rather than at cross-purposes. Regardless of the goal, professional roles might include sharing information and planning with a parent or colleague, holding a staff or interagency conference, preparing newsletters, setting up referral services, and so on.

Improving Institutional and Agency Environments

Implicit in much of the previous discussion has been attention to the physical and emotional "climate" of agencies and institutions. Climate includes the full range of attitudes and messages conveyed to people nonverbally through tone of voice, facial expression, body language, garb, the wording of written rules and regulations, the physical layout and furnishings, and so on. It behooves professionals to be aware of that climate in their own office surroundings and interpersonal communications, and to be role models for making it as human and helpful as possible. There is more, however, that they can do to help others build a positive climate in an organization.

Underlying attitudes. The goal, of course, is to help the physical structure and staff behaviors reinforce the attitudes that the "helpers" wish to convey. Some thought, then, must be given to what those attitudes are, how helpful they are, what changes are needed to make them more helpful, and how needed changes can be made. One would hope for consensus that the general attitude to be conveyed is that of respect and concern for both the staff of an institution and the people it serves. All people have the right to be treated with dignity, to achieve self-fulfillment and responsibility for their own actions in accordance with their own needs and abilities, and to enjoy reasonable degrees of privacy and physical comfort. (The term "reasonable," of course, is subject to interpretations that in themselves convey attitudes.) For our purposes, we must also specify the need for a sex-positive attitude that includes the right to *sexual* fulfillment and responsibility in accordance with individual needs and abilities.

When staff attitudes and institutional policies interfere with or negate such attitudes, they also interfere with helpfulness. Depending upon one's role with an agency, a professional may modify attitudes through education (in-staff training, consultation, etc.) and by attempting to initiate policy changes that affect programs, personnel, or clients. Thought must be given to staff attitudes in hiring and selecting personnel for a particular program (for example, a sex education program in an institution). In some cases, when attitudes of staff cannot be modified, the climate can be changed only by removal of that staff.

Physical layout and furnishings. The need for creating privacy in existing institutions has already been stressed. The need to plan for privacy ahead of time can hardly be stressed enough, and professionals can help facilitate building or remodeling that truly conveys the desired messages. Appreciation of "personhood"—with the right to sexual relationships—can be conveyed by careful design, rather than the usual dormitory arrangements or sterile cubicles found in institutions for aged, physically disabled, or mentally handicapped persons. Even hospitals and nursing homes could provide wings for married couples (partners or lovers).

Furnishings also convey messages. Offices can create an atmosphere of warmth through the choice of chairs and sofas, with desks and files, if they must be used, placed in an unobtrusive spot. The choice of books or brochures strewn around or in the bookshelf, the wall furnishings, the announcements or cartoons on a bulletin board—all can be deliberately planned to fit the needs of a specific population, or to generally say "sex is spoken here," "dignity is spoken here," "humor is spoken here," "homosexuality is spoken here," and so on.

Development of New Resources

For the most part, previous discussion has focused on the utilization or enhancement of existing community resources. In some cases, however, the community simply does not have the necessary resources. Professional knowledge, coupled with creativity, can be employed to help create resources.

Given such hidden, isolated, and stigmatized populations as, for example, victims of sex abuse or married homosexuals and their families, a support network can be implemented. Try starting hotlines, interagency referral and information systems, newsletters, or speaking in call-in radio shows. A support group can be initiated individually through an existing agency, or even through an ad in the paper. Sometimes community organizations that are not primarily service oriented can be helped to become resources. One social worker, for instance, noted the number of suicides occurring in her high-rise condominium building. She convinced the board of directors to exchange her rent for counseling and for organizing rap groups for building residents. The concern of just one team of doctors, psychologists, and social workers recently led from a small informal support network to the establishment of an AIDS foundation, which will provide a full range of medical, legal, psychological, and social services. Initial funding came from a group of gay and gay-supportive businesses.

Whether the goal is a simple one of establishing an informal support and information network or a complex one of establishing a complete program or agency, there are many processes and skills to consider. Professionals must know existing community resources, officials, and indigenous leaders both within and outside the targeted population. They may need to know or be able to assist others in understanding and using such program development skills as fundraising and grant writing, administration, and obtaining needed publicity. They need to be aware and increase others' awareness of potential legal issues, to communicate desired values such as the need for confidentiality, the right to sexual expression, etc., and to help others be aware of their own limitations. They may need the group leadership skills to help form a cohesive group with identified goals, one able to withstand disappointments and critique itself. They need not be experts in all areas—they simply need understanding of where and how to obtain the needed experts and how to tap the resources of those already willing to help. In short, the innovator needs to have or develop leadership skills.

Employing Advocacy and Social Action

Implicit in many of the interventions heretofore discussed has been the use of advocacy and social action. Acting on behalf of an individual or group—whether as an interpreter of needs, a defender of rights, an arbitrator or mediator—is a form of advocacy. The end goal is to give individuals and groups access to resources needed for achieving their right to self-fulfillment. Those "resources" may be as tangible as adequate medical service or as intangible as "understanding." A practitioner might act as advocate in a court, for a retarded person's right to marry or have an abortion, or in a welfare agency, for the financing of a recipient's birth control measures. Usually, although not always, the advocacy carries an implicit message that one is championing people whose rights have either been denied or overlooked, who are either unable to speak for themselves or whose messages, unless supported by others, will not be given credence by those in authority. Those in penal or mental institutions, the very young or very old, the poor, the handicapped—all those groups we have termed the sexually oppressed—are often in need of people to speak in their behalf at review boards or legislative hearings, to stand up for them in dealing with bureaucrats, and to help them cope with "helpers" who are less than helpful.

Some advocacy, of course, cannot be carried out alone, nor can the requested service be authorized by one single authority. To a large extent, systems services are those services aimed not at helping individuals but at changing society to fit the needs of all its citizens. Even when an individual client's cause is being championed, it is as a case in point, with the advocate engaging in a symbolic (or sometimes literal) "class action" suit. It is this kind of advocacy that we call social action. Because even small changes in institutional policy may at times run into political interference, conflict with state or national laws, or require the changing of community attitudes and the organization and cooperation of a total community, even some of the seemingly innocuous interventions we have illustrated earlier may require social action or be part of a social action process.

The need for commitment to social action can hardly be stressed enough. Doctors and therapists, for example, may be persuaded to donate services for one poverty stricken AIDS patient. They can hardly do the same for every patient. Nor should any patient have to depend on the benevolence of an individual. The right to adequate professional care is hampered by a dearth of knowledge, discrimination and prejudice, public hysteria, lack of funding or facilities for the prevention and cure of a new disease, and political forces bent on oppression.

Professional strategies include public education, lobbying or political pressure to obtain federal funding and backing for research, legislative testimony, grant writing, providing leadership to or participating in forming community coalitions and collective action. In short, social action utilizes the full complement of personal/social/political activities possible to ensure that our society lives up to the principles embodied in its Constitution and serves to provide the framework within which individuals can be helped to meet their own needs.

Attempts to effect policy changes, then, are at the macrolevel of social planning, with changes that may in turn affect the policies of community organizations and agencies. Passing ERA, legalizing homosexual marriages, mandating the right to sex education in school, including sex therapy in health insurance coverage are just a few more examples of policy changes which professionals might help to effect.

Education. Whether formal or informal, a wide range of educational options is available. Education can range from micro- to macrolevels, reach a specific target or general population, contain general information about a wide range of sexual behaviors and lifestyles, or specific information about a specific population or sexual behavior. It can serve one or many functions and can be the only intervention used or part of a combination of interventions. The targeted "student(s)" might be one's own client, significant people in the client's life, colleagues, students in a public or professional school, legislators, or a mass audience. The education provided might serve as a "preventive" step or a "curative" step.

In an earlier illustration of advocacy—a family agency trying to separate a young child from her welfare mother—simply correcting misinformation about masturbation was the key to the effectiveness of the advocacy. More comprehensive sex education, however, might be appropriate in a special education school, coordinating in-service training for the teachers, a workshop for parents, and classroom instruction for the students.

At base, all education is simply the transmission of information and values. No matter what the subject at hand, messages are automatically given and received about society's (or the teacher's) views of the two sexes—their characteristics, expected roles and behaviors, and their behavioral relationships with each other. Even in formal sex education classes, attitudes about sexual behaviors are transmitted unconsciously. The amount of education received or given formally or even with any planning is minimal. Most learning is picked up through a sort of osmosis, powerful precisely because it is so unnoticed, so seldom subjected to objective scrutiny, and so often contradictory to stated values.

Professionals who wish to be effective educators, then, must give careful thought to the messages they wish to impart, do some planning for how they will try to transmit those messages both formally and informally, verbally and nonverbally, and make use of the many options open to them.

The possibilities are almost endless. Besides acting as teachers and in-service trainers, professionals can assist others in planning courses or act as consultants to schools, school boards, or entire public education systems. Often overlooked are such strategies as giving speeches, appearing on television or radio talk shows, writing articles and books. Professionals can influence mass attitudes by acting as consultants to movie and television producers or programmers.

Some potentially useful options are too often deliberately discarded. Some journal editors, for example, are disdainful of articles that are not research oriented, and many practitioners are afraid to submit "think" pieces or bits of practical wisdom. Both forget, perhaps, that research itself stems from personal experiences and shared ideas. Similarly, practitioners are apt to be intimidated by the thought of writing. Some scholars who write for professional journals are disdainful of writing for a mass audience and, in effect, talk only to themselves. Yet articles for popular magazines, newsletters, or even letters to the editor reach thousands of people at a time, and can help to prevent more problems than the contributing writer could either prevent or cure by direct intervention alone.

No matter what the intervention, the underlying goal must be to encourage a positive view of sexuality that helps people increase their options for sexual fulfillment, enhances self-esteem, recognizes and respects difference, facilitates personal and social responsibility, and regards access to correct information and new ideas as a citizen's basic right.

CONCLUSION

This chapter has dealt with a number of interventions in which the goal is less that of changing oppressed populations than of changing the policies, behaviors, perceptions, and attitudes of the surrounding society. It should be evident that these interven-tions overlap considerably. Often they share many of the same strategies and differ only in the focus of immediate attention or long-range goal. They all have one common approach—a systems approach that treats individuals, groups, community organizations, or agencies and social institutions in relation to each other, rather than as separate entities unto themselves. They all have one underlying value—that societies form for the collective well-being of individuals and hence must be responsive to the needs of their citizens.

REFERENCES

DULANEY, D., AND KELLEY, J. Improving services to gay and lesbian clients. *Social Work,* 1982, 27(2):178–183.

HEPWORTH, D. H., AND LARSEN, J. A. *Direct social work practice: Theory and skills.* Homewood, Ill.: Dorsey Press, 1982.

PART II
Meeting the Needs of Specific Oppressed Groups

CHAPTER
5

WOMEN
Jean S. Gochros
Wendell Ricketts

Among the list of oppressed groups, the category of women must certainly be considered unique. No other group comprises 53 percent of the country's population, is so evenly dispersed throughout it, is so apt to live with and love its oppressors, benefits so much by its oppression, or stands to lose so many "secondary gains" by its liberation from the "sickness" of oppression. Hence no other group faces such extreme opposition to change from within its own ranks.

With no other group does true change so completely affect the rest of society, changing the distribution of wealth, uprooting the foundations of our social institutions, and cutting across divisions of class, religion, and race. Hence no other group (not even ethnic or racial groups) evokes such widespread and extreme resistance to change from outside its ranks. Also, ironically enough, in the

oppression of no other group does the "oppressor" become such a victim in his own right.

With other groups, it is relatively easy to differentiate between sexual oppression per se, and economic/political/social oppression that is either rooted in or extended to sexual behavior. With women, however, *every* problem—indeed every thought and behavior, problematic or not, is to some extent defined by their gender (biological sex) and by how society characterizes the qualities and defines the roles of that gender. Moreover, all of society's institutions are rooted in differential expectations of women and men. Both sexual oppression and liberation, then, must be considered holistically: that is, socially, politically, and economically, as well as in terms of erotic gratification.

There seems little point, in this chapter, in

painstakingly documenting the oppression of women. As Safilios-Rothschild (1972) has stated,

Those who still remain unconvinced [of sexism] cannot be convinced by factual evidence because their resistance is emotional. (p. 2)

Given such a large domain this chapter will simply try to provide an overview of problem areas, with examples of especially pertinent or new problems, and some estimate of the progress made in overcoming sexism. It will then focus on the women's movement: where it has been, where it seems to be going in its development of theory, goals, and design for social change, and the implications of those trends for the helping professions. It will conclude with a section on suggested professional interventions based on those trends.

HAVE WE PROGRESSED?

It has been over twenty years since Betty Friedan's *The Feminine Mystique* (1963) proclaimed that women were oppressed. By now "Women's Liberation," "sexism," "male chauvinism," and "sex role stereotyping" have become household words.

There is little doubt that progress has been made. Not only have women entered the work force in unprecedented numbers, they have entered and done well in many traditionally male trades and professions. They have become better educated. They have risen to executive ranks in business, commanded higher salaries, and have achieved the passage of significant anti-discrimination legislation. They have entered the political arena, made changes in dress, in the language, in education, in child care, and in credit and insurance policies.

Women have become more sexually assertive, sharing the once "male only" right to sexual gratification in or out of the marital bed. They have helped society to pay attention to the problem of sex abuse, fostering changes in legislation, preventive programs, and treatment of sex abuse victims. Finally, they have brought about changes in such areas as abortion rights and sterilization policies, family law, and have made medical and mental health care more responsive to their needs. Pointing to such signs of progress, many in today's society feel that women have secured their rights and that nothing more need be done. In fact, some would say that women have gone beyond all reason in their demands.

Such obvious signs of progress, however, are deceptive. One of the most insidious manifestations of women's oppression continues to be economic. In fact, contrary to any notion that they control the nation's wealth, women are invariably at the bottom of the economic ladder. At the beginning of the 1980s, women were in roughly the same earning position as they were at the beginning of the 1970s. Surprisingly, that position was lower than it had been in the 1920s (Freeman, 1975). Women earn, on the average, $6 for every $10 brought home by a man (*Perspectives on Working Women*, 1980). Women comprise 94 percent of bank tellers, but only 37 percent of bank officers and financial managers; 99 percent of legal secretaries but only 22 percent of lawyers. They comprise 96 percent of registered nurses, but only 22 percent of physicians. That 22 percent is mainly in the areas of obstetrics and pediatrics, each of which is low on the medical salary scale. They comprise 2 percent or less of mechanics, construction workers, and carpenters, and 5 percent of engineers (where they earn $.68 for every $1.00 male engineers make). Of the ten occupations that earn men the highest median weekly income, women make up an average of only 14 percent of workers (Rytina, 1982). Although highly visible, the comparatively few women who achieve high salaries and prestige are frequently still tokens.

The majority of women work, as do men, because they and/or their families need the income. For the most part, however, they still command lower salaries than men, suffer sexual harassment on the job, and are subject to discrimination in hiring, firing, and promotion.

In 1971, Miller, Roby, and Joslin's research indicated that when discrimination because of ethnicity or gender interact, gender is the salient factor. That fact remains true today. At the same time, discrimination because of race or ethnicity packs a potent charge when combined with sexism. In annual income, white men are on top, followed by black and then Hispanic men. White women come in a poor fourth. But it is nonwhite women who suffer the most (*Perspectives on Working Women*, 1980).

Women comprise the bulk of those falling below the poverty line. Although 43 million women accounted for 60 percent of the labor force by the end of the 1970s (Kesler, 1982), the incomes of one-fourth of these women were not enough to lift them above the poverty level. Between 1970 and 1980, the number of single-parent households maintained by women grew by 55 percent to 8.5 million (*Perspectives on Working Women*, 1980). Neither welfare legislation nor income maintenance programs have been responsive to such changes in women's status.

Despite a few programs to help single mothers and displaced homemakers enter or return to the labor market, women—even highly educated ones—still lack marketable skills or reenter the labor market at a disadvantage because of the time they have taken out to raise children. Child-care facilities are still inadequate, and those that exist are often financially prohibitive. Many women are faced with only two choices: whether not to work and risk poverty, or to work and create a "latchkey child," thereby running the risk of censure for child neglect.

Progress has been made in the distribution of power and division of labor within marriage. Many men now are willing to help with both child care and household duties. Some have even taken the role of "househusband" while their wives worked, or have given highest priority to their wives' employment needs and opportunities. Yet for the most part, help with children and home has been just what the word implies: helping *her* with *her* duties, as it suits *his* convenience, and often accompanied by a hint of criticism that *she* has been incompetent. Moreover, recent research suggests that working wives—even at the highest executive level—pay for the privilege of working by having two full-time jobs. They may still have to battle the notion that outside employment is a frivolity and that a woman's *real* job—in the home—must not be interfered with by outside interests. Finally, work in the home is still not given the status of "work" at an office.

Sex Role Stereotyping

Stereotyped notions about the differential characteristics of men and women have softened. Women are increasingly apt to see themselves as assertive and to be considered and treated as logical, strong, intelligent, and capable human beings. Men are apt to see themselves as tender and to show such emotions as grief and hurt (Bem, 1974).

But have traditional stereotypes truly changed? Research is inadequate. Yet anecdotal experience suggests that such changes are tenuous at best. Attitudes toward crying are particularly illustrative. In the process of studying such attitudes, one of the authors hears countless stories to suggest that crying evokes conflicted feelings, that it is still considered a feminine behavior equated with loss of control, weakness, irrationality, manipulativeness, incompetence, passivity, and so forth.

Moreover, efforts to combat stereotypes about crying have led to contradictory factions with contradictory approaches. One faction insists that women should eradicate their "feminine," "passive" crying and substitute "masculine assertiveness." The other faction defends "femininity" and touts crying as a behavior that men should emulate. It would seem that stereotypes are still alive and well, that "femininity" is still considered a negative, and that gender rules have broken down only enough to create confusion and double messages.

A study on wives of gay men (Gochros, in press) yielded other evidence of the ambivalent attitudes held in our society toward the expression of traditionally feminine qualities. Women married to gay men were stereotypically perceived to have chosen their husbands because of their own masculinity, assertiveness, or inability to cope with sexuality. When they expressed anger, they were seen as aggressive, "unladylike," and controlling. When they cried, however, they were accused of being overly feminine, passive/aggressive, manipulative, or irrational. Stigma based on male chauvinism and sex role stereotyping—coming from many sources, including husbands, friends, and professionals who had been presumed nonsexist—was one of the biggest problems faced by women who had unknowingly married gay or bisexual men (Gochros, in press).

This study, of course, was of a special segment of the population. But the values revealed in it mirror dramatically those held in other parts of society. Clinical experience with women in therapy and with heterosexual couples suggests that this is, indeed, the case.

Sexuality

There is no question that women today have increased rights and abilities to find sexual fulfillment and to refuse sexual advances. A continuing problem, however, has been the confusing messages in information and practical advice to women, particularly heterosexual women, who want to be both good feminists, successful in the work and professional world, and to have satisfying love relationships with men. The message of much of the information promulgated by the earlier women's movement was to get out of the house, throw off the chains of wifedom and motherhood, and make it on your own in the "real" world. The cry was taken up by the media and by popular magazines that

combined articles on "Success at Work" along with ones that advised women to transform themselves into sex kittens the moment they punched the time clock at the end of the day. No doubt many women have felt caught in a particularly untenable situation: the messages they receive about being strong and assertive in the work world often make little sense in the context of sexuality. In the bedroom, men often accept women's new rights only when they fit men's fantasies without making demands or posing a threat to a male sense of power and ownership.

Many clinicians, for example, report seeing more men who have become more sexually passive, disinterested, and even dysfunctional as women have become more assertive and orgasmic. Such men complain that they lose interest once they have "won" or now that they have less need to enter the "chase." Some husbands push their wives into a sexually open contract or a "swinging" group, in order to relieve their sense of guilt about infidelity, real or fantasied. Yet, when their wives try it and like it, the husbands are not so accepting. As one man told his wife, "In my head, I know you have the right. In my guts, I can't take it" (Gochros, 1982).

At the same time, information women receive about sexuality often seems designed to create an image of women not only as sexual, but as supersexual. As more women have become orgasmic, one generation's liberation has become another's oppression. Not only are women allowed to have orgasms now, many feel compelled to have *at least* one, and often multiple orgasms, either to prove their own sexual adequacy or to reassure their partner about his. The term "preorgasmic" devised by Barbach (1975) and widely used in groups designed to help women attain orgasm, was meant to give hope by suggesting that "any woman *can*" (have orgasms). The despair and shame with which people come to such groups, however, suggests that it may give an unintended message of "every woman *must*."

The emphasis in such groups is that women should take more responsibility for their own orgasms. However, the tendency to exclude men from such groups, and the difficulty in persuading them to participate when they are included in the planning, suggests that men still take the stance, with inadvertent reinforcement, that if a woman is unable to reach orgasm, it is purely *her* problem. Yet when women do try to define and explain their sexual wishes in lovemaking, they are often met with accusations of being controlling and mechanical.

Even advances in sex research and therapy have often had the effect of imposing on women a new model of sexual normalcy, rather than freeing people from stereotypes of sexual adequacy. Zilbergeld (1983) notes the tendency of professionals to create as many problems as they solve. Freud, for example, was the first to recognize women's right to sexual pleasure but made them feel guilty about clitoral stimulation and orgasm. Masters and Johnson (1966) freed them from that guilt by noting the lack of difference, physiologically, between vaginal and clitoral orgasms. In no time at all, however, women who did indeed have vaginal orgasms and who did not like clitoral stimulation began to feel guilty and abnormal.

The recent controversy over the rediscovery of the Grafenberg spot (Ladas, Whipple & Perry, 1972), and its putative association with orgasmic expulsion of fluid by women (promptly named "female ejaculation"), have created new expectations for women. The Perry and Whipple group originally disseminated information about the G-spot and female ejaculation to demonstrate that there is no single genital focus of arousal in women, and to alleviate the anxieties of women who had considered their orgasmic expulsions to be abnormal (supported in this belief by physicians who performed surgery to cure "urinary incontinence"). Soon, however, therapists began receiving frantic calls from women who now felt abnormal because they couldn't locate their G-spot. Women rightly felt discouraged by a hierarchy of expanding expectations that seemed to require them first to be orgasmic, then multiply orgasmic, and finally even to have G-spots and perhaps to ejaculate.

Women's right to say no is acknowledged intellectually, but women are still subjected to subtle pressures to have intercourse on demand. The woman who works outside the home is usually still a full-time homemaker as well. Her participation in sex may serve the purpose of fulfilling perceived obligations rather than genuinely meeting her sexual needs. Men may pressure women into sex by using the rhetoric of the "new sexuality" against them: "You're liberated; you should want sex as much as I do." Sometimes the pressure is not so subtle. Despite changes in both legislation and attitudes, rape victims are still suspected of "asking for it," either because they are "provocative," "flaky" or because they somehow look like victims. It is not clear whether the increase in reports of rape, incest, and wife battering is due to increased societal responsiveness to women, or whether there is a rise in such crimes. But it is very clear that there is still a tremendous amount of violence toward women, and that to be a sexual victim is still to be suspect.

Have women stopped being sex objects? Certainly, to some extent. Yet men—even highly educated, nonsexist men in the helping professions—still talk about women as if they were simply walking genitals and breasts, deliberately embarrass them with public sexual jokes, categorize them according to their sexual attractiveness, and brag about "scoring." In one city, for example, men term going to a singles' disco "checking out the Prime Heifers."

The issues of body image and sexual attractiveness, and the debilitating effect on women who are made to feel worthless as human beings or inadequate sexually because they do not fit whatever standard of physical beauty is current, are beginning to be addressed more widely by the women's movement. Partly this is because the manifestations of this insidious form of sexual oppression are increasing. So much emphasis is put on beauty and slimness that such emotional disorders as anorexia and bulimia once relatively rare and considered the product of disturbed parenting, are now common. The connection between ideals of female attractiveness and sexual oppression is also being recognized by feminist writers who take on the issue of obesity (such as in Orbach's *Fat Is a Feminist Issue*, 1983).

The New Oppressors

It could once be said that women were oppressed by men. As in other liberation movements, however, the need to obtain group cohesiveness, consensus, and power can result in intimidation of the oppressed group by its own members. This feature may be accentuated in women's oppression, for several reasons.

With most oppressed groups, resistance from within is based mainly on fear of reprisal. Members often have at least some consensus on what they want and differ mainly in how to reach their objectives. Frequently, moreover, they live in geographic clusters and have some bonding against one common enemy. Obtaining both a broad base and group consensus, although not easy, is possible once the potential for group action is demonstrated. Working for change does not necessarily tear apart families, and may increase their cohesiveness. Reprisal may serve to increase both group and family bonding.

Although some of these same features are part of women's liberation efforts, the even population distribution of women in intimate relationships with an "enemy" they love accentuates fear and prevents group unity. When the group comprises 53 percent of the country's population, it is difficult to obtain consensus over either goals or methods. For some women, for example, "liberation" may mean the freedom to work; for others, it may mean the freedom *not* to work. For some it may mean the exemption from military duty, while for others it may mean the expectation of equal responsibility even for unpleasant and dangerous duties.

Whether in the area of employment, sexual behavior, or social behavior, then, many women have felt intimidated and devalued by other women's insistence that the values, lifestyles, and behaviors they enjoy are worthless and unacceptable. It seems obvious that in many areas oppression is in the eye of the beholder. Liberation obtained by legal, physical, or psychological coercion, then, is no liberation at all.

Another kind of oppression is also becoming apparent. This time, however, it is not oppression of women but of men, in what one might call a "liberation ethic" (Gochros, 1982) that substitutes female chauvinism for male chauvinism. Any oppressed group member must wear some blinders in order to escape excessive guilt in establishing independence from an oppressor. Liberation ethics, however, is a stance that makes it permissible to be insensitive to the feelings and needs of anyone who poses a real or imagined threat to liberation and punishes men simply for being symbolic oppressors.

As noted in one of the introductory chapters, it has led to such situations as the wife who establishes her liberation by holding her husband responsible for (and expecting him to magically solve) all the problems society has created for her. She is angry at him no matter what he does or doesn't do, becomes inconsiderate and insensitive, and considers any protest "male chauvinism." She may leave him abruptly without attempts at problem solving, and be indifferent to any pain that he might feel. Ironically enough, men are beginning to complain that *they* are being treated as sex objects, good for stud service without attention being paid to their total personality. Moreover, men, as well as women, are being stereotyped, insulted, and dumped without explanation. It is tempting to say to men, "Ha! Now you know how it feels! You can dish it out, but you can't take it." Such a solution, however, is unsatisfactory. Just as men become oppressed by their oppression of women, so women's liberation cannot be obtained by reversing the procedure. Oppression in the name of liberation, whether directed at men or women, has fueled the fires of the inevitable backlash forces.

Backlash and Backward Movement

In any liberation movement, there are periods during which progress is tenuous and often stopped in its tracks, as well as times when ground is even lost. There is evidence that such is the case with the women's movement.

Although some people point to the defeat of the Equal Rights Amendment as a message that women's liberation has lost, it had always been clear to ERA activists that the passage or failure of the amendment would hinge more on political maneuvering in Washington than on the usefulness or fairness of such legislation. Like the Fair Employment Practices legislation in the 1960s, it was never expected to provide more than a reaffirmation (albeit one with legislative teeth) of existing constitutional principles.

The failure of the ERA constitutes, then, primarily a psychological defeat. Its main dangers lie in discouraging committed fighters for women's rights, and in the potential that a future push for its passage will divert attention away from other needed reforms, as the suffrage issue did many years ago.

Other backward steps, however, are more directly oppressive to women. On the economic front, Equal Opportunity Commission (EOC) officials have told the authors that affirmative action for women is going backward, and that women—particularly ethnic women—are the last hired and the first fired. Government statistics reveal that while women's salaries are rising, the gap between men's and women's salaries is spreading. In the attempt to halt inflation through budget cuts, it is those programs that most affect women that are cut most drastically.

Fundamentalist religious groups and conservative political forces have made steady inroads into undoing women's newly attained right to control over their own bodies. The right to abortion is being successfully infringed on in many states and local communities. Even though 1983 Supreme Court rulings have prevented some infringements, antichoice forces working on the local and regional level have been able to set up tough barriers for women who want abortions.

Only a minority of states cover abortion in their Medicaid programs, and 1976 legislation added new restrictions on Medicaid funding of abortions. In practice, the right to abortion has been all but eliminated for the poor. The National Abortion Rights Action League (NARAL) warns that even the right to adequate family planning and medical care in the areas of sterilization and temporary contraception is continually threatened by such proposed legislation as a constitutional ban on abortions and the use of the IUD.

So Where Are We?

Although space has permitted discussion of only a few pertinent areas, we have presented a complex, often contradictory picture: women have progressed, women still have problems, they have swung the pendulum perhaps too far, and they have gone backward. So where exactly are women today?

We would suggest that women are still in a state of transition and probably will be for some time to come. They have made a surprising amount of progress in twenty years. In fact, it has become something of a joke in the women's movement that such opposition leaders as Phyllis Schlafly have essentially become liberated women in order to fight liberation. Changes, however, have been tenuous at best. It would probably be unreasonable to expect more change in such a short time, given such a diverse population and such firmly entrenched societal values.

Much of what passes for liberation is simply the superimposition of new contradictory and rigid rules upon old ones. Both men and women find themselves caught in double-bind situations, confused, still struggling to define exactly what liberation means in a pluralistic society and how to achieve it in a way that truly respects individual, religious, and cultural values.

Despite resistance, the women's movement does seem to have brought about at least widespread recognition that sexism exists and must be eliminated. Few people—particularly in the helping professions—would dare disagree on that score today, no matter how they might complain that women are going too far. But where are they going? Where should they go?

A NEW LOOK AT OPPRESSION

At this point, we face a dilemma. We have described some of the problems women still face; we could now proceed directly to providing practical suggestions for professional interventions. To do so, however, is to treat women as merely one of many oppressed groups, their social movement as simply one among many civil rights movements. Suggestions for interventions, then, could be limited to a few strategies, like helping to pass ERA and helping women to achieve orgasms.

We consider such an approach an error, as serious as it would be to suggest techniques for treatment of medical symptoms without ever discussing the intent of the treatment, its relationship to the health of a patient, or indeed without even being sure who the patient is and what medical condition is being treated. Women are *not* merely one more "rights" group. The women's movement, which did indeed start out as such a group, has evolved over the past twenty years into a true social movement that fundamentally challenges existing views of society and the human beings who compose it. It is potentially as revolutionary and as powerful a force for changing the future as the concepts of democracy, capitalism, or communism were for the past.

That may seem like a grandiose statement. We are convinced, however, that if it is an inaccurate one, the inaccuracy is on the side of understatement, not overstatement. We are further convinced that failure to take the movement seriously has led to token, uncoordinated, often directionless and contradictory professional interventions. Conversely, there may be some professionals who are unwittingly aiding and abetting societal changes that they would never knowingly support.

One model for social change called "muddling through" (Lindblom, 1959) suggests that in today's complex world, it is impossible to plan truly informed, rational changes. Change agents should simply plan small incremental changes for immediate benefits, without worrying about where they might lead or how helpful they will be in the long run. Somehow, society's checks-and-balance system will prevent serious mistakes in the process.

For the most part the helping professions have used a "muddling through" approach to dealing with sexism. Although we appreciate Lindblom's good-natured acceptance of human inadequacies, we cannot accept muddling through as a desired approach to problem solving.

Our first suggestion for professional interventions, then, must be that professionals take the women's movement seriously enough to educate themselves and their future generation about the evolution of its goals, strategy, and behavioral theory. After all, whether we take time out to think about it or not, all of our social and clinical interventions are based on and framed within our understanding of the evolution of American democracy: its institutions, its theories of individual and collective behavior, its areas of consensus and of disagreement. That framework has been a part of our education from childhood on. Its importance has been recognized in our professional training through required courses linking the evolution of our professions to the evolution of our society and comparing differing approaches created by differing systems of government. Similarly, we consider the evolution of the women's movement so essential a framework for discussing interventions, that while space limitations allow for only a brief, over-simplified discussion of that framework, we feel obliged at least to provide that much.

The women's movement is composed of two branches that have led (in somewhat linear progression) to three overlapping paradigms concerned with (1) the critique of society's institutions and values, and (2) the concept of oppression.

The Egalitarian Paradigm

The first faction was indeed simply one more "rights" group. Its perspective on oppression was an egalitarian or "integrative" one that presented no challenge to traditional thinking. It saw male thinking and behavior as good, felt that if it was good for men it was also good for women, and saw oppression simply as exclusion from the male world. Mainly, then, efforts at change held limited goals directed at a few specific attitudes or policies (for example, helping men to accept women's right to work, adding daycare centers, ERA, etc). In some ways, the insistence on paid employment *in addition to,* rather than instead of, women's traditional roles created new oppression, putting women in role conflicts and making them feel guilty if they did not wish to work. Moreover, it helped mainly upper- or middle-class, white, heterosexual women.

The Liberation Paradigm

The second strand presented the first real challenge to the traditional pie. Instead of simply seeking a few changes in order to allow male values and privileges to be shared by women, it began to challenge those values, to seek institutional change, and to reevaluate and discard traditional assumptions about sex role differentiations.

It was this strand that coined the terms "sexism" and "male chauvinism" to identify two core concepts in traditional theories of sex role differentiation: (1) men are more important (significant or worthwhile) than

women, and (2) women are here for the pleasure and assistance of men. Such concepts become translated into such ideas as "Men do the most important work and *whatever* they do is important work," "Women should take care of trivial chores so that men can carry on their important work," and "A woman should make a man feel like a man" (Freeman, 1975).

In rejecting such ideas, this strand, composed of many groups, took on an active and vocal critique of society's insistence on heterosexuality; violence directed at women both in reality and in the media; the use of women as sex objects; stereotyped views of female characteristics; sex abuse; inattention to female sexual needs; and the oppressive role distinctions built into such social institutions as marriage and the nuclear family, the legal system, the education system, the labor market, and so on. Moreover, it broadened the base of the movement, addressing the concerns of women who were poor, uneducated, inarticulate, and/or non-white.

Within this faction, some subgroups became antimale, antiheterosexual, and separatist. Ironically, despite declarations to the contrary, in many ways male behaviors and values were retained and simply ascribed to women rather than men. Freeman (1975) views these subgroups as changing from an "egalitarian ethic" to a "liberation ethic" in the approach to eliminating oppression.

Synthesis: Androgyny

Most analysts of the women's movement agree that neither the egalitarian nor the liberation paradigm alone is sufficient to explain or eliminate the oppression of women. A third paradigm, which in many ways forms a synthesis of the others, has been increasingly called "androgny." It is emerging as the road the feminist movement will travel, taking society with it.

Pitted against a traditional view that men and women are essentially different and should serve different functions, and that their roles and status merely reflect such differences, the androgynous perspective starts with this major premise: the two genders are constitutionally equal and share the same human capabilities. Hence, observed differences demand a critical analysis of the social institutions that cause them (Freeman, 1975).

The traditional view insists that the two genders are so different that individual personality traits identify one as masculine or feminine and, moreover, that sex role traits are polarized and dimorphic. Such a view dictates not only that "feminine" traits are good for women, but also that "masculine" traits are bad for them. In doing so, it rigidly proscribes behavioral roles according to these differentiations and punishes exchange or blurring of sex role traits.

An androgynous view on the other hand values both genders equally, looks only at "desirable" traits, and considers them equally desirable for both genders. The formulation of androgynous theory is still in progress, with many divergent views being debated. One hypothesis, for example, suggests that masculine and feminine traits coexist in individuals, each acting as a moderating force on the other. Another (and one with which we agree) suggests that the traits in question vary according to individual personality rather than strictly by gender and may vary over time within one individual (Rebecca et al., 1976). For our purposes such fine points, which are the subject of considerable ongoing research, need not be argued. What authorities agree on is that:

1. No matter what biological differences there may be between men and women, they are not sufficient to warrant different personality or role expectations. Proscribed sex roles, then, must go, leaving people equal opportunity to develop interests, careers, sexual relationships, and partners according to their individual needs and abilities.

2. Sexism can be a two-way street: the oppression of women also oppresses men. There is no meaningful choice for members of either sex so long as there are socially proscribed sex roles and social penalties for those who deviate from them.

3. Sexism must be redefined as the entire range of policies, attitudes, beliefs, practices, policies, laws, words, and concepts that either deliberately or unintentionally assign characteristics, lock people into arbitrarily and rigidly defined roles and behaviors, devalue attributes, or unequally limit social, sexual, and economic opportunities on the basis of sex.

The goal, then, is *not*, as many people fear, to develop a unisex homogeneous society. Rather, it is to develop a society so equitable in its expectations and opportunities that one cannot tell the gender of a person merely by knowing his or her work, interests, roles, sexual behaviors or partners, or income, nor can one assume anything other than gender simply by knowing a person's biological sex. The movement seeks diversity within unity, with an androgynous stance asking only that people have true choice in deciding how they wish to live their lives.

INTERVENTIVE STRATEGIES

The strategy for developing such a system is holistic, because both institutional, group, and individual change must occur to achieve such a goal. Although the objective may be a radical change in the foundations of society, violent revolution is not seen as a way of reaching that objective. What is sought instead is planned and coordinated change in every sphere, ranging from sweeping policy changes to incremental steps, mass interventions to individual ones.

Such changes are already taking place on many levels. Legislative lobbying, agency reform, innovations in psychotherapeutic counseling, and even the efforts of nonprofessional consciousness-raising groups are all essentially aimed at remedying the same social injustices. But well-coordinated planning, with cooperation between professionals and lay persons, seems to be missing.

For example, the "bandaid" activities of some self-help groups resemble those of social work in its earlier history. In such a situation, social work might well provide consultants to prevent their own earlier errors from simply being repeated. In general, uncoordinated efforts may interfere with each other and may block the formation of broadscale, organized interventions. The helping professions can conceivably act, through their input, services, and advocacy experience, as agents of coordination.

Broad Scale Interventions

Safilios-Rothschild (1974) delineates four major dimensions of social policy changes needed:

1. Policies that liberate women. For example, professionals might work for legislation that establishes women's right to make their own decisions about birth control and abortion and gives access to adequate counseling and medical care regardless of income. Professional efforts might include lobbying, education, and helping clients to connect with appropriate organizations. They might also include helping a particular hospital or agency effect such a policy, advocating with a doctor, hospital, insurance company, or even a husband or parent on behalf of a particular woman.

2. Policies that liberate men. Professionals might engage in similar activities to effect such legislation as ERA not only to help women, but to free men from having sole responsibility for military duty. Professional effort might also be directed toward legislative, insurance, or social agency policies that allow single or gay men to adopt children and that do not discriminate against fathers in alimony or custody suits.

3. Policies that liberate marriage and the family. For example, professionals might work to promote legislation and agency policies that give both parents equal responsibil- ity for and access to child care. One might, for instance, work for legislation requiring places of employment to have child-care facilities, help a particular place of employment voluntarily offer such a facility, work for legislation to provide state or federally funded facilities, advocate for a couple's or single parent's right to receive financial assistance for child care.

One might urge insurance companies to offer divorce insurance to enable marriages to dissolve without the financial hardships (and hence legal and emotional struggles) that so often occur. One might encourage both legislative and agency policy changes that allow for job sharing, job flexibility, and parental leaves without penalty. One might also work for changes in welfare and social security policies that unintentionally create "Catch-22" situations in which both men and women are penalized for working, for not working, for getting training and education, and for not having training and education.

4. Policies that liberate the society from sexism. For example, one might work with editorial boards to eliminate sexist attitudes and language from books, journals, movies, television, newspapers, and so on. One might work for legislation mandating school sex education programs, help professional schools to include discussion of sexism in their curriculum, help schools, hospitals, community organizations, places of employment, etc., examine their hiring, firing, and promotion practices, help a community develop new services aimed at preventing and coping with violence toward women (including various forms of sexual harassment on the job), and so on.

This broad, interactive model recognizes that areas and levels of intervention interact with each other. Interventions can and should take place at each level and in each area simultaneously. Helping professionals might serve as lobbyists for legislation, as educators providing specific information or stimulating new thought and discussion, as agency or legislative consultants, community organizers, or advocates for specific clients or groups of clients.

Clinical Interventions

Clinical interventions using an androgynous framework start, of course, with a commitment to helping individuals free themselves from rigid sex role expectations in their self-evaluations, their interpersonal relationships, and their daily functioning, to helping them increase their options for self-fulfillment and behave as equal partners in their relationships with others. The reader is reminded that our use of such terms as "androgyny" and "equality" is not meant to insist on one particular behavioral model, but to provide choice.

A new form of therapy, however, called "feminist" therapy, has begun to emerge from the women's movement. Feminist therapy suggests that to simply be nonsexist or androgynist is not enough. In order to help clients attain equality, a more activist stance must be taken, helping people to understand the oppressive elements that have shaped their problems, using a wide range of treatment modalities which may involve peer help as well as professional help, helping them to become more politically conscious and active, and treating them as equal partners within the therapeutic relationship (Franks & Burtle, 1974).

For example, it is common for married partners to seesaw between self-blame and blaming the other partner for marital or sexual problems. Although the clinician often warns against assigning blame, the structuring of how the therapist sees the problem is often limited to outlining intrapsychic and interpersonal processes that may, in more subtle fashion, continue to assign blame and lead to excessive defensiveness. One might, however, discuss with the couple how society has "set them up" for problems and made solutions difficult to find, particularly in the confusing "transitional" era. The partners can be asked to help each other change what

they themselves can change and to be empathic with each other about what they cannot change. Helping them to separate one from the other can often set a whole new climate for change. That same approach can be used in individual therapy. There are countless possibilities for useful interventions. Many have already been used by some therapists. One might, for instance, help a woman (or man) explore new career opportunities and be supportive of choices that are not sexually traditional. One might help a couple "liberate" their marriage by helping them to take equal responsibility for household and child-care chores, creatively dividing their labor, not in broad divisions like cooking, child care or housework, but in more detailed and specific tasks based on their own interests, time, and abilities.

One might need to act as advocate and interpreter, helping both partners to express their feelings, assert their rights, establish their individual identities, and achieve economic independence. One might help both partners to consider work in the home as productive, worthwhile, and important as work outside the home. Not only is this important for wives, it may become increasingly important for husbands who are either unable to find paid employment, who prefer to be "househusbands," or who are willing to act as househusbands to allow their wives to take advantage of a job opportunity.

Obviously, we have been stressing the idea that it is not enough simply to help women modify their attitudes and behaviors, that an androgynous stance requires attention to the needs and responsibilites of both men and women. Professionals may, however, need to help a family recognize that a family version of an "affirmative action" program may be necessary to enable a wife to "catch up." For example, helping a wife to return to school may require sacrifices from the family. Even skill and training may not make up for an older woman's years spent out of the labor market. Professionals may need to help all concerned recognize and find realistic ways to cope with the fact that no matter how non sexist a husband may be, wives are still at a distinct disadvantage in ability to achieve equality.

Professionals must also be aware of subtle forms of sexism and sex role stereotyping. One might, for example, need to help a woman be more assertive in expressing her feelings, thoughts, and rights at work, at home, and in social relationships. Yet one might also need to validate crying as one constructive way of coping with tension, help a crier to explain the feelings and thoughts behind the tears, and help a "responder" to respond by empathic listening rather than tuning out because of immediate and often inaccurate assumptions about what the crying means. (We might note here that therapists themselves may need to examine their own potential for making stereotyped *a priori* assessments.)

Often therapist interventions are not enough. Time limitations may also prevent a single therapist from dealing with all of a client's problems. Helping a woman to find additional support systems may expand the areas of help, reinforce a therapist's own interventions, or in some cases give a client help in being more assertive and honest with the therapist. A therapist might well make referrals to, create, or even lead support groups. Such groups relieve the sense of stigma and isolation and allow a degree and kind of help that a therapist alone might not be able to provide.

Treating sexual problems. Despite the almost fadlike attention given to the treatment of sexual dysfunction in the past few years, many professionals remain hesitant to help with sexual issues and, even when willing, fail to communicate their willingness to women who may be too embarrassed to initiate discussion of sexual concerns. Whether as doctors, nurses, marriage counselors, psychotherapists, or pastoral counselors, professionals need to open more doors to communication. Pregnant women and new mothers, for example, often have questions about sex that cannot be answered by the cursory "instructions" issued by obstetricians. The aftermath of birth may create sexual problems for both partners. A professional could open doors to discussion simply by noting those facts, and inviting discussion as needed. A physician fearful of doing so because of either time or knowledge limitations, might consider hiring an expert to hold periodic seminars or rap sessions, or to deal with problems as they arise.

In treating sexual dysfunction, it is important to remember that the end goal is to help people find fulfillment, not to cure "plumbing" problems. The professional needs to look beyond a presenting complaint and to guard against making the achievement of orgasm a new form of oppression. One may need to provide information about sexuality, to help a couple clear away roadblocks to solving "their" problems rather than "his" or "hers," help a wife to clarify and communicate her wishes in sex, pinpoint a husband's subtle guilt-provoking behaviors that serve to prevent honest communication. Often one may need to intervene in a double standard regarding extramarital sex, or clarify and help a woman cope with the many double messages she receives about her sexual rights.

Use of the PLISSIT model (Annon, 1976) may be helpful here. Many pregnant or newly delivered women and their husbands, for example, need "permission" to be sexual, need limited information about changes in sexual response during and immediately after pregnancy. Such specific suggestions as using added lubricants, trying new positions, or ways to achieve sexual gratification without intercourse may prevent or solve many sexual concerns. The therapist might need to explore both partners' ideas about sex and sex roles, and expectations based on myths about how good parents are supposed to feel and act.

Menopausal and aged women similarly are often in need of information about changes that aging brings to sexuality. Many women are not aware that women as well as men masturbate. Both men and women may need help in understanding both their own sexual needs and those of their partner. Therapists may need to act as educator, advocate, interpreter, as well as therapist.

Whether or not one adopts the title of feminist therapy (we ourselves question the appropriateness of such a term), its principles hold much merit. It is important, however, to be aware of its potential for becoming as oppressive as traditional therapies have often been in the past.

It is also important to avoid a heterosexual bias in counseling. We would suggest that homophobia is one symptom of sex role stereotyping. Freeing people from homophobia might mean helping gay, lesbian, or bisexual clients to accept their homosexual feelings and behaviors, helping to increase understanding between such clients and their relatives, peers, or colleagues, helping them to connect with support networks and political action organizations, helping people to see themselves as sexual beings, with many options in sexual partners, rather than as categories marked homosexual or heterosexual.

The Need for Research

Many of our present attitudes, policies, and interventive strategies are based on inadequate information. One form of intervention, then, must be research to provide new information. More research to determine the extent of biologically determined sex-linked behaviors and traits, to understand differences and similarities in male and female sexual response, to determine how sexual orientation is formed, and to determine the effectiveness of specific treatment modalities are just a few of the possibilities. Professionals must guard against their own sexism, however, not only in planning research designs, but also in interpreting findings, evaluating studies, and even in determining what is worth researching.

In summary, this chapter has presented a broad conceptual framework for viewing both the sexual oppression and liberation of women. We have presented possibilities for interventions at various levels. For some they may seem old hat, while for others they may appear radical. What is important, however, is that they be viewed simply as a few examples of many interventions needed not only to enhance female sexuality or to change women, but to change society. The interventions should be made with some attempt at thoughtful assessment, planning, and coordination of efforts.

We are convinced that only within such a holistic framework can single interventive strategies, clinical strategies in such areas as sexual functioning, or indeed, the strategies to be suggested in succeeding chapters, be meaningful.

CONCLUSION

Women today are in a state of transition. They have achieved an amazing amount of change in the past twenty years. Yet they are often caught, as are men, by conflicting role expectations superimposed on each other, by institutional structures that oppress even when individuals are willing to change, and by a pluralistic society that holds many different views of what liberation means.

The women's movement itself is in a state of transition. That it has not reached its ultimate goals is not surprising. As a movement for social change, it has evolved in only twenty years from a narrow, traditional perspective to challenging a theory of behavior that has existed for over 2000 years. Its blueprint for change is more comprehensive than any that has ever existed. It is our opinion that only to the extent that the women's movement succeeds will other oppressed groups achieve the full measure of their liberation. That is the potential for reform it carries. The helping professions need to both utilize it more fully and offer their own knowledge and insights in a joint effort to create a truly democratic society that is fully responsive to the needs of all its citizens.

REFERENCES

ANNON, J. *The behavioral treatment of sexual problems.* Hagertown, Md.: Harper and Row, 1976.

BEM, S. L., AND LENNEY, E. Sex typing and androgyny: Further explorations of the expressive domain. *Journal of Personality and Social Psychology* 34 (1976): 1016–1023.

FLEXNER, E. *Century of struggle.* New York: Atheneum, 1974.

FRANKS, V., AND BURTLE, V., EDS. *Women in therapy: New psychotherapies for a changing society.* New York: Brunner/Mazel, 1974.

Freeman, J., ed. *Women: A feminist perspective.* Palo Alto, Calif.: Mayfield Publishing Co., 1975.

FRIEDAN, B. *The feminine mystique.* New York: Dell, 1963.

GOCHROS, J. Wives' reactions to learning that their husbands are gay or bisexual. *Journal of Homosexuality,* in press.

KESLER, L. Behind the wheel of a quiet revolution. *Advertising Age.* 53 (1982):M–11, M–14.

LADAS, A., WHIPPLE, B., AND PERRY, J. *The g-spot and other recent discoveries about human sexuality.* New York: Holt, Rinehart and Winston, 1982.

LINDBLOM, C. The science of muddling through. *Public Administration Review* 19 (1959):79–99.

MASTERS, W., AND JOHNSON, V. *Human sexual response.* Boston: Little, Brown, 1966.

MILLER, R., ROBY, P., AND JOSLIN, D. *Handbook on the study of social problems.* Chicago: Rand-McNally, 1971.

ORBACH, S. *Fat is a feminist issue.* Berkeley, Calif.: Berkeley Publishers, 1983.

Perspectives on working: A databook. U.S. Dept. of Labor, Bureau of Labor Statistics, Bulletin 2080. USGPO, Oct. 1980.

REBECCA, M., HEFNER, R., AND OLESHANSKY, B. A model of sex-role transcendence. *Journal of Social Issues* 32 (1976):197–207.

RYTINA, N. F. Earnings of men and women: A look at specific occupations. *Monthly Labor Review* April 1982:25–31.

SAFILIOS-ROTHSCHILD, C., ED. *Toward a sociology of women.* Lexington, Mass.: Xerox College Publishing, 1972.

YATES, G. *What women want.* Cambridge, Mass.: Harvard University Press, 1975.

ZILBERGELD, B. *The shrinking of America: The myth of psychological change.* Boston: Little, Brown, 1983.

CHAPTER
6

MEN
Linda Perlin Alperstein

SOURCES OF OPPRESSION

For a man to write a chapter on men as a sexually oppressed group is a challenging endeavor. For a woman, it is an act of blind courage. There is little argument among both men and women that men are much less oppressed sexually than women. Feminists especially would find the idea of male sexual oppression absurd. There is virtually no body of literature, no profession, no national organization, nor center of research to address the subject.

Nevertheless, men can clearly identify ways in which they feel truly oppressed as individuals, even though they may not identify with an acknowledged population, such as gays or the aged. As early as 1963, one writer (Goffman, quoted in Pleck) said:

In an important sense there is only one complete unblushing male in America: a young, married,

white, urban, Northern, heterosexual Protestant father of college education, fully employed, of good complexion, weight and height, and a recent record in sports . . . Any male who fails to qualify . . . is likely to view himself—during moments at least—as unworthy, incomplete and inferior. (p. 153)

This chapter addresses middle and working-class, heterosexual American men and the ways in which they experience sexual inadequacies and oppressions. It does not focus on men with other issues of oppression *per se,* except as those men also identify with "middle American" sexuality. Likewise, this chapter will not focus on men whose social-sexual lives are such that their capacity for any relationship is seriously lacking.

As this author has listened to male clients, teachers, male friends, and colleagues, and as she has read men's writings about themselves and interviewed male experts on men,

I have been struck by the many painful ways in which men suffer in their sexual lives. Men are often articulate and clear as to their sexual concerns. They have many common problems such as performance anxieties, sexual dysfunctions, loss of interest or desire, as well as general sex-related concerns—for example, lack of partner, loneliness, poor communications, or jealousy. Although most men clearly identify their own individual problems, there is little evidence of a group identity and little agreement as to the causes of these concerns or the roots of sexual oppression. Men, as a group, have not developed a way of clarifying, categorizing, or understanding these common problems.

The sources of oppression that men do describe range from their individual partners to all of womankind, the women's movement, the men's movement, macho scripts, feminist expectations, their fathers or lack of fathers, and other innumerable and contradictory causes. And it is possible that all of the above may be sources of sexual oppression. Nevertheless, what is missing are the vehicles through which men can connect with one another for mutual support for these common concerns, regardless of the disagreements as to their origins. Compared to women's books and magazines, women's organizations, television shows, conferences, and personal support systems, heterosexual men lack a sense of community. There is no brotherhood in which they can talk openly about social/sexual/emotional concerns, and in which they can help each other through the benefit of their own experiences. Gay men have been developing such systems for years now, but the formal avenues through which heterosexual men can talk personally with each other, and learn from one another, are few and far between.

Although it is stereotypical that women share their lives with each other verbally while men are strong and silent, oddly it is the *fathers* of modern psychiatry who gave us the basic mental health techniques of free association and ventilation via talking about oneself. Yet even such organizations as Fathers for Equal Rights, which has been an active advocate for men's legal rights, may provide no opportunity for personal disclosure and support in accomplishing its goals.

Perhaps a major source of sexual oppression of men stems from complex societal forces that have isolated men from one another over the years. These are profound social, political, and economic evolutions. Economics alone, for example, and the industrial revolution, have caused huge changes in family relationships. Fathers work away from home, and boys no longer apprentice to the world of men and work by learning their father's trade. Yet regardless of these societal evolutions, one cannot help but compare men's many individual concerns with the almost nonexistent number of men's groups or other support systems. Men face their private anxieties alone, and few have male friends with whom they can unburden, commiserate, or gain comfort. And barely a handful have a sense of a supportive male community with which to identify. In the literature that does exist, however, three major themes emerge as the commonly mentioned sources of sexual oppression: sex role stereotypes and norms, feminism and the women's movement, and lack of male mentors or intimate friendships.

SEX ROLE STEREOTYPES AND NORMS

Sex role stereotypes and *norms* can be defined as widely shared beliefs about what men and women are actually like or should be like. Although these beliefs tend to change or evolve with economic, military, and other societal realities, whatever the current norms are, they do have a deep effect on both sexes, creating a requirement of conformity that is not always congruent with the individual. As Julty (1979) has noted, "It might be said that sexuality in all parts of the world is influenced more by social traditions than by hormones. In some cultures, the natural and cultural factors are in harmony. In our society 'male' sexuality (biological sexuality) and masculine sexuality are often incompatible. . . ." Writers such as Julty, Zilbergeld (1978) and Castleman (1980) discuss at length the oppressive models of masculine sexuality. In fact, Castleman says, "you need to read *Penthouse* or *Playboy* in order to understand the fantasies and expectations of the average guy" (interview by author, 1983.)

Although male authors characterize masculine sex roles in their own style, their descriptions are remarkably similar. First and foremost is the assumption that there *is* a "normal" way to have sex and that way requires penis/vagina intercourse. Chapter 1 of this book discusses in detail this reproductive bias, and for men especially the burden to "perform" sexual intercourse is most oppressive. Simply put, the American concept of male sexuality necessitates the "efficient management of intercourse" (Julty, 1979).

A second common sexual script is that men should be interested in sex and ready to perform whenever a sexual scenario is possible. This "Ready Teddy" syndrome assumes that men are of high libido by nature—certainly more so than women. Lack of sexual interest is not compatible with masculinity, regardless of a man's feelings, health, morals, or the practicalities involved.

A third myth claims that men must be leaders. They must initiate, engineer, and conduct the sexual experience. They need to develop universal techniques for pleasing women, not to mention guiding inexperienced women toward sexual pleasures. Furthermore, the job must be done spontaneously, confidently, and not too quickly! A large penis is preferable and a firm erection is mandatory. During this process, moreover, a man's sexual wants should be entirely satisfied, so that he becomes aroused, erect, and otherwise performs without any special attention to his own needs.

These sexual scripts change somewhat with racial, religious, and economic differences, but few men grow up or grow old in this culture without experiencing pressure concerning their sexual feelings and functions. These rules are particularly oppressive to men who are virgins or who choose sexual abstinence. They are also oppressive to men as they become middle-aged and elderly. Even if they once fit these sexual expectations with ease, most have some difficulty in accepting the natural changes in sexual patterns that come with age.

For many men these scripts prevail in one form or another, despite our supposed "age of enlightenment." One might say that penis envy (or rather penis-performance envy) is a major *male* sexual concern. One writer points out: "Much of the explicitness of recent film and fiction serves only to give more detailed presentations of the same old myths, thus creating even more pressure to do it right . . . . You need only to go to one pornographic film to check this out" (Zilbergeld, 1978). Yet the male experts themselves are not always in agreement. In his book *Sex and the Liberated Man*, Albert Ellis (1976) for example lists nine major rules for satisfying highly intelligent women, and he devotes an entire chapter to "The Art of Sexual Persuasion." Although each individual point may have some merit, Ellis's sum total gives the clear message to men that they are responsible to guide and manage the sexual act and take care of women in the process.

For many men these sex role expectations work in opposition to their physical and mental well-being. One would hope that masculine sexual scripts would be flexible enough for a great variety of men and allow for a wide range of acceptable masculine behavior. However, the reality in this culture is quite different. Here we provide sexual role models that confuse instead of enlighten and diminish instead of enhance.

MEN AND FEMINISM

Confusion is often the basic hallmark of communication between men and women. Moreover, communication regarding sex is frequently accompanied by anger and disappointment as well. There are not many situations as subject to embarrassment, vagueness, innuendoes, or silence as when sexual intimates are troubled with their sexual lives. Even sophisticated men and women have great difficulty expressing themselves. To tell your lover such feelings as loss of interest midway during a sexual encounter, or to ask to be touched in a specific way or place, are words not spoken with ease, even by the articulate.

This difficulty for human beings to level with each other and talk openly about sexual feelings once again reflects the powerful sexual scripts instilled within us. For men expecially, measurements of masculinity do *not* include requests for help with arousal or sexual fussiness of any sort. Sexual isolation from women, wives, or lovers is inevitably felt by many men at one time or another. In her book, *Worlds of Pain,* Lillian Rubin says that for both middle and working class individuals, sex therapies can "be useful in dealing with some specific dysfunctions. . . . But the kinds of sexual conflicts to be discussed here (between men and women) are so deeply rooted in the socio-cultural mandates of our world that they remain extraordinarily resistant regardless of how able the psychotherapeutic help we can buy" (Rubin, 1976).

A major shift in men's attitudes toward sex has occurred during the past thirty years. By the 1970s men were feeling much more responsible for mutual pleasure in sex rather than for individual satisfaction. Compared to Kinsey's findings in 1948, Rubin cites a *Playboy* study in the 1970s by Morton Hunt which indicates that both college and noncollege educated men have changed their sexual practices and begun to use a greater variety of sexual activities and spend more time on foreplay. Hunt notes that the most significant changes occurred among the noncollege educated (Rubin, 1976).

These changes brought about some new issues of conflict for men. As men have integrated the idea that sex is better if their partner shares the enjoyment, they have felt increasingly more responsible to give pleasure.

Thus they now suffer not only from their own conflicts, but from the problems of women as well. Many men feel incompetent and subsequently disappointed or resentful if their partners are not eager or orgasmic. Other men describe a disconcerting loss of control in the sexual arena and feel that sex is sometimes given manipulatively as a punishment or a reward for non-sex-related behaviors. This feeling is underlined by one woman's comment that, "He gets different treats at different times, depending on what he deserves. Sometimes I let him do that oral stuff . . . when he is *very* good, I do it to him" (Rubin, 1976).

It has been said that men beg for sex and women beg for love or emotional intimacy. Herein lies another form of male sexual conflict and oppression. In talking about his partner of seven years, one 37-year-old man says,

When we have sex, I feel the closest to her. There is something about our bodies being so close that makes all the other kinds of distance disappear. It's the best way for me to feel that emotional connection that she's trying to get to by talking. I just can't get there with words.

For many men physical sex is the avenue toward emotional intimacy and an acceptable route toward emotional vulnerability. For women, the opposite is often true: the desire for physical sex is more likely to develop after they first feel emotionally connected. It is ironic that the ultimate goals of having both physical and emotional intimacy may be identical for men and women; however, the order in which to obtain these goals is reversed.

A variety of explanations is offered for this conflict, although most experts make reference to early sex role expectations put upon men in their childhood. Boys are expected to be exploratory in general and to take risks. As adolescents and young men they are not discouraged from experimenting with and experiencing sexual contacts. In fact a teenage boy who is open about his sexual accomplishments is admired by his peers. A teenage girl, however, would be viewed as a tramp for the same behavior (Julty, 1979). Thus men learn to separate sex from emotional commitment, because sex, like other activities, can be promoted as an adventure. Men are not expected to be cautious because they might be vulnerable to hurt. In fact, they are not even to admit the possibility of being vulnerable. In contrast, for women the risk of pregnancy alone necessitates caution.

Some men are, indeed, quite split-off from the emotional/expressive side of themselves, not only sexually but in other ways as well. It is difficult for anyone to know what sex means to them symbolically, or to know the emotional significance of such specifics as intercourse, hugging, cunnilingus, masturbation. Obviously, sexual desire is not a simple expression of biological urge for either men or women. Perhaps for men, sex can be an opportunity to be vulnerable, tender, and expressive. In any event, there is often great disparity between men and women about the meaning of sexual experiences and about their reasons for wanting sex. A man is often so oppressed by the demand for constant sexual interest that his feelings of sexual desire are linked to the role of initiator rather than to any examination of inner needs.

Interestingly, a significant number of married men who had previously complained of their wive's lack of interest, and who had always been functional, experienced their first erectile problems *after* their wives had "discovered their sexuality" and became more eager and orgasmic (Rubin, 1976). This extra pressure, coming as a direct expression of their partner's interest, upset a delicate balance. Now as some men look at the past decade, they point an angry and confused finger at the women's movement in an effort to identify a very different source of sexual oppression. What is the reason for the emergence of this new set of sexual woes?

As women have begun to participate in an economy that had previously shut them out, men are feeling invaded. One 51-year-old man said in comic exasperation, "Women are everywhere! They're in the locker room. They're even into weight lifting and muscles!" Although he was not a man who basically objected to the advancement of women, he was certainly expressing a very poignant anxiety beneath his mock complaint. If women *are everywhere,* and can *do everything,* the question then for men is, "What have I got left? If I am not a leader or aggressor, then who am I?" (Julty, interview by author, 1983).

This loss of a clearly defined role can be a source of considerable confusion and resentment in men's lives. As women become less dependent upon men economically and as the risk of social censure for being a single women diminishes, men may wonder what, if not dependency, will keep their partner with them? In an attempt to cope with this uncertainty, some men have made great efforts to follow the guidelines of behavior that their consciousness-raised partners have set out for them. Yet men complain that despite their struggles to please feminist partners, they somehow fail to do so. No matter how many toilets they clean or how much quiche they eat, they still have a sense of alienation and disappointment from their partners. And the men themselves feel no particular enhancement of self-esteem or joy.

No matter what the given social scripts— from macho to mushy—an extraordinary number of men are never really in sync with the sex role expectations. They do not know what rules to follow and are caught in the middle of transitions that deeply upset and confuse both sexes. This discomfort is demonstrated in numerous ways when it comes to sex. Frequently discussed are the difficulties that men experience as women want more sexual satisfaction. As Gore Vidal has observed, "The tyranny of the female orgasm is really going to drive male heterosexuality to the wall" (in Rubin and Leonard, 1980). An eloquent description of this oppression comes from Milan Kundera, the Czechoslovakian novelist, in his *The Book of Laughter and Forgetting* (1979). A middle-aged man is describing a woman he dated, whom he met at a store that rents sporting goods:

She was an orgasm fanatic. The orgasm was her religion, her only goal, the primary rule of hygiene, a symbol of health; but it was pride as well, because it distinguished her from less fortunate women, like having a yacht or a famous fiancé. . . . It wasn't easy to give her one, either. "Faster," she'd urge him on, "faster," and then "take it easy, take it easy," and then again "harder, harder." She was like a coxswain shouting orders to the crew of a racing shell. Completely caught up in her erogenous zones, she would guide his hand to the right place at the right time. Whenever he looked at her, he would see her impatient eyes and the feverish thrashings of her body—a portable apparatus for manufacturing the minor explosion that had become the meaning, the goal of her life." (pp. 204, 205)

In a way this description is much more a statement of sexual alienation than an opinion about women's sexual rights and pleasures. The real tyranny of woman's sexual wants is not the "wants" themselves, but the discomfort and anxiety that men experience due to the demands upon them. In an article in *New Age Magazine* (May 1983), poet Robert Bly is quoted as saying, "The male in the past 20 years has become more thoughtful, more gentle, but has *not* become more free. He's a nice boy who not only pleases mother but also the woman he is living with." Men do not know where to place themselves on this "macho-wimp" scale. Many have echoed the angry exclamation of one 32-year-old man: "I don't want to be a sexist pig, but I certainly don't want to be pussy-whipped either!"

MEN TOGETHER

The men's liberation movement of the 1970s, which occurred mainly in a few urban centers, made a serious attempt to deal with sexism and to unite men for both personal and political change. In a collection of articles called *Male Pride and Anti-Sexism* (Wernette et al., 1983), the authors point out that "The roles we are taught as men are designed to support economic structures and keep other people down." The article suggests that men need to confront themselves, individually and collectively, with their own hatred and fear of women, very much as the civil rights movement mandates that white people confront their own bigotry against blacks. It also makes a distinction between men's liberation and male antisexism. Men's liberation is defined as becoming freer at a personal, emotional level, whereas antisexism is more of a political stance, seeing the oppression of *anyone* as an insult to *everyone's* feelings of caring and justice. These are fine and valuable ideas. One wonders, however, why men's unity and movement toward them has been so miniscule?

One man says very simply, "We were unwilling to put out much energy or attention, or even emotion to each other. We are unwilling to expose ourselves in much of a real way" (Pleck & Sawyer, 1974). A 45-year-old single father attended one meeting of a men's group; he found it interesting, but said he would prefer a mixed group (men and women) because it would be more fun. When pressed for other reasons, he added that he had some discomfort with feelings of competition. It is very difficult to network cooperatively when one has been taught from birth to compete. Men are taught to compare themselves to other men in all arenas, and strive for money, job, athletic, and sexual successes—the gridirons of power. If heterosexual men have anything to learn from women, it is not how to be more like women *per se*, but perhaps how to network for support within a male community.

In her book *In A Different Voice*, Carol Gilligan (1982) researches and explains the complexities of a serious yet subtle disparity between men and women regarding the ways in which they value relationships.

The elusive mystery of women's development lies in its recognition of the continuing importance of attachment in the human life cycle. Woman's place in men's life cycle is to protect this recognition while the developmental litany intones the celebration of separation, autonomy, individuation and natural rights. (p. 23)

Gilligan asserts that both dimensions of human development—individuation and attachment—are essential.

Daniel Levinson, author of *The Seasons of a Man's Life,* observes this lack of attachment in male relationships.

In our interviews, friendship was largely noticeable by its absence. . . . A man may have a wide social network in which he has amiable, "friendly" relationships with many men and perhaps a few women. In general, however, most men do not have an intimate friend. . . . We need to understand why friendship is so rare and what consequences this deprivation has for adult life. (p. 335)

Many men express an envy of women's closeness and ability to talk openly—to be dependent on each other. Yet should women really be men's mentors for emotional and social well-being? To add to the quandary, men spend most of their childhood learning *not* to be feminine. Ironically, they scorn things womanly but are largely under the control of women. For many boys their fathers are absent, and peers become their mentors of masculinity, emphasizing physical and athletic strength ". . . with almost a complete omission of tender feelings or acceptance of responsibility towards those who are weaker" (Pleck & Sawyer, 1974). In light of this statement, one sees the obstacles to becoming a loving father or friend.

One wonders if the difficulty for men to nurture and protect each other is linked to a rejection of weakness. Sally Woods (1983) of the Sex Abuse Hotline in Knoxville, Tennessee, has found in preliminary research that many men had negative childhood and adolescent sexual experiences, which, based on their descriptions, were clear situations of sexual abuse. Nevertheless, most men re-jected the term "abuse," and not one of the hundred individuals she interviewed had disclosed their victimization to anyone. How can one be part of an oppressed group without admitting a lack of power or control?

Psychologist James Gardiner, in his book *The Turbulent Teens* (cited: *Sexuality Today,* 1983), suggests further that boys need both instruction and support from a warm, empathic older man. He notes one example of this need is evidenced by an increase in sexual dysfunction among adolescent males.

Many young men feel that women are experienced and that they expect a degree of sophistication or sexual technique that a young man knows he does not possess. Under such pressure, failures of erection or premature ejaculation are highly likely . . . (yet) . . . the youngster is often simply suffering from beginner's anxiety.

The question is: Who should be men's teachers?

Robert Bly (Thompson, 1983) has lectured at length on the subject of men and expands this theme. He feels that young males need initiation into the rites and rituals of manhood by a community of men, not by their mothers. Although he emphasizes that men need to learn male strength from each other, he makes it clear that it is *not* that women have been doing the wrong thing. The problem, Bly claims, is that men are not doing their jobs, and he underscores the absence of close male relationships. Sons need to be together with their fathers and other men, especially at adolescence, to see what men do and to understand it. Yet the American industrial revolution has separated fathers from their sons at a critical time of initiation into masculine rites of sexuality and work.

Bly elaborates further. He believes that men should take responsible leadership for the good of the community and not for personal aggrandizement. Bly develops a concept of "compassionate authority" that emerges from positive male energy and promotes robust health, intelligence, and goodwill. He describes the "soft male" (the 1960s male) as antiwar, procooperative, valuable, and vulnerable, but without much energy or happiness. He says, "They are life preserving but not exactly *life-giving*." Men have learned to be receptive and nurturing but are not able to show something fierce, yet something deeply male and fierce is needed once in a while. Keith Thompson, editor and founder of a men's wilderness/consciousness network, says, "It seems as if many of these soft young men have to come to equate their own natural male energy with being macho" (Thompson, 1983). Some men are unable to be assertive without being oppressive. Others hold back this show of "something fierce" for fear of offending women.

A different perspective might be considered: the idea of a nonhostile strength in contrast to the polarized position of beast versus jellyfish. Bly characterizes this concept describing a deep and primitive masculinity in which forceful actions are taken with both compassion and resolve. He thinks men need to distinguish between showing strength and hurting someone—displaying their swords, so to speak, but not killing. John Skow (*Time* November 7, 1983) furthers the idea, suggesting that men connect to a basic "animal" ability to be ferocious, but not really do harm. These concepts of masculinity may set a valuable direction for men, but they might be difficult for the average guy to live up to without a suitable role model.

In Joseph Pleck's *The Myth of Masculinity* (1981), a fascinating and complex book, the author questions the very origins of sex role norms and very carefully criticizes the conventional male sex role identity paradigm. He suggests that this traditional paradigm is not useful because it assumes that sex roles stem from a basic, innate psychological need. What he proposes instead is a sex-role strain paradigm which assumes that sex roles develop for reasons of social approval and situational adaptation. Pleck very specifically analyzes a variety of psychological tests of masculinity, in particular noting that the

Minnesota Multiphasic Personality Inventory (the most frequent test of male sex role identity) was originally based on comparison of 45 male soldiers, 67 female airline employees, and 13 male homosexuals! Similarly, many other sex-typing scales are also based on oddly selected samples.

Pleck further criticizes the use of a bipolar scale, claiming that it is not as useful to differentiate and compare masculine and feminine traits as it is to describe a variety of traits that characterize each sex. He suggests the use of a "dual-unipolar scale," an androgenous concept of sex typing. "The traditional focus on sex differences obscures the fact that women and men are more alike than different," having "masculine and feminine traits" (p. 137).

Pleck offers a number of propositions based on his research. Like others, he thinks that sexrole expectations have been contradictory and inconsistent. He finds, moreover, that a high proportion of individuals violate them. Classically defined sex roles are not only based on unreliable research, but also generate considerable stress. Sex role violations lead to both societal and self-condemnation, as well as the emotional strains of attempting to live out roles that do not fit. Interestingly, Pleck sees the violation of these expectations as having more severe consequences for men than for women.

A changing society has a dramatic effect on traditional sex roles, and the ideas of Robert Bly have mirrored these caustic words of Pleck: "While in an earlier age males became men by participating in an all-male social life and holding a job, they now come to do so by learning from psychologists that they must act in certain ways if they are to have male sex-role identities," (Thompson, 1983, 159).

Another researcher also discusses the benefits of a concept of androgyny. In an article in the *Journal of Sex Research*, Hooberman (1979), like Pleck, claims that measurements of masculine gender identity should take into account personality characteristics that are both masculine and feminine by tradition. Utilizing the BEM Sex-Role Inventory, he describes typical masculine attributes as "instrumental" or "action" in character, whereas feminine attributes are more "expressive." Hooberman proposes that having both the masculine and feminine characteristics may provide men with a greater repertoire of qualities with which to interact more effectively with the world. He finds that this androgenous self-image of men who accept masculine traits *without a concomitant rejection of the feminine* is positively correlated with higher self-esteem.

BROADSCALE INTERVENTIONS

If, indeed, men are to consider a change of sex role expectations, both men and women may have to change their thinking. As Bly suggests (Thompson, 1983), the first step toward any such transformation might be a campaign to educate men on the skills and importance of being fathers and close friends. In this culture, in these times, parenting is one of the most challenging and frustrating tasks, yet neither men nor women earn money or power for doing it well. One practical way, for example, to give public recognition to the importance of fatherhood might be for employee unions to lobby for paternity leave, certainly a departure from traditional thinking. Although both formal and informal support systems exist for women as mothers, there are barely such resources for men.

The emotional separation of boys from their fathers often causes grave but unconscious sadness in men. Men of all ages in men's groups or therapy usually suffer anger or grief over this loss as they become more aware of feelings. Older men, in addition, mourn lost opportunities for closeness with their sons. Yet few men choose to enter therapy over problems of "fathering." Perhaps, through popular television, literature, or movies, men could experience models of fatherhood and friendship who, creative in their approaches to male relationships, nei-

ther abandon masculine strength nor imitate the feminine. How might men have been affected if John Wayne had routinely hugged not only his women, but his best male buddies, too!

In addition to promoting more positive father-son and male-mentor relationships, there is a great need for change in sex education for boys. Not only is there far too little, but the emphasis is often wide of the mark. Girls, not boys, are taught to be protective of themselves. Yet there is considerable evidence that men suffer from a variety of early, negative experiences and from the unwanted pregnancies and abortions of their partners as well (Leo, 1983). Boys are given the idea that early sexual activity is normal and masculine, but they receive few messages that it is O.K. to say "No," or that it is O.K. to require love or affection with sex. If sex equals intercourse, there is only one goal. Yet this pressure for boys and young men to "get laid" creates anxiety and feelings of inadequacy without any specific skills of setting individually comfortable limits regarding sexual interactions.

Fatherly mentors and specific sexual guidance are not likely to develop in the societal structures that already exist. One major mode of male relating, for example, is through the vehicle of sports and competition. Not only does this mode exclude significant numbers, but it is no playground of kindly support and personal exploration. Neither are the Boy Scouts, the schools, most boys' clubs, or Friday night poker games. This is *not* to say, however, that these connections have no meaning. They are often intensely important, but their value emotionally is rarely acknowledged at a conscious level or verbalized as part of the general conversation. Although a few agencies and community centers offer social activity clubs for boys, it has become the job of the mental health profession to recognize and be responsive to male sexual and social concerns.

In contrast, the gay community has begun to develop a literature and network of grassroot services to help boys, men, and their families with the social/sexual issues of coming out and being gay. Gay college professors, gay bosses and ministers, gay peers in all walks of life offer support even where the gayness is secret. Like the women's movement, there is a growing number of hotlines, professional groups, church groups, hangouts, community centers, private clubs, and so on, in smaller towns as well as urban environments. These individuals have a group identity and can work collectively to fight oppression.

There are almost no clubs or structures for the socialization and sexual guidance of heterosexual males. Perhaps their homophobia is too great to allow them to follow the example of their gay brothers. Perhaps it is unacceptable to acknowledge a need for leadership and counsel when one is already cast in the role of leader. Nevertheless, the energy and charisma of a few individual men can develop important grassroots connections. One man, for example, in Berkeley, California, began an organization in the early 1980s for single men and women that provides social, political, and personal activities with a special emphasis valuing male friendships. Yet most men are on their own, with *Playboy* and *Penthouse* as their educators and mentors.

DIRECT SERVICE INTERVENTIONS

Since men have such a minimal collective identity as an oppressed group, and since the impetus for change at a broadscale level has had so many obstacles and such little support, it might be wise to consider a very different territory for interventions. Most people are not receptive to changes, unless they are consciously hurting in some way. And the way in which men inevitably experience the discomfort of these sex-role expectations is in the bedroom.

Male sexual concerns have always been described in terms of function instead of feeling, by men themselves, as well as by the mental health profession. Men almost always define their sexual problems in terms of the action or nonaction of their penis. Impotence, ejaculatory incompetence, premature and retarded ejaculation are the classic terminologies for male sexual problems. All describe performance. Men who have never considered therapy of any sort will seek sex counseling for "dysfunctions." A profound vulnerability for men is experienced in bed, when their physical, sexual lives are unhappy and beyond their control. Thus, concerns over dysfunctions may provide the best domain for interventions that address needed changes in attitude and thinking. This is the time when men consciously feel the most frustrated and helpless. This is the time when "trying harder" simply does not work.

In any case, the major focus of sex therapy itself is education, specific information, and attitudinal remodeling, as well as behavioral assignments. Without dwelling on the details of intensive sex therapy techniques and behavioral procedures, there are a number of significant concepts transmitted to clients as part-and-parcel of sex therapy. These are crucial to changes in their normal lives.

In reality, these concepts can be imparted to men in a great variety of settings and not just within the boundaries of sex therapy. Mental health professionals in almost any setting can be very helpful in addressing sexual and sex-related concerns. Although one doesn't have to be a trained sex therapist, one must be sufficiently *educated* about the wide range of human sexual needs and activities that do exist. Further, one must be *accepting* of the fact that sexual interest, arousal, function, and feeling naturally differ from man to man. Finally, one must also be *comfortable* with one's own sexual life. This does not mean the same as "satisfied." One can experience various eras of sexual troubles (loss of partner, loss of desire, medical problems, etc.) and still live comfortably enough with the notion that sex is not always fabulous or even good.

The first and most basic concept addresses the issue of diagnosis: Consider two men, Leo and Jim, of similar age, family status, health, and occupation. Both men describe identical conditions under which they have trouble obtaining erections when they are making love and wanting to have intercourse. When this trouble occurs, Leo claims that he and his partner "just do something else" sexually that does not require an erection. Jim, however, after five months, telephones a sex therapy clinic for treatment of impotence. Leo does not even consider the notion that he has a sex problem. Should Leo be told that he is ignoring a basic problem of impotence and be referred for sex therapy? Or should one tell Jim that he is taking things too seriously and really has no problem? The real question is: *Who* is to decide when a so-called "dysfunction" is truly a problem? Sam Julty asserts that "real oppression is the word 'dysfunction' itself" (interview by author, 1983).

Sex problems are part of the human condition. No one goes through life 100-percent functional at every era. Thus acceptance of these problems is a second basic concept. Since sexual response is emotional as well as physiological and interactive, there is plenty of room for complications. The fact is that some men experience these problems of dysfunction as a betrayal of the body. They have limited tolerance for the feelings of helplessness that occur when, no matter how hard they try, they cannot perform. They often feel a serious loss of self-esteem and think the penis should be counseled, nagged, cajoled, brow-beaten, or otherwise whipped into proper action. These men usually suffer in silent shame. Single men, especially, are likely to withdraw from a social and sexual life without discussing their difficulties with anyone.

Other men deal with changes of sexual function with an easier acceptance, for these ups and downs (pun intended) are only natural. Obviously, the less desperate one feels, the better off one is. The range of response to these problems is as varied as the range of responses men have to the natural process of aging. Sometimes just the opportunity to describe one's sexual feelings and behavior to a caring and nonjudgmental person can be very relieving and comforting. This is especially true when a man receives some assurance that he is not the first person in the world to have ever suffered thusly.

A third, vital aspect of male sexual concerns is the acknowledgment of medical issues. The American Urological Association reported recently that 65 percent of male sexual problems have an organic component (Julty, 1983). For example, erection concerns can be symptomatic of any illness that affects the circulatory or neurological system, such as diabetes and hypertension. One must also consider other illnesses, injuries, medications, and drugs (prescribed and recreational). Ejaculation and orgasm further can be affected by medical problems such as sickle cell anemia, prostatitis, and cancer of the prostate, or even more obscure conditions such as pituitary tumors. A great number of concerns are both organic and psychogenic. It is *always advisable* for a man to be evaluated by a urologist or other physician who is trained to screen for medical problems masked by changes in sexual function or chronic dysfunctions. Most doctors have no expertise in this field, and a qualified sex therapist can usually recommend one who does. The real problem is the difficulty involved in discerning organic from psychogenic factors. It is unethical to assume a psychogenic cause alone, even if the emotional evidence is strong.

Zilbergeld has made a very important contribution to men's sexual lives with a fourth concept, his theory of "conditions for good sex" described in his book, *Male Sexuality* (1978). "A condition is anything at all . . . that makes you more relaxed, more comfortable, more confident, more sexual, more open to your experience in a sexual situation." Conditions can involve many aspects, including one's physical environment, emotions, health, relationship, etc. They can be mundane and practical issues such as room temperature, cleanliness, or privacy. They can also be complex issues such as being angry at one's partner or feeling upset about a flareup of herpes and not knowing how to raise the subject. Again, traditional "Ready Teddy" scripts make it difficult for men to acknowledge sexual sensitivities and personal conditions for good sex. One 63-year-old man said he was very embarrassed to admit that he preferred having sex in a completely dark room because of his self-consciousness about a gall bladder scar. A 28-year-old man realized he usually had trouble getting an erection if he went to bed with a woman before he knew her well enough. He was always secretly relieved when the woman herself wanted to postpone sex. Still he felt obliged to be "ready" by the end of the first date, and it never occurred to him that he could be the one to delay sex.

Even if men take the time to recognize their conditions, they often do not respect or follow them. Castleman (1980), adding to this concept, says the major key to enjoyable sex is the reduction of anxiety. But what reduces anxiety? The overwhelming opinion of writers on this subject is that anxiety diminishes when a man takes care to have sex under the conditions that are optimal to him. This requires the encouragement and opportunity to think through and evaluate positive as well as negative aspects of his own sexual experiences. This process is a basic tool of all mental health professionals. Usually, however, sex is not raised as the subject of such a careful and detailed scrutiny. A useful sex therapy technique is to ask a client to compose a list of his own particular conditions for good sex. These conditions can then be discussed in terms of how they might be met or ignored and why.

For many men it is the expectations they have about their sexual performance that causes the most anxiety. It is difficult enough to flirt, seduce, arouse one's partner, stay erect, delay ejaculation, or generally conduct the show. It is virtually impossible to accomplish these jobs if in addition you are worried about whether your equipment is reliable! One might compare the situation to driving a car that is likely to conk out in dangerous traffic. Anxiety prevails instead of excitement. Men are more likely to attend to the warning signals and needs of their cars, however, than they are to their own bodies. No one expects a car to function without maintenance or to perform well under hazardous conditions.

Sex therapists often help anxious men to verbalize their worries to partners *in advance of* actual sex. Assertive communication skills, such as personal disclosures, can be practiced with the clinician so that a man can find an appropriate way to raise uncomfortable subjects and relieve both himself and his partner from the strain of unspoken tensions. For just this purpose a workshop called "Speaking Up While Lying Down: Assertive Communication in Sexually Intimate Relationships" (Alperstein, 1979) was developed in the Human Sexuality Program of the University of California School of Medicine, in San Francisco. Here, assertive skills and basic education about sexual attitudes, physiology, and behavior were blended to address problems of unrealistic expectations, poor conditions, and anxieties of men and women.

The idea that good sexual performance is equated with good mental health is *not* an accurate and useful concept. Actually, a fifth concept considers the relationship between sexual performance and mental health as much less predictable. At times it is true that general problems of anxiety or depression, for example, can create sexual problems. Conversely, it is true that sexual concerns can create anxiety, depression, or a variety of other emotional problems. Emotionally stable and happy men as well as men troubled with serious mental disorders can have any number of sexual problems or none at all. The most helpful attitude is to consider each individual situation. In fact, perfect sexual performance under adverse emotional conditions might be symptomatic of a rigid defense system in which angry or sad feelings are compartmentalized. In this case, good performance is automatic but not necessarily appropriate. In his book, Apfelbaum (1980) discusses how men who are automatic performers for many years suffer from enormous feelings of helplessness at the point their body malfunctions and underlying anxieties break through. He specifically suggests that couples agree to express their negative thoughts during sex in an effort to counteract the oppression of having to feign enjoyment and the burden of going through the motions.

To borrow an expression from Goldberg (1976), a sixth useful concept might be called "the wisdom of the penis." Most men believe they should be turned on, and few feel free to say "I'm not interested" or "I'm not aroused." Therefore, their penis says it for them. As much as men do protect their eagerness to perform, Goldberg suggests that a sexual dysfunction can be an expression of resentment or other negative feelings. It is a comfort to men to be reminded that they have the right *not* to be interested, and that there are many understandable reasons for not wanting sex. Sometimes the penis just says "no" when a man cannot figure out how he feels. Unfortunately, there is a dearth of research and literature on male problems of low desire and arousal, despite an abundance of writing on sexual plumbing and mechanics. Nevertheless, most situations of sexual disinterest stem from relationship conflicts and sex role expectations. When a man is convinced that he is *entitled* to be disinterested, the pressure to perform can be greatly reduced. Then he is free to decide if sex is really what he is wanting at that moment.

The final concept? Whereas some men do not give themselves permission to be turned off, others, to the contrary, do not allow themselves to experience a full range of sensual pleasures. Men often define their role as the doers, but rarely the receivers. A 48-year-old man said, "I always feel guilty after a few minutes when my wife is stroking me. I like it all right, but I feel that I should be doing something to her too. Like I'm lazy to just lie there." Men are not scripted to be in a passive role. Moreover, if a man is anxious about sex, he may simply be unable to feel

much at all, either physically or emotionally. That is not uncommon with men who ejaculate rapidly and who lack a sense of control. Instead of reaching an orgasm because of a build up of great pleasure, they may be too anxious to maintain various levels of sensual arousal. Instead, they may ejaculate without much feeling of intensity, pleasure, or release. Since men have been taught that their sexuality is limited to the genitals, it is a new idea for many to explore other erogenous zones as a source of sensuality and pleasure. Zilbergeld (1978) gives some specific and excellent assignments for men to follow in order to learn more about their levels of arousal and their ability to control or delay an orgasm.

These concepts or ideas may not address men as a united oppressed group, but they can help in making men's sex lives more individually enjoyable and comfortable. Additional details of behavioral methods to deal with specific sexual problems can be found in the writings of Zilbergeld (1978), Castleman (1980), and others previously mentioned. Yet there are really no fancy techniques or magical cures. Even intensive sex therapy is based upon attitudinal changes and the willingness to become better acquainted with the workings of one's mind as well as one's body.

Bernie Zilbergeld (1978) speaks very plainly on the subject:

. . . we are suggesting that changing your sex life may not lie in the direction you think. What is needed is not more exotic practices, techniques, or equipment, but rather a willingness to let go of the sexual script you learned and to create new ones that are more relevant to you. Will this, then, lead to passion-filled sex and the ultimate orgasm? Probably not. But it can lead to sex that accurately reflects your values, your body, and your personality—your self. Sex, like everything else, is limited in what it is and what it can produce. The secret, however, is . . . to . . . participate fully in whatever sexual expression and activities seem appropriate to you. Such experiences are more likely to occur when you are aware of your sexual needs and wants and are able to get them. (p. 68)

BROACHING THE SUBJECT

These concepts of sex therapy can be very helpful to men with many different kinds of sexual concerns. The onus is on the mental health professional to find some manner in which to broach the issue of sex. Most men will not discuss anxieties or risk asking questions that show sexual ignorance unless they feel the conditions are quite safe. Men need to feel assured that sex is a welcome and natural subject along with the other issues being discussed. They need, moreover, to be certain the responses they get will be reassuring and nonjudgmental.

One of the greatest worries men have about discussing their sexual lives is the fear that somehow they are not normal. Sexual naivete and lack of experience are other anxieties too. All of which create a reluctance to speak. Here then are some specific conversational examples of ways that helping practitioners can broach the subject of sex and open the doors for discussion in a variety of settings:

Medical Setting: "Many men have questions or concerns about the effect of their cancer (illness, surgery, disability, etc.) or the treatments upon their sex life. I hope you will feel welcome to ask me any questions, you, yourself, might have—even if it's a question you think you ought to know. I'll be happy to answer it or just talk to you about any sex-related issues. If it's a question that I can't answer, I'll try to find the answer for you. The whole field of sexuality could still use a lot of research."

Mental Health Clinic: "I know we have a number of different issues to think about; however, I'd also like to add sex to the list, if needed. It's natural for a lot of men in your situation (of your age group, with your particular problems, etc.) to be concerned about your sex life too. And I just want you to know that I think it's an important subject, even if it's uncomfortable to discuss."

Group or Workshop Setting: "Although our purpose here is to discuss personal problems related to work (school, business, etc.) there's one subject that rarely gets raised, but it concerns almost everyone, at least some of the time. And that's the subject of sex. Believe it or not, a lot of the personal problems that men have affect their love life—and vice versa. Problems with your sex life can really affect your work and other relationships in general. Therefore, I want everyone to realize that sex certainly can be included as one of the issues for discussion. Lord knows it can be on our minds enough."

The above examples are door openers that can be adapted for different clients as well as for their significant others. They do not insist upon or demand a discussion of sex; however, they certainly apprise people in a natural and casual way that the subject is open. These door openers do not assume everyone suffers from sexual dilemmas, but neither do they imply that sexual problems do not exist. Moreover, they do not assume that helping professionals have all the answers! It is quite important to find the appropriate words and ideas for each particular client or group. The utilization of warmth and humor can be extremely important. Silence about sex fosters the notion that it should not be discussed. And if clients never respond to an invitation to speak up, it is a good idea for practitioners to reexamine their words and tone for personal bias, discomfort, or unconscious reluctance. The more one reads and becomes accustomed to talking about sex, the easier it is to encourage others to speak openly.

CONCLUSION

When men are asked to talk about sexual oppression, the most common response is to deny that the word "oppression" applies. One 42-year-old psychologist said incredulously, "I never think of myself as part of an oppressed population." Later, however, he talked at length about his fears of performance failure and a long-held worry that women might ridicule him sexually, even though he had never had such an experience. Although many share such common fears, the word "oppressed" is usually rejected. What makes this concept so uncomfortable? Perhaps because it is the complete antithesis to all that is masculine in this culture. To be downtrodden, persecuted, or victimized is too shameful to even be acknowledged.

In this book about helping the sexually oppressed, each chapter deals with a population that clearly identifies with a specific legacy of disadvantage or handicap. There is no such fraternity for heterosexual American men. There is no well-established affiliation for nurturance and support. At best, men seem to be at the very beginning of a journey toward change, if on the road at all. It is clear that the sex role expectations and norms are breaking down as men, like women, question their validity. But these times of transition are disquieting. The old rules fit poorly. New rules are embryonic, and men are having to be more thoughtful and creative about their sexual guidelines. How men will evolve is a question mark. It does not seem likely that a burst of enthusiasm for a brotherly coalition is in the near future—except for a handful. It does seem, however, that men as individuals will feel increasingly dissatisfied with their sexual scripts—with or without group support. In any event, both men and women are in need of a societal balance that provides the efficient security of sex role norms, yet encourages independent choices and diversity.

REFERENCES

AHRONS, P. Quoted in Teen males: Influences on contraceptive use. *Sexuality Today* 6 (1983).

ALPERSTEIN, L. Speaking up while lying down. Unpublished paper delivered to the Social Work Program for the Study of Sex, University of Hawaii, School of Social Work, Honolulu, July 1979.

ANNON, J. *The behavioral treatment of sexual problems,* vols. I and II. Honolulu, Enabling Systems, 1974.

APFELBAUM, B., ED. *Expanding the boundaries of sex therapy,* rev. ed. Berkeley, Calif.: The Berkeley Sex Therapy Group, August 1980.

BARBACH, L., AND LEVINE, L. *The intimate male.* New York: Doubleday, 1983.

BARRET, R., AND BRYAN, E. Teenage fathers: Neglected too long. *Social Work* 27, November 1982.

BIERNBUAM, M., MOSSMILLER, T., ET AL. Gentleman for gender justice. *The Los Angeles Men's Collective* 10, Spring 1983.

BRADLEY, M., ET AL. *Unbecoming men.* Albion: Time Change Press, 1971.

BRENTON, M. *The American male.* New York: Fawcett, 1966.

CASTLEMAN, M. *Sexual solutions.* New York: Simon and Shuster, 1980.

DAVID, D., AND BRANNON, L. *The forty-nine percent majority: The male sex role.* Reading, Mass.: Addison-Wesley, 1976.

EHRENREICH, E. The male revolt. *Mother Jones* 8, April 1983.

ELLIS, A. *Sex and the liberated man.* Secaucus, N.J.: Lyle Stuart Inc., 1976.

FARRELL, W. *The liberated man.* New York: Random House, 1974.

FRIDAY, N. *Men in love: Men's sexual fantasies.* New York: Delacorte, 1980.

GARDINER, J. Quoted in Sexual dysfunction in teen males. *Sexuality Today,* 6, September 12, 1983.

GILLIGAN, C. *In a different voice.* Cambridge, Mass.: Harvard University Press, 1982.

GOLDBERG, H. *The hazards of being male.* New York: Signet, 1976.

HITE, S. *The Hite report on male sexuality.* New York: Alfred Knopf, 1981.

HOOBERMAN, R. Psychological androgyny, feminine gender identity and self-esteem in homosexual and heterosexual males. *Journal of Sex Research* 15, November 1979.

JULTY, S. *Men's bodies men's selves.* New York: Dell, 1979.

KAHN, A. Gone with the wimp. *East Bay Express,* May 6, 1983.

KINSEY, A., POMEROY, W., AND MARTIN, C. *Sexual behavior in the human male.* New York: Saunders, 1948.

KOLODNY, R., MASTERS, W., AND JOHNSON, V. *Textbook of sexual medicine.* Boston: Little, Brown 1979.

LEO, J. Sharing the pain of abortion. *Time*, September 26, 1983.

LEVINSON, D. *The seasons of a man's life.* New York: Alfred A. Knopf, 1978.

NETWORK SERVICE COLLECTIVE, EDS. *Off their backs . . . and on our own two feet.* Philadelphia: New Society Publishers, 1983.

NIETO, D. Aiding the single father. *Social Work* 27, November 1982.

NOWINSKI, J. *Becoming satisfied: A man's guide to sexual fulfillment.* Englewood Cliffs, N.J.: Prentice-Hall, Inc., 1980.

PIETROPHINTO, A., AND SIMENAVER, J. *Beyond the male myth.* New York: Times Books, 1977.

PLECK, J. *The myth of masculinity.* Cambridge, Mass.: MIT Press, 1981.

PLECK, J., AND SAWYER, J., EDS. *Men and masculinity.* Englewood Cliffs, N.J.: Prentice-Hall, Inc., 1974.

RUBIN, J., AND LEONARD, M. *The war between the sheets.* New York: Richard Marek Publishers, 1980.

RUBIN, L. *Worlds of pain.* New York: Basic Books, Inc., 1976.

———. *Intimate Strangers.* New York: Harper and Row, 1983.

SKOW, J. In California: Roar lion roar. *Time*, November 7, 1983.

SMITH, M., *When I say no, I feel guilty.* New York: Bantam, 1975.

SNODGRASS, J., ED. *For men against sexism.* Albion: Time Change Press, 1977.

THOMPSON, K. What men really want: Interview with Robert Bly. *New Age Magazine,* May 1982.

WERNETTE, T., ACACIA, A., ET AL. *Male pride and anti-sexism,* 3/e. San Francisco: Anti-Sexist Men's Political Caucus, 1983.

WOODS, S. Quoted in Telephone research on male sexual abuse. *Sexuality Today* 6, October 24, 1983.

WYLDER, J. Including the divorced father in family therapy. *Social Work* Vol. 27, November 1982.

ZILBERGELD, B. *Male sexuality.* New York: Little, Brown, 1978.

CHAPTER 7

CHILDREN AND ADOLESCENTS
H. Lawrence Lister

The dictionary definition of *oppression* as "unjust or cruel exercise of authority or power" and "a sense of heaviness—in the body or mind"—has been cited as justification for the designation of adolescents as one of the groups of the sexually oppressed (Lister, 1977). By the more liberal criterion discussed in the opening chapters of this book—which views the oppressed as all of those whose sexual behavior cannot lead to a socially approved pregnancy—then all children, and most adolescents, would be sexually oppressed. When sexuality is considered in its wider "spheres" of identity, sensuality, physiology/reproduction—that is, in the more encompassing framework than simply behavior—then the possibilities of child and adolescent oppression seem unlimited (Lister, 1981).

The purpose of this chapter is to discuss some examples of the sexual oppression of children and adolescents and to present information about intervention approaches in selected problem areas. It would be impossible to provide examples of interventive activities for all of the possible types of child/adolescent oppression; in fact, no general listing of what is the range of oppression of this population exists. Instead of full coverage, a number of examples of problems and interventive approaches will be presented.

THE INTERVENTION PROCESS

The approach to changing any social problem involves a process which consists of a number of components. These components include at least the following: data gathering about a problem or issue; an assessment of the facts in order to arrive at understanding; problem formulation; goal setting to guide the direction of change activity; intervention planning and actual intervention; evaluation; and follow-up.

Of particular relevance to this chapter are the components of data gathering, problem formulation, and intervention. These aspects of the basic intervention process will be briefly identified here, since the remainder of this chapter will consist of discussion related to each of them.

Data Gathering

Data gathering always consists of the means of accumulating information (that is, empirical research, interviewing, literature search) and the actual facts which emerge. Especially in the area of sexuality, both the means and the resultant data are highly influenced by the values and attitudes of both those who gather and those who provide the information. For the present chapter, data have come from personal observations and experiences, from professional practice, and from a range of literature (theoretical, empirical, and the popular press).

Problem Categories

Problem categories have been established for this chapter based on an intent to present broad theoretical issues (for example, changing theories) as well as to focus on discrete examples of oppression (for example, incest). Problem categories change over time. For example, in an earlier paper, this author discussed adolescent conflicts over "petting" as one example of how society encourages suppression yet provides few acceptable alternatives for sexual expression for youths. Although petting can of course still be an issue, it simply cannot be considered a problem sufficient for extensive discussion in the 1980s. Thus, problems identified in this chapter may a few years from now be considered only "issues" or simply "subjects for discussion," while other emerging issues (for example, impact of technology on the deter-

mination of gender at conception) may be identified as major problems.

Intervention

Intervention—the actual process of implementing change strategies with a client system—can be considered from a number of perspectives. These perspectives will be briefly discussed here, since several will be referred to at various points in the later discussion. The first way to think of intervention is in terms of system levels. As previously discussed, intervention focuses on activity at either the "micro," "mid," or "macro" levels.

Secondly, intervention takes place at various points or times in the development of problems, such as before a problem is manifested (primary prevention); once there is a problem, but when it may be reversed or ameliorated (secondary prevention); and finally, when a problem has caused irreversible damage but when intervention may prevent further deterioration or ill effects (tertiary prevention).

Third, intervention may be considered in terms of the change approaches which are used at any of the three points in time discussed above. Approaches include psychotherapy or casework, group work or group therapy, family therapy, community organization, social planning, and other such types of change strategies. Each of the approaches is influenced by different theories about human functioning (for example, behavioral theory, psychoanalytic theory) and each is also directed to different "target systems" (for example, an individual, a total family system).

Fourth, there are intervention models for specific types of problems. Case management, discussed in Chapter 4, is an increasingly documented model for organizing the total intervention process, in the focus of this chapter, on behalf of children needing protective services.

Fifth, there are intervention strategies and techniques (advocacy, role-playing).

Thus, a role-play exercise may be devised wherein the change agent uses verbal instruction to help a child anticipate a court appearance at which the child will be required to testify about a sexual molestation.

Finally, for many problem categories, there are cycles or stages during which certain intervention approaches and techniques are most appropriate. Several examples will be given later of structured intervention approaches that are organized to provide intervention techniques in a progression based on the ongoing assessment of client needs and responses.

PROBLEMS AND INTERVENTION PERSPECTIVES

Problem categories are based on current values and on definitions of what are both the sources and consequences of oppression. Sources of oppression range from those which are the most covert, subtle, and omissive (for example, the lack of sex education for children) to those which are the most overt, clear-cut, and commissive (rape of a child). Some of the sources are found at the microlevel (for example, within the family, as with incest), while other sources are at the macrolevel (society's changing values). Most problems, of course, may be traced to numerous sources, but causation usually is attributed to the level at which the intervention is to take place. For example, adolescent unwed pregnancy may be related to society's changing (and inconsistent values) or it may be related to conflicts within the family of the pregnant teen. Where the change agent has the ability to intervene to effect positive change will guide the assessment of what are the causal forces. It is therefore imperative for all human service professionals to not become only wedded to the intervention methods which they know, but to also search for intervention possibilities at different system levels—and at different points in time in the development of problems—which may yield novel solutions.

Although the judgment of which problems discussed in this chapter actually are attributable to sexual oppression may be somewhat arbitrary, data will be offered to support the contention that each problem area is indeed an example of oppression. It needs, nonetheless, to be reiterated that even the choice of data and the weight given to one piece of information over another is influenced by values. Consequently, readers must screen the information presented here through their own personal value and perceptual systems and take into consideration the social systems which influence their use of the data provided (for example, the norms of the work setting in which the reader may want to implement any of the interventive approaches to be described).

The remainder of this chapter will consist of a discussion of six problem categories ranging from the macro (the changing American social values) to the micro (incest) levels. For each problem category, there will be discussion of theory and data about the nature of the problem and description of interventive methods, models, or strategies. As will be shown in the discussion, interventions become more diverse, focused, and precise as problem categories are conceptualized toward the micro end of the system levels.

America's Changing Social Values

One source of oppression, generally covert and omissive in nature, stems from the rapid change of values, lifestyles, and role expectations in modern urban life. Sexuality in the 1980s continues to represent an explosion of ideas, dicta, mandates, and prescriptions. As an illustration, consider the following example of one family's experience in the past 10 years:

Ten years ago the oldest granddaughter took up residence with a male musician who was blind and with whom she had a platonic relationship. Grandmother was not told. About five years later, another granddaughter began living with her older boyfriend—the granddaughter being 18 and the boyfriend in his 30's. It was decided that if grandmother asked, then grandmother had a right to know with whom this granddaughter was living. Grandmother asked, and she was able to come to terms with the reality of her granddaughter's living arrangement. Several years later, grandmother's own daughter and her husband suddenly separated preparatory to a divorce. The daughter returned to the hometown where grandmother lived and soon the daughter was living with an old boyfriend from long ago. Within a week, grandmother was having them over for dinner!

The changes in sexual mores illustrated in the above vignette are far-reaching in their implications. In many respects, today's children are being programmed for a world which adults barely understand or, unlike the grandmother in the example, cannot accept. In Margaret Mead's formulation of what she calls a "prefigurative culture," our children inhabit a world that in part excludes the adults (Mead, 1970). Of course, one of the functions of adolescence as a developmental stage in western society has been to provide a subcultural environment from which youths may exclude their parents as youths push for emancipation and separation. Consequently, the newer concepts and tools of technology—which children are mastering from preschool on up—help them to more easily understand ideas of frozen sperm and egg banks, embryo transplants, surrogate mothers, genetic selection and modifications, predetermination of sex, artificial wombs, cloning, technological sex through brain stimulation, vaginal transplant, and test-tube babies (Delora, 1977). On the level of social interaction, youths are exposed to concepts of open marriage, sexual choice from sexuality to polymorphous perversity, sexual utopias ranging from the communal model of the nineteenth-century Oneida community to contemporary models of "sex spas" (Talese, 1980). What is invoked is an environment for child-rearing which is possibly best expressed by Comfort's future vision of

a society in which pair relationships are still central, but initially less permanent, in which childbearing is seen as a special responsibility involving special life styles, and in which settled couples engage openly in a wide range of sexual relations with friends, with other couples, and with third parties as an expression of social intimacy, with no more, and probably less, permanent interchange than we see in the society of serial polygamy that now exists. (Delora, 1977)

Although Comfort envisions this as a possible positive scenario for the future, warnings are currently being voiced about how children are being victimized under contemporary circumstances. In a review of a recent book by Marie Winn, *Children Without Childhood,* Scarf (1983) refers to Winn's comments as

a big concoction of complaints about the way we raise our children today. The author . . . argues that childhood, which since the late Middle Ages has ideally been a period of happy innocence and protected nurturance, has become an "Age of Preparation" for the grim realities of adult life. We used to shelter our children . . . from the "knowledge of sexuality . . . suffering, injustice, deceit, sorrow, death." Nowadays, she argues, most American parents not only let their children know about their grief, but also use their children as counselor/confessors from whom both consolation and absolution are sought. What she terms a "truly new parental style"—in which adults seek to relate to their children as equals—is robbing the current generation of children of their childhood (p. 8).

Scarf goes on to point out instances of Winn's use of data and deduction to show the plight of children as related to exposure to drugs, sex, fantasy-retarding television viewing, and role-reversed family relationships. But the issue is capped by Scarf's plaintive question: "But it is not clear what she would have us do—prohibit divorce, send all working mothers home and pull the plug from every television set in the nation?" (Scarf p. 26)

Both Winn and Scarf well express the essential point: What impact do the wider changes have on children (and for children's sexuality), and what is anyone to do about it? It is not the intent (or presumption) of the present author to suggest interventions for this macrolevel of oppression. However, all persons who work with or on behalf of children and adolescents should have some awareness that: (1) the large-scale changes and models for the future are impacting on children; (2) that these changes bring benefits (for one, the validation that what youth feel and experience sexually is not pathogenic); (3) but they also are sources of oppression (for example, when they offer— through the impersonal sorcery of mass media—the promise of new sex-role definitions, in the face of the reality that sexism continues in the workplace, in the legal process, and even in the minds of "helping professionals") (*Social Work,* 1976).

Intervention at the macrolevel must consist of collective action directed toward changing those laws, policies, and social values that perpetuate oppression. At the midlevel, an example comes from a newspaper article. It described a high school honor student in Pennsylvania fighting her dismissal from the National Honor Society, an expulsion which occurred because she "bore a child out of wedlock" (*Star-Bulletin,* 1984). Although American society has come to a certain acceptance of the fact of unwed pregnancy, a new source of oppression seems to be the definition of such young women as non-"Honorable." The very fact that this story from a distant part of the country was reported on the front page of a local newspaper illustrates one way in which prevailing values may be challenged on the midlevel.

Changing Theories and New Data

At another macrolevel of influence are theories and empirical data currently available which guide helping professions so that choices in policy formulation, in the development of resources, and in the structuring of services may be as free of oppressive consequences as possible. As in the previous discussion of changing social values, this category of oppression does not lead to focused choices of intervention. Nonetheless, oppression may stem from the inadvertent— not to mention the avowed—adherence to theories or data that may provide wildly varying forms of intervention from one service delivery system to another.

As referred to previously in the Scarf review of Winn, there are diametrically opposed ideas of how contemporary life is influencing children. Some would view current trends—and the promises they bring of future liberalization—as benefiting children by enhancing their capacities as humans, capacities which have long been stifled in our culture's view of childhood as a period of prolonged impotence. From this view come such radical proposals as an advocacy of children's rights which would essentially

grant to children most . . . of the primary and secondary rights now enjoyed by adults, including the right to choose guardians and living arrangements, to exercise political and economic power, and to receive information (Constantine & Martinson, p. 256).

Rarson, Foster, and Freed are cited as having

effectively shown that the arguments for restricting rights of minors are essentially the same as those used to rationalize oppression of women and racial minorities (Constantine & Martinson, p. 256).

Macrolevel proposals such as these for children's rights could lead—if carried to their logical conclusion—to policies which would allow children the right to even contract and negotiate sexual contacts with adults. Such proposals seem to invoke a model of family life and child-rearing where the old power balance—weighted in favor of the parents— is equalized if not reversed. There are numerous examples in current policy and in the law where many children's rights have been greatly extended in recent decades, though none to the degree cited above (Lister, 1977).

Thus, new theories lead to innovative or

even extreme (again, depending on one's values) proposals for macrolevel intervention. What, for example, might be some consequences of liberalizing policies of children's rights? If children could choose their guardians and their living arrangements, then what would be the boundaries of sexual behavior? In the face of some data which indicate that many child sexual experiences once thought always traumatic are not—even incest, as presented in some data by Meiselmen (1979) and Constantine and Martinson (1981)—where would policies and laws place the limits on child sexuality? For if incest taboos have, in part, served to maintain some of the power balance in families in the past, then freeing children to have rights in many respects coequal to adults could lead to a new view of incest, as some type of negotiable choice between children and their adult relatives.

How this position, (viewing children as more or less free agents) can be reconciled with every theory which shows the need of children for care and nurturing as they progress through developmental stages—and what would be the presumed outcomes in terms of the personalities of the adult persons who would evolve—has not been worked out. Nonetheless, the boundaries of what will be allocated as rights to the child and what will remain in the province of the parent(s) continues to be debated. For participation in that debate, the human service professional needs to be informed about the theories and the empirical supports on both sides of the issue.

That there remain both sides is reflected in a recent summarizing comment by a psychoanalyst (Lampl-DeGroot, 1982):

Many "modern" women leave their babies in daycare facilities, sometimes for a whole day, not realizing how much harm this may do to the baby's development. It requires an emotional understanding and empathy with a little child's experiential world, combined with well-balanced deliberations between both parents to achieve a reasonable, effective result in bringing up a child.

This view is but a mild reflection of the strongly held position that our society is abdicating its responsibility to its children—that rather than write of children's rights, what is lacking is parental responsibility, what Duhl referred to as "process parenting" as opposed to "symbolic parenting" (Duhl, 1976). The process-oriented perspective would suggest that children's sexuality (in all of the "spheres" mentioned at the beginning of this chapter) only develops within an ongoing combination of experiences which are embedded within an enduring relationship with a parent(ing) person. Thus, the capacity to touch and be touched; to identify with both the instrumental and the expressive components of adult functioning; to maintain the capacity for trust and intimacy; to be capable of sexual vulnerability and to allow for the vulnerability of a sex partner; to be able to take on the nurturing of another; to have the energy and the freedom from emotional blinders to be able to learn;—these and other capacities of the human being are best developed within a process which is guided and overseen by a consistent, caring adult. Child-rearing such as this would be antithetical to an option for children to "choose their own guardian."

Of course, the child-rearing model discussed above is an ideal that probably rarely exists and which probably actually engenders mainly guilt in parents who feel unable to live up to it. It may even be that as a result of the inability to live up to impossible past models—and in view of the inability of "experts" to find empirical support for any workable model of childhood or child-rearing which relates to a predictable adult sexuality—parents may simply raise their children in whatever fashion suits them with respect to issues of sexuality.

And what better child-rearing information do the "experts" have? Speaking at the secondary level of intervention at this point, we have much we can offer when problems have already arisen. This is because each case is complete with all of the practices that a parent did *not* carry out, practices which can then constitute the repertoire of new activities to be suggested they carry out in the future. But what information do professionals have to offer at the primary level?

An incipient controversy seems on the horizon for one of the cherished theories of the present century: that is, the seduction versus the oedipal theory of childhood neurosis. The oedipal theory is well known; the seduction theory held that parents actually sexually molested, seduced, or in some manner involved themselves in sexual activity with their children. As discussed by Malcolm (1983), the controversy centers around the possibility that Freud abandoned the seduction theory in part because of Freud's denial of his own observation of his father masturbating. The implications of this theoretical issue are indeed profound. Not only have patients since Freud's time had to come to terms with their fantasies (that is, what they otherwise recalled as "real" seduction), but models of child-rearing and family life have been constructed around this concept of psychosexual development. If indeed a true sexual experience does underlie adult "neurosis," then the incidence of incest must be much greater than ever suspected. And, to refer again to that research which finds some benign outcomes for incest victims, then society's and the professional's overreactions to the uncovering of incest in any given family itself may constitute the childhood trauma—more than the incest itself—as is proposed by some investigators (Constantine & Martinson, 1981).

The practical consequences of this discussion for helping professionals has to do with intervention possibilities and choices, since few will have much opportunity to redo the theories of Freud. Thus, when incest is discovered, do professionals descend in a multidisciplinary phalanx, isolating the father (in the most commonly reported situation, father-daughter incest), blaming the mother for unconscious collusion, and traumatizing the victim daughter? The belief that incest is one of the more aberrant forms of child oppression may itself structure the type of intervention, creating a "social iatrogenesis" or "system-induced trauma" where the "cure" may be more devastating than the crime (Conte, 1984).

As an example, a case encountered by the author involved the accusation by a young girl that an adolescent neighbor boy made sexual overtures to her and that he had also had sexual activity with his own sister. Without the parent's knowledge or permission, the sister was taken from her classroom at school and interviewed by members of a sex-abuse crisis team. The sister denied any involvement with her brother, but members of the intervention team were skeptical because theirs and other's research data show that, in nearly all reports of this type, the accusations are true (Sturkie, 1983). However, the outcome in this case was that both the brother and sister continued to deny the accusation, the parents were livid about the form of intervention, the neighbor girl's "seductive behavior" and possible lying were the subject of neighborhood gossip, and no case of child sexual molestation was established.

This is admittedly an unusual case, but it serves to illustrate the impact of changing theory as well as the impact from emerging new data. For who, in the above example, emerged as the victim? From where did the sexual oppression emanate? Who was an ultimate beneficiary?

Sexist Child-Rearing

Doubtless the most pervasive form of sexual oppression in our society occurs in our child-rearing practices, which create gender-organized categories into which children are programmed to fit. To the extent that this thwarts the talents, inclinations, and aspirations of the growing child—and forces the parents and other social institutions into the roles of oppressors—that is the extent to which everyone is caught in an oppressive matrix which all sectors of society have some ability and responsibility to influence. The pervasiveness of sexism in our society may be simply drawn with some of the following examples: the increasing desire to determine the sex of a child at conception; the first or second question asked at the birth as to the sex of the infant; the studies which show male infants are handled more aggressively—and after age two less nurturantly—than females (Sprung 1978); the very early discouragement of certain toys for different sexes (Sprung, 1978); the encouragement of a more exploratory use of the environment by boys (Sprung, 1978); the stereotypical portrayals of woman and men on TV—for example, a study of TV commercials where females displayed 82 percent of the nurturant behavior and where only men were aggressive (Carmichael, 1977); and in the very fact that our language is considered, according to one expert, "the most positively expressively masculine" of all the languages he knows: "the language of a grown-up man, with very little childish or feminine about it" (Carmichael, 1977).

Increasingly, a literature is accumulating which suggests that the traditional dichotomy of the sexes in our society portrays females as experiencing an interconnectedness and capacity for intimacy and, for males, an autonomy and separateness, and that both sexes are the losers at most points in the life cycle because of this division. Women lose out because most definitions of "adulthood" favor autonomous thinking, sharp decision-making skills and action—qualities for which men are programmed or scripted from childhood. Women, as a consequence, may feel threatened by experiences of separateness and by demands for individual initiative, such as are called for in the traditional workplace.

On the other hand, men may be the losers when they fear that situations calling for intimacy and closeness may lead to "entrapment" or a smothering loss of individuality and self (Gilligan, 1982). As stated by Gilligan:

The sexual stereotypes suggest a splitting of love and work. Expressive capacities are assigned to women, instrumental abilities to men. Yet these stereotypes show an adulthood that is out of balance, favoring separateness over connection, and leaning more toward an autonomous life of work than toward the interdependence of love and care (p. 70).

The outcome of the severe restriction on men's capacities for interrelationship (certainly "learned incapacities," not something innate) was well expressed in a book by Paul Auster, written almost compulsively upon the sudden death of his father; Auster feared that "if I do not act quickly, his entire life will vanish along with him" (Merwin, 1983). About his perception of his aloof father's relations with him, the son wrote:

It was not that I felt he disliked me. It was just that he seemed distracted, unable to look in my direction. And more than anything else, I wanted him to take notice of me . . . . The more aloof he was, the higher the stakes became for me . . . . I realized that even if I had done all the things I had hoped to do, his reaction would have been exactly the same. Whether I succeeded or failed did not essentially matter to him . . . his perception of me would never change . . . we were fixed in an unmoveable relationship, cut off from each other on opposite sides of a wall. Even more than that, I realized that none of this had anything to do with me. It had only to do with him. Like everything else in his life, he saw me only through the mists of his solitude" (p. 10).

Men lose out in relationships with their daughters as well, when they feel they must squelch the nurturant parts of themselves. And, when they do nurture, it need not be the stereotype of the patronizing daddy to his "little girl," because when fathers treat their daughters as interesting people, worthy of respect and encouragement, the young women benefit in terms of their ability to be self-determining (Carmichael, 1977).

Efforts by professionals have been exerted in many of society's social structures to break down old sexist patterns. For example, many hospitals now allow fathers to be present in the delivery room. Some schools are examining curriculum and textbooks for sexist biases. TV programming is increasingly presenting diverse gender roles in meaningful contexts. Recruitment and hiring practices in businesses and the professions are subject to equal opportunity criteria. Day-care programs for children provide activities and equipment available to both sexes. Leaves of absence from work make it possible for both parents to take part in their children's lives, either when children may be ill and require parental attention or when children are participants in those benchmark occasions of life such as birthdays, graduation celebrations, and award ceremonies.

Sex Education

One covert area of child and youth oppression is the frequent lack of sex education, either at home or at other extrafamilial social systems. Of course, there are currently organized curricula in schools across the country designed to provide sex education. However, when sexuality is defined in the wider "spheres" of identity, sensuality, and physiology/reproduction, then it is clear that systematic sex education in areas beyond biological and reproductive content is not guaranteed. Teachers are not always secure about how much information they should impart, both because of their own personal reactions and because clear guidelines are not always provided in educational policy:

An example of how sex education programs may not be well carried out was reported by a substitute teacher who encountered—in a classroom of sixth graders—a lesson plan which included a film on human sexuality. Following the film, the substitute began to elicit reactions and, because of her own comfort with the subject and her openness to a discussion, the classroom became alive with questions, discussion, interaction between the students (boys and girls) and the teacher. When the substitute later told one of the regular teachers in the school, the latter was non-plussed at the fact that children had been so active in the discussion and was somewhat abashed at all that

had been discussed, since no such discussion ever took place with the regular teachers.

In a variation on the traditional teacher-student sex education program, Kirby et al. (1982) reported on a joint parent-child sex education program which was initiated by the school but which subtly opened up the subject for parents and children so that it might be more readily followed-up at home. In this series of five or six evening sessions, 10 parent-child pairs (fathers-sons, mothers-daughters) are appropriately grouped according to age and receive cognitive input through lectures, films, and discussion of subjects relevant for the age-range of the youths (reproduction and body changes for the younger group and pelvic/breast exam and birth control information for the older). Use is also made of games designed around sex information, of feeling cards ("I feel embarrassed when . . ."), and of "Dear Abby" vignettes, which stimulate discussion of value issues.

A number of examples are in the literature of sex education programs which have been designed for youths who are in institutions. That we are in the midst of a sexual "evolution" is clear when contrasting the current reports with the earlier example of this author's (Lister, 1981) of the institution for adolescents which had the policy that "sexual language—should not be accepted by any staff member."

Two recent examples appear in a report by Gitelson (1977) of a symposium on sex education in residential child care settings. In one report, Partok and Berner (1977) note that prior sex education had not met the needs and perceptions of the kids, since onlookers heard them trying to match the words taught in their sex education classes with their own street language, and badly mismatching concepts. A program was thus designed to provide information in nine areas: (1) accuracy in sexual terminology; (2) female reproduction (using films, passing around a sanitary napkin); (3) the male reproductive system; (4) conception, development, birth, and aftercare; (5) pregnancy; (6) contraception; (7) venereal disease; (8) dating; and (9) attitudes, consequences, and responsibilities. The authors point out the need for staff who are comfortable with the subject area since, for example, single staff members were uncomfortable responding to personal questions directed to them by the kids.

Another example (Housler, 1977) provided information about the steps in a training program which included an initial survey and training of staff and use of staff to communicate similar content to that which is discussed above. A before-after knowledge test indicated no significant difference in knowledge among the youths; however, there seemed to be more open and positive discussion by the residents as a result of the educational program.

Programs such as these illustrate the need for adequate training of staff because there can be discrepancies between professional staff's expectations for both the knowledge and attitudes which they desire to have communicated and program staff's own attitudes and information and their means of conveying these. Work with youth forces clarification of attitudes and requires various levels of staff to come to terms with some of their own feelings and to make clear their means of communicating. This author recalls an example from some years ago when a psychiatric consultant was going into lengthy discussion about the handling of the "self-stimulation" and "erotic" behavior of an adolescent in an institution for delinquents. It was not really clear to anyone what the message was until one of the resident staff persons—implementing the consultation—told one of the boys in his cottage: "Hey, quit beatin' off!"

Adolescent Pregnancy

One of the consequences of poor or inadequate sex education is unplanned pregnancy by adolescents. Intervention strategies must be considered from three perspectives when considering this issue: primary prevention, pregnancy decisions (abortion, adoption, retention), and postdelivery planning. Every social institution with which adolescents interact has a role to play in one or more of the interventive approaches mentioned above. However, for purposes of the present discussion, only three will be discussed.

A comprehensive effort at primary prevention was reported by Schinke et al. (1981). Based on data which indicate that two-fifths of girls age 15 and under do not use contraceptives; that one in five deliveries is now of an adolescent and that the majority of these was an unplanned pregnancy; that neonates of teenagers are at higher risk for birth complications and various malformations; and that the psychosocial prospects for teenage parents include higher divorce rates, risk of child abuse, economic disadvantage, and poor occupational prospects— Schinke et al. implemented a cognitive-behavioral preventive program that included problem-solving and decision-making strategies and communication skill training. Teams of male and female social workers met with mixed groups of 8 to 12 teenagers in 14 one-hour meetings, using media, guest speakers, and Socratic exchanges. Basic to the program was the implicit knowledge that the teens would likely be sexually active. What was taught were strategies to recognize potential problems, possible outcomes, and various solutions. For example, the boys were taught communication skills that would help them take responsibility for forestalling further sex activity unless there was contraception, on the basis of the conviction that neither the boy nor his partner wanted a pregnancy. A follow-up in two controlled studies validated the retention of the knowledge taught, the positive attitudes toward family planning, and the appropriate use of birth control.

At a different level of intervention, Chiaradonna (1982) reported a group-work approach to treatment of teenage girls who gave up their babies for adoption. According to the data provided by Schinke et al. (1981), less than 7 percent of teen mothers surrender their babies, thus reflecting the enormous increase in abortion as a solution to unplanned pregnancy. For those mothers who do relinquish, however—and to avoid their only choosing retention or abortion for lack of other services—group approaches to help them work through their reactions may be important, since the young mothers in the present sample described the act of leaving the hospital without their babies as the "most trying experience of their lives."

During the course of 10, hour-and-a-half sessions of 2 groups of 6 and 3 members respectively, the following themes emerged:

1. Experiences during the pregnancy (hiding the pregnancy, feelings of isolation and loneliness, attitude of parents and issues of autonomy and dependence).
2. Reactions to the decision to surrender the infant.
3. Grief and loss (including some feelings of the need to suffer and some feelings of guilt if the girl did not feel unduly depressed).
4. Self-image and readjustment (which included a meeting with an adoptive couple who expressed how they held the birth-mothers in high regard and did not look down on them as the group members feared might happen. However, a question about whether the adoptive mother could give up her own birth-child and to which the adoptive mother understandably could not answer yes, did leave some question about the ultimate impact of this type of meeting).

A final example, at a macrolevel, was described by Palmer (1981) as a long-term effort at creating a community resource for those adolescents who kept their babies but who were not being provided medical and educational and related services. What was created in Detroit—after four years of study and planning—was a multidisciplinary staff of social workers, teachers, child care workers, aides, and clerical personnel, backed up by the consultation of psychiatrists, nurses, dietitians, lawyers, and similar resources. The social service component, for example, included:

1. Helping the girl—and often the father, since over 340 fathers were served on a yearly average—break the news of the pregnancy to her parents.
2. Helping the family deal with their reactions, within a family therapy or other mode of intervention.
3. Helping the couple come to the best decision for them regarding the pregnancy.
4. Outreach efforts, since early failed appointments were common.
5. Concrete services, such as layette, money, transportation.
6. Educational planning at the center for those girls not electing to continue in regular school.
7. Parenting classes, divided into two phases—the first which included content on pregnancy and the first 12 months in the baby's life and which taught about nutrition, play, health care, safety and developmental needs; and a second phase which focused on the social and emotional development of the child from one to three years.

Incest

Classically, incest is regarded as the extreme in sexual abuse of children. Incest violates one of the most universal of taboos found in any society, it calls for extreme approbation of the perpetrator, and it leaves a stigma that the victim may never be able to eradicate. In spite of some of the research and opinion referred to earlier, the overwhelming evidence is of untoward consequences both in the young child at the time of involvement as well as lingering consequences affecting the adult adjustment of the former victim. These data come from both treated samples (Meiselmen, 1979), from samples of women seeking help for other conditions (Caldiorla et al., 1983), and from nontreated research samples elicited through the media and other sources. For example, in a study comparing child incest and rape victims with adult rape victims, the trauma scores of child incest victims (the scores based on initial interview assessment of behaviors, emotions, and cognitions) indicated that child incest victims showed the greatest signs of trauma (at the time of interview) among the three groups (Ruch & Chandler, 1980). In another study of 36 women age 18 or more who responded to an ad seeking subjects, 53 percent indicated they had not disclosed the incest experience at the time of its occurrence. Most indicated that the immediate effects of the incest experience were moderate or worse, and, in terms of long-term effects, more than 70 percent felt they were "moderate" to "severe" in the categories of social, psychological, physical, sexual, familial, and in terms of their sense of themselves (Courtois, 1980).

Other reports indicate other types of problems for adult women who were incest victims in their own childhood, though the perfect study seems not to have yet been constructed to help separate out what are the outcomes for incest victims that differentiate them from any other groups of women. For example, Meiselman compared a small psychotherapy sample of incest victims with a psychotherapy group with no incestuous experiences in their history and found that in many nonsexual areas (depression, anxiety, suicidal thoughts, problems with their children and phobias) the groups did not differ (Meiselman, 1979).

Given the varied findings cited above, several perspectives may be taken by human service personnel when addressing incest at the wider levels of intervention (policy and primary prevention). First, it would appear that many women have experienced incestuous relationships in their childhood that they did not report and that—for some—seemed to have no dire long-term consequences. Thus, it may be that an insistence on rooting out every instance of incestuous involvement may not be the public policy stance to advocate. However, there should be continued research directed to-

ward refining the accumulating data cited earlier and which helps to enlighten both about the impact of incest as well as the impact of various intervention approaches. Secondly, each community should have an array of services available for the multimethod and multidisciplinary approaches that are needed for secondary-level intervention. Basic to this level of intervention are individual psychotherapy, group therapy (for both victims and perpetrators), family therapy, self-help groups such as Parents United, and arrangements among police, schools, courts, health, and welfare services that facilitate communication, referrals, and proceedings so as to minimize the secondary trauma (social iatrogenesis) of incest.

The accumulating reports on intervention approaches with incest seem to agree on a number of points: intervention must be (1) multifaceted, including varied approaches as above; (2) interdisciplinary; (3) directed toward the family system in toto as well as subparts of the mother-child, father-child, marital pair; and (4) long-term in duration, though crisis intervention may be appropriate in the early phase (Deaton and Sandlin, 1980).

Pioneering work with incest has been done in Santa Clara County, California. In an evaluation of their family-oriented approach, 84 percent of families were found to have positive results after about a year of intervention (Kroth, 1979). In an introduction to the therapeutic model followed by the Santa Clara program, Kroth notes:

Reconstitution of the family involves a process of forming new boundaries and coalitions amongst its members. Vital steps in the process involve the perpetrator's accepting his responsibility for the molestation, and acknowledging this to other family members, and a process of reassuring the child-victim that she is not responsible for the molestation. The parents must review their marital relationship and develop patterns of behavior that allow them to meet their needs without renouncing the protective and nurturing responsibilities of parenthood. Cross-generational boundaries must be delineated, while same-sex coalitions are generated. When both parents are willing to accept and admit their joint responsibility for the molestation, and the child perceives the parents as her protectors, reunion of the family may occur (p. 17).

In a recent summary of approaches to incest intervention, Hoorwitz (1983) outlines four stages that might constitute a paradigm for the intervention process. In the first stage (orientation-engagement) the therapist must establish roles and authority relationships through separate meetings with the family members. The protection of the child must be first guaranteed by, if necessary, the removal of the perpetrator from the home (rather than the child, who would thus be punished). The denial by either the father or mother or both must be attended to from the beginning and is best handled by acknowledging "the situation" and that changes in the family have to take place. Ultimately, the father must acknowledge his incestuous activity, but at this early stage denial is worked with—as in all other therapy—by not reinforcing it and by not insisting on its premature removal. The early work must also include attempts to secure the family's commitment to therapy; this is facilitated by the continued involvement of the court.

Basic life needs must be attended to (housing, food, employment), since many of these life systems may have been disrupted during the crisis of disclosure. In Kroth's report, for example, over 65 percent of the families needed welfare, housing, and employment assistance as an aftermath of the disclosure (Kroth, 1979).

The individual emotional reactions of each family member need attention. There may be certain characteristic reactions for the three principals in this family triangle for which a therapist should always be looking. The child may feel shame and guilt about the incest itself and anxiety about the possible breakup of the family. She needs to feel the support of an ally—preferably her mother—and may need concrete planning for testify-

ing in court. The father may feel guilt, shame, and despair, or he may be angry or still denying and projecting blame; either way, he needs a therapeutic relationship where he can sense that he will not himself become victimized. The mother may still be experiencing shock and anger or denial, but a key component in treatment is her involvement in her role as mother to her daughter and as wife to her husband. Her anger, when present, needs to be recognized; it is possibly directed at either her husband (as the abuser) or may be more diffusely directed toward the daughter or other family members—or even the service providers—because of the upsetting of the family balance by the revelation of the abuse. It is with respect to some of these reactions that the service providers sometimes need to deal with their own reactions, since they may feel any reactions by adults in the family, other than guilt and remorse, are unacceptable.

The second stage involves intensive work with the individuals in the family. The child, based on an assessment of her individual needs and problems, will usually have the need to sort out family roles, to enhance her feelings of self-esteem, to learn to trust, to even begin to modify any "seductive" or "stylized sexual" behavior (Burgess-Groth, 1980) which she has learned has brought special privileges in the family. For the mother, she may need to learn assertive skills, to deal with her anger toward her husband, to take on the nurturing role with her daughter—possibly first needing extensive nurturing herself through the therapeutic relationship—sex education, and possible treatment for the often common depression such women face. The father usually falls into a category of either dependent or dominating personality. He may need help to identify and appropriately express his anger at his wife (who he feels has either failed him or dominated him). He may also need to learn stress-reduction techniques—especially for men whose incestuous behavior is related to a regression in functioning rather than an arrested development (Sgroi, 1982)—and possible alcohol treatment.

The third stage of intervention is directed toward creating the healthy boundaries and alliances among subsystems in the family. Mother-daughter sessions allow for expression of feelings of disappointment, anger, and abandonment, while focusing on new rules and arrangements in the family that will strengthen the mother-daughter bond. Marital therapy must be directed toward bringing the couple together affectively, sexually, and in terms of their ability to develop communication and problem-solving skills.

In the last stage, at least one father-daughter session should be arranged where the father can apologize and where new rules can be articulated. The remainder of the fourth stage involves family sessions where the mother's power is enhanced, tasks are assigned and reviewed, realignments are reinforced, individual needs are expressed, and understandings about each other are shared among the family members.

In conjunction with the foregoing stages of intervention, family members should be receiving help through other means such as father's groups, Parents United, and therapeutic groups for the child victims. Several examples of group treatment with incest victims illustrate intervention through that medium (Delson & Clark, 1981). These groups involve expressive therapy, didactic teaching, art work, psychodrama and role-playing to achieve goals which include working-through, normalizing, and sharing in order to overcome feelings of pejorative uniqueness. In a group treatment approach incorporating art therapy, Carozza and Heirsteiner (1982) outline five stages, as follows:

1. "Gathering"—where girls identify commonalities among themselves and are helped to feel comfortable expressing themselves, and where the medium of art is offered as a resource.

2. "Self-disclosure"—where a film on incest, guided imagery, and a "group scribble" are used to facilitate disclosure.

3. "Regression"—where paint is used to facilitate the freeing of regressive trends.

4. "Reconstruction"—where a collage helps the group members place themselves in the group and in the world.

5. "Ending"—which takes about four sessions, terminating with all art work of the girls returned to them.

Results indicated that attendance was good, the girls felt less isolated, their dealings with their families was improving (and family treatment was an adjunct), functioning was improved in other systems such as school, and the pre- and post-artwork showed a changed perception of self by the girls.

In another structured group treatment approach, Sturkie (1983) identified eight treatment themes that have proved always important to child sex-abuse victims. The group treatment was organized into 8-week therapy cycles of 90 minutes per evening session. The eight themes are: believability, guilt and responsibility, body integrity and protection, secrecy and sharing, anger, powerlessness, other life crises, tasks and symptoms, court attendance, and a terminal "ninth night"—an experience of having fun together borrowed from Parents United. Without elaborating all the intervention strategies and techniques used to work on each theme, "guilt and responsibility" may serve to illustrate how each subject area is worked with therapeutically. Assessment has shown that victims—because of the ego-centricity of their stage in development or because of parental, or even service providers', attributions—often blame themselves for the incest. Thus, guilt and responsibility are dealt with in four ways:

1. Through education and discussion, the message is repeated that sexual activity between an adult and child is the *adult's* responsibility to prevent.

2. Because incest has often precipitated a division of loyalties in a family, the next tactic is for group members to express their feelings (for example, fear of abandonment) associated with family conflict.
3. Due to the fact that many perpetrators are gentle with the victim, the child may have experienced pleasure in the incestual activity. Consequently a technique developed by Rosensweig-Smith is used whereby the children are given the analogy of how, when they are tickled by another person, they respond in spite of their desire to have the tickling terminated. Thus the effort is to separate compliance from involuntary physical responses and to maintain the child's developing capacity for pleasurable body responses in the future and on an elective basis.
4. To feelings that the child chastises herself for not better defending herself, the inability of a child to easily say no to an adult is discussed and children are encouraged to externalize their feelings and redefine them as anger.

Most of these approaches are appropriate to family systems that remain intact. Many families break apart when the incest is revealed, with current opinion strongly favoring the removal of the father if separation of family members must occur, in order not to further victimize the child. To determine when families can be reconstituted, Server and Janzen (1982) suggest the following criteria:

1. The father has taken responsibility for the incest.
2. All family members have expressed reasonable assurance that the child is safe.
3. The girl has expressed the ability to seek help in the future (should she ever need it).
4. The mother has demonstrated the ability to protect both her child and herself.
5. The family and the therapist are confident that sufficient progress has been made toward both short- and long-term goals.
6. The mother-daughter bond is secure and the mother does not hold the girl to blame for the incest.
7. The generational boundaries have been strengthened and appropriate marital and parental roles have been demonstrated.

CONCLUSIONS

This chapter has been concerned with children and adolescents as a population of the sexually oppressed. The oppression of this group originates at various levels of society: at the macrolevel it occurs because of rapidly changing social values, because of changing theories and information available about children and their sexuality, and because of our society's enduring sexist child-rearing patterns. At the mid-level, oppression occurs because of our approaches to sex education, and this leads to at least one untoward consequence in many instances—adolescent pregnancy. And finally, oppression occurs at the microlevel of the family, where information continues to accumulate about the prevalence of incest as one of the most clear-cut examples of sexual oppression. Also presented in this chapter was a discussion of several of the elements in the basic intervention process and examples of intervention approaches were offered for each of the types of oppression which were selected for this chapter.

Obviously, there are numerous other ways in which children and adolescents are oppressed, both sexually and otherwise. This chapter was designed to show how the basic intervention process may be utilized to explore various sources and types of oppression and to illustrate—with only a few of the numerous examples available—how human service professionals must use varied means to help prevent and ameliorate the oppression of youth, so that youths may continue to grow into fully functioning adults in all spheres of their sexuality.

REFERENCES

Burgess, A., and Groth, N. Child sexual abuse. Keynote speech presented at the Third National Symposium on Violence in Families, Hot Springs, Arkansas, October, 1980.
Caldirola, D., Gemperle, M. B., Guzinski, G., Robert, G., and Doerr, H. Incest and pelvic pain: The social worker as part of a research

team. In *Health and Social Work* 8: (1983) 309–319.

CARMICHAEL, C. *Non-sexist childraising.* Boston: Beacon Press, 1977.

CAROZZA, P., AND HERISTEINER, C. Young female incest victims in treatment: Stages of growth seen with a group art therapy model. *Clinical Social Work Journal*, 10: (1982) 165–175.

CHIARADONNA, W. A group work approach to post-surrender treatment of unwed mothers. *Social Work with Groups* 5: (1982) 47–68.

CONSTANTINE, L., AND MARTINSON, F. *Children and sex: New findings, new perspectives.* Boston: Little, Brown, 1981.

CONTE, J. Progress in treating the sexual abuse of children. *Social Work*, 29: May–June, 1984, 258–263.

COURTOIS, C. Studying and counseling women with past incest experience. *Victimology: An International Journal* 5: (1980) 322–334.

DEATON, F., AND SANDLIN, D. Sexual victimology within the home: A treatment approach. *Victimology: An International Journal* 5: (1980).

DELORA, J., AND WARREN, C. *Understanding sexual interaction.* Boston: Houghton Mifflin, 1977.

DELSON, N., AND CLARK, M. Group work with sexually molested children. In *Child Welfare* 60: (1981) 175–182.

DUHL, B. Changing sex roles—Information without process. *Social Casework* 57(1976): 80–86.

GILLIGAN, C. Why should a woman be more like a man?. *Psychology Today*, June 1982, 68–77.

GITELSON, P., ED. Symposium: Sex education and residential child care. *Child Care Quarterly* 6 (1977).

GOCHROS, H., AND GOCHROS, J. *The sexually oppressed.* N.Y.: Association Press, 1977.

———. *Honolulu Star-Bulletin*, January 17, 1984, p. 1.

HOORWITZ, A. Guidelines for treating father-daughter incest. *Social Casework* 64: (1983) 515–524.

HOUSLER, R., AND SCALLON, R. Sex education in a residential child caring agency. *Child Care Quarterly* 6: (1977) 211–221.

KIRBY, D., PETERSON, L., AND BROWN, J. A joint parent-child sex education program. *Child Welfare* 61: (1982) 105–114.

KROTH, J. *Child sexual abuse, analysis of a family therapy approach.* Springfield, Ill.: Charles C. Thomas, Publisher, 1979.

LAMPL-DE GROOT, J. Thoughts on psychoanalytic views of female psychology. *Psychoanalytic Quarterly* 51: (1982) 1–18.

LISTER, L. Adolescents. In Gochros and Gochros, eds., *The sexually oppressed.* N.Y.: Association Press, 1977, 41–53.

———. Chronically ill and disabled. In Shore and Gochros, eds. *Sexual problems of adolescents in institutions.* Springfield, Ill.: Charles C. Thomas, 1981, 223–235.

MALCOLM, J. Trouble in the archives (parts I and II). *New Yorker Magazine*, December 5 and 12, 1983.

MEAD, M. *Culture and commitment.* Garden City, N.Y.: Natural History Press/Doubleday and Co., 1970.

MEISELMAN, K. *Incest: A psychological study of causes and effects with treatment recommendations.* San Francisco: Jossey-Bass, Publishers, 1979.

MERWIN, W. S. Review of The invention of solitude, by Paul Auster. *New York Times Magazine Book Review*, February 27, 1983.

PALMER, E. A community-based comprehensive approach to serving adolescent parents. *Child Welfare* 60: (1981) 191–197.

PARTOK, L., AND BERNER, G. Sex education and the behavior problem child. *Child Care Quarterly* 6: (1977) 204–210.

RUCH, L., AND CHANDLER, S. The impact of sexual assault on three victim groups receiving crisis intervention services at a rape treatment center: Adult rape victims, child rape victims, and incest victims. *Journal of Social Service Research* 5: (1982) 83–100.

SCARF, M. *New York Times Book Review Magazine*, July 24, 1983.

SCHINKE, S., BLYTHE, B., GILCHRIST, L., AND BURT, G. Primary prevention of adolescent pregnancy. *Social Work with Groups* 4: (1981) 121–135.

SERVER, J., AND JANZEN, C. Contradictions to reconstitution of sexually abusive families. *Child Welfare* 61: (1982) 279–288.

SGROI, S., ED. *Handbook of clinical intervention in child sexual abuse.* Lexington, Mass: D. C. Heath and Co., 1982.

SOCIAL WORK. Special Issue on women. 21: November 1976.

SPRUNG, B., ED. *Perspectives on non-sexist early childhood education.* New York: Teachers College Press, 1978.

STURKIE, K. Structured group treatment for sexually abused children. *Health and Social Work* 8: (1983) 299–308.

TALESE, G. *Thy neighbor's wife.* N.Y.: Doubleday, 1980.

8

THE AGED

James J. Kelly
Susan Rice

THE PROBLEM

The purpose of this chapter is to discuss the aged as a sexually oppressed population and to suggest a variety of means of intervention to deal with and change this situation. In approaching the sexual problems, the normal physiological changes relating to aging are discussed, as arc a number of common physical, emotional, and social problems that elderly people encounter. In analyzing the forms of intervention, this chapter presents the policy behind direct service as well as the results of research on what direct service is being practiced today.

Who Are the Elderly?

In the United States at the end of 1984 there were over 26 million people age 65 or over, or slightly more than 12 percent of the population (U.S. Government Printing Of-

fice, 1984). The population is growing daily since 5000 Americans become 65 every day, and only 3400 Americans over 65 die every day. In 1979 older women numbered more than 14.6 million compared to 10 million men. Women in the United States live an average of 7.8 years longer than men from birth, and 4.4 years longer from age 65. Statistics on marital status reveal even more dramatic differences between men and women: 77 percent of elder men are married, while 52 percent of older women are widows. In 1980, the number of men and women over age 65 who were divorced was 49 and 88 per 1000 married individuals, respectively (Christenson, 1984). Statistics on living situations also show differences between men and women. Women are three times more likely than men to live alone or with nonrelatives. Twenty percent of all older people receive nursing home care at some point, although only 5 percent are institutionalized at any one time. Seventy percent of older people live in families, and only 25 percent live alone or with nonrelatives. Poverty is typically associated with old age. In 1978, half of the families headed by an older person had incomes of less than $10,000 while the median income of older persons living alone was $4303 (Butler & Lewis, 1982).

Sexual Oppression of the Aged

The elderly, as a population, are sexually oppressed because of general attitudes toward sexuality and aging. Sexuality is a concept that incorporates sensuality as a personal perception and intimacy as interpersonal experience. Sexuality is really an expression of one's total being. However, besides sexual touching, touch can be seen as an overt expression of closeness and intimacy and can offer the aged (and everyone else) a sense of well-being. In fact, sexuality can validate the lifelong learning that the individual is a man or a woman who can give to others and have that offering appreciated. In examining the notion of healthy sexuality, one must remember that it is individually defined and is wholesome if it leads to intimacy (not necessarily coitus) and enriches all involved parties (Ebersole and Hess, 1981). Schwartz (1974) ties this concept of sexuality into specific needs of the elderly:

Another important and highly sensitive area of concern with respect to compensating is the need for attention, love, affection, particularly as this involves sexual activity. The price one pays for survival into the later decades of life is the gradual loss of family, friends, even spouse. And, not surprisingly, one of the most pervasive hazards of old age is loneliness. The need for affection is universal. . . . Most especially in the late years, when many of the self-esteem factors diminish, does the need for affection, for love, for "stroking" become more, not less, intense.

Yet, when we examine our societal attitudes about sexuality and aging, we find them to be directly contradictory to the above statements. Our society sees age as equated to sexlessness. *The Myth and Reality of Aging in America* (1975) surveyed 4254 people, including a representative cross section of the American public over age 18 and an additional sample of people 55 to 64 years of age. In questions relating to sexuality, of the total public surveyed, only 5 percent saw "most people over 65" as very sexually active, and 28 percent saw them as somewhat sexually active. Older people themselves share this attitude to some degree, as only 11 percent of the group over 65 saw themselves as very sexually active and, at the same time, they saw only 6 percent of "most people over 65" as being very sexually active.

These attitudes have come from a number of sources. The Victorian ethic of being productive as an integral part of the equation of worth has made us see old people as generally valueless. Then, our own fears of growing old lead to stereotyping to create distance between "us" and "them." Furthermore, general misinformation about sexuality leads to ignorance, disguised by silence.

Murphy (1979) points to yet another attitudinal norm that effectively eliminates sexuality from the life of the elderly. That is the notion in our society of romantic love, which is equated to intense physical love. Its only appropriate sexual expression is characterized by passionate love-making and the achievement of sexual union through simultaneous orgasm. Neither older people nor younger ones can consistently measure up to these expectations, and thus the belief is fostered that "real" sexual pleasure is only for a privileged few.

Yet, the evidence regarding sexuality directly contradicts these attitudes. There are three major clusters of research studies dealing with sexuality and aging, in addition to numerous individual studies. The Kinsey studies (1948) included research on 14,084 males and 5940 females. However, of these subjects only 87 males and even fewer females had sexual histories adequately detailed for examination purposes. Nevertheless, the findings that did emerge pointed to the ability and existence of sexual expression in old age. At age 60, only 1 out of 5 men were no longer capable of sexual intercourse. At age 80, this proportion had risen to 3 out of 4 men. However, Kinsey also concluded that the rate of decline in absolute frequency of sexual outlet (including sexual intercourse, masturbation, and nocturnal emissions) did not decline any more rapidly in old age than it did at ages between 30 and 60. Kinsey's conclusions about women represented extrapolations from changes observed at younger ages. He noted a gradual decline in frequency of sexual intercourse between ages 20 and 60, but felt that this decline was probably related to aging processes in the male, rather than an independent phenomenon.

Masters and Johnson (1966, 1970) have done a number of studies of sexuality and aging. Interview data from 133 males above age 60, including 71 in their sixties, 37 in their seventies, and 15 in their eighties were studied, as were data from 54 women above age 60, including 37 in their sixties, and 17 in their seventies. For males Masters and Johnson found that the most important factor in the maintenance of effective sexuality was consistency of active sexual expression. For women too, the likelihood of engaging actively in sexual expression is greater if they have done so earlier in life.

A group of longitudinal studies at the Duke University Center for the Study of Aging and Human Development showed that 70 percent of aging men in their sample continued to have regular sexual activity. Another supporting statistic was that 15 percent of the group showed increased patterns of sexual activity as they grew older (Verwoerdt et al., 1969).

Additionally, recent studies have attempted to examine sexual expression in older people. Martin (1981) examined male members of the Baltimore Longitudinal Study of Aging. Of 313 males between the ages of 60 to 79, 62 (19.5%) were considered very active sexually (more than 51 sexual events in the past year had occurred, includ-

ing coitus, masturbation, nocturnal emission, and homosexual activity), and an additional 63 (20.1%) were considered moderately active (22 to 50 sexual events in the past year).

Even more interestingly, a study of 106 cultures, using Human Relations Area Files (Winn & Niles, 1982) showed sexual activity to have cross-cultural patterns of variability. In 70 percent of the societies for which data were available, men continued to have sexual activity of various kinds as they aged. For females 84 percent of the societies showed strong sexual interest as aging occurred.

All of the above studies point to the fact that sexual expression can and does exist in old age. The last study cited especially points to the fact that culture plays a part in the extent and kind of sexual expression utilized.

Most of the research on sexuality and aging focuses on performance. The studies measure direct sexual activities such as intercourse, masturbation, nocturnal emissions, orgasm, and so on. However, the definition of sexuality is broader than specific activities, and in fact old age can *lead* to an increase in those activities. As defined previously, sexuality is a form of human intimacy, of being aware that one is a man or a woman, and that others respond to him or her as such.

Towards that end, there is a need to distinguish sexual activity from sexual interest. A series of studies by Pfeiffer, Werwoerdt, and Wang (1968, 1969) initially examined 254 subjects, and at later dates examined 190 and 126 subjects. This decline in numbers was due to death of some subjects and serious illness in others.

The degree of activity, as measured by frequency of sexual intercourse, tended to decline over time, but not in a statistically significant way until the late eighties. The degree of sexual interest also showed a significant negative relationship to age in all of the three studies. This incidence of interest, however, is not as clear as an age-related decline in activity because, although *strong* degrees of sexual interest are absent after age 75, mild-to-moderate sexual desire may persist far beyond that age.

Additionally, the effects of marital status are important in relationship to sexual activity. Findings showed that for unmarried women the incidence of sexual activity was very low, but unmarried women retained their sexual interest; thus the difference between married and unmarried women's sexual *interest* was much smaller. Unmarried men maintained both sexual activity and sexual interests at levels roughly similar to married men.

When sexual activity was no longer operative, subjects were asked the reasons for its cessation. Male subjects tended to assign responsibility for stopping to themselves, while the women attributed blame to their spouses, thus demonstrating agreement that in general the husband was the determining factor in cessation of sexual intercourse in marriage.

The range of sex-related problems encountered by the elderly is extremely varied and can fall into any of the physical, emotional, and/or social categories. These categories are, however, integrally intertwined and will be discussed in relationship to their effects on the client, their partners, and significant others.

To understand the problems, one must also understand the normal, physiological changes in sexual response that are part of the aging process. In males a number of changes occur over time as a result of less production of the sex hormone, testosterone. In response to overt sexual stimulation, older men take longer to achieve erection. For males another important physical change is that the incidence of spontaneous erection diminishes when confronted with visual or overt sexual stimuli. When younger, men often get erections when attractive others come close to them; with advancing age, direct physical genital stimulation is required to reach full erection. There is a decrease in the expulsive pressure and volume

of seminal fluid during the ejaculatory experience, and there is also an occasional reduction in or loss of ejaculatory demand. The level of interest can continue to be high, but since the demand to ejaculate is lessened, older men can maintain erection for a longer period before orgasm. There is also a longer refractory period during which a second erection and/or ejaculation cannot be achieved.

For females, there is a slowing in the rate of production and volume of lubricating fluid in the vagina. The vaginal walls also become thinner and less elastic so that, to avoid painful sensations, more time is necessary for precoital stimulation. There is also a reduction of duration in orgasm time and a slower reaction of the clitoris to stimulation. Furthermore, for females, breast and buttock tone decreases.

For both males and females, the changes that occur point to a slowing down in performance time rather than intensity of enjoyment. However, if older men and women do not make allowances for these subtle kinds of changes, they may feel less capable and desirable, and this kind of feeling increases incidences of impotency and sexual withdrawal (Davis & Davis, 1978).

Masters & Johnson (1970) point to a group of important factors that relate to the loss of potency. They include:

1. Boredom stemming from the monotony of a repetitious sexual relationship.
2. Preoccupation with economic and occupational goals to the exclusion of communication and sexual energy.
3. Fatigue.
4. Overindulgence in food or alcoholic beverages.
5. Physical or mental deprivations of either the person or the partner.
6. Fear of sexual failure (the vicious cycle of fear of failure producing failure.)

A number of changes in sexual belief and practice would probably occur if older clients were aware of the normality of the aging process as it relates to sexuality. For example, when conception is not even a theoretical possibility, the expectation that every episode of sexual interaction terminates with the penis placed in the vagina would be altered, and alternate sexual approaches could be explored (Masters & Johnson, 1981). Also, when on any particular occasion only one parner may be involved to the level of orgasmic demand, the obsession of providing mutual sexual release would be altered, and the warm sensual experiences of holding and touching would not be viewed as a failed sexual experience. Finally, sexual expectations would alter more realistically as people alter. The adage of "I'm too old for sex" can be translated into "I'm too frightened about how well I can perform now as compared to how I used to perform, instead of realizing that I am different now and want and need different things." This attitude would change, as clients become more aware of the process of aging in respect to sexuality.

INTERVENTION

Intervention can occur at the level of changing societal attitudes by creating policies and can also occur at the direct service level in terms of intervening with clients and other helping professionals.

One of the factors making intervention so complex is that, in the process of dealing with the issue of sexuality and aging, at least three sets of values are present—those of society in general, those of the client, and those of the helping professional—and all of these set of values are constantly changing (Shomaker, 1980).

First, societal norms, as related to sexual expression, dictate who shall be allowed the privilege of sex, when, and under what circumstances it is appropriate. As we have said, some of the norms that today's elderly population have grown up with include the attitudes that sex should occur between married men and women for the purpose of procreation rather than recreation and that sex is only for the "young and beautiful." These norms give a clear message to older adults that once their reproductive capacity terminates, once their marital partner is no longer available, or once they are no longer "young and beautiful," sexual expression is no longer appropriate. They receive that message from society as a whole and from their own subgroups. One commonly finds middle-aged children of older adults shocked to hear the suggestion that their parents are pursuing or might want to pursue active sexual gratification.

Second, the norms of the client affect intervention. To the degree that the older person has absorbed societal norms, he or she too may be convinced that sexual expression is inappropriate. At a time when loss is a significant theme in their lives—emotional losses of family members and friends, social losses of opportunities, economic losses of income, and the career losses associated with retirement—sexual activity is one (unnecessary, perhaps) loss that is accepted without exploration. The physical changes discussed, along with health problems, may influence the client's idea that this loss too is inescapable and irreversible. The taboos of sexuality among aged people, reinforced by phrases such as "dirty old man" and "lecher," are often swallowed hook, line, and sinker by older people themselves, so that they feel guilty and embarrassed about the feelings they may have.

Lastly, the norms of the helping person are also influenced by society. To the degree that we have absorbed societal norms, we too may be concerned that sexual expression is inappropriate for older people. Therefore examining one's own attitudes is an essential first step for supportive intervention.

Helping practitioners are encouraged to answer the following questions and examine some of their attitudes about sexuality and the aging. Are the following questions true or false?

1. Males between the ages of 60 and 80 experience a steady decline in their capacity to be sexually active.
2. Females between the ages of 60 and 80 experience a steady decline in their capacity to be sexually active.
3. There are no established data to demonstrate that the physiological response of men to sexual stimulation clearly diminishes past 60 years of age.
4. The capacity among women for sexual performance at "orgasmic response levels" clearly diminishes past 60.
5. The most important factor in the maintenance of effective sexuality for the aging male is consistency of active sexual expression.
6. Among aging men, interest in sex first diminishes, then ceases by age 70.
7. Sex does not play an important role in the lives of elderly people.
8. A pattern of decline in sexual activity for both men and women has been identified by researchers as integral to the aging process.
9. A very high level of sexual activity in youth generally results in a sexual "burning out in the old age."
10. Sexual activity is unheard of among people in their 90s.

Questions 1, 2, 4, 6, 7, 8, 9, 10 are all false. Questions 3 and 5 are true. Answering these questions incorrectly reflects, to some degree, the incorporation of stereotypes into the mindset and attitudes of the helping practitioners. Before intervention can take place, in terms of helping the aging population to become *less* sexually oppressed, individual attitudinal change needs to occur.

On the broader level of intervention, care can be taken to avoid agist references to sexuality in our institutions and media. The Grey Panthers offers guidelines for nonagist portrayals of sexuality in the media that incorporate the idea of elderly people *being* sexual.

DO use words like elder, old, old age, and, in context, words such as experienced, wise, mature, and weathered.

DON'T use words or expressions like balding, granny, hag, old bag, peppery, spry, old goat, old fogey, little old lady, dirty old man, sagging breasts or face, cranky, cantankerous, grouchy, or housewife (if not applicable).

DO try to emphasize the positive aesthetic aspects of growing old: a face wrinkled with beauty, gray hair blowing in the wind.

Be careful, in general, of age-related adjectives. DON'T use the word senile as a general adjective. Instead of saying, "She's acting senile," be more specific: "She's acting confused and disoriented"; instead of saying, "Their love affair was almost adolescent in spite of their advanced age," say, "Their love affair was wild and fresh."

DON'T assume that all elders are heterosexual; as with all ages, a significant proportion of elders are Lesbians, gay men, and bisexuals.

AVOID portraying old men as needing young women for potent and vital sex. Include the portrayal of sexually active elders with contact with each other. Be careful in portraying old women in relationships with young men as "news"—you may be helping to generate yet another myth.

All of the above apply to humorous depictions of elders. Avoid implying that sex for elders is absurd by snickering or being oblique about their lives or sensuality. [Davis (1980), pp. 83–84]

Another means of mid- and macrolevel intervention can be the development of specific programs for the elderly to help them become more comfortable with sensitive topics such as sexuality. Boyer and Boyer (1982) describe a program entitled "Remaining Vital," given at a senior citizen center, which covered a variety of topics including changing family relationships, loneliness, altered sexual expression, and dealing with death and dying. During three offerings, 111 people participated ranging in age from 55 to 92. The number of women (mostly single or widowed) greatly exceeded the number of men (94 women, 17 men). The format included poetry, slides, excerpts from the literature, and a coffee break followed by group discussion. Several handouts were used including pages of reading material, quotations relevant to the topic, and questionnaires to be anonymously completed and used in subsequent discussions. The participants responded positively, mostly because they received reassurance that their own feelings were normal. An examination of participants' feelings demonstrated that the range of past and present sexual experience was considerable, but lack of information about sex fostered inappropriate fear and pain. Curiosity continued, but the aging person's definition of the sexual experience was more diffuse than younger people's, and feelings were normal. One of the concepts, it was felt, that made this group successful was that it incorporated sexuality into a holistic perspective. This perspective allowed for participants' inhibitions to be dealt with in a respectful and dignified method.

Older people want and need information on the sexual attitudes of their cohorts, as it eliminates a great deal of the guilt and anxiety felt by them.

Direct Intervention

If we examine direct intervention with clients, the kind of intervention must relate to the specific problems encountered. Specific medical treatments for specific physical sexual dysfunctions will not be discussed here. However, working with physicians as an advocate for the elderly is important. Assisting the physician to have a fuller understanding of the patient as a sexual human being can increase the doctor's attempt to alleviate sexual dysfunction rather than shrugging it off as a part of normal aging. Additionally, sensitizing physicians to the emotional damage done by prescribing medications with sexual side effects would also decrease the situations in which it occurs. Table 8-1 includes some of the more common drugs that affect sexual activity.

In general, the advocate role of the helping professional includes the involving of medical personnel and facilities in viewing the client in the psychosocial perspective,

TABLE 8-1   Drugs That Affect Sexual Activity (Long, 1979)

Drug name or family	Possible effects
alcohol	reduced potency in men, delayed orgasm in women
amphetamine	reduced libido and potency
bethanidine	impaired ejaculation
clonidine	reduced libido
debrisoquine	reduced potency, impaired ejaculation
dextroamphetamine	reduced libido and potency
disulfiram	reduced potency
guanethidine	reduced potency, impaired ejaculation
haloperidol	reduced potency
levodopa	increased libido (in some men and women)
lithium	reduced potency
methyldopa	reduced libido and potency
oral contraceptives	reduced libido (in some women)
phenothiazines	reduced libido and potency, impaired ejaculation (occasionally)
phenoxybenzamine	impaired ejaculation
primidone	reduced libido and potency
reserpine	reduced libido and potency
sedative and sleep-inducing drugs (hypnotics) when used on a regular basis	reduced libido and potency
thiazide diuretics	reduced libido (occasionally, in some men)
tranquilizers (mild)	reduced libido and potency
tricyclic antidepressants	reduced libido and potency

taking into consideration the client, significant others, and the way a specific medical problem may affect the person or the person's environment.

As people age they do develop many acute and chronic kinds of health problems. With proper information and care, however, most problems do not necessarily indicate cessation of sexual activity. A large part of the helping professional's intervention needs to be in the form of educating the elderly client both about the physical condition itself and the effect that it might have on functioning. Specific health problems that are common include heart diseases, prostate problems, hysterectomies, urinary problems, and menopause.

There are 13 to 20 million people with functional or psychogenic heart disease in the United States. Although this does not necessarily result physically in cessation of sexual activity, many people *feel* that such is the case and do curtail their sexual activities (Bloch et al., 1975).

Many heart patients, even after recovery, view themselves as fragile, vulnerable, and sickly. There is a widespread myth that coitus is such a strenuous activity that it can provoke a heart attack and cause the death of the cardiac patient. This myth arose from a number of sources: the emphasis in the media on a public figure who dies in the arms of a lover, the fact that disinterest or weakness is often a side effect of prescribed medications, and the fact that the anxiety and depression that often follow a heart attack can cause temporary impotence.

In reality, during the orgasmic stage of intercourse there is a short-timed elevation of the blood pressure and acceleration of the heart which rapidly returns to normal. The energy spent seems equivalent to climbing a flight of stairs or performing any other average daily living activity.

Intervention by human service professionals needs to be directed toward the patient and his or her partner in a number of ways. The professional can serve as a facilitator to discussions between patient/family and physician. Sexual activity is often ignored because of uncertainty or embarrassment unless the patient and family is encouraged to discuss it openly. Additionally, supportive counseling includes debunking the myths regarding sexuality and heart disease and engendering a sense of hope that a sexual relationship can and will resume.

The *prostate gland* is integrally related to sexual ability in the male because seminal fluid is largely a product of that gland. Problems usually stem from bacterial infections causing inflammation, congestion (an age-associated degenerative process), or prostatic enlargement. This can lead to premature ejaculation, pain on ejaculation, or varying degrees of impotence, which can often be alleviated by prostatic massage, antibacterial preparations, and reduction in alcohol intake. If surgery is required for prostatic enlargement, there is usually no change in capacity. One significant change, however, is that there will be retrograde ejaculation as a result of the surgery—that is, the ejaculate flows into the bladder and is excreted later. If a carcinoma of the prostate is found and treated surgically, total impotence can follow. However, the resultant lack of erection should not be equated with lack of libido, the mental and emotional desire for intercourse, and a penile prosthesis can be inserted.

The explanation of possible consequences and symptoms and reduction of anxiety help patients to have more favorable sexual outcomes (Roen, 1983). The interventions called for with clients undergoing hysterectomies are similar to those discussed above for women. The most frequent emotional responses to hysterectomy are feelings of depression and loss of femininity. These emotions stem from (physically) groundless fears, myths, and apprehensions about what might occur. Huffman (1969) described one account of such fears:

She wanted to know what the hysterectomy would do to her. Was it true that women had emotional crises, lost their sexual libido, ceased to be attractive to their husbands, had nervous breakdowns, became fat and lethargic, found their hair turning gray, became irritable and developed antisocial tendencies after a hysterectomy? (p. 48)

Both the client and her partner need to understand that there are no anatomical or physiological reasons for the removal of the uterus to affect normal sexual response. Even if one's ovaries are also removed, a woman can enjoy normal sexual relations because the vagina is the source of lubricating secretions during sexual activity, not the uterus or the ovaries. Estrogenic hormones are *not* essential for sexual response (Filler & Hall, 1969).

Elderly, sexually active women are particularly susceptible to urological problems because of the changes taking place in their genitals as a result of aging. The resulting pain during intercourse discourages sexual activity, which, aside from presenting emotional problems, tends to reduce further the body's production of estrogen and exacerbates the problems. The solution is to request medical intervention to minimize the effect of the aging process on the genitals (Solnick & Corby, 1983).

Menopause, not in itself a disease, is often treated as such by clients and their families. *Menopause* is the irregularity, followed by cessation, of menstruation and is a clear signal of decreasing ovarian function (conception of offspring is no longer possible). The research on menopause effects is mixed because symptoms vary so widely from woman to woman. What actually occurs is that the ovaries stop producing estrogen, sometimes leading to hot flashes, sleeplessness, or atrophy of the vaginal walls that can cause discomfort during coitus and subsequent withdrawal from sexual activity. Oral estrogen is prescribed in severe cases, but there are risks involved related to increased incidences of cancer of the endometrium, hypertension, and gall bladder disease. Physically, the use of a lubricating cream is often sufficient to deal with the problem.

However, as with many facets of aging, the emotional impact of menopause causes far more problems and is the area where intervention can be most helpful. Anticipation of menopause is often anxiety provoking because women see themselves as less physically desirable and thus are prone to diminished self-regard and to depression. Intervention in the form of exploration, sup-

portive counseling, and possible use of antidepressant medication can help the client focus on some of the more positive results of menopause. Many women experience a resurgence of sexual interest because of relief from anxiety about possible pregnancy, gradual resolution of earlier sexual conflicts, and shifts away from concerns with child raising toward renewed intimacy with the sexual partner.

Additional intervention with partners of menopausal women can often be a necessary support at a time when they are struggling with their own midlife *emotional* adjustment, although not accompanied by physical symptoms. Career concerns, and the *normal* physiological sexual changes discussed above (if not understood) can lead to alienation and estrangement between sexual partners. For women without *regular* sexual partners, supportive intervention legitimates the wish to find new partners for sexual release, or to find alternative means, such as masturbation for obtaining sexual satisfaction.

Other common ailments that affect sexuality in old age are arthritis, strokes, Parkinson's disease, and so on. In all cases, open, honest discussion between the client and his or her significant others can help deal with the psychic stress and also encourage innovative efforts for relief of sexual tension. Again, touching, caressing and use of different parts of the body for sexual arousal may also be a comfort to clients. Reassurance of "normality" is a crucial factor in most cases. All other diseases too, of course, even those with no direct physical effects, affect sexuality because they affect feelings of self-esteem and the ability to interact intimately with other people. In addition to physical illness, the emotional illness of depression leads to cessation of sexual interest and activity. Depression, caused by a variety of losses—such as of loved ones, jobs, friends, or health—should be distinguished from normal grieving processes so that appropriate intervention can be taken.

Recognizing the helplessness, outrage, and sense of impotence that follows loss will allow the client to move beyond those feelings. Jacobs (1982) notes that:

Depressive symptoms—even a full depressive syndrome—may occur as a normal part of grief and, in themselves, are no cause for concern. The differential diagnosis of depressive disorder and grief is a difficult clinical judgment for which the following rules of thumb serve as guidelines. If depressive symptoms (such as dysphoric mood, pessimistic thinking, sleep disorder, anorexia, irritability, and poor concentration) include psychomotor retardation or morbid preoccupations with guilt, the occurrence of supervening depressive disorder is likely. Talk of self-injury or death in these patients is particularly worrisome and requires close monitoring. Another criterion involves the emergency of depressive syndrome accompanying pathologic grief. The pathologic grief is the criterion that strongly suggests the diagnosis of depressive disorder. (p. 69)

SPECIAL POPULATIONS

Single Older Women

There are a number of special populations that merit attention because they face special kinds of problematic situations. The single older woman, for instance, far outnumbers her male counterparts. For women in their 60s and 70s, there are very few male partners. By age 75 there are approximately 156 women for every 100 men. As a result, tolerance of the idea of masturbation as an acceptable outlet is growing and can be encouraged, as well as the exploration of alternative lifestyles. Bernard (1968) identified five types of relationships aside from traditional courtship and marriage that are as applicable to older as they are to younger people (Peterson & Payne, 1975). First, there are the unrelated seniors who live independently in a subculture of people of their own generation. The many retirement villages and communities are examples of places set up to assure opportunities for intimacy apart from marriage. Second, there are semiserious, semicommitted, semistable relationships, often with a partner who is un-

available because of another marriage. However, these relationships afford opportunities for women or men to have close relationships with another. Third, the companionship model involves men and women living together either before formal marriage or as a substitute for it. For older adults, this seems to be the most popular alternative to marriage, as it provides constant and intimate companionship on a live-in basis. Fourth, there is a model of the household with three or more unrelated individuals. This represents an informal change in our standards of monogamy and an adjustment to the fact that if there are a majority of women, group relationships may be a viable option. It affords the opportunity to reestablish a meaningful family group and to feel needed and wanted. Last, the one-sex community is a model in which people depend exclusively on others of the same sex for their emotional satisfaction. This alternative includes those who seek companionship *without* intimate contact and those who seek sexual experiences of a homosexual type.

As we have said, the effects of marital status on sexual activity have been clearly documented for women. Very few unmarried women report regular sexual activity in later years. The primary obstacle seems to be the double standard that says older women are not attractive to younger men and cannot participate in sexual activities without a *sanctioned* partner. Older women commonly feel guilt and anxiety over having sexual feelings. To intervene effectively, the professional needs to be comfortable with sexuality in the aged for intervention with both men and women. The professional also needs to be aware of feelings of transference in this situation so as not to allow feelings about his or her own parents to prevent candidly exploring the client's sex life and sexual activities.

The Institutionalized

What happens to sexuality in institutions? In most institutions, the residents are expected and *forced* to live a life of celibacy. First of all, privacy (or lack thereof) becomes a major issue. In most residential settings, there are single-sex rooms, regardless of marital status. Double beds are almost non-existent, and even solitary expressions of sexuality, such as masturbation, are unavailable because of the lack of privacy.

However, hospitalized elderly patients do become confused at night, especially in unfamiliar surroundings (Burnside, 1973). When some crawl into bed with another person, the "diagnosis" is that of confused and disoriented, rather than recognizing the great need for touch and closeness because the staff refuses to recognize that the elderly still want and need physical closeness. Additionally, the social expressions of sexuality, such as flirting, kissing, dancing, hugging, hand-holding are also frowned upon, as if desire was completely inappropriate.

Intervention can be both on the policy and direct service levels. On the policy level, changing the institutional milieu so that privacy is available for people to express their own sexuality, for husbands and wives to sleep together and touch each other, and for staff to be more aware of the need for human contact will all have the desired effect of increasing the aged person's potential outlets for sexuality.

Further suggestions include changing any policies that cause married people to be separated against their will. Breaking up a marriage should be illegal, even if one member requires full-time nursing and the other does not. Health facilities could accept both partners if the one who was not ill was allowed to help care for the other spouse. Additionally, if not vigorously resisted the bureaucracy and Medicaid, Medicare, and Social Security regulations can separate people who have lived together for a number of years without being married. All of these changes call for intervention on the part of professionals advocating for those who are sexually oppressed (McKinley & Drew, 1977).

There are, however, more elderly single people than married who are suffering from sexual isolation.

Often the single person is placed in an institutional setting more quickly because there are not as many financial support systems within the community. Furthermore elderly singles encounter a stronger barrier than elderly marrieds because the idea that old people can desire new partners and new sexual relationships is another that is repulsive to many institutional personnel.

On the direct service level, discussing sexuality openly legitimizes the clients' feelings. Touching, to emphasize once again, is an extremely significant form of intervention and helps to compensate for a variety of other losses. This is one of the most elemental forms of sexuality that professionals can practice with their clients to demonstrate that they are indeed sexual human beings. If we uphold aged people as individuals with dignity and worth, we and the institutions that serve them need to provide them the opportunity to live out their lives with dignity, worth, and the same personal rights that younger people exercise.

Older Lesbians and Gay Men

Homosexuals in later life also face some special problems in terms of adjustment. Chapters 12 and 13 address the oppression of homosexuals in general, but the specific needs of older homosexuals will be examined here. A recent estimate (Berger, 1982) was that over 1.75 million people in the United States today are homosexuals over the age of 65.

There are specific issues related to homosexuality that need to be addressed for purposes of intervention, together with issues of aging. First, the stereotype of aging gay men and lesbians as frustrated lonely people who are isolated from the world because they have lost their physical appeal to younger people is untrue (Kelly, 1977; Berger & Kelly, 1982). The fact that the stereotype exists, however, has damaged the self-esteem of many older gay men and lesbians and must be addressed. Second, the issue of the extent to which older clients are "passing," or concealing their homosexuality from parts of their world, should be focused on. Helping professionals must be sensitive to clients who carry a need for concealment, based on their growing up and living in a more oppressive era when discovery often meant loss of job, family, and friends. Some people choose to "come out" in later life, but there are no guarantees that this will not lead to negative consequences for the client.

An additional issue is that many older gays are likely to have been married at one time or another because of intense social pressures in past decades when these clients were of marriageable age. For the helping professional, their contact may involve emotional issues of separation from a heterosexual spouse and related legal and financial issues.

There are also some positive aspects of aging homosexuality. The suggestion has been made that the experience of growing older as a homosexual has become less stressful since the gay rights movement began in 1969 (Huyck & Hoyer, 1982). Furthermore older homosexuals have less trouble coping with age-related changes in life because they have tested their abilities to adapt by the experience of coming out. The norm for older homosexuals, as for heterosexuals, is that of continuing sexual interest and activity, and their ability for having such encounters is enhanced because of the typical relationship patterns and living arrangements of older gay men and lesbian women today. Actually, older gays have more options in this area than their heterosexual counterparts. A study of 112 gay men, 40 and over, found only 39 percent of them to be living alone (Berger, 1982), and most had active friendship networks. Love relationships between older lesbians are not disrupted as frequently or as early as their heterosexual counterparts are by widowhood and, additionally, are not devalued by their lesbian partners for being "old." In general homosexual love relationships are characterized by diversity since, in the absence of social constrictions, a greater variety of forms has been explored.

In intervening with the emotional, legal, and financial problems mentioned above, as well as with special institutional problems, the professional must examine some special issues. Emotionally, when a long-term relationship is ended because of death, agencies do not often think of bereavement counseling for a homosexual partner. Practitioners however need to be aware of this need and counsel from a nonjudgmental basis for the purpose of resolving the grief process and starting new relationships.

The legal system discriminates against homosexuals for whom marriage is not an option. Therefore, if a will is not made (as is often the case because of so few lawyers' being familiar with the needs of homosexual couples), all property and assets can be claimed by the deceased partner's family in case of death. Even when wills are made, they can be challenged by hostile families who contend that the surviving partner exercised "undue influence." Practitioners can help homosexual couples to plan ahead to prevent some of these problems.

Institutional policies in hospitals and nursing homes also create extra problems for aging homosexuals. For example, in most intensive care units, only immediate relatives are allowed to visit. And if the patient is unable to make decisions about treatment, only blood relatives are allowed to give consent. As Berger notes (1982), "this puts the elderly homosexual in the unenviable situation of having life-and-death decision making entrusted to an estranged or distant relative rather than to a longstanding partner. Nursing homes, too, exacerbate relationship problems. Although, as discussed previously, space for conjugal visits is too seldom provided for heterosexually wedded couples, private space for gay/lesbian couples is never considered (Raphael & Robinson, 1981).

Advocacy Roles

An extremely appropriate role for human service practitioners to play in intervention on behalf of the aged is that of advocate. If professionals advocate for clients' rights to be sexually active to whatever degree and in whatever ways the clients find appropriate, professionals also will be supporting their clients' right to self-determination.

Major areas of advocacy deal with working with institutional staff, working with medical personnel, and working with family members in an advocacy/educational role.

Working with families of the elderly can be examined in terms of spousal intervention and intervention with their adult children. Children of the elderly often have anxieties about parents' engaging in sexual activities because of misguided concerns about health issues and/or unresolved feelings about parents indulging in intercourse. These anxieties are related to the role reversal that takes place as parents age. Although greater degrees of support are needed in a variety of areas as parents age, parents and children should not suddenly reverse roles. That is, middle-aged children should not treat their parents like children, because they are *not* children. The unresolved feelings adult children have about their parents' sexuality also can be explored in this type of situation.

Another problematic area for adult children occurs with age-discrepant relationships (that is, when an aging person finds a substantially younger love partner). The older partner is assumed to be making a last grasp at youth (Berardo, Vera & Berardo, 1983). In our society, rampant age segregation creates difficulties in making meaningful relationships for people involved in age-discrepant relationships. Adult children are often concerned if their parents become involved in these relationships because the children experience a conflict of interest. On the one hand they want the parent to be happy, on the other they may worry about how this relationship will effect their inheri-

tance. The professional, however, is an advocate for the older person's right to live his or her own life and to help the adult children see the appropriateness of the parent's right.

In direct intervention with couples a number of factors should be considered. There are a variety of kinds of marriages that one encounters in dealing with the elderly, and each has its own unique problems of adjustment related to sexuality (Peterson & Payne, 1975). First marriages that persist into old age need to deal with complicated feelings surrounding role shifts, power-balance shifts, and basic changes in patterns that have become deeply ingrained after forty or more years. For many males in our society (and especially for people in that age group) a man's self-esteem still depends largely on what he accomplishes in and by his work. When he retires, he loses power and undergoes a drastic change in lifestyle that causes drastic adjustments in marriage.

Middle-age marriages are usually between divorced or widowed persons. In these marriages problems sometimes occur when remarriage is looked at as a solution to the problems of growing old. The new marriage can easily slip into habitualized patterns too, a process which causes disillusionment.

Another expanding group is people who marry in old age. Here too, marriage is not the answer to problems—in fact the reverse is true: the degree to which elderly people adjust to the aging process is important in predicting how likely their marriage will be successful.

Again, there is also a difference between ability and desire for sexual relationships in marriage. Even though the research has shown that most older people have the physical capacity to continue sexual activity, they may not prefer to do so.

In dealing with sexual problems, the professional must also remember that sexual problems on the surface often mask much more profound problems of human relationships and of individual psychological problems, such as depression, which should be addressed.

Specific Intervention Skills

Various approaches have been suggested to elicit concerns about sexual matters with clients. As part of a general initial assessment of client's needs, learning to include the topic of sexuality also legitimizes the feelings that clients have and the concerns they may want to explore. A brief question as to possible problems with sexuality might suffice. Woods (1979, p. 79) suggests three questions that can be easily integrated into a health history:

1. Has anything (illness, surgery) interfered with your being a (mother/wife, father/ husband)?
2. Has anything (heart attack, injury) changed the way you feel about yourself as a (man, woman)?
3. Has anything (disease, physical changes) changed your ability to function sexually?

In a fuller psychosocial interview, Burnside (1981, p. 378) suggests questions that could be included as part of a sexual history:

1. What was your parents' attitude toward sex, nudity, and touching?
2. How would you rate or describe your parents' sexual adjustment?
3. What is the effect of your parents' sexual adjustment on your sexuality and present sexual functioning?
4. What physical traits do you like in a person of the opposite sex?
5. What physical traits do you like in a person of the same sex?
6. Describe one thing that sexually excites you or "turns you on." Describe one thing that "turns you off."
7. How would you rate or describe your present sexuality? What about it would you like to change?
8. What is one thing you would like to tell a present or past partner about your relationship (sexual and otherwise) that you were (or are) afraid to tell him or her?
9. What is it like—how does it feel—to ask and answer these questions?

Annon (1976) suggests a four-pronged approach to intervention in sexual issues that is as applicable for older adults as any other population. The first level of achieving an atmosphere in which a humanistic, pleasure-oriented (rather than performance-oriented) view of sexuality can be presented. This view conveys the assumption that sex is an expression of the self. At this level, helping clients describe their sexual lives accurately and being aware of clients' sense of comfort and their value systems are very important. The second level is providing information in a limited way to dispel myths and provide key information about sexual anatomy and normal physiological changes that occur in aging. On the third level, the professional makes specific suggestions as to changes clients can make. These can include readings, self-stimulation procedures, and alternative sexual positions or activities. The fourth level involves referral to a qualified sex therapist.

In terms of explicit sexual therapy, some older couples develop a marked avoidance of sexuality after treatment success, which is a psychosocial defense against depression related to realization of the sexual limitations due to the normal physiological changes of aging. Therefore it is important to continue treatment until both partners have integrated mutual self-acceptance without devaluation (Reckless & Geiger, 1978).

The following outline summarizes specific guidelines for professionals intervening in the area of sexuality with older adults. It is designed to assist professionals working with older individuals who may need sexual counseling (Steffi, 1978).

I. Communication skills.
   A. Examine awareness of your own beliefs, values, and attitudes toward aging and the aged and sexuality.
   B. Assess interpersonal skills necessary to:
      1. Initiate communication with the elderly.

2. Create an atmosphere conducive to discussion of sexual concerns.
3. Listen for nonverbal cues of sexual concerns.
4. Elicit verbalization of underlying concerns.

C. Review knowledge of sexual physiology and functioning.
D. Assess client's perception of his/her sexual concerns.
E. Ask yourself, "What kind of nonverbal messages am I sending?"

II. Helps in assessing the problem.
A. Is the problem a request for information about anatomy and physiology?
B. Is the need a specific sexual problem?
C. Is the problem a clinical situation directly or indirectly related to sexual functioning?
D. Is the problem organic or situational requiring alterations in preferred mode of functioning?
E. Is it a crisis or a long-term problem?
F. Is the person trying to live up to some preconceived performance expectations and creating his/her guilt for failure?
G. Assess for physical illness or disorders and medications.
H. Always look at what is left, not what is gone.

III. Points of departure for initiating discussion on sexuality with older persons.
A. Consider finding out the client's early orientation to sexual behavior.
B. Look for feelings (residual) about masturbation as a child, which may be present unconsciously.
C. The "first time" seems to have great significance, so consider it as a point of departure in discussion.
D. "The second time around" is often described as being better, so one might use that as a point of departure for discussion.
E. Tie sexual behavior and history in with other social activities and/or

religion; and remember, it may take time to come around to the topic and questions or problems.
F. Listen for a double message: "I don't think about that," "I would if I fell in love."
G. Remember, there may be increased preoccupation (conscious or unconscious) with sexuality in old age, particularly in certain settings.
H. Keep approach "confidential, private, personal."
I. You don't have to know all the answers to counsel, you just need to help old people find their own answers, and sometimes they have them but need your sanction and/or support.
J. Avoid avoidance of the subject.

IV. How do you limit overt sexual exposure and improper advances?
A. Look at circumstances: night, fantasy, etc.
B. Examine precipitating events.
C. Look for need to prove masculinity or sexuality.
D. Assess for sensory deprivation.
E. Look for health in the situation: for example, is a man trying to prove something?
F. Recognize needs.
G. Recognize the ability and need to live and function as a man or woman.
H. Direct to a healthy outlet in an appropriate place.
I. Do not punish.

V. How do you handle "the dirty old man"? Consider how you handle your own peers. Young women may encourage similar behavior from a 6-foot football player and not expect to go to bed with him, but what makes it so "dirty" when an 80-year-old, 100-pound man stares at her from the feet up, or reaches for her bosom?

Anxieties like these are not easy to handle. They are the result of conflicts in a departure from our culture, our lifestyle, and our comfortable cohort group. We may need help in handling them. Unfortunately, this help is usually sought after the fact; nevertheless, it helps to share experiences and do problem solving as a team.

VI. How shall we deal with masturbation?
   A. Recognize it as acceptable and healthy.
   B. Examine our own attitudes.
   C. Certain aspects of sex are private—so is masturbation; so encourage proper time and place.
   D. Do not punish or ridicule.

VII. Mechanical stimulation. Whether counseling or simply educating older individuals, health and helping professionals should be informed about the availability, prevalence, and use of vibrators and other mechanical devices used to stimulate the genitalia and other erotic zones of the body. The use of various kinds of vibrators and intrusive devices is quite common: for example, an electric toothbrush has been used. A nurse told me in confidence that when one of her aged nursing home patients was no longer able to masturbate, the administrator obtained a vibrator for her. No doubt personnel in institutions, especially those giving direct care to patients, could tell us much about coping strategies and innovations, but our taboos have made it too dangerous for them to do so.

Counseling should be centered around the importance of alternatives to intercourse, including caressing, touching, and exploring ways of pleasing both oneself and/or one's partner. The physical act of orgasm is not essential for sexual satisfaction at any age. Since the research clearly shows that the most effective way to achieve pleasurable sexuality in old age is through continual use in earlier years, we can support a client's use of masturbation and other alternatives to sexual intercourse.

In regard to masturbation, SEICUS (Sex Information and Education Council of the United States) holds the position that:

Sexual self-pleasuring, or masturbation, is a natural part of sexual behavior for individuals of all ages.

It can help to develop a sense of the body as belonging to the self, and an affirmative attitude toward the body as a legitimate source of enjoyment.

It can also help in the release of tension in a way harmless to the self and to others, and provide an intense experience of the self as preparation for experiencing another.

Masturbation, and the fantasies that frequently accompany it, can be important aids in maintaining or restoring the image of one's self as a fully functioning human being. (Brashear, 1974)

Brashear further discusses the question of how to communicate this message to all individuals. She notes that the use of such formerly taboo words as masturbation usually elicits shock or puzzlement. Still, people are eager for information and comfort about their sexuality and sexual behaviors. Giving that permission in a supportive manner can open the door for acceptance of masturbation as an alternate form of sexuality rather than as a substitute for something better. At the very least, it can give permission to clients who would like express themselves sexually but have closed themselves off from exploring this type of behavior.

CONCLUSION

Why then are aged people considered a sexually oppressed population? Even though, physically, sexual expression is achievable, our attitudes—our agism, as it were—have effectively negated that expression of what is physically achievable and neutered the aging population.

What is needed is a consideration of what

our attitudes toward aging and sexuality are and in examination of how to change them. There are a great variety of physical changes that occur in the sexual area—what is not realized is that the blanket we throw over them—tends to negate all sexuality.

Butler and Lewis (1978) suggest a number of functional and positive results of sexuality in later years including:

1. The opportunity for expression of passion, affection, admiration, loyalty, and other positive emotions
2. An affirmation of one's body and its functions—reassurance that our bodies are still capable of working well and providing pleasure
3. A way of maintaining a strong sense of self-identity, enhancing self-esteem, and feeling valued as a person
4. A means of self-assertion—an outlet for expressing oneself when other outlets for doing so have been lost
5. Protection from anxiety as "the intimacy and the closeness of sexual union bring security and significance to people's lives, particularly when the outside world threatens them with hazards and losses"
6. Defiance of stereotypes of aging
7. The pleasure of being touched and caressed
8. A sense of romance
9. An affirmation of a life that has been worthwhile because of the quality of intimate relationships that have been developed
10. An avenue for continued sensual growth and experience

The important thing to realize is that lessened sexual activity results from specific reasons—whether they be social, physical, or emotional, rather than from the aging process itself. Additionally, sexual activity is only one form of sexual expression, which is a lifelong process since it is an affirmation of life itself.

In summary, what are the sexual needs of older people?

They are exactly the same kinds as those of younger people, with equivalent variations in intensity, kinds of expression, other persons to express with. As human beings at any stage of life, we long for other human beings to respond to us and to be responsive with whether in touch, in shared pleasures, joys, sorrows, intellectual interchange, or from time to time in sexual responsiveness at many levels including the purely physical. (Calderone, 1971)

As professionals working with a group of people who are sexually oppressed, our task is to lift that oppression and to offer them the opportunity to live complete, sexual lives.

The purpose of our intervention is not to foster new criteria about how much, how often, and what kind of sexual activities should occur with older people. Its purpose, rather, is to encourage a sense of life and living that includes sexuality in all its diverse forms.

REFERENCES

ANNON, J. S. *Behavioral treatment of sexual problems.* Hagerstown, Maryland: Harper and Row, 1976.

BERARDO, F., VERA, M., AND BERARDO, D. Age-discrepant marriages. *Medical Aspects of Human Sexuality* 17(1983):57–76.

BERGER, R. A. *Gay and gray: The older homosexual man* (Champaign, Ill.: University of Illinois Press, 1982.

———. The unseen minority: Older gays and lesbians. *Social Work* 27(1982):236–242.

——— AND KELLY, J. J. Where do old gays/lesbians go? Clinical issues and strategies. *Paper presented at the NASW Clinical Practice Conference,* November 18–21, 1982, Washington, D.C.

BERNARD, J. Present demographic trends and structural outcomes in family life today. In James A. Peterson, ed., *Marriage and family counseling perspective and prospect.* New York: Association Press, 1968.

BLOCH, A., MALDER, J. P., AND HAISSLY, J. C. Sexual problems after MI. *American Heart Journal* 90(1975):536.

BOYER, G., AND BOYER, J. Sexuality and aging. *Nursing Clinics of North America* 17(1982):421–427.

BRASHEAR, D. Honk! If you masturbate! *SIECUS Report* 3(1974):1.

BURNSIDE, I. *Nursing and the aged* New York: McGraw-Hill, 1981.

BURNSIDE, I. M. Sexuality and aging. *Medical Arts and Sciences* 27(1973):13–27.

BUTLER, R., AND LEWIS, M. *Aging and mental health: Positive psychosocial and medical approaches*, 3/e. St. Louis: C. V. Mosby Co., 1982.

———. The second language of sex. In *Sexuality and Aging*, R. L. Solnick, ed. Los Angeles: University of Southern California Press, 1978.

CHRISTENSON, R. Plight of elderly divorced. *Medical Aspects of Human Sexuality* 18(1984):206.

DAVIS, L., AND DAVIS, V. Golden sexuality. *Behavioral Medicine* 5(1978):16–19.

EBERSOLE, P., AND HESS, P. *Toward health aging*, chap. 12. St. Louis: C. V. Mosby Co., 1981.

FILLER, W., AND HALL, W. C. Castration in the female. *Medical Aspects of Human Sexuality* 3(1969):33.

HARRIS, L. *Myth and reality of aging in America.* Washington: National Council on Aging, 1975.

HUFFMAN, J. W. Sexual reactions after gynecological surgery. *Medical Aspects of Human Sexuality* 3(1969):48–57.

HUYCK, M., AND HOYER. *Adult development and aging.* Belmont, Calif.: Wadsworth Publishing Co., 1982, Chap. 10.

JACOBS, S. Clinical management of grief following a spouse's death. *Medical Aspects of Human Sexuality* 16(1982):69–70.

KELLY, J. Aging male homosexual—Myth and reality. *Gerontologist* 17(4):328–337, 1977.

KIMMEL, D. C. Adult development and aging—Gay perspective. *Journal of Social Issues* 34(3):113–130, 1979.

KINSEY, A. C., POMEROY, W. B., AND MARTIN, C. R. *Sexual behavior in the human female.* Philadelphia: Saunders, 1948.

———. *Sexual behavior in the human male.* Philadelphia: Saunders, 1948.

LONG, JAMES W. *The essential guide to prescription drugs: What you need to know for safe drug use.* New York: Harper and Row, 1979.

MARTIN, C. E. Factors affecting sexual functioning in 60–79 year old married males. *Archives of Sexual Behavior* 10(1981):399–420.

MASTERS, W. M., AND JOHNSON, V. E. *Human sexual inadequacy.* Boston: Little, Brown, 1970.

———. *Human sexual response* Boston: Little, Brown, 1966.

———. Sex and the aging process. *Journal of the American Geriatrics Society* 29(1981):1385–390.

MCKINLEY, H., AND DREW, B. The nursing home: Death of sexual expression. *Health and Social Work*, August 1977, 180–187.

MOGUL, K. Effect of menopause of libido. *Medical Aspects of Human Sexuality* 16(1982):37–42.

MURPHY, G. Human sexuality and the potential of the older person. In *Sexual issues in social work: Emerging concerns on education and practice*, Kunkel, Dale, eds. Honolulu: University of Hawaii, School of Social Work, 1979.

PETERSON, J., AND PAYNE, B. *Love in the later years: The emotional, physical, sexual and social potential of the elderly.* New York: Association Press, 1975.

PFEIFFER, E. Sexual behavior. In *Modern perspectives in the psychiatry of old age*, John Howells, ed. New York: Brunner/Mazel, 1975.

PFEIFFER, E., VERWOERDT, A., AND WANG, H. S. Sexual behavior in aged men and women. *Archives of General Psychiatry* 19(1968):756–758.

RAPHAEL, S., AND ROBINSON, M. Lesbians and gay men in later life. *Generations*, Fall 1981, 16–18.

RECKLESS, J., AND GEIGER, N. In *Handbook of sex therapy*, Lopiccolo, J. & L., eds. New York: Plenum Press, 1978.

ROEN, P. Changes in sexual function due to prostatic diseases. *Medical Aspects of Human Sexuality* 17(1983):176–179.

SCHWARTZ, A. W. A transactional view of the aging process. In *Professional obligations and approaches to the aged*, Schwartz, A., and Mensh, T., eds. Springfield, Ill.: Charles C. Thomas, Publisher, 1974.

SHOEMAKER, D. Integration of physiological and sociocultural factors as a basis for sex education to the elderly. *Journal of Gerontological Nursing* 6(1980):311–318.

SOLNICK, R., AND CORBY, N. Human sexuality and aging. In *Aging: Scientific perspectives and social issues*, Woodruff, D., and Birren, J., eds. Monterey: Brooks/Cole Publishing, 1983.

SOLNICK, R., ed. *Sexuality and aging: Implications for nursing and other helping professionals.* Los Angeles: University of Southern California Press, 1978.

STEFFL, B. M. Sexuality and aging: Implications for nurses and other helping professionals. In *Sexuality and aging*, Solnick, R. B., ed. Los Angeles: University of Southern California Press, 1978.

U.S. GOVERNMENT. *America in transition: An aging*

society Washington, D.C.: U.S. Government Printing Office, 1984.

VERWOERDT, A., PFEIFFER, E., AND WANG, M. S. Sexual behavior in senescence. *Geriatrics* 24(1969):137–154.

WINN, R., AND NILES, N. Sexuality in aging: A study of 106 cultures. *Archives of Sexual Behavior* 11(1982):283–292.

WOODS, N. F. *Human sexuality in health and illness.* St. Louis: C. V. Mosby, 1979.

CHAPTER

9

VICTIMS

LeRoy G. Schultz

The sexual victimization of humans, one of the oldest problems in western civilization, is partly related to western views of sexuality. That our generation has not come to grips with this problem will be painfully evident throughout this chapter, although some gains have been made. This chapter will cover the incidence of sexual victimization and the current professional interventions designed to treat, control, and prevent the problem. The theme of this chapter will be that professionals could do a much more effective job, costing less, if they would take the time and energy to delimit definitions of sexual victimization to those worthy of intervention in a multivalue democratic society, and if they would focus their attention on those interventions that, at least tentatively, indicate some success. We need to broaden our perspective on interventions themselves as victimogenic or iatrogenic. Note how long it took to eliminate two iatrogenic interven-

tions from standard practice: removal from the home of victim-children or offender-parents. We will need to mount and fund broadscale research, with longitudinal and control group rigor, that will help us decide on neutral, positive, or sex-educating types of child/adolescent/adult sexual interactions, with effective result diffusion. This chapter will be an unromantic report of the state of intervention art, devoid of hyperbole and the usual professional propaganda.

CHILD VICTIMS

Incidence

Society usually pays little attention to small problems. Indeed, it socially constructs the problems it chooses to focus on, ignoring other important problems that are equally costly. Professionals have the status and resources to influence what problems society faces up to. One method of harassing a weak, rather fluid social concern is by marshaling data on the incidence of the problem and educating the required "publics" regarding it. In the case of sexual abuse and victimization, such education has involved the media with "war stories" and show-biz hype based to some degree on distortion and exaggeration (Robinson, 1982; Whelen & Stanko, 1983). As a result, no reliable data have been shared with the public, since official incidence figures are collected in the United States in such a way as to provide an unclear guide to legislative, administrative, or professional practice. There is no professional consensus on definitions of sexual abuse for children and adolescents (Schultz, 1980). Such incidence figures as are available are loaded with softness, hype, regional differences, class biases, and general unreliability (see Table 9.1). Part of this problem is related to the manner in which sexuality has evolved in western society, surrounded by secrecy and shame (Money, 1979), and another part is due to the elastic definitions, over time, which have creeped into popular usage. Today, such definitions of child/adolescent sexual abuse may include parental touching while bathing one's child, sexual harassment, verbal sexual flirtation, circumcision, iatrogenic interventions by professionals, and french kissing of children. This politicalization of child/adolescent sexual activity has only surfaced recently in professional literature (Lee, 1981; Schultz, 1982).

All definitions of sexual victimization are time-related, reflect differences in state laws, and are subject to political definition of a given value orientation. All professionals have private sets of beliefs, myths, social constructions, and labels of the problem, its cause and its appropriate intervention. Recently, some professionals have spoken of "epidemics" of sexual abuse and rape and have furthered the loss of objectivity and credibility. Although some children and adolescents are without question sexually abused, professionals' continued broad-

TABLE 9-1   Child/Adolescent Sexual Victimization Incidence

High Estimates	*Low Estimates*
336,000 cases yearly (Sarafino, 1979)	44,700 cases yearly (NCCAN, 1981)
INCEST ALONE	
509 cases yearly (A.H.A., 1978)	200 cases yearly, extropolating from Virginia's figures (Eudailey, 1981)
CHILD PROSTITUTION	
300,000 cases yearly (Robin, 1976)	250 cases yearly for large cities (Enablers, 1978)
CHILDREN IN PORNOGRAPHY	
30,000 cases yearly in large cities (Densen-Gerber, 1979)	290 cases yearly in large cities (I.L.I.C., 1980)
ADULT RAPE	
6 percent of all adult crime (LEAA, 1973)	0.3 percent of all adult crime (FBI, 1977)

brush methods of informing the public may actually backfire at a time of staff shortages and fiscal conservatism in those agencies most responsible for intervention.

Some professionals may take advantage of the feeling that we cannot wait for more honest and rigorous measuring techniques to catch up with our moral imperative to "do something."

Effects of Sexual Victimization on Children/Adolescents

Historically, the sexual abuse of children and adolescents was seen as responsible for every known pediatric problem (Schultz, 1982). We have changed only slightly today. In going through the professional literature of the past 20 to 30 years, the following are presumed to be postoffense behaviors in victims warrenting professional attention (or related to attracting the adult abuser):

debilitating trauma	suicide
neurosis	sexual acting-out
psychosis	excessive
depression	seductiveness
mental retardation	drug addiction
multiple personality	runaway reaction
immaturity	somatic symptoms
seizures	sexual precocity
prostitution	sexual dysfunctions

No other single human act or experience by a child claims such universal etiological power. Such continued reductionism must be resisted by every concerned professional. Most of the professional literature on cause and effect lacks the most basic ethic of research and violates simple objectivity, and cannot inform professionals today. The presumed effects of sexual abuse are as varied as there are political actors, professional biases, trauma ideologies, and moralists. Sexual abuse can produce anything we want it to.

The postsexual events vary among victims and participants. Although most reported incidents of child sexual abuse are brought to the attention of Protective Services, a few incidents come to the attention of hospitals and clinics. Most of the literature on aftereffects is written by professionals in medical settings and therefore cannot be used to generalize to the whole population of victims. Typical negative symptomatology reported from medical settings include: pregnancy, venereal disease, somatic complaints, guilt, unpleasant dreams, runaway reaction, truancy, heightened sexual interest, enuresis, pelvic pain, encopresis, clinging behavior, and the sexualization of affection. Some of these symptoms existed before the sexual event, and the sexual event triggered latent conditions. Some symptoms are incurred by the intervention used. Much of the intervention technology is based upon sexism, political positions regarding power usage and presumptions of guilt, responsibility, causability, labeling, and attribution. Only recently have some professionals come out of the closets we have forced them into; they are now speaking of possible nondamaging,

neutral, or positive aspects of some sexual events involving children, adolescents, and adults (Constantine, 1982; Nelson, 1981; Courtois, 1980; Ingram, 1981; Bernard, 1981; Tsai, 1979; Simari & Baskin, 1982; Finkelhor, 1980; Henderson, 1983). No professional is educationally or experientially prepared to effectively deal with children's sexual choices or children's rights in this respect. The variant nature of victim response creates conflict and ambiguity for Protective Service workers who must, *by law*, intervene in every reported case of child sexual abuse. Even if professionals knew how to intervene in positive child sexual behaviors, society or its social control agencies will not give sanction to nonintervention, much less fund research into positive sexual behaviors between children, adolescents, and adults. Sexual involvement with children and adults is illegal no matter what it does for or to the participant, postevent. Some responsible agencies give "under the counter" approval or selective oversight of some types of adult-child sexual behaviors (Johnson, 1978). In summary, the research and practice that has evolved regarding post-abuse reaction descriptions of child victims of sex abuse is overblown, pretentious, and meddling.

INTERVENTIONS WITH CHILD/ADOLESCENT VICTIMS

Macrolevel

There has been a legal explosion in recent years regarding new legislation to protect and intervene with the sexually abused, misused, or exploited child. Much of this is symbolic and attempts to spread the umbrella of physical abuse over sexual behaviors without much success. Considerable professional opinion differs on whether to invoke the legal system in cases of family incest, or other forms of family sexual behaviors, or to depend upon voluntary forms of client involvement in treatment, or if the incarceration of the labeled offender is required (Response,

1979; Hoorwitz, 1982). Most protective agency professionals (Baily & Baily, 1983) feel that legal intervention may be required for some offenders who are not motivated for voluntary treatment, but that legal intervention is not required for treatment of all offenders. Invoking the legal system also invites contrary opinion among professionals as to the risk of trauma in child testimony (Libai, 1980; Journal, 1981; Berg, 1982), and those who feel that such trauma assumptions are not absolute for at least some victims (Rogers, 1982; Jones, 1982). Very few child victims are processed through the entire justice system, thus reducing some risk. Most professionals avoid the legal system entirely (Besharov, 1981–82) if possible, although the legal system provides a last line of defense if all else fails. Books written to detraumatize court proceedings have been developed for children (Beaudry & Kitchum, 1983) or mock trials with friendly others can be behaviorally rehearsed (Schultz, 1973), and the movie *Double Jeopardy* (MTI Teleprograms, Inc., 1979) has started a professional drive toward more sensitivity.

Public awareness campaigns have been launched in many parts of the nation to educate the public on the nature of child sexual abuse and resources for attacking the problem; however, success is difficult to gauge. One thing is sure: such campaigns may have deluged human service agencies with sexual abuse complaints, far beyond what such agencies' staffs and resources can mount to solve the problem. Child-protection agencies are assigned responsibilities beyond any person's or organization's competence. (Examples of public awareness campaigns in this area are Pat Boone's "Interfaith Committee Against Child Molestors"—Glendale, California; "Save a Lass and Help a Lad"—Louisville, Kentucky; or the broadside approaches of the U.S. Children's Bureau or the National Committee for Prevention of Child Abuse in Chicago.)

Other broadscale interventions involve prevention and advocacy. Since there is considerable confusion over children's sexual knowledge and who is responsible for its dissemination and its content, "sex education" has proven an elusive means to control sexual abuse (Goldman & Goldman, 1982; Lewin, 1983; Fox & Inaza, 1980). Not all adolescents can be assumed to have criminalized some sexual behavior as some adults do. Adult interpretations of the meaning of sexual conduct, forced upon innocent children, may themselves be traumatizing, but this issue has not been seriously addressed by any of the helping professions. Sex education for parents of abused children, or parents in general, is still in its infancy (Gilbert & Bailis, 1980).

Prevention of sexual abuse is the most popular intervention being proposed by the helping professions, although many do not know enough about child sexual development to proceed safely (Constantine & Martinson, 1981; Cook & Wilson, 1979; Oaks et al., 1976). Perhaps the most used preventive intervention method is that proposed by Kent (1979), employing the use of Illusion Theatre staff and materials (1980) for children K through 8th grade in St. Paul, Minnesota. Using theatrical scenarios, children are educated to the limits of "acceptable" touch from others. Although this approach assumes children have the power to say "no" to unacceptable sexual touching from others, it may overlook the power to say "yes" (Yates, 1980).

Another program was developed by Levy and Guerrero-Pavish (1979) for a Hispanic setting through a public school, using bilingual social workers as teachers. Both the above programs are based upon an assumed violence-aggression theory and may overlook the fact that most child molestors do not use or need aggression to gain victim cooperation. A few school districts in the United States allow portions of regular sex education, health, or safety courses to include some aspects of sex abuse prevention. Some private programs have been developed in large cities where both sexual molestation and child-snatching are prevalent (SAFE in New York City for example). Since all the above programs require parental permission before a child can be enrolled, their efficacy remains questionable in view of the incidence of sexual abuse in the home itself. The school remains a critical point for detecting and assessing sexual abuse, since it is the one institution reaching children outside the family. Many schools do not have adequate staff, such as social workers and psychologists, to assist overworked teachers and nurses with this problem.

Other professionals, equally sensible, are addressing some of the possibly positive aspects of sexual touching, or previously tabooed behaviors at home (Ramey, 1980; Jobin, 1981).

Many professional efforts at prevention fail to address important issues such as ethnic differences in sexual development, and social-class and cultural differences in "touching" boundaries. The use of fear in teaching about sexuality has not been addressed by preventionists (Kirkendall, 1964), nor has the problem of needs versus rights been dealt with (Rappoport, 1980).

Another broadscale intervention consists of integrating systems within the network of agencies and services addressing the problem. But integrating so many different agencies, with different funding sources, different perceptions of victimization, and with tendencies to "turf building" may be impossible (Schultz, 1982; Blose, 1979; Bander, 1982; Weiss, 1981). Policy makers must agree on what is to be coordinated on behalf of victims. If the multiple objectives of all the relevent constituencies (police, courts, mental health, and public welfare) are negotiated into a focused, limited set of purposes, planners and administrators are in a much better position to create a workable program targeted appropriately. Fortunately, the sexual abuse of children involves less life-threatening acts than most kinds of physical abuse; thus professional rivalries are not that critical. Other efforts include prevention manuals and movies for parents. Some teach parents how to be nontraumatizing after the sexual event has occurred; others inform of

self-defense for children (Tegner & McGrath, 1976); still others teach parents to build good self-images in children (Sanford, 1982) or teach self-assertion to potential victims (Adams & Fay, 1981). Many parents would disagree with even these few efforts (Westin, 1981).

Microlevel

Professionals differ in their explanations and theories about the causes of child sex abuse and so their treatment perspectives also vary. There have been few new microlevel interventions for sexually abused children or adolescents, with the exception of the Giarretto model (described below; Giarretto, 1982), with this model limited to father-daughter incest. In fact, most professionals attempt to place the client's problem within their currently used modality, the one or two methods of intervention for which they have been educated or trained. Since protective service workers, no matter what their education, prefer that other agencies treat the family or victim through referral (Johnson, 1978), the burden falls on professionals outside the public welfare services. This very lack of professional intervention by an agency *outside* public welfare may account for a conviction rate of 5 times higher for sexual offenders over physical abusers, chronic referral to psychiatrists if available (Kaplan & Zitrin, 1983), and more placement of sex victims in foster homes than battered children (Finkelhor, 1983). Since protective service workers in public welfare receive all hot-line phone calls for suspected sexual abuse, and since they are the only agency legally mandated to intervene, it appears incongruous that they, in turn, refer family and victim therapeutic interventions to private agencies, mental health agencies, or private practitioners (MacFarlane & Bulkley, 1982). Applying standard mental health interventions to sex victims may be inappropriate and wasteful (Lalley, 1980). The burden is still on whether various professionals and public welfare workers can develop swift, short-term, effective intervention arrangements that reflect community services levels and complexity, with or without the use of legal authority, or whatever is in the best interests of the child or adolescent victim.

Perhaps the most popular model of intervention is that developed by Henry Giarretto and his students, known as the CSATP approach (Giarretto, 1982). He uses a conjoint family therapy approach based on humanistic psychology principles, in an authority setting, with good success (Kroth, 1979), and his model is now taught in several parts of the country. Other microlevel interventions deal with anger control (Novaco, 1975), dysfunctional helplessness (Seligman, 1975), guilt reduction (Stein, 1969), trauma reduction (Furst, 1967), tightening sexual boundaries in families (Perlmutter, 1982), prolonged sex education (Renshaw, 1982), and standard crisis intervention (Funk, 1980), to name a few.

Many communities and social service agencies now use former victims or offenders and volunteers (David, 1984) for so called self-help groups. Examples include Parents United, Parents Anonymous, Adults Molested as Children, and the Pomona Project. All these groups attempt to use standard group treatment models and ventilation techniques, the sharing in postvictim problem solution and peer-support methods, and finding meaning to life events. Although such group work to help individual victims does not appear to harm them, they are not particularly helpful (Coates & Winston, 1983; Silver et al., 1983).

Since any professional—and in some states, layman—may call the child abuse hotline with a suspected sex abuse complaint, the worker who investigates is risking iatrogenesis on one hand by using his or her own definitions and interventions or, on the other, being charged with malpractice for not doing what is "right." Since there are no *a priori* grounds for refusing to intervene in areas that are politicized as protective services is, human or other resource constraints

are not accepted as excuses for nonintervention.

ADULT SEXUAL VICTIMIZATION: THE EFFECTS

Some professional literature and media talk shows have muddled postrape effects to such a degree that professionals are not being given support in providing effective intervention. Indeed, intervention may deal primarily with societal distortion in restoring the victim. Many of the reported postrape symptoms are a reflection of the time and point at which professionals encounter the victim, as well as which victims they see and which they don't. Thus crisis centers and hospital emergency rooms see victims in early postrape stages, and family service agencies, private practitioners, and sexual dysfunction treatment agencies are encountering victims 6 months to 20 years afterward. The result is confusion over time-frames, vague, ill-defined sets of symptoms, and minimal regard for postrape adaptation made by victims who never see a professional.

General fear is the most consistent first effect reported by victims, although this subsides within 30 days (Kilpatrick et al., 1979a). Some victims indicate no postrape symptoms that are visible to professionals (Schultz, 1975). The fears most reported by victims one week following rape are: fear of venereal disease or pregnancy, problems they anticipate with law enforcement or testifying, medical treatment, and vulnerability to future attack. At 3 to 6 months postrape, fears include being alone, being in strange places, sudden awakening at night, and tension over tough-looking persons. The victim's tendency is to generalize specific cues learned by week 1 of the postrape stage to the sixth-month stage. By the sixth month, only three fears remain constant: fear of being alone, sudden awakening at night, and dating new people (Kilpatrick, 1979b).

Another postrape reaction may be sexual

dysfunction, although the evidence is ambiguous (Schultz, 1975; Belcastro, 1982) since some victims were sexually dysfunctional before the rape and others are not after the rape (Becker et al., 1982). If dysfunctional postrape, the victim behaviors manifested are a general fear of lovemaking with another person, loss of arousal capacity, or loss of sexual desire. In the author's experience some female rape victims report sexual problems with a husband or boyfriend, if the male's sexual behaviors resembles the rapist's (for example, excessive assertion, oral sexual requests, and anal sexuality).

The last reaction to rape is anger. It has both positive and negative costs depending on how and when it is employed by the victim and/or the practitioner working with the victim.

INTERVENTIONS WITH ADULT RAPE VICTIMS

Macrolevel

The assault on the rape problem is a national campaign that arose very quickly compared to other social problems. Considerable professional and legislative attention to the rape problem has occurred in books, magazines, movies and TV. A rash of new laws regarding evidence and consent issues has emerged. Women sexually abusing boys, or women as aggressors, has only recently been recognized, thus reducing some of the sexist nature of the rape literature (Sarrel & Masters, 1982; Beattie, 1983; Ellis & Beattie, 1983). The reader should be aware that there are large differences in postrape reaction between victims, depending on which of three categories the victim falls within: those who come to rape-crisis centers and hospital ERs; those who do not ask for any help; and those who report rape some twenty years or so later, after intense probing during therapy for some other problem. Other significant differences affecting intervention break down into several other categories: rape vic-

tims in public institutions, spousal rape in marriages or in separation or legal proceedings (Russell, 1982), victims who precipitate victimization, date-rape, males who are raped, and victim recidivism.

The problem of child sexual abuse surfaced after 1950 due to changes in pediatrics (Pawluch, 1983). Rape, however, became a socially significant problem due to the reemergence of the feminist movement (Rose, 1977). The feminist perspective holds, in part, that rape is a reflection of a maldistribution of power between the sexes, and interventions have been so shaped. Macrolevel interventions have included campaigns to change rape mythologies. Movies and programs on rape prevention have been produced, and college courses in victimology are now available. Other interventions include: lectures to young people in public schools on rape prevention, the establishment of rape-crisis centers, and the passage of federal legislation establishing a National Center for the Prevention and Control of Rape and forcing community mental health centers to treat rape victims (PL. 94-63, 1975). There have been changes in state criminal laws (Bienen, 1983) regarding rape evidence and courtroom inquiries, and some new state victim compensation programs on behalf of rape victims (as in Tennessee for example).

Microlevel

Direct services to female adult rape victims are of two types. The first type views self-help through the feminist movement as the best ideological approach. This approach assumes the major cause of rape is related to the maldistribution of power in society and that a more equitable balance of power between the sexes is part of the solution to the rape problem. Thus sex role resocialization programs, self-assertion methods, empowerment techniques, career planning, physical self-defense courses, and general consciousness-raising constitute the main interventions. To the degree that these methods are individualistic in focus they may not be very effective (Anderson & Rinzetti, 1980), although they have preventive potential.

The second type of intervention consists of the standard therapies adapted to postrape problems, exemplified by Forman (1980) and Ruch et al. (1980) and the pioneering efforts of the social worker Sutherland (1970). All three postulate the stages that a rape victim experiences, with suitable interventions at each stage. Crisis intervention may prove the most efficient method since many female victims (adult or children) do not maintain contact with treatment resources (Binder, 1981; Byrne & Valdiserri, 1982). Although individual interventions have made many gains recently, many problems still remain unrecognized or overlooked. Such approaches do not deal with interactionist factors, since the offender is not apprehended or is incarcerated. Mediation techniques are still untried. Male victim treatment is almost unheard of today (Groth & Burgess, 1980). The problems in loss of family privacy in spousal rape receives scant attention, yet may be more costly to couples and society (Hilf, 1980–81). Sex biases in rape interventions are little explored (Bassuk & Apsler, 1983). Rape victim recidivism, victim precipitation, and the disabling impact on the professional of working with rape victims all remain relatively untouched problems (DeVasto et al., 1980). Although our values will not let us stand still, many interventionists are simply taking chances and hoping for the best.

Future Practice-Research Requirements

There remains a great deal of confusion among the helping professions regarding semantics, the meanings of behavior of both victim and offender, what is effective intervention, professional role requirements, and possible iatrogenisis. New, simplistic, reductionist explanations continue to appear in the literature and in the media. When old rationalizations can no longer be supported, new ones take their place. Therapeutic paternalism abounds, and the term "trauma" has lost all clinical meaning. Some professionals are guilty of ideological incest within their agencies (White, 1978), while others are forced into iatrogenic roles through burnout (Helmer, 1983). Continued overloading of social services and protective agencies, while cutting operational funds, hastens burnout among professionals and does not fare well for victims in the future (Sobell, 1982). It appears that the evolution of the now overextended "sex-victim syndrome" has occurred, in part, because of the didactic and philosophic poverty in professional training, coupled with the inherent vagueness of diagnostic criteria and intense social pressure to "do something" about the sex abuse problem. New agents are implicated daily, and another null hypothesis is presented to the research community. No one wants to throw the baby out with the bath water.

There are victims who require our best intervention. This author's plea is for recognition of the fact that uncritical use of intervention can have unintended consequences. All professionals have a legitimate and important role to maximize development for all persons; however, increased expertise and sophistication in practice must accompany our interventions. It is in this spirit that the following recommendations are made:

1. All professionals involved in intervention could be substantially aided by their development of a working, operationalized definition of "sexual abuse" that clearly reflects the modern world and times, today's sexual expression and development, and the minimum standard of sexual conduct for a multivalued democracy. Today, professionals find a confusing, vague, ill-defined array of sexual interactions labeled abuse, with hundreds of private meanings, that add confusion to intervention efforts and in some cases raise the prospect of iatrogenisis (Schultz, 1980; Besharow, 1981; Bixler, 1983; Saragin, 1977). For example, a recent national study (NCCAN, 1981, p. 23) indicated some 8400 cases of "sexual abuse" of children or adolescents in which no sexual

contact occurred. In addition, it appears that even the basic issue of consent in sexual encounters with children and adolescents, and in cases of adult rape, has never been adequately dealt with (Harris, 1976).

2. "Truth squads" should be formed by selected professionals in each community to help correct misleading information and half-truths communicated to the public by so-called experts on sexual victimization. The scarcity of documented facts, the tendency to confuse facts, theory, and value, the hyping of statistics, misuse of war stories, and moral entrepreneuring characterize much of the TV and radio talk show material on sexual abuse (Robinson, 1982), and in magazine articles as well. Since popularization is probably the principal way recent findings are transmitted to the public, professionals need to be more actively involved in correcting distortion (Zimmerman, 1983). Truth squads should demand debates with these so-called experts and demand equal time, write letters of rebuttal to newspapers and magazines, and call in with challenging phone rebuttals on talk shows that allow this.

To stand back and permit the media to distort information on sexual victimization (as entertainment) is an error of professional omission that could prove sociatrogenic (Loeb & Slosar, 1974). Admittedly, there are hazards to truth telling in all professions (Katz, 1979), and many professionals hide behind conventional wisdom.

3. Child/adolescent sexual abuse should be divorced from physical abuse in treatment policy, in research and practice, and in funding because they are different from each other. Blending the two, as is currently done, produces confusion, erroneous comparison, faulty etiology, and useless interventions. Sexual interactions with children and adolescents are seldom physically violent and rarely physically damaging. Sexuality, unlike violence, is a child's/adolescent's right, if voluntary (see Chapter 7). Claiming that all sexual activity between persons of different ages and of differing amounts of power is *always* motivated by the need to dominate, humili-ate, or overpower, as in forcible rape, does not cover all the reasons for sexual interaction between family members, and at some point is counterproductive to further advances in intervention.

4. Responsible research, funded by respectable organizations and/or foundations, governmental and private, should be commenced to discover why so many families are not incestogenic, and why most family adults are not sex abusers. Why does intimacy in early life diminish mutual sexual attraction for some family members but have no retarding effect upon the appeal of cousins, uncles, and nieces for each other? Would more prepubescent sexual activity decrease the likelihood of such individuals to form a reproductive pair (Bixler, 1981)? What are the factors that provoke resistance in adolescents after they have previously engaged in "incest?" Our obsession with pathology, deviance, and morality may have obscured the one area offering the best preventive potential.

5. Research is required on nontraumatized minors involved in sexual activities with adults and siblings. The word "trauma" often is invoked in a cavalier fashion by many professionals, with little regard for its true clinical meaning, or its effect on the victim during intervention. The adaptive capacity of children has been sadly underestimated and their invulnerable potential has not been harnessed in interventions (Cass & Thomas, 1979; Clarke & Clarke, 1976; Wolens, 1974). Should values, rather than cause-effect knowledge, determine program and policy on sexual abuse? Some of the most accepted "traumas" of yesteryear have been abandoned by professionals today (Schultz, 1980).

6. The intervention effects upon victims have not been seriously questioned or researched to date. Professional iatrogenisus, labeling, and attribution effects on victims are unknown (Morgan, 1978; Blom, 1984; Fisher et al., 1983). The labeling of a sex victim is a perception, a social construct, and a prediction, all based more on ideology than

empiricism. Metaphors in lieu of facts can be self-fulfilling projections that negatively impact intervention. All the helping professions should seek out data-based criticism of the possible iatrogenic dimensions of their effects on victims. Overintervention can be a remediable deficiency of the service delivery system (Morgan, 1983; Torry, 1977; Arnhoff, 1975) with research help. Fragile defenses may be damaged unwittingly, or a shaky defense through reaction-formation or stoicism, disturbed. Some forms of iatrogenic damage are well known (Kernan, 1970; Lesnik-Oberstein, 1982; Mathis, 1981) and can be prevented. Even if our interventions are not effective but do no harm, they still may not be justified in terms of scarce intervention resources. All intervention becomes a human experience as it is interpreted, evaluated, and communicated (Waxler, 1981) to the victim, and we have made excessive claims prematurely (Sarason, 1981). As one mother put it in the *New York Times Magazine* (July 3, 1983), "A son is a son, a home is a home, and a parent is an idiot to open the door each week to admit a different expert freshly arrived to paint a ring of voguish woe all around." Researchers investigating intervention should distinguish between wrong and damaging interventions and between null effects, side effects, and reverse effects (Sieber, 1981).

7. New interventions that are more effective and less costly must be developed through safe and ethical means with transfer to agencies most responsible for intervention. Efforts should be made to bridge the gap between the specialized literature and the practical applications demanded by those in the field. Intervention applications under safe and controlled conditions should be experimentally tried with positive redirection (Ganam, 1982), positive reframing (Jessee et al., 1983), or recasting victims as perpetrators (Bergner, 1981), inducing therapeutic crisis (Minuchin & Barcai, 1969), or use of positive labeling (Cornell, 1983). More efforts are required in the areas of sex therapy, marriage counseling, or mediation in in-

trafamily sexuality. Controlling seduction during intervention (Krieger et al., 1980) and addressing the interlocking problems between important agencies and professionals is critical (Furniss, 1983). Effective integration of services on behalf of child victims (Bander et al., 1982) and adolescent victims (Thomas & Johnson, 1979) and for adult rape victims (Hardgrove, 1976) is long overdue. Since research seldom informs practice, more effective in-service training and workshops are needed, where education is interactional rather than didactic.

8. A large resource gap exists for the victims of sexual abuse in rural areas. Although rural populations support child protective services (Sargent et al., 1982) they do not have the service infrastructure necessary to combat what is the largest percentage (46%) of sexual abuse in children in the United States (NCCAN, 1981, Table 5-4). Marked efforts to build services in rural areas have to be made, with the Department of Welfare or Department of Human Services in each state taking responsibility for initiating and maintaining interagency linkages. Professionals have little incentive for practicing in rural areas at present, at a time when public agencies in those areas admit they are not trained to treat victims (Johnson, 1980; Davanport, Davanport, 1979).

9. One of the largest sexist gaps in research, the results of which would assist professionals in the field, is the whole problem of male-victim intervention. What little literature exists is one-sided and value-laden, or involves such small samples as to make generalizations dangerous, imprudent or iatrogenic. As skimpy as the current research is, significant differences already are noted between male and female victims that call for carefully orchestrated interventions in some male cases, and no intervention at all in others (Schultz & Jones, 1983; Sandfort, 1983; Taylor, 1981; Jason, 1982). Marked efforts at nonsexist research with good control groups and longitudinal comparisons are essential, so that the current rash of research/practice mistakes now impacting

female molestation (Didi Hirsch, 1982) do not burden male children in the future.

CONCLUSION

Although treatment and prevention services are being initiated here and there, usable information on program/service trends, dynamics, and outcome remain inadequate. Researchers and practitioners must continue to explore the complexities of sexual abuse and share their findings across professional boundaries. Interventions currently employed by professionals remain constrained by an inadequate foundation of theory and practice, or they increase professional burnout (Henry-Pfifferling, 1984). The concerns most central to practitioners are seldom phrased in ways that provide focus to research. Research results are seldom in a form that guide intervention. Well-conceived, controlled, longitudinal studies hold the best promise for the practitioner in the future.

As Eisenberg stated in 1975, ". . . therapeutic intervention is hampered only by the extent to which the state of the art and our individual skills fall short of what is needed" (p. 104).

REFERENCES

ABRAMSON, P. *Sarah: A sexual biography*. Albany: State University of New York Press, 1984.

AMERICAN HUMANE ASSOCIATION, CHILDREN'S DIVISION. *National study*. Denver: American Humane Association, 1981.

ANDERSON, M., AND RENZETTI, C. Rape crisis counseling and the culture of individualism. *Contemporary Crisis*, 1980, 4:323–339.

BAILY, T., AND BAILY, W. *Criminal or social intervention in child sexual abuse: Review and viewpoint*. Denver: American Humane Association, 1983.

BANDER, K., ET AL. Evaluation of child sexual abuse programs. In Sgroi, S., ed., *Handbook of clinical intervention in sexual abuse*. Lexington, Mass.: Lexington Books, 1982.

BARON, R. Heightened sex arousal and physical aggression: An extension to women. *Journal of Research in Personality*, 1979, 13:91–102.

BASSUK, E., AND APSLER, R. Are there sex biases in rape counseling? *American Journal of Psychiatry*, 1983, 140:305–308.

BEAUDRY, J., AND KITCHUM, L. *Carla goes to court*. New York: Human Sciences Press, 1983.

BECKER, J., ET AL. Incidence and types of sexual dysfunction in rape and incest victims. *Journal of Sex and Marital Therapy*, 1982, 8:65–74.

BEHLMER, G. *Child abuse and moral reform in England, 1870–1908*. Stanford, Calif.: Stanford University Press, 1982, p. 73.

BELCASTRO, P. Comparisons of latent sexual behavior patterns between raped and never-raped females. *Victimology*, 1982, 7:224–230.

BERGNER, R. Recasting victims as perpetrators. *Journal of Strategic and Systemic Therapies*, 1981, 1:1–90.

BERNARD, F. Pedophilia: Psychological consequences for the child. In F. Constantine, F. Martinson: *Children and Sex*. Boston: Little, Brown, 1981, pp. 189–199.

BESHAROV, D. Toward better research on child abuse and neglect: Making definitional issues on explicit methodological concern. *Child Abuse and Neglect*, 1981, 5:383–390.

BIENEN, L. Rape reform legislation in the U.S.: A look at some practical effects. *Victimology*, 8(1983):139–151.

BINDER, R. Difficulties in follow-up of rape victims. *American Journal of Psychotherapy*, 1981, 35:534–541.

BIXLER, R. Incest avoidance as a function of environment and heredity. *Current Anthropology*, 1981, 22:639–654.

————. The multiple meanings of incest. *Journal of Sex Research*, 1983, 17:197–201.

BLOSE, J. *The sexual abuse of children in Massachusetts: A preliminary study of system response*. Boston: Statistical Analysis Center—Massachusetts Committee on Criminal Justice, July 1979.

BRASSARD, M., ET AL. School programs to prevent intra-familial child sexual abuse. *Child Abuse and Neglect*, 1983, 7:241–245.

BYRNE, J., AND VALDISERRI, E. Victims of childhood sexual abuse: A follow-up study of a non-compliant population. *Hospital and Community Psychiatry*, 1982, 33:938–939.

Carozza, P., and Hiersteiner, C. Young female incest victims in treatment: Stages of growth seen with a group art therapy model. *Clinical Social Work Journal*, 1983, 10:165–175.

CASS, L., AND THOMAS, C. *Childhood pathology and later adjustment*. New York: John Wiley & Sons, 1979.

CLARKE, A., AND CLARKE, A. *Early experience: Myth and evidence.* New York: Free Press, 1976.

COATES, D., AND WINSTON, T. Counteracting the deviance of depression: Peer support groups for victims. *Journal of Social Issues,* 1983, 39:169–194.

CONSTANTINE, L. The effects of early sexual experiences: A review and syntheses of research. In L. Constantine, F. Martinson: *Children and sex.* Boston: Little, Brown, 1981, pp. 217–244.

COOK, M., AND WILSON, G. *Love and attraction.* New York: Pergamon, 1979.

CORNELL, D. Gifted children: The impact of positive labeling on the family system. *American Journal of Orthopsychiatry,* 1983, 53:322–335.

COURTOIS, C. Studying and counseling women with past incest experiences. *Victimology,* 1980, 5:322–334.

DAVENPORT, J., AND DAVENPORT, J. The rural rape crisis center: A model. *Human Services in the Rural Environment,* 1979, 1:29–39.

DAVID, M. Teaching and preaching sexual morality: The new right's anti-feminism. *Journal of Education,* 1984, 166:63–72.

DENSEN-GERBER, J. Sexual and commercial exploitation of children. *Child Abuse and Neglect,* 1979, 3:61-65.

DEVASTO, P., ET AL. Caring for rape victims: Its impact on providers. *Journal of Community Health,* 1980, 5:204–208.

DIDI HIRSCH COMMUNITY MENTAL HEALTH CENTER/LAPS. *Child sexual assault: Issues and interventions.* Culver City, Calif.: SCRPSC Training Series, vol. 3, 1982.

EISENBERG, L. The ethics of intervention: Acting amidst ambiguity. *Journal of Child Psychology and Psychiatry,* 1974, 16:93–104.

ELLIS, L., AND BEATTIE, C. The feminist explanation for rape: An empirical test. *Journal of Sex Research,* 1983, 19:74–93.

ENABLERS. *Juvenile prostitution in Minnesota.* Minneapolis: Enablers, 1978.

EUDAILEY, B. *Region 3 Recap,* 6(1981).

FBI. *Uniform crime reports.* Washington, D.C.: Government Printing Office, 1978.

FINKELHOR, D. Sex among siblings: A survey of prevalence, variety and effects. *Archives of Sexual Behavior,* 1980, 9:171–194.

———. Removing the child—Prosecuting the offender in cases of sexual abuse. *Child Abuse and Neglect,* 1983, 7:195–205.

FISHER, J., ET AL. *New directions in helping.* New York: Academic Press, 1983.

FORMAN, B. Psychotherapy with rape victims. *Psychotherapy: Theory, Research, and Practice,* 1980, 17:304–311.

FOX, G., AND INAZU, J. Mother-daughter communication about sex. *Family Relations,* 1980, 29:347–352.

FUNK, J. Management of sexual molestation in preschoolers. *Clinical Pediatrics,* October 1980, 686–688.

FURNISS, T. Mutual influence and interlocking professional-family process in the treatment of child sexual abuse and incest. *Child Abuse and Neglect,* 1983, 7:207–223.

FURST, S. *Psychic trauma.* New York: Basic Books, 1967.

GANAM, C. Positive redirecting. *Family Therapy,* 1982, 9:155–161.

GIARRETTO, H. *Integrated treatment of child sexual abuse: A treatment and training manual.* Palo Alto, Calif.: Science and Behavior Books, Inc., 1982.

GILBERT, F., AND BAILIS, K. Sex education in the home: A empirical task analysis. *Journal of Sex Research,* 1980, 16:148–161.

GOLDMAN, D., AND GOLDMAN, J. *Children's sexual thinking.* Boston: Routledge, Kegan Paul, 1982.

GORDY, P. Group work that supports adult victims of childhood incest. *Social Casework,* May 1983, 300–307.

GROTH, N., AND BURGESS, W. Male rape: Offenders and victims. *American Journal of Psychiatry,* 1980, 137:806–810.

HARDGROVE, G. An interagency service network to meet the needs of rape victims. *Social Casework,* April 1976.

HARRIS, L. Towards a consent standard in the law of rape. *The University of Chicago Law Review,* 1976, 43:613–645.

HELMER, D. Iatrogenic intraorganizational process as a mediator of burnout. In R. Morgan: *The iatrogenics handbook.* Toronto: IPI Pub., Ltd., 1983, pp. 375–382.

HENDERSON, J. Is incest harmful? *Canadian Journal of Psychiatry,* 1983, 28:34–40.

HENRY PFIFFERLING, J. The role of the educational setting in preventing burnout. *Family and Community Health,* February 1984, 68–75.

HILF, M. Marital privacy and spousal rape. *New England Law Review,* 1980/81, 16:31–44.

HOORWITZ, A. When to intervene in cases of suspected incest. *Social Casework,* 1982, 374–375.

ILLINOIS LEGISLATIVE INVESTIGATION COMMITTEE. *Child molestation: The criminal justice system.* Chicago, Ill.: 1980, p. 3.

ILLUSION THEATER. *Touch (and) no easy answers.* Minneapolis: 1980.

INGRAM, M. Participating victims. In L. Constantine, F. Martinson: *Children and sex.* Boston: Little, Brown, 1981, 177–187.

JASON, J., ET AL. Epedemiologic differences between sexual and physical child abuse. *Journal of the American Medical Association*, 1982, 247:3344–3348.

JESSEE, E., ET AL. Positive reframing with children. *American Journal of Orthopsychiatry*, 1982, 52:314–322.

JOBIN, J. The family bed. *Parents*, 1981, 56(3):57–61.

JOHNSON, C. *Child sexual abuse case handling in Florida.* Athens, Georgia: Regional Institute of Social Welfare Research, Inc., 1978, pp. 7, 55.

————. *Child sexual abuse case handling through public social agencies in the southeast.* Athens, Georgia: Regional Institute of Social Welfare Research, Inc., 1980.

JONES, R., ET AL. Incidence and situation factors surrounding sexual assault against delinquent youth. *Child Abuse and Neglect*, 1982, 5:431–440.

JOURNAL OF LAW REFORM. Proving child-parent incest. 1981, 15:131–152.

KAPLAN, S., AND ZITRIN, A. Psychiatrists and child abuse. *Journal of the American Academy of Child Psychiatry*, 1983, 22:253–256.

KATZ, J. Concerted ignorance: The social construction of cover-up. *Urban Life*, 1979, 8:295–315.

KENT, C. *Child sexual abuse prevention project.* St. Paul, Minn.: Sexual Assault Services, Hennepin County Attorneys' Office, 1979.

KERNAN, J. Iatrogenic learning disabilities. *Academic Therapy*, 1970, 5:305–309.

KILPATRICK, D., ET AL. The aftermath of rape: Recent empirical findings. *American Journal of Orthopsychiatry*, 1979a, 49:658–669.

————. Assessment of the aftermath of rape: Changing patterns of fear. *Journal of Behavioral Assessment*, 1979b, 1:133–148.

KIRKENDALL, L. The arousal of fear: Does it have a place in sex education? *Family Coordinator*, 1964, 13:14–16.

KNITTLE, B., AND TUANA, S. Group therapy as primary treatment for adolescent victims of intrafamilial sexual abuse. *Clinical Social Work Journal*, 1980, 8:236–242.

KRIEGER, M., ET AL. Problems in the psychotherapy of children with histories of incest.

American Journal of Psychotherapy, 1980, 34:81–88.

KROTH, J. *Child sexual abuse: Analysis of a family therapy approach.* Springfield, Ill.: Charles C. Thomas, 1979.

LALLEY, T. Some research perspectives on evaluation of services to victims. *Evaluation and Change*, Special Issue on Services to Survivors, 1980, 90–93.

LEAA—LAW ENFORCEMENT ASSISTANCE ADMINISTRATION. *Criminal victimization surveys in the nation's five largest cities.* Washington, D.C.: Government Printing Office, 1975.

LEE, J. The politics of child sexuality. In *Childhood and Sexuality.* Quebec, Canada: Editions Etudes Vivantes, 1981.

LESNIK-OBERSTEIN, M. Iatrogenic rape of a 14 year old girl. *Child Abuse and Neglect*, 1982, 6:103–104.

LEVY, B., AND GUERRERO-PAVICH, E. Prevention of sexual assault for children and parents in the hispanic community. Culver City, Calif.: Didi Hirsch Community Mental Health Center, 1979 (mimeo).

LEWIN, B. Attitudes among adolescents in a Swedish city toward some adult sexual crime. *Adolescence*, 1983, 18:159–168.

LIBAI, D. The protection of the child victim of a sexual offense in the criminal justice system. In L. Schultz: *The sexual victimology of youth.* Springfield, Ill.: Thomas, 1980, pp. 187–245.

LOAB, P., AND SLOSAR, J. Sociatrogenic dysfunctions: A concern for social work education. *Journal of Education for Social Work*, 1974, 10:51–58.

LUBELL, D., AND SOONG, W. Group therapy with sexually abused adolescent. *Canadian Journal of Psychiatry*, June 1982, 311–315.

MACFARLANE, K., AND BUKLEY, J. Treating child sexual abuse: An overview of current program models. In J. Conte, D. Shore: *Social work and child sexual abuse.* New York: Haworth, 1982, pp. 69–91.

MORGAN, R. The iatrogenic psychology of practitioners defeatism. *Psychological Reports*, 1978, 43:963–977.

MATHIS, J. Iatrogenic sexual disturbances. *Medical Aspect of Human Sexuality*, July 1981, 15:96–108.

MICHELSON, L., AND WOOD, R. A group assertive training program for elementary school children. *Child Behavior Therapy*, Spring 1980, 1–9.

MINUCHIN, S., AND BARCAI, A. Therapeutic induced family crisis. In J. Masserman, Grune and Stratton, 1969, pp. 199–205.

MONEY, J. Sexual dictatorship, dissidence and democracy. *International Journal of Medicine and Law*, 1979, 1:11–20.

NCCAN, NATIONAL CENTER FOR CHILD ABUSE AND NEGLECT. *Study findings.* DHHS 81-30325, Washington, D.C., 1981.

NELSON, J. The impact of incest. In L. Constantine, F. Martinson *Children and sex.* Boston: Little, Brown, 1981, pp. 163–174.

NOVACO, R. *Anger control.* Lexington, Mass.: Lexington Books, 1975.

OAKS, W., ET AL. *Sex and the life cycle.* New York: Grune and Stratton, 1976.

PAWLUCH, D. Transitions in pediatrics: A segmental analysis. *Social Problems,* April 1983.

PERLMUTTER, L., ET AL. The incest taboo: Loosened sexual boundaries in remarried families. *Journal of Sex and Marital Therapy*, 1982, 8:83–96.

RAMEY, J. Positive socialization of incestuous desires. Family Sexuality Symposium, University of Minnesota Medical School—Minneapolis, 1980 (mimeo).

RAPPAPORT, J. In praise of paradox: A social policy of empowerment over prevention. *American Journal of Community Psychology*, 9(1981):1–25.

RENSHAW, D. *Incest: Understanding and treatment.* Boston: Little, Brown, 1982.

RESPONSE. Using the law to help incestuous families. *Response*, 2(1979):1–3.

ROBIN, L. *Boy prostitution in America.* New York: Vanguard, 1976.

ROBINSON, B. Family experts on TV talk shows: Fact, value, and half-truths. *Family Relations*, 1982, 31:369–378.

ROGERS, C. Child sexual abuse and the courts. In J. Conte, D. Shore: *Social work and child sexual abuse.* New York: Haworth, 1982, pp. 145–153.

ROSE, V. Rape as a social problem: A byproduct of the feminist movement. *Social Problems*, 1977, 25:75–89.

RUCH, L., ET AL. Life change and rape impact. *Journal of Health and Social Behavior*, 1980, 21:248–260.

RUSSELL, D. *Rape in marriage.* New York: Macmillan, 1982.

SANDFORT, T. *The sexual aspect of paedophile relations.* Amsterdam, Netherlands: Pan/Spartacus, 1982.

———. Paedophile relationships in the Netherlands: Alternative lifestyles for children? *Alternative Lifestyles,* 1983, 5:164–183.

SARAFINO, E. An estimate of nationwide incidence of sexual offenses against children. *Child Welfare*, 1979, 58:127–134.

SARAGIN, E. Incest: Problems in definition and incidence. *Journal of Sex Research*, 1977, 13:126–135.

SARASON, S. *Psychology misdirected.* New York: Free Press, 1981.

SARGENT, M., ET AL. Attitudes toward family services in a rural state. *Family Relations*, 1982, 31:91–97.

SARREL, P., AND MASTERS, W. Sexual molestation of men by women. *Archives of Sexual Behavior*, 1982, 11:117–131.

SCHULTZ, L. Psychotherapeutic and legal approaches to the sexually victimized child. *International Journal of Child Psychotherapy*, 1972, 1:115–128.

———. The emotional aftermath of rape: Social work implications. *Journal of Humanics*, 1975, 2:23–26.

———. Victim-helpers as hostages to ideology: The case of adult-minor sexual interaction. Paper delivered at the First World Congress of Victimology, Washington, D.C., August 23, 1980.

———. Child sexual abuse in historical perspective. In J. Conte., D. Shore: *Social work and childhood sexual abuse.* New York: Haworth Press, 1982, pp. 21–36.

——— *The sexual abuse of children and adolescents in West Virginia: A social policy analysis of system response.* Morgantown, W.V.: School of Social Work, West Virginia University, 1982. (On michrofiche—U.S. Department of Justice.)

SELIGMAN, M. *Helplessness.* San Francisco: 1982. Freeman, 1975.

SGROI, S. Sexual molestation of children: The last frontier in child abuse. In L. Schultz, ed.: *The sexual victimology of youth.* Springfield, Ill.: Charles C. Thomas, 1980, pp. 25–35.

SIEBER, S. Fatal remedies: The ironies of social intervention. New York: Plenum, 1981.

SILVER, R., ET AL. Searching for meaning in misfortune: Making sense of incest. *Journal of Social Issues*, 1983, 39:83–102.

SIMARI, C., AND BASKIN, D. Incestuous experiences within homosexual populations. *Archives of Sexual Behavior*, 1982, 11:329–344.

SOBELL, S. Child and youth services: A vanishing

species. *Professional Psychology*, December 1982, 797–804.

STEIN, E. *Guilt: Theory and therapy.* London: Allen and Unwin, 1969.

SUTHERLAND, S., AND SCHERL, O. Patterns of response among victims of rape. *American Journal of Orthopsychiatry*, 1970, 40:503–511.

TAYLOR, B. *Perspectives on Paedophilia.* London: Batsford, 1981, pp. 59–76.

THOMAS, G., AND JOHNSON, C. Developing a program for sexually abused adolescents: The research-service partnership. *Child Abuse and Neglect*, 1979, 3:683–691.

TSAI, M., ET AL. Childhood molestation: Differing impacts on psychosocial functioning. *Journal of Abnormal Psychology*, 1979, 88:497–417.

WAXLER, N. The social labeling perspective on illness and medical practice. In L. Eisenberg, A. Kleinman: *The relevance of social science for medicine.* Boston: Reidel, 1981, pp. 283–306.

WEISS, E., AND BERG, R. Child victims of sexual assault: Impact of court procedures. *Journal of the American Academy of Child Psychiatry*, 1982, 513–520.

WEISS, J., ET AL. *The plea for coordination of services to young children.* Paris, France: Center for Education Research and Innovation, 1981.

WESTIN, J. *The coming parent revolution.* New York: Bantam, 1981.

WHELAN, E., AND STANKO, S. Medically muddled media. *JAMA*, October 28, 1983, 2137.

WHITE, W. *Incest in the organizational family.* Rockville, Md.: HCS, Inc., 1978, p. 14.

WOLINS, M. Developmental research and public policy: A commentary. In J. Romanyshyn, ed. *Social science and social welfare.* New York: Council on Social Work Education, 1974, pp. 183–193.

YATES, A. The eroticized child. First World Congress on Victimology, Washington, D.C., 1980 (mimeo).

ZIMMERMAN, J. Psychologists multiple roles in TV broadcasting. *Professional Psychology*, 1983, 14:266–269.

10

THE POOR
Arthur Schwartz

The demoralizing effects of poverty upon sexuality are too frequently overlooked in volumes aimed at providing guidelines to helping professionals. The "poor" are all too often ignored as clients because they are frequently difficult to work with. Indeed, poverty has many consequences, not the least of which is a numbing effect which often shows clinically as depression (Hirschfeld & Cross, 1982).

When poor people *are* seen by human service practitioners, their sexual needs are often either overlooked or not considered relevant areas for intervention. Perhaps there are too many other pressing needs. Perhaps there are also racial and ethnic biases. A great many poor people are also black, Native American, displaced Applachian mountaineers, Mexican immigrants, migrants from Puerto Rico, patois-speaking Haitians, and so forth.

Also prominent among the poor are the

mentally ill, often prematurely released from psychiatric hospitals into the jungles of the crowded city streets. The poor, as a collectivity, also includes a disproportionate number of the aged, of the mentally handicapped, the physically disabled, and others who are included elsewhere in this book. Furthermore, our view of the poor is often confounded by myths, which shall be discussed below.

Clearly, the "poor" is not a homogenous grouping. This chapter, in dealing with both the nature of the problems the poor face and upon recommendations for intervention, will cut across many boundaries.

THE SEXUALITY OF THE POOR AS SEEN BY THE LARGER SOCIETY

There most certainly are myths about the sexuality of the poor, and these myths reflect the way we view and treat the poor. In truth, these myths may very well serve a function. Some of us rationalize that the life of the poor really isn't that bad, that there are compensations not available to those of us more privileged, such as freer and more open sex characterized by an almost Rousseau-like innocence and lack of responsibility. An example of this glamorization of the poor is seen in the myth of lower-class sexuality, the indulgence in Saturday night frivolity, with a "to hell with tomorrow, live for today" feeling, so antithetical to the self-denial and asceticism of the Calvanist-ridden morality of the middle classes.

Being poor, to state the obvious, means not having enough money to meet one's needs. Not having enough money often means that one does not eat a nutritionally adequate diet and becomes malnourished; people on improper diets not only are lacking in energy but, too often, are in poor health and often not that much interested in sex. Certainly, there is not the excess of energy for the free-swinging sexual, "sporting life" behavior.

Being poor also means that one's choices about a great many matters are limited. Not able to exercise options, one thus is often (or feels often) helpless to change things. This lack of options, this helplessness in the face of fate, has been called "learned helplessness" by Seligman (1975). Poor people learn that there is often no connection between any action they may take and changing their life circumstance. This learned helplessness is often a precursor of, and contributory to, psychological depression. Poor people are often depressed, not only by lessened physiological reserves but by psychological pressures, with all that implies, the sadness, pessimism, helplessness, and the view of an equally bleak tomorrow. One of the most widely observed symptoms of psychological depression is a loss of libido (DSM-III). Depressed people just don't feel sexy. Furthermore, depressed people often suffer from loss of self-esteem, and people with low self-esteem do not feel attractive to other people, nor to themselves.

A further complication of the issues of sexuality, poverty, and racism, tied to self-esteem, is the often widespread unemployment among poor men while women are more often able to work (albeit often at low-paying domestic jobs). There is often role reversal, the woman being the breadwinner and the man staying home, doing housework and child care. In the extreme, there may be an interruption in family life, and, consequently, in the esteem of people for each other, reflecting decreasingly satisfactory sex; this happens when the man is forced to abandon his family so that the family can be eligible for welfare payments. The "feminization" of poverty has disastrous consequences for sexual relations, confounding communication between men and women and making relationships based on an equal exchange of trust and intimacy most difficult.

Kinsey (1948), among others, has stated that the "lower" classes begin sex earlier and engage in sexual relationships more frequently. These generalizations of earlier and more frequent sexuality, based on earlier data, may very well not hold up with developments since the "sexual revolution" of the 1960s. In fact, a recent review of these studies (Chilman, 1980) has stated that "findings are equivocal concerning the effects of SES [socioeconomic status] on the sex behavior of adolescents" (p. 141). Several studies have shown an increasing number of adolescents of all social classes engaging in intercourse while still in their teens.

There *is* a high rate of single parenthood among poor teenagers, but much of the black single parenthood may be more a reflection of social and familial disorganization and lack of information about contraception rather than evidence of a loose and pleasurably careless sexuality. (The rate of white single parenthood, incidentally, is increasing while that among blacks is declining.) Having babies, and having babies out of wedlock, does not necessarily mean the same as enjoying sex. In fact many of these mothers report a lack of pleasure, almost to the point of abhorence, about sex (Seiden, 1982). Participation in early sex (indeed regardless of class) is explained better by loneliness, a desire to be needed and wanted, and, increasingly, peer pressures than it is by economics or social class alone.

The brutal facts are that poor people *do* have different views on sexuality, and that these differences tend more to the dysfunctional, to the pathological, than to the pleasurable, free, careless couplings so often fantasized by the larger majority.

What Kinsey (1948) found—which many of us have observed while working as human service practitioners—is that poor people, rather than being loose and free about sex, are actually inhibited and quite uptight about sex. Many variations of sexual activities, such as oral-genital sexuality and most certainly homosexuality in any form, are considered perversions and deviations to be questioned if not condemned. Kinsey in fact stated that the higher the person's education or SES, the greater the diversity of his or her sexual practices and the more experimental they are (Kinsey, 1948; also Berelson & Steiner, 1964).

The cumulative, devastating effects of poverty, of poor diet, interwoven with psychological depression, are often manifested in physical illness or a low level of health, hence the lack of energy (libido) for sexual interest. Poverty produces illness, and illness is often characterized by discomfort and sometimes by pain. No one in pain feels very much like having sex. All diseases, but especially the diseases of poverty, specifically have effects upon endocrine systems, effects too numerous to detail here. Thus poorer people are sick more often, and these illnesses in many ways lessen the desire, the frequency, and the quality of sexual relationships[1] (Woods, 1975).

Many of poverty's effects are dehumaniz-

ing. One of the most dehumanizing directly affecting sex is that of physical overcrowding. Poor people live closer together and in housing that is obviously undesirable because they cannot afford good housing. Poor people, often unemployed, are sometimes forced to double up with relatives. Thus there is even more crowding, even more lack of privacy—privacy for intimacy, for sex. This physical crowding and lack of space also increases "uncontrollability" and contributes to learned helplessness, as demonstrated by Rodin, who showed that crowding (among other factors) lessened the ability of urban ghetto children to make choices and to solve problems (Rodin, 1974; in Seligman, 1975).

Physical crowding, unemployment, bad health, and psychological depression can be so depleting that a result is often anger. Sometimes the feeling of loss of control is due to not being able to show one's feelings in front of the children, of fear of losing that control in front of them. Children see such parents not as role models of successful adults but as frustrated, often sick and depressed people. This affects—negatively—their own views of what love and marriage are. Furthermore, frustrated parents unable to overcome their environments, to do anything about their conditions, succumb not only to learned helplessness but often rebel against their helplessness by railing against their fates, by lashing out, sometimes blindly. The targets for this lashing out, for this anger and hostility, are often those nearest to them, their children and their spouse. Thus, poverty often is characterized by increased violence, hardly an aphrodisiac. And ironically, because of the crowded conditions and denser populations, there is less police protection, less protection against the violence. In extreme cases, the cycle of depression and violence and anger results in increased suicide and homicide, both numerically more common among the poor, as is divorce. (Contrary to public belief, the divorce rate is highest in the lowest SES and inversely correlated with education, which, in the United States, usually means income; that is, the

---

[1]Needless to say, women burned out by too many children and/or the fear of pregnancy, manifest lower sexual desires.

more money, the lower the divorce rate), (Stuart, 1980, p. 4).

It goes without saying that this picture of poverty is one of deprivation that has effects not only on the parents involved but upon the next generation. Despite the theoretical debates as to whether or not there is such a thing as a "culture of poverty," about the influences of poverty upon the behavior learned by the next generation is undeniably real.

The effects of poverty—the continual, humiliating grind that seems so much the antithesis of the so-called carefree life of the poor—has been called "endemic stress" by Fried (1982). Fried uses the term to describe those threats, deprivations, and frustrations that are continuous and have an additive effect; they grind the individual down. These stresses, which may be of many kinds, characterize the life of the poor. They are most certainly a contributing factor to much of the erratic behavior, the violence, the wife and the child beating. Stress, *per se,* has psychological and physiological effects, and many of these effects are antiaphrodesiac. As Fried says, although "catastrophic" stress may gear up and mobilize the individual "endemic stress" grinds the poor down, producing apathy, alienation, and withdrawal. These are effects all similar to Seligman's learned helplessness or what we call psychological depression. Again, depression is characterized by a lack of interest in sex. Thus we come full circle to the negative effects of poverty on people's sexual expression.

WHAT CAN WE DO ABOUT IT? GUIDELINES FOR INTERVENTION

The first and most obvious thing that one can say when talking of intervention with the "poor" is that poverty should be eliminated. This has been a goal of social workers and social philosophers for a very long time. It is a very big order, heady in its implications. Certainly there have been many attempts, and the interpretation of the success or failure of these attempts often rests on whether the interpreter is a politician in or out of power. Whether there are fewer or there are more poor people at any point in time is beyond the scope of this chapter. This author merely trusts the results of his own observations in the major cities of this country to state that "more or less" is not the issue. There are still many poor people, there are still many hungry people and there are still many depressed people. The poor are still with us, and the consequences of poverty are still all too visible.

The strategy and approaches to poverty on a macro-, policy level, are beyond the scope of this chapter. Perhaps this limitation stems from a sense of "learned helplessness," living as we do during a federal administration that claims that poor people utilize soup kitchens just to get a free meal. Perhaps it is the realization that it is precisely because it *is* more comforting to talk in broad policy terms that we thus avoid any sort of accountability. However, action is the antidote to learned helplessness, action that is possible on the small scale, more precisely with the clients—individuals, couples, and even families—who constitute the clientele of the professional.

Assessment

In dealing with the sexual problems of the poor one must first remediate if possible the direct effects of poverty: malnutrition, poor health, depression, and so on, all of which are antithetical to sexual health. With *every* client, regardless of problem or class, one should inquire into the person's physical health. With poorer clients it is particularly important to do so. What is that state of their nutrition? Are they getting enough to eat? Are they healthy or sick, or—perhaps more accurately—how *well* are they? When was the last time an individual had a medical checkup, including blood tests, x-ray for tuberculosis (still, unfortunately, quite prevalent), and examination of eyes, ears, and—too often overlooked—teeth. Aching teeth, rotting teeth, are not only an aesthetic draw-back: who can feel warm and loving, like having sex, when they have aching molars?

As important as the physical status of clients, is an assessment of their immediate social field, or social system. This usually means the family. An individual is either part of and connected with a family or partner or, equally important diagnostically, he or she is *not* part of a family or ongoing relationship. More often than not, unless one is working with an isolate, or a homeless individual, it will be the former. Questions also should be asked about clients' relationships with their family, spouse, or lover, and if indicated children and other significant others in the immediate picture. There is an excellent diagnostic tool which is particularly adaptable to individuals, and their families, who are poor. These are the scales of family and community functioning devised by Ludwig Geismar (1980). They cover nine areas: family relationships and family unity; individual behavior and adjustment; care and training of children; social activities; economic practices; home and household practices; health conditions and practices; relationship to social worker or other practitioner; and the use of community resources.

The scales may be used as a complete package, or the practitioner may elect to use only certain subscales. Of particular interest to us is the first set of scales, "family relationships and family unity." This set focuses on "present functioning," including the following topics: degree of love and compatibility (of tastes, interests, etc.); closeness of emotional ties; independence (interdependence); source of satisfaction and dissatisfaction; arguments and disagreements; sexual adjustment; responsibility for financial support; and others. The scales for the "individual"—both as partner and as parent—are also useful, as are those for obtaining information on health conditions and on the use of community resources by the individual and family. Assessments may be made on a seven-point scale, ranging from "inadequate" through "marginal" to "adequate."

The instruments may obviously be used for the assessment of change during intervention as well as for diagnostic and assessment purposes. Geismar (1980) provides anchoring for the scale points and illustrations of the use of the scale. One advantage of the use of the scales, when intervening in this area, is the implicit assumption of relating the assessment, and the intervention, to community standards not of a utopia but "where the . . . actions . . . meet the needs of [the family or the individual]" (Geismar, 1980, p. 189).

Assessing clients' employment and economic status and their knowledge of community resources, and encouraging their use, at least presents some options and works toward decreasing learned helplessness and depression.

Any assessment of poorer clients must be viewed within the reality that *very few*, if any, will initially present complaints that are specifically sexual. Clients will present any combination and permutation of the usual conditions associated with poverty. Frequently the problems might be associated with a domestic situation and, not infrequently, the client will be involuntary. For example, the referral might be one of marital discord, where the couple is coming to remedy a difficult domestic situation. Here the approach is one of marital counseling, with the dyad as the unit of attention and intervention. There are numerous texts and guides for dealing with dyads, such as Stuart (1980) and Satir (1983), though neither is aimed specifically at the poorer client. Another useful guide would be the numerous publications of Geismar (particularly Geismar, 1980).

As with couples from *all* socioeconomic strata, the main problems will often be communication in one form or another. One form of communication, or lack of it, will be of course about sex. It cannot be overemphasized how little the sexual interactions of the poor (both white and minority) resemble the popular myths mentioned at the beginning of this chapter. The focus of intervention with a poorer couple, as with a couple from any SES, will probably begin, and most certainly include, discussion of communication. The resources available to the lower-SES couple will be less, and the felt (and realistic strains) will be greater, such as the effects of illness, depression, endemic stress, and so forth. As Kinsey found the sexual practices of the poor to be more constricted than those of the nonpoor, so will the practitioner working with the poorer family often find that they are unaware of some of the basic facts of physiology and anatomy and of human sexuality. In short, as with many couples, the practitioner must also be an educator and teacher, providing some basic sex education. This education might include not only the elements of sex and procreation but—very importantly—information on birth control and how to use whatever health facilities are available. Practitioners might also have to help the client often overwhelmed by bureaucracies in dealing with these health agencies; the professional must be a broker and, often, an advocate in helping these clients obtain health care for themselves and for their children.

The practitioner might also have to be an educator on budgeting, helping the client to stretch the all-too-few dollars, including advice on shopping, money management, and so forth. Education also includes nutrition, not only teaching the elements of a balanced diet, but also the least expensive way to achieve that diet and thus, indirectly, raise the general level of health—on a small amount of money.

We have also mentioned that there are negative effects of crowding and lack of privacy, both of which obstruct intimacy and sex. The practitioner might again have to be broker and advocate to help clients obtain better, more spacious, and more adequate housing and shelter if the clients want it.

Intervention

Assessment and treatment of any couple or individual will have to include the various factors mentioned above. Of primary importance, of course, as with any client, is the nature of the presenting problem. Since violence and abuse (or perhaps *reported* violence and abuse) may occur more frequently in lower-income groups, these will have to be the first order of business. There are a number of works giving guidance on abuse and violence which provide specific procedures for dealing with these problems (for example, Conte and Halpin, 1983). In addition, the couple, or often the husband of the pair, may be involuntary clients, so the practitioner will have to be skilled in the use of authority (Murdoch, 1980).

The couple may be exhibiting sexual dysfunction. For example, "inhibited sexual desire" (Kaplan's term) may very well be due to depression, and/or it may be reflective of the greater difficulties in the relationship between the pair. Following Kaplan (1979), the intervention may have to be of a more conventional psychotherapeutic nature, with talking and the examination of communication problems (Stuart, 1980; Satir 1983; Lederer & Jackson, 1968).

The couple, however, may also exhibit sexual dysfunction not of frequency but of function, disorders either of the excitement phase or the orgasmic phase, or residual complaints such as dyspareunia (both sexes) and vaginismuss (for the woman). The interventions here may very well be the now-popular sex therapy of Masters and Johnson (1971) or the new sex therapy of Kaplan (1974, 1979). (Frieda Stuart and D. Corydon Hammond have an excellent summary chapter on procedures for dealing with sexual dysfunction in Stuart, 1980.) These direct procedures, primarily behavioral but combining elements of cognitive and other approaches, most certainly will work well with clients of lower SES and, particularly, with clients of lower educatonal attainment. The specificity of the assignments has been well received by many clients. However, since some of the procedures—such as Sensate Focus—do require privacy and some time, neither freely available in a crowded home, these adverse conditions may very well present therapeutic obstacles that will have to be overcome.

The more difficult conditions may well call for ingenuity on the part of the practitioner and the possible shortening of such exercises as sensate focus. The need for adaptation, though, does not eliminate the use of the whole range of techniques subsumed under the rubric of sex therapy. The practitioner should engage in the standard diagnosis and assessment of the sexual problems, bearing in mind the reality that, as with the nonpoor, consideration of sexual problems cannot and should not be made without assessment of the total relationship. This viewing of sex within a relationship is as important as the assessment of physical and health factors. Equally important are such diagnostic information as whether the problem is primary (lifelong) or secondary (recently acquired), whether generalized (under all conditions) or selective (only in specific situations or with specific people), whether partial or total. These techniques should be used (as sometimes they are not) with the realization that a slow rate of sexual activity may be less an "inhibited sexual desire" than an indicator of endemic stress and depression. Similarly, low libido may be an indicator of poor nutrition and physical illness, such as diabetes, more than a reflection of intrapsychic stress.

Part of the reluctance of many practitioners to work with the poor is because they may, although not necessarily, have low verbal skills. So they may tend to verbalize less. Some authorities hold that persons with lower educational levels may tend to be less introspective, but we have to regard this generalization with a great deal of caution; it may very well be that in the crowded milieu in which so many live, talking about or sharing one's troubles may violate certain cultural taboos. There is evidence that some working class subcultures *do* share more with friends (for example, talk over family troubles with the neighbors next door); but they may be reluctant to discuss such topics in more formal settings, such as clinics, and with therapists who are obviously middle class and may be viewed as authority figures able to apply some sanctions upon the family. However, there are also authorities who feel that the above are merely rationalizations used by middle class professionals to avoid contact with either lower-class clients or clients from cultural groups that are strange or unknown to the worker (Fantl, 1961; Miller, 1983).

Intervention with poorer clients is, as we have stated, frequently not offered. The poorer client is often avoided, for the poorer client is often considered less desirable. This is often related more to practitioners' prejudice and resistance than it is to the actual ability of clients to utilize help. Poorer clients most certainly are amenable to help and to intervention, albeit there is often the necessity to attend to external matters, such as ensuring they have enough to eat and giving attention to their physical condition.

Needless to say, diagnosis and treatment of any of the various symptoms of depression is also a necessity. With careful thought and with flexibility of approach, poorer clients may also be treated. Wortman (1981) has made a number of suggestions, which we shall summarize. He stated that poor people have lower amounts of energy, due to depression, illness, and so forth, and because of these factors their "patience [is] already sorely tried." The practitioner must be realistic both in demands of the client and also realistic on how much and how soon the practitioner may engage the client in change. He stresses that practitioners should avoid raising either their own or a client's hope unrealistically. Missed appointments should be made up immediately. If weekly appointments are unrealistic, try spacing them differently. Above all, do not refer clients out after they have spent some time with you, for many of these people have already been bounced around various agencies. Wortman comments that referrals ". . . are a recipe for a lost case." Intervention should be kept direct, centering on the major facts and problems, and clients treated with courtesy and without conning them. Wortman recommends that practitioners use medication for depression, if indicated, in order to get people functioning as soon as possible. (However, this recommendation must be balanced against the alleged antiaphrodesiac qualities of some of these medications.) Poor people can use a variety of therapies, especially those that are more action oriented (Goldstein, 1973), but sometimes including the more insight-oriented (Lorion, 1978; Shapiro, 1983). Wortman ends with a caution that practitioners try to be realistic and not become as discouraged, and potentially as depressed, as their clients.

Another factor that complicates therapeutic work with poorer clients is that many of these clients are simply unaware of what therapy is, and of what behaviors will be asked of them in therapy. This is even more complicated when the therapy focuses on an area of such extreme sensitivity as sexuality. Orlinsky and Howard (1978) report on a number of studies that "trained" applicants to be clients, the so-called role-induction procedures. They report a great deal of success with many different types of clients using these procedures, but particularly with clients from the lower SES. Role-induction procedures, along with films, video tapes, and other audiovisual techniques, could be used either to supplement or to replace the standard interview techniques. They may, in addition, be used for general education in these areas.

SUMMARY

There are numerous myths and misconceptions about the sexuality of poor people. Poor people are often also members of minority groups such as racial, ethnic, and age groupings discussed elsewhere in this book. The poor, as a category, often have massive health, physical, and morale problems, often to the point of diagnosable depression. They tend to live in rundown, less desirable housing, especially in the cities. This may mean overcrowding and lack of privacy. Depression and poor health often mean demoralization and a rise in fatalistic, apathetic views toward life, a learned helplessness where sexual drives are either low, or where sexuality is translated into power and exploitative relationships.

In offering help to these clients, it is important that practitioners pay attention to the reality of the client's lives, and to the high possibility that many of these clients will be experiencing learned helplessness and either depression or near-depressive states. This does not mean that they are unworkable or resistant to help; adaptations may have to be made in the helping modalities, with practitioners showing a high degree of flexibility. Above all, it is important, in working with poorer clients, to approach them as individuals, to be aware of one's own feelings, to be careful to identify one's prejudices, and be able to view "what is actually happening" not within the framework of unfounded myths, but in terms of what is actually known about and useful to the sexuality of poor people.

REFERENCES

BERELSON, B., AND STEINER, G. A. *Human behavior: An inventory of scientific findings.* New York: Harcourt, Brace and World, 1964.

CHILMAN, C. S. *Adolescent sexuality in a changing American society: Social and psychological perspectives.* Washington, D.C.: U.S. Department of Health, Education and Welfare, 1980.

CONTE, J. R., AND HALPIN, T. M. New services for families. In A. Rosenblatt and D. Waldfogel, eds. *Handbook of clinical social work.* San Francisco: Jossey-Bass, 1983.

FANTL, B. Casework in lower class districts. *Mental Hygiene,* 45(1961):425–438.

FRIED, M. Endemic stress: The psychology of resignation and the politics of scarcity. *American Journal of Orthopsychiatry,* 52(1982):4–19.

GEISMAR, L. L. *Family and community functioning: A manual of measurement for social work practice and policy*, 2nd rev. ed. Metuchen, N.J.: The Scarecrow Press, 1980.

GOLDSTEIN, A. P. *Structured learning therapy: Toward a psychotherapy for the poor*. New York: Academic Press, 1973.

HIRSCHFELD, R., AND CROSS, C. K. Epidemiology of affective disorders. *Archives of General Psychiatry*, 39(1982):35–46.

KAPLAN, H. S. *Disorders of sexual desire*. New York: Brunner/Mazel, 1979.

———. *The new sex therapy*. New York: Brunner/Mazel, 1974.

KINSEY, A. C., ET AL. *Sexual behavior in the human male*. Philadelphia: Saunders, 1948.

LEDERER, W. J., AND JACKSON, D. D. *The mirages of marriage*. New York: Norton, 1968.

LORION, R. P. Research on psychotherapy and behavior change with the disadvantaged: Past, present and future directions. In S. L. Garfield and A. E. Bergin, eds. *Handbook of psychotherapy and behavior change*, 2nd ed. New York: John Wiley & Sons, 1978.

MASTERS, W. AND JOHNSON, V. *Human sexual inadequacy*. Boston: Little, Brown, 1971.

MILLER, S. O. Practice in cross-cultural settings. In Rosenblatt, A., and Waldfogel, O., eds. *Handbook of Clinical Social Work*. San Francisco: Jossey-Bass, 1984.

MURDACH, A. D. Bargaining and persuasion with non-voluntary clients. *Social Work*, 25 (1980):458–461.

ORLINSKY, D. E., AND HOWARD, K. I. The relation of process to outcome in psychotherapy. In S. L. Garfied and A. E. Bergin, eds. *Handbook of psychotherapy and behavior change*, 2nd ed. New York: John Wiley & Sons, 1978.

SATIR, V. *Conjoint family therapy*, 3rd ed. Palo Alto, Calif.: Science and Behavior Books, 1983.

SEIDEN, A. Depression and women. In E. R. Val, et al. *Affective disorders: Psychopathology and treatment*. Chicago: Year Book Publishers, Inc., 1982.

SELIGMAN, M. E. P. *Helplessness: On depression, development and death*. San Francisco: W. H. Freeman and Company, 1975.

SHAPIRO, J. Commitment to disenfranchised clients. In A. Rosenblatt and D. Waldfogel, eds. *Handbook of Clinical Social Work*. San Francisco: Jossey-Bass, 1983.

STUART, R. B. *Helping couples change: A social learning approach to marital therapy*. New York: The Guilford Press, 1980.

WOODS, N. F. *Human sexuality in health and illness*. St. Louis: C. V. Mosby, 1975.

WORTMAN, R. A. Depression, danger, dependency, denial: Work with poor, black, single parents. *American Journal of Orthopsychiatry*, 51(1981):662–671.

11

ETHNIC MINORITIES
Noreen Mokuau

Ethnosexual oppression is a form of social control of the sexual freedom of ethnic minority peoples. It is manifested by a set of beliefs about ethnic minorities to justify individual and institutional sexual discrimination against these groups. In a sociological analysis of minority-dominant relations, Davis (1976) reviews beliefs of racism that could be seen to underlie ethnosexual oppression:

1. The belief that some races are physically superior to others
2. The belief that some races are mentally superior to others
3. The belief that race determines temperament
4. The belief that racial mixing lowers biological quality.

Beliefs such as these provide rationalizations for oppressive acts ranging from slavery to antimiscegenation laws to the creation and use of stereotypes that classify sexual attitudes and beliefs of ethnic minority persons in an inaccurate and undesirable way.

The literature is rich in analyses of the etiology and scope of racist beliefs (Daniels & Kitano, 1970; Knowles & Prewitt, 1969; Blauner, 1972; Davis, 1978); however, accounts of the ideology and effects of ethnosexual oppression are limited (Hernton, 1965; Gochros, 1979; Williams, 1972), and documentation of the sexual oppression of specific minority groups is even more scarce. This chapter is an attempt to extend this literature by describing the nature of sexual oppression for three ethnic minority groups in the United States, and discussing possible intervention strategies to overcome some of this oppression.

Specifically, this chapter presents a conceptual framework for viewing the impact of racism and sexual oppression on cross-cultural relations, provides a descriptive profile of Black Americans, Hispanic Americans, and Asian and Pacific Islander Americans, with reference to sexually oppressive acts, and discusses the conceptual and practice implications for intervention strategies at both the individual and social system levels.

A CONCEPTUAL MODEL

Ethnosexual oppression functions in a context of cross-cultural relations. However, there are few models in the literature that adequately conceptualize the variations inherent in any definition of ethnicity, ethnic identity, and cross-cultural relations. Green (1982) reviews several major conceptual models that account for ethnicity and classifies these models into two broad areas: (1) categorical models which explain ethnicity according to the degree to which individuals or groups manifest specific, distinctive traits; and (2) transactional models which explain ethnicity according to the values, signs, and behaviors that signify cross-cultural encounters. When viewed separately, both classifications are limited and do not sufficiently contribute to an understanding of cross-cultural relations. An examination of both areas, however, lends to a more complete understanding of the dynamics of cross-cultural interactions and provides a framework for describing and assessing ethnosexual oppression.

Categorical models of cross-cultural relations focus on the identification of specific traits such as skin color, food preferences, retention of native language, and musical styles as indicators of ethnic identity and intergroup interactions. There is some merit in acknowledging that visible physiological traits such as skin color, hair texture, and slant of eye may affect one's self-image, how one projects an identity to others, and how others respond to that individual. The easy identification of visible traits leads to an instant categorization which shapes much of the initial interaction in a color conscious society (Kitano, 1974, p. 120). Denial of the

importance of a specific trait such as skin color is destructive if it also means denial of differences in experience, culture, and psychology of ethnic minority persons (Bass, 1982, p. 69). Although specific cultural traits are important, they are not sufficient to a total understanding of ethnic identity and cross-cultural relations. For example, it is conceivable that a third-generation Asian American woman with Asian physiological traits (for example, dark hair, slanted eyes) may maintain world views that run counter to the values of her parents and may demonstrate behaviors that are perceived as more culture-general than culture-specific. It is necessary then, in any conceptualization of cross-cultural relations, to include a component that emphasizes these values and world views which impact on transactional behaviors.

In the transactional approach to ethnicity, Green (1982) notes that the examination of values, signs, and behavioral styles that influence the relations between the larger society and persons who identify themselves with an ethnic group are of central interest. A pattern of values, signs, and behavioral acts signifies the development of social boundaries that distinguish one group of individuals from another. These boundaries develop in an ongoing manner subject to socio-political-economic factors and, in many instances, tend to be highly stereotypic and ritualized. Serving as markers of inclusion and exclusion, these boundaries are formulated based on a group's sense and maintenance of cultural distinctiveness. The transactional model's indicators of cross-cultural relations are, by their nature, more difficult to identify than the specific traits of the categorical models; however, an understanding of a group's values and world views is vital to any assessment of cross-cultural transactions.

A categorical-transactional model of cross-cultural relations may be useful as a tool in understanding ethnosexual oppression. If categorical traits sometimes serve as cross-cultural indicators, then in cases of sexual oppression there may be the association of traits with stereotypic beliefs. For example, for many black American males, skin color connotes hypersexuality. Socially imbued stereotypes of hypersexuality can have an impact on self-image as well as on intra- and intergroup relations. Thus the categorical traits have assumed increased importance as they are associated with certain values, signs, and behaviors. Black American men who have internalized stereotypes of hypersexuality may attempt to match sexual performance with stereotypic expectations. If they are successful, they reaffirm the maintenance of stereotypes. If they are not successful, behavioral and psychological problems ensue. Other persons who have internalized those stereotypes of hypersexuality for Black American men may define their transactions according to these generalized expectations. Such an understanding of cross-cultural relations underscores the importance of the eradication of racist ideology and stereotypes for treatment success. Human service professionals working with different ethnic minority members, therefore, need to be informed of and sensitive to the cultural background and experiences of the client in order that appropriate assessment and effective treatment might be offered.

POPULATION DESCRIPTION

The Population

Appropriate assessment and effective treatment of problems of sexual oppression for ethnic minority peoples is founded on an informed awareness of cultural background and experience. This informed awareness is the somewhat paradoxical seeking of evidence of uniformities within and between groups as well as an appreciation of the differences. Davenport (1978) suggests that studies of sexuality in a cross-cultural perspective will be more profitable if intercultural constants are identified within the matrix of cultural variety.

The labels "Black American," "Hispanic American," and "Asian and Pacific Islander American," connote a homogenous character among the individuals who comprise the various ethnic communities. In a very global sense this homogeneity is attributed to physical visibility, the sharing of common geographic and cultural origins, a universal respect for specified beliefs and traditions, and similar adjustment experiences in the United States in terms of racism and prejudice. The merit in utilizing a label with such homogeneous connotations lies in providing a broad-based foundation from which the helping professional can initially begin to assess the circumstances of the ethnic minority individual. In providing a broad foundation, however, the label is limiting in that it fails to identify or project the many differences that exist among the groups that it attempts to classify. By virtue of group membership, sexual oppression will affect all ethnic minority peoples; however, the degree and experience of oppression may vary according to specific ethnic group association and individual variation. This section highlights similarities and differences of and between black Americans, Hispanic Americans, and Asian and Pacific Islander Americans through the presentation of a profile of sociodemographic information and a discussion of oppressive experiences for each of these various groups.

Sociodemographic Profile

In 1980, the three largest ethnic minority groups in the United States were blacks, 26.5 million (11.7%); Hispanics, 14.6 million (6.4%); and Asian and Pacific Islanders, 3.7 million (1.5%), (United States Department of Commerce, Bureau of the Census, 1980). These ethnic classifications are comprised of a diverse array of subcultural groups. The category "Black" includes persons who indicated their race as Black, Negro, Jamaican, Black Puerto Rican, West Indian, Haitian, or Nigerian. Persons of Spanish origin are those who classified themselves as Mexican,

Puerto Rican, Cuban, or Hispanic. The Asian and Pacific Islander category included persons who indicated their race as Japanese, Chinese, Filipino, Korean, Asian Indian, Vietnamese, Hawaiian, Guamanian, and Samoan. When compared with census statistics in 1970, the Black population showed only a moderate increase in population size in 1980 (17%). In contrast, Hispanics (40%) and Asian and Pacific Islander populations (over 100%) showed dramatic increases in population size in the last ten years. The increase in Hispanic population is difficult to interpret because persons of Spanish origin in the 1980 census reported their race differently than in the 1970 census; this difference in reporting may have an important effect on the counts. The high increase in the 1980 count for Asian and Pacific Islander peoples reflects a high level of immigration during the 1970s as well as census classification changes for race.

The distribution of sex for each ethnic minority group is fairly balanced, with the largest discrepancy showing for Black Americans. Census reports show a count of 12.5 million Black males and 13.9 million Black females; 1.8 million Asian and Pacific Islander males and 1.9 million females; and an even representation of 7.3 million Hispanic males and females. The median age is 24.9 years for Blacks, 23.2 years for persons of Spanish origin, and 28.6 years for Asian and Pacific Islanders.

Other important sociodemographic variables include mean family income and family types. The 6 million Black American families living in the United States have a mean income of $15,721, the lowest among all groups. The 3.3 million Hispanic families report a mean income of $17,360, and the 828,000 Asian and Pacific Islander families show an average income of $25,681. It is further reported that persons living at the poverty level include 7.8 million Black Americans (out of 26.5 million), 3.4 million Hispanic Americans (out of 14.6 million), and 503,000 Asian and Pacific Islanders (out

of 3.7 million). Of these ethnic families residing in the United States, 2.3 million, 650,000, and 90,000—for Blacks, Hispanics, and Asian and Pacific Islanders, respectively— are headed by females with no husband present.

Census data allows for a general description of population traits that will enhance our understanding of these various ethnic groups.

Black Americans

Sexual oppression for Black Americans is wedded to racist ideology. The beliefs that Blacks are intellectually and physically inferior to the white population justified sexual exploitation during the slavery years. In the early years of the slavery period, there were a greater number of Black men then Black women, so sexual relations between Black male slaves and indentured white women were initially encouraged to augment the slave population (Williams, 1972; Staples, 1971). This practice was later prohibited with antimiscegenation laws. Black women on the other hand, were subjugated to their slave masters as soon as they were introduced into America and were used as breeders of more slaves (Wyatt, 1982).

Sexual exploitation was also justified with the racist belief that race determines temperament. The equation was drawn between the Black race and hypersexuality and bestial instincts. Thomas (1901) states that:

Negro nature is so craven and sensuous in every fibre of its being, that negro manhood with decent respect for chaste womanhood does not exist. . . . Women unresistingly betray their wifely honor to satisfy a bestial instinct . . . so deeply rooted in immorality are our negro people . . . (in Johnson, 1977; p. 174)

Black women, believed to be loose and immoral, were the antithesis of white women, who were perceived as being virtuous and demure. The sexual availability of Black women allowed white men to see white women as sexually chaste individuals and to put them on pedestals (Wyatt, 1982). Black men, were believed to possess supersexual powers physiologically exemplified by their large penises. Carter (1979) suggests that the myth about the Black man's sexual superiority had been intended to discourage and frighten white women away from Black men; however, it may have backfired because it inadvertently created a situation in which sex is an area where Black men can compete with white men.

The myth of Black hypersexuality has been challenged with opposing stereotypes of emasculation for Black men (Kardiner & Ovesey, 1951; Staples, 1971) and images of hyposexuality for Black women (Wyatt, Strayer & Lobitz, 1976). Staples (1971) suggests that the stereotypes of the Black male as psychologically impotent and castrated may have its origins in slavery, in which the slave husband and father was deprived of his sociological and economic functions, and may have been perpetuated through the systematic denial of socio-economic-political opportunities. As legitimate as these reasons may seem, Staples (1971) contends that the real genesis of the myth of impotence is the white man's fear of the Black man's supposed hypersexuality. Similar to the contradictory statements offered on Black men's sexuality, Wyatt, Strayer, and Lobitz (1976) note that various studies have projected Black women in a diametrically different image from that of hypersexuality. Accounts of Black female sexuality have suggested that they are "frigid" and more sexually restrained and traditional than white women.

Sexual oppression is also associated with the racist belief that racial mixing lowers biological quality. An assumption of anti-miscegenation laws (found unconstitutional in 1967) is that the product of a white-black union is someone who is intellectually and physically deficient. Williams (1972) notes that such statutes forbidding racial intermarriages were inaccurate in that they only related to white women and non-white men. Black men were forbidden to have sexual relations with white women. White men, on the other hand, sexually exploited Black women. The belief that racial mixing lowers biological quality is perhaps best reflected in the treatment of the mulattoes. Children of white and Black unions sometimes had slightly preferential treatment over children of Black parents; however, they were still considered to be slaves.

The creation and maintenance of such racist beliefs destructively influences self-perceptions and intra- and intergroup relations. In those situations when a person's beliefs contribute to the development of contradictory stereotypes (for example, hyper- and hyposexuality), then greater confusion might be anticipated. Negative self-images may be the result of the incorporation of negative stereotypes and, as Poussaint (1974) notes, may contribute to the development of self-hatred among Blacks. This self-hatred is easily transferred to Black marital and sexual partners. Carter (1979) suggests that a most sorrowful issue is the relationship of Black men and Black women. Black women place on Black men economic and emotional demands that cannot be met because of institutional racism. Black men treat Black women in devalued ways because of their own lack of self-esteem. In a case study provided by Wyatt, Strayer, and Lobitz (1976), a Black American couple was experiencing sexual difficulties due to internalization of sexual stereotypes. One expectation, for both partners, was that the male be sexually aggressive and skilled. When he failed to be sexually demonstrative and aggressive, he felt inadequate and inferior and she was disappointed and disillusioned.

There is no truth to racist ideology. However, the negative influence of racist beliefs on Black sexuality, historically and today, is a truth. Attempts to clarify the misconceptions are slowly emerging in the literature, but much more needs to be done before public consciousness is changed and the true sexual freedom of Black Americans can be considered a reality.

Hispanic Americans

Racism exists within the diversity and complexity of Hispanic culture. The subjugation of and discrimination against Hispanic Americans can be traced to the immigration experiences of these major groups: Mexican Americans since the 1600s, Puerto Ricans since the 1920s, and Cuban Americans since the 1960s. LeVine and Padilla (1980) report that the history of Hispanic immigration to the United States is illustrative of how many Mexican and Puerto Rican Americans are institutionally locked into poverty through exclusion, and also how many skilled and professional Cubans are barred from middle- and upper-class status. The underlying assumption justifying all this is that Hispanic Americans are inferior and, therefore, their subordinate status is appropriate and really their own fault (Simmons, 1971). Associated with this racist belief of superiority-inferiority, is the ideological distortion of the relationship between ancestry and temperament. Common stereotypes characterize Hispanics as criminally inclined and deceitful, lazy and undependable. Two of the most frequently publicized and commonly exaggerated stereotypes of Hispanic Americans are related to their sexuality: machismo and mariasmo.

Machismo, and its root, *macho*, are Spanish words for male with an emphasis on superiority and dominance. These words are not fabricated constructs, but rather derive from the mythological literature of Latin American cultures. Macklin (1980) notes that ethnographic research on supernatural models of gender validates the general description of the male Hispanic role as one of virility and aggressiveness. However, the terms have tended to acquire stereotypic distortion with time. Machismo, as the term is commonly misconstrued, "expresses itself through multiple sexual conquests, sensitivity to insult, and a latent capacity for

violence" (LeVine and Padilla, 1980, p. 32). Furthermore, machismo is conceptualized as a Hispanic male's self-esteem in relationship to how many children he procreates (Andrade, 1980). LeVine and Padilla (1980) state that this kind of description is an exaggeration of the more accurate notion that traditional Hispanic males have a less restrictive role than the Hispanic female. Another perspective, offered by Cromwell and Ruiz (1979), asserts that the image of macho dominance in decision making in Hispanic families is not an exaggeration, but a myth lacking substantive empirical evidence.

The impact of machismo on self-image and intra- and intercultural relationships might be paralleled by that of the Black man's image of hypersexuality. A Hispanic American male, like a Black American male, who internalizes beliefs that ethnosexuality locks him into actions of sexual expertise and domination, may develop unrealistic expectations of his sexual performance and sexual role. He may, with others who have internalized sexual stereotypes, demand of himself unrealistic behaviors of the machismo image (Maccoby, 1971). Inability to conform to machismo may lead to a dissatisfaction with sexual patterns and sexual partners.

Machismo has also been frequently cited as a pathological attempt of Hispanic Americans to meet cultural needs by producing large families (Andrade, 1980) and is perceived by many as a cultural deterrent to fertility regulation (Urdaneta, 1980). The nature of such descriptions as reported in the social science literature has broad implications for cross-cultural relations. Perhaps the most obvious implication is that whites and others in positions of societal dominance and power may well choose to control Hispanic Americans' sexuality through fertility regulation.

Mariasmo is the female counterpart to machismo. It is a stereotype of the ideal Hispanic woman with derivations from Latin American mythology (Macklin, 1980). *Mariasmo* is moral superiority, spiritual strength, humility, and sacrifice, and submissiveness to men (Stevens in Macklin, 1980). Like machismo, there may be some validity to the characteristics of mariasmo if tracked back to mythological and historical origins; however, the current promotion in the literature tends to be grossly generalized, stereotypic, and inaccurate. Mariasmo has become a stereotypic explanation of large Hispanic American families and is perceived as "culturally pathological" and "socially deficient" in any conceptualization of family structure and functioning (Macklin, 1980).

The most sexually oppressive act resulting, at least in part, from the perpetuation of stereotypes such as machismo and mariasmo has been the physical sterilization of Hispanic American women. Velez-I (1980) notes that, in 1977, sterilization procedures were performed on nonconsenting "Chicana" women. In an extreme act of racism, a Los Angeles court legitimized the "sterilization of the physical ability of a group of ethnic minority women to procreate and the resultant cultural sterilization of that same group" (p. 247). The women suffered severe depression and, in many situations, the marital and family relationships deteriorated.

Cultural sterilization as an act of sexual oppression is a violation of the most basic human rights. It is inexcusable and racist in orientation. The prevention of such an act happening again begins with the diligent battle of all Americans against our racist legacy through the promotion of cultural information and reeducation.

Asian and Pacific Islander Americans

The literature regarding sexual oppression of Asian and Pacific Islander Americans is almost nonexistent. What is available tends to be isolated accounts of sexually oppressive acts scattered in reports of racism, historical immigration, and acculturation experiences of Asian Americans and Pacific Islanders. While the census label, "Asian and Pacific Islander," connotes some broad commonalities between the two major subcultural groups, for the most part the life experiences of Asian Americans and of Pacific Islander Americans are very different. For example, the major Asian groups such as the Chinese, Japanese, and Filipinos immigrated to the United States as laborers from the mid-1800s to the 1930s. Pacific Islanders, such as Native Hawaiians, Samoans, and Guamanians, however, primarily inhabit their land of origin, with some persons living in various parts of the continental United States. Such differences in history and geographical origin preclude the possibility of making descriptive generalizations of sexual oppression for Asian Americans and Pacific Islander Americans. This section, then, focuses on the experiences of the earliest Asian groups to the United States.

The racist ideology that permeates the cross-cultural relations of Black Americans and Hispanic Americans somehow seem less vitrolic when applied to Asian Americans. The "model minority" thesis, suggesting that through their hard work and perseverance Asian Americans have successfully adapted to the American lifestyle, may account for the seemingly positive image in the American public consciousness. Although more recent reports qualify, revise, and sometimes discredit the model minority thesis (Kitano, 1974; Murase, 1979; Suzuki, 1980), all reports acknowledge that Asian Americans continue to be victims of a subtle, insidious white racism. Thus, racist ideology is again a factor in sexual oppression.

Sexual issues undergird the racist anti-Oriental movement in the early immigration experiences of the Chinese, Japanese, and Filipinos. Similar to accounts for Black Americans and Hispanic Americans, racist ideology of white intellectual and physical supremacy was manifested in the fears revolving around relationships between non-white men and white women. A fear in the white mind was the "ravishing of pure White women by lascivious Oriental men" (Daniels & Kitano, 1970, p. 67). Relationships between white men and Asian women aroused little opposition as Chinese and Japanese prostitutes had been a feature of West Coast brothels since the gold-rush days (Daniels & Kitano, 1970).

Sexually aggressive stereotypes depicted Asian men as having immoral temperaments. Ogawa (1971) notes that in an 1892 *Sacramento Daily Record Union* article, Japanese were portrayed as "men who know no morals but vice, who sit beside White daughters and debauch and demoralize them" (p. 15). These stereotypes were sometimes propagated by political figures, such as Grover Johnson in 1909:

I am responsible to the mothers and fathers of Sacramento County who have their little daughters sitting side by side in the school rooms with matured Japs with their base minds, lascivious thoughts, multiplied by their race and strengthened by their mode of life. . . . I have seen Japanese twenty-five years old sitting in the seats next to the pure maids of California. . . . I shudder . . . to think of such a condition. (in Ogawa, 1971, p. 15)

Evidence of fear that a yellow-white union would result in lower biological quality is amplified in accounts justifying American racism. The following quote best captures this racist fear:

Colored migration is a universal peril, menacing every part of the White world. . . . The whole White race is exposed, immediately or ultimately, to the possibility of social sterilization and final replacement or absorption by the teeming colored races. There is no immediate danger of the world being swamped by black blood. But the White stock can be swamped by Asiatic blood . . . unless the [white] man erects and maintains artificial barriers [he will] finally perish. (in Daniels & Kitano, 1970, p. 55)

The impact of sexual oppression on Asian Americans today takes many forms. The racist stereotype from the historical past influences an individual's self-image and perceptions, and interactions with others. For example, in an autobiographical text Carlos Bulosan, a Filipino immigrant states:

We were suspect each time we were seen with a White woman. And perhaps it was this narrowing

of our life into . . . a filthy segment of American society, that had driven Filipinos inward, hating everyone and despising all positive urgencies toward freedom. (in Daniels & Kitano, 1970, p. 68)

This kind of hostility directed both internally and externally exemplifies a destruction to self and others resulting from racist and oppressive acts. Another form of sexual oppression today is the comparison of white and Asian physiology. The ideal American—both male and female—as characterized by the media is tall, blond, and blue-eyed. A variety of opposing viewpoints on American beauty are currently being promoted, but for the most part the standard images still are predominant. For Asian men and women who tend to be short, dark-haired, and dark-eyed, the realization of "American beauty" can never be fully attained. Consequently, "between the ideal which the Asian American is seeking and the reality of what he/she looks like, frustrations and anxieties can result" (Ogawa, 1977, p. 193). Asian American males may take up weight lifting to build muscle strength as a form of compensating for lack of height. Asian American women utilize Scotch tape to make their eyes appear rounder and fuller and more Caucasian-like (Ogawa, 1977). With such actions, the outcome is a dissatisfaction with self and a dissatisfaction with intracultural and cross-cultural relations.

It is acknowledged that while the nature of physical stereotypes tend to be consistent for the Asian male, the image of the Asian female also has an opposing perspective. This image is characterized as the slim, sexy, lovable, "Suzy Wong" types of American movies (Weiss, 1973). The stereotype of Asian women as being the antithesis of the American beauty, as well as being "Suzy Wong" exotic, are cross generalizations, inaccurate and destructive to Asian women who attempt to meet these stereotypic expectations.

Internalization of stereotypes has led to a debilitating effect on Asian American self-image that eventually transmits itself to relations with sexual partners. For example, in a study of interracial dating, Weiss (1977) found that Chinese American girls prefer Caucasian males who were perceived as being "good-looking," and "sexy," to Chinese males who were portrayed as "sexually inept."

The minimal attention paid to the sexual concerns of Asian and Pacific Islanders in the literature is a kind of oppression in itself. The information available is not systematized nor is it comprehensive. What is evident is the impact of racist ideology on sexual oppression. As with the discussions of Black Americans and Hispanic Americans, the road to sexual freedom resides in the dispelling of sexual stereotypes and the reeducation of all peoples.

Summary

Racism underlies sexual oppression for Black Americans, Hispanic Americans, and Asian Americans. As illustrated in the descriptive summaries, ethnosexual oppression has historical roots and current-day manifestations. What is known about sexual oppression for these groups is best understood in the context of transactional relations—how one individual, or group of individuals, responds to others. Ethnic minority persons suffer sexual oppression because of their ethnic heritage, but they also experience the same degree of oppression suffered by other groups as well. It is not a mutually exclusive situation. There are physically disabled Black Americans, homosexual Hispanic Americans, and elderly Asian Americans. The problem of sexual oppression for ethnic minority members, therefore, seems to be compounded. Although racism and sexual oppression originates with the acts of dominant group members against minority group members, it is perpetuated by dominant group members as well as minority group members who internalize sexual stereotypes and live accordingly. The need is for human service professionals to be informed of and sensitive to all ramifications of ethnic minority concerns in order to provide accurate assessments and appropriate treatment.

INTERVENTION

Intervention for problems of sexual oppression may involve direct services to individuals and small groups or it may entail providing service on the broader level of social systems. At the heart of such intervention is the attempt to eliminate the cancerous effects of racism that create and sustain sexual oppression. In cases of oppression of Black Americans, Hispanic Americans, and Asian and Pacific Islander Americans, the theme that has been promoted throughout this chapter is that appropriate assessment and effective treatment is predicated on understanding the individual in the context of his or her culture.

Information about and sensitivity to cultural background and experience is important, yet it is also vital for the human service professional to be able to translate the cultural information into specific intervention strategies. The problem of attempting to correlate the dynamics of the client's background with effective treatment is not necessarily peculiar to work with ethnic minority persons but applies to all members of oppressed groups. It is succinctly reflected in Ivey's (1978) question, "Which treatment for which individuals and under what conditions?"

Inherent in any response to such a question is the acknowledgement that a complex interplay of factors influences the determination and appropriateness of intervention strategies to be used with problems of sexual oppression for ethnic minority clients. It would be impossible to delineate all factors revolving around broad and complex topics such as human nature, interpersonal relationships, and social institutions, or to project the infinite and dynamic interconnections of such factors. It would, furthermore, be simplistic to isolate and identify, "laundry-list" fashion, a few of these factors and then attempt to prescribe direct practice and social-systems intervention strategies without further thought to a more comprehensive framework. Complexity of practice and heterogeneity of ethnic group composition precludes such actions. It is the intent of this discussion to recommend some broad guidelines for working with ethnic minority clients with the understanding that appropriate treatment will originate from the clear assessment of an individual's, group's, or community's unique world views, needs, and styles of functioning.

This section on intervention addresses direct practice and social systems strategies as they relate to the institution of mental health. It is well documented that mainstream mental health facilities have been underutilized by ethnic minority clients (Pedersen et al., 1981; Sue & McKinney, 1975; Levine and Padilla, 1980; Wagner and Haug, 1971; Atkinson, Morten & Sue, 1979). A variety of explanations have also emerged in the same literature to account for underutilization, ranging from practitioners' biases in working with the ethnically different, to clients' preferences in seeking assistance from sources other than mental health facilities, to systems deficiencies such as geographical inaccessibility of facilities and lack of bilingual/bicultural staff. The major underlying assumption of such explanations is that the structure of and services provided by mainstream mental health facilities conflict with ethnic minority cultural values and, thus, detrimentally affect the process and outcome of treatment for ethnic minority clients. The development and provision of culturally responsive services derives from an understanding of the interface of such conflicts, and an aggressive attempt to change services and systems to more closely accommodate clients' needs and world views. Three strategies of intervention that may be useful in addressing such concerns, counseling, social action, and social planning, will be discussed, with implication for application to ethnosexual problems.

Direct Service Intervention

Cross-cultural counseling is that dynamic process between persons of culturally different backgrounds in which one person seeks help and another individual is trained to provide assistance. Despite the fluid and complex nature of the relationship, broad parameters of the interaction might be highlighted through a discussion of general principles of cross-cultural counseling and a more extensive examination of practitioner and client world views.

The appropriate and sensitive delivery of counseling services to ethnic minority persons with problems of sexual oppression is predicated on the assumption that all persons have a right to responsible sexual expression. This assumption connotes a commitment on the part of the practitioner to understand and accept cultural variation among people, and to expedite services that are consistent with people's varying background, world views and experiences. There are several general principles that address these concerns. These principles, not necessarily mutually exclusive, are offered as guidelines to enhance counseling for problems of ethnosexual oppression.

1. Knowledge of the impact of racism on individuals and their intra- and cross-cultural relationships. Racism exists in American society. Practitioners are asked to be informed about the impact of racism on a client's development, self-image, and relationships. Information about racism from a historical perspective as well as current-day manifestations will be instrumental to a more accurate definition of ethnosexual problems, and useful to treatment planning.

2. Knowledge of the dynamics of sexual oppression and the specific relationship to ethnic minority peoples. Ethnosexual oppression as a form of social control needs to be understood by practitioners. Specifically, information on the nature and scope of sexually oppressive acts for Black Americans, Hispanic Americans, and Asian and Pacific Islander

Americans, and the effect of this form of oppression on self-image and interpersonal relationship is needed.

3. Awareness of the potential barriers to cross-cultural counseling. Cultural differences between the practitioner and client may precipitate counseling barriers. Vontress (1981) points out that cultural differences may detrimentally affect the ability of the counselor to relate to, communicate with, diagnose, and treat ethnic minority clients. Some of the potential barriers that he identifies include language differences, relationship problems of transference and counter-transference, and psychosocial problems stemming from differing socialization experiences. Practitioners are encouraged to gain information on such barriers in an effort to reduce the possibility of occurrence in practice.

4. Knowledge of cultural-coping and help-seeking behaviors. Different individuals and different ethnic groups may demonstrate varying means of coping with life stresses. The practitioner is urged to recognize the possible differences in cultural definition of health and illness, and to identify culturally relevant coping styles. LeVine and Padilla (1980) suggest that while maladjustment occurs in all cultures, the pattern of symptoms may vary across cultures. Furthermore, the ways people cope with maladjustment may also be culturally determined. Practitioners need to be aware of the variations in definition and coping, and open to the notion that a client's experience may be expressed in forms of sexual dysfunction different from one's own.

5. Knowledge of and ability to demonstrate a variety of verbal and nonverbal responses in a culturally appropriate way. Communication is all important in counseling. Practitioners must be aware of the cultural nuances of verbal and nonverbal language as well as have the ability to generate and accurately receive a variety of responses in a culturally sensitive way. Atkinson, Morten, and

Sue (1979) suggest that information on postures, gestures, and eye contact as part of body language and verbal language systems are crucial to cross-cultural counseling.

6. Knowledge of and ability to transpose a variety of theories and techniques of helping in a culturally appropriate way. Effective treatment for problems of ethnosexual oppression must be based on a careful selection of theories and techniques that best fit the client's needs. In order to do this practitioners must have a knowledge of the multitude of theories and techniques that exist and, most importantly, be able to modify and translate these theories and techniques so that they are consistent with the world views and concerns of the client.

7. Awareness of indigenous forms of helping and the availability of folk-healing resources in a community. Insight into indigenous forms of healing may provide practitioners with added information on what is culturally acceptable to ethnic minority clients. This type of information on folk healing may be used in conjunction with or to modify mainstream theories of counseling.

8. Continual examination of one's racial world views and attitudes in terms of counseling relationships. A practitioner's racial world views and attitudes will influence the counseling relationship. As members of a society in which racism exists, human service professionals are encouraged to examine how racist ideology affects their practice with ethnic minority clients. They are cautioned against bringing their own racial prejudices into the counseling relationship and are urged to engage in continual self-examinations as a means to decrease the likelihood of generalizing and stereotyping.

9. Understanding of the varying world views and experiences of the client, and the extent to which a client identifies with his or her cultural group. Clients' world views and experiences vary tremendously and will directly impact their responsiveness to treatment. The totality of an individual's experiences—which includes values, attitudes, and preferences—might be referred to as ethnic identification (Ruiz & Casas, 1981). Practitioners are advised to be aware of the varying degrees of ethnic identification, and how this should influence assessment and choice of treatment.

10. Focus on the individual in the context of his or her culture. The focus for cross-cultural counseling should always be on the individual. Although people may share similar cultural world views and experiences, the manner of integrating them is unique and most clearly a personal endeavor. Ethnosexual oppression effects all ethnic peoples, but appropriate assessment and sensitive treatment should be based on the unique circumstances of the individual.

As guidelines these general principles have different areas of emphases, ranging from institutional racism and ethnosexual oppression, to the dynamics of cross-cultural counseling and an understanding of helping strategies, to a focus on the practitioner and the client. These principles assume greater significance and applicability through an extended discussion of practitioner and client world views. World views, people's conception of the world, are important in that all other traits and characteristics derive from, contribute to, or, in some way, are related to them. The world views of a practitioner will dictate ideas of self-image as well as influence perceptions and interactions with others. These perceptions subsequently will have an impact on the practitioner's assessment of client functioning and treatment planning. The world views of the client will similarly affect his or her perceptions of self and influence perceptions and interactions with others. These perceptions ultimately affect how responsive and receptive a client will be to a particular form of intervention. An examination of these world views is the preface to any discussion addressing the enhancement of cross-cultural counseling for problems of ethnosexual oppression.

The practitioner's world views. A practitioner brings a unique set of world views to the counseling relationship. An ideal perspective of world views would reflect a flexible balance and appreciation of two opposing frames of reference: *etic* (culture-general), which views cultural information in light of categories and concepts external to the culture but universal in their applicability, and *emic* (culture-specific), which views cultural data as indigenous or unique to a culture (Draguns, 1976, p. 2). The culture-general perspective assumes that there is a single, universal definition of mental health, and the culture-specific perspective assumes intercultural variation (Pedersen, 1981). The ideal, therefore, is an integration of both perspectives so that there is a respect for the universal dimensions of human functioning with an understanding, if not sharing, of world views of a specific ethnic group.

The reality of the underutilization of mental health services by ethnic minority clients is sometimes attributed to practitioners who fail to integrate the culture-general/culture-specific perspectives and, instead, emphasize one perspective over the other. An overemphasis toward the culture-general is one in which the worker defines the dynamics of the relationship and prescribes treatment according to a monocultural set of assumptions. As products of a racist society, Vontress (1981) notes that counselors bring to the therapeutic relationship preconceived ideas and attitudes about ethnic minorities. These preconceptions often manifest themselves as barriers to the therapeutic relationship because counselors apply their own "self-reference" criteria to clients who are culturally different. For example, Vontress (1981) states that the lack of recognition of, and respect for, the importance of machismo, could serve as a psychosocial barrier to counseling the Hispanic male. White female counselors who are overly assertive, or the combination of Hispanic males and females in group counseling, may be perceived as inappropriate for certain Hispanic clients who believe in machismo.

The polar opposite of this imbalance is the overemphasis toward the culture-specific. Here, overemphasis in counseling focuses on the culture, not the individual. Draguns (1976) suggests that a culture-specific over-emphasis results in dangers of cultural stereotyping as all members of a cultural group are perceived as being alike and the personal attributes of an individual are glossed over. Counselors are strongly cautioned against seeing all ethnic minority clients as stereotypic caricatures—the hypersexual Black male, the reserved and acquiescent Asian female, the Hispanic couple who use procreation as a means to maintain family relationships; treatment must never be based on these stereotypic notions.

In essence, a counselor's deliberate effort to understand how one's world views may impact on his or her perceptions of, and interactions with, ethnic minority clients is crucial to cross-cultural counseling. Continual exploration, even changing of world views, can contribute positively to cross-cultural interactions. The flexible integration of the culture-general and culture-specific perspectives has relevance in counseling ethnic minority clients with problems of sexual oppression.

Through an integration of culture-general and culture-specific perspectives, a practitioner will be committed to accepting aspects of the client's experience which might be expressed in forms of sexual behavior culturally different from one's own. Although it is important to understand how sexual behavior may be influenced by cultural background, the practitioner must also acknowledge that sexuality is one dimension of a socialization experience in which we all participate (Wyatt, 1982).

Client world views. In much the same manner that a practitioner brings a unique set of world views to the counseling relationship, so does the client. These world views affect how an ethnic minority individual constructs a self-image, and how he or she perceives and interacts with others. This discussion attempts to project the scope of client world views by organizing them into three frames of reference that tend to correspond with perspectives provided for practitioners' world views: culture-general, culture-specific, and bicultural. These world views might be visualized as markers on a continuum ranging from culture-general to bicultural to culture-specific, with an infinite number of varying world views in between. Unlike the discussion on practitioner world views, this discussion does not recommend or project any particular world view that is ideal for the cross-cultural relationship. Rather, the intent is to further define the parameters of cross-cultural counseling by delineating three major perspectives which will have import for assessment and treatment planning. Concurrent with self-awareness, a practitioner must strive for an understanding of the client's world views. Pedersen (1981) notes that several major organizations, the National Institute of Mental Health, the American Psychological Association, and the President's Commission on Mental Health, have emphasized the responsibility of all counselors to "know and attend" to the client's cultural world views.

An individual with a culture-general outlook is highly committed to the values and traditions of a dominant culture. This perspective may manifest itself in a categorical way, such as the ability to speak only the dominant culture's language, and/or a transactional way, such as the preference for egalitarian male-female relationships. Offering a list of modern values for Hispanic Americans, LeVine and Padilla (1980) comment that these values are antithetical to traditional Hispanic values in many respects and reflect a motivation for adjustment and advancement in a rapidly changing society. They predict that ethnic minority clients with a high commitment to Anglo culture may be effectively assisted by the Anglo practitioner. The implication is that treatment provided in mainstream mental health services may be appropriate and useful for this kind of clientele.

An ethnic minority client with a bicultural perspective holds simultaneous membership in two different cultures (Ruiz & Casas, 1981), and thus there is a commitment to the values of both the dominant and ethnic cultures. Biculturality may manifest itself in bilingual capabilities and/or in the mixing and switching from culture-general world views to culture-specific. The struggle for practitioners is to separate the generalized traits from the culturally particular elements of experience (Draguns, 1976). LeVine and Padilla (1980) predict that the bicultural client may be effectively assisted by bicultural practitioners (or practitioners integrating the *emic-etic* perspectives), as well as by Anglo practitioners. The implication is that mainstream mental health services may be appropriate if restructured to take into account the needs of ethnic minority clients, and if restaffed by persons with cultural knowledge, training, and sensitivity. If only by degree of American citizenship, Black Americans, Hispanic Americans, and Asian and Pacific Islander Americans are to a certain extent, bicultural. It would seem, therefore, cogent to concentrate on treatment concerns for this group of clientele.

Clients with a culture-specific world view are highly committed to the values and traditions of a specific cultural group. Indicators of a culture-specific perspective may include use and preference of a specific language, preference for certain diets and costumes, and cultural perceptions of law and religion (Ruiz & Casas, 1981). In terms of interpersonal relationships, culture-specific clients may reside in ethnic enclaves and tend to sustain transactions primarily from the culture group membership. Bilingualism and biculturalism, according to LeVine and Padilla (1980) may not be sufficient qualities to satisfy the treatment needs of this clientele. They imply that the services of mainstream mental health facilities may be inap-

propriate, unless indigenous forms of helping are incorporated into the system.

Treatment. The enhancement of cross-cultural counseling, dependent on numerous variables, is associated most significantly with the congruence of assessment and treatment with the world views and experiences of the client. In taking into account the varying world views of ethnic minority clients, several treatment strategies might be proposed for working with ethnosexual problems. Solomon (1982) states that what is needed for delivering effective direct service are not new theories but additional concepts which take into account the Black American experience in this society. The statement might be generalized to Hispanic Americans and Asian and Pacific Islander Americans. It is possible, therefore, to modify culture-general theories and techniques to more closely match the world views and needs of ethnic minority clients.

In a review of treatment programs for sexual dysfunctions, Wyatt, Strayer, and Lobitz (1976) note that, although many treatment procedures are amplifications of behavior therapy, other aspects of treatment derive from cognitive and humanistic psychology. In discussing the appropriateness of such treatment programs for Black Americans, they suggest that such strategies are useful if modifications are made. For example, an educational model in which discussions of how myths of Black sexuality affect self-image and interpersonal relations may precede the identification of treatment goals and actual treatment planning. Support therapy, role-playing, and homework assignments may comprise other dimensions of treatment. The following vignette, taken from a case study provided by Wyatt, Strayer, and Lobitz (1976), demonstrates an appreciation of world views and cultural experience in the prescription of treatment.

VIGNETTE I

Clients A and B: Bicultural, Black American couple.

Presenting Problem: Sexual dysfunction due to internalization of hypersexual stereotype. Client A felt inadequate and inferior because his body build and sexual performance did not match the hypersexual black image. He experienced premature ejaculations which restricted his ability to bring his wife, Client B, to orgasm.

Intervention: The female-male, black-white cotherapy team combined educational discussions on the effect of myths of Black sexuality with a more directive behavior approach to sexual activities. Client A was instructed to explore areas of his body which increased his sexual arousal and to communicate this to Client B. Client B was instructed to lessen her partner's performance anxiety by giving him supportive verbal statements. Homework assignments were given to be carried out in the privacy of their own home.

Mokuau-Matsushima, Tashima, and Murase (1982) conducted a study of Asian and Pacific Islander practitioners working with Asian and Pacific Islander clients. They found that practitioners tended to use cognitive-behavioral theories with sexual concerns, and use psychodynamic and existential (phenomenological) theories with intrapsychic problems such as depression and low self-esteem. The selection of theories by the practitioners was based on the assumption that basic values relating to the family, interpersonal relationships, and role status and expectations should be taken into account.

VIGNETTE II

Client C: Culture-general world views; third-generation Japanese female residing in Los Angeles, California.

Presenting Problem: Client reports depression and communicates a low self-image. She feels unable to "compete" with the American ideal of physical beauty as typified by media models who are tall, "busty," and blonde. Diminutive and dark, she will never be the stereotypic blue-eyed and blonde California beauty.

Intervention: Once the worker-client relationship was engaged, techniques from the existential-humanistic and psychodynamic schools focusing on client self-exploration were used. Through the use of techniques such as reflection and clarification, the client was encouraged to see how external factors (e.g., media, friends) influenced her perceptions of physical beauty. More importantly, she was encouraged to see how she also contributed to her own sense of physical inferiority by validating the stereotypic concepts of beauty. With the identification of "causal" factors, came an opportunity to express feelings. The worker also utilized behavioral rehearsal and assertiveness training to get Client C to gain a sense of confidence in her social interactions, and concurrently, a sense of confidence in herself.

For those ethnic minority clients who maintain culture-specific world views, more drastic modifications of counseling theories may be needed. Black, Hispanic, and Asian and Pacific Islander cultures have evolved folk systems to explain illness, which some members of these groups adhere to. It is possible and feasible to demonstrate culturally relevant practice by integrating professional theories of intervention with these folk system treatment strategies. For example, it is appropriate to combine *curanderismo* (folk medicine practiced by some individuals of Mexican descent) and psychotherapeutic treatment for some Hispanic clients (LeVine and Padilla, 1980); herbal medicine and cognitive-behavioral therapy for Asian and Pacific Islanders; and spiritual healing with the vast array of psychodynamic therapies for Black Americans (Mendes, 1982). In cases of integration, it would be ideal to have a bicultural/bilingual worker who could maintain comprehension as the client shifts from one culture to another (Ruiz and Casas, 1981).

The degree to which folk-healing resources are actually utilized by ethnic minority persons is not extensively documented, and those reports reviewed indicate low utilization (Manzanedo, Walters, Lorig, 1980; Mokuau-Matsushima, Tashima, Murase, 1982; Karnos & Morales, 1971); however, these accounts may be more a reflection of research design and sampling than actual utilization, and it would behoove the practitioner to at least be familiar with indigenous systems and open to the possibilities of collaborating with community folk and spiritual healers.

Among some Blacks, religious beliefs

have been a sustaining factor in dealing with social and psychological needs. In contemporary Black American communities, religious beliefs are manifested in many different ways, including—in addition to mainstream perspectives—guilt meditation, chants, whispered prayers to saints, spirit possession, and "holy dances" done to syncopated rhythms of trumpets, drums, and tambourines (Mendes, 1982, p. 204). In addition, Mendes (1982) has illustrated how some Black Americans burn candles, purchase charms, and consult spiritualists located in storefront churches.

Among Hispanic Americans, some Mexican Americans subscribe to folk beliefs or *curanderismo,* Puerto Rican to *espiritismo,* and some Cubans to *santeria* (LeVine & Padilla, 1980). It is believed that physical or supernatural events can contribute to illness by upsetting the body's balance. The body maintains a balance between hot and cold—illness results when an excess of heat or cold destroys the equilibrium (Macklin, 1980). Commonly recognized illnesses include *mal de ojo* (evil eye), characterized by headaches and nausea; *susto* (soul loss or severe fright), characterized by decreased appetite, restlessness, and withdrawal; and *embrujado* (bewitchment) characterized by constipation and nervousness (LeVine & Padilla, 1980; Macklin, 1980).

LeVine and Padilla (1980) noted that treatment employs herbal tonics, elaborate ritual (e.g., housecleaning practices), massage, ventroliquism, confession, prayers, sacrifice, admonitions, and may be utilized without any reference to psychological causes.

In Asian and Pacific Islander culture, many diverse forms of culture-specific treatment exist including herbal medicine and spiritual therapy. Herbal medicine and spiritual therapy are strongly influenced by a holistic approach to health in which the mind and body are inseparable. Herbal medicine is treatment that attempts to restore a balance of functioning. Spiritual treatment may involve consultation with spirit doctors, folk healers, and religious leaders in order to exorcise or appease offended spirits (Moon, Tashima & Murase, 1982).

The family is important in Black, Hispanic, and Asian and Pacific Islander cultures, and folk-healing treatment tends to emphasize the role of the family. Treatment procedures revolve around familial role expectations and obligations, and, as such, family members may be actively and directly involved in the treatment process.

Knowledge of folk-healing systems provides the practitioner with information from which a more accurate assessment might be made and appropriate treatment planned. For example, what practitioners assume to be sexually deviant may in fact be a normal manifestation of coping within the client's culture. A practitioner may choose to work collaboratively with a folk healer, or refer the client to work exclusively with the folk healer.

VIGNETTE III

Client D: Culture-specific world views; first-generation, Mexican-American female.

Presenting Problem: Severe depression resulting from a medical procedure in which she was sterilized without her consent. Depression manifested itself through withdrawal, decrease of appetite, and fatigue.

Intervention: Client D was referred by hospital staff to a bicultural/bilingual counselor. The worker decided to seek the assistance of a community folk healer because of the client's disillusionment with the Western medical system, and her spiritual belief of "susto," an experience being influenced by supernatural events. Client D believed that her sterile state was related to her vision of a supernatural event several years prior in which she recalled the traumatic death of an infant. Treatment lasted for several weeks and involved a combination of behavioral procedure with prayer, and herbal tonics. Client D's husband was directly involved throughout the process.

In summary, the provision of culturally responsive counseling services derives from an integration of several variables:

1. A practitioner's understanding of self, and the impact of his or her world views on the therapeutic relationship
2. A practitioner's understanding of the variations of ethnic minority clients' world views
3. A practitioner's knowledge of mainstream theories and techniques of counseling as well as folk-healing systems
4. A practitioner's ability to transpose all this information into appropriate assessment and treatment

Inherent in this integration is the practitioner's commitment to helping and the basic belief that, by helping ethnic minorities achieve their right to responsible sexual expression, we will also be addressing the reduction if not eradication of ethnosexual oppression and racism.

SOCIAL SYSTEM INTERVENTION

Effective intervention for problems of ethnosexual oppression must be flexible and comprehensive in its incorporation of two, closely related forms of intervention: services to individuals and families as well as strategies directed at the social systems level (macrolevel). Sexual oppression against ethnic minority peoples is interrelated and enmeshed in the various social systems. Attempts to change these systems would necessitate a comprehensive understanding and working knowledge of major institutions such as law and politics, business and labor, economics, education, health and mental health, and the interrelationships of these various systems. As Davis (1978) suggests, patterns of discrimination involve interlocking institutional arrangements, and it is difficult to know where to begin in efforts to change such systems. It is beyond the scope of this chapter to describe all the systems that impact on ethnosexual oppression; however, by overviewing one institution, mental health, it is believed that strategies of intervention specifically focused on sexual oppression could be generalized to all major

institutions. For example, a human service worker may assume roles of planner, advocate, or educator for developing, modifying, or completely changing services available in the various social systems. Although content and direction of services may vary from one system to another, the roles of the worker and the means of intervention will tend to be the same.

Miranda and Kitano (1976) attribute the low utilization of mental health facilities by ethnic minorities to an inefficient service delivery system characterized as fragmented, inaccessible, and unaccountable. *Fragmentation* implies an ineffective organization of mental health services in which human services agencies operate according to singular goals without adequate linkages to other resources. The result is the compartmentalizing of clients' needs and difficulties in providing services for clients with multiple problems (Baker & Northman, 1981). Inaccessibility *refers* in large part to the geographical placement of mental health facilities outside of ethnic communities. LeVine and Padilla (1980) state that because mental facilities are often divorced from the Hispanic community, residents may not be aware of existing services (p. 141). Further, virtually all ethnic minority communities have experienced difficulties in influencing the structure and processes of mental health systems. Two intervention strategies that are useful in addressing such concerns at the systems level are social action and social planning.

Social action. The social activist must aggressively advocate several reforms—a redistribution in power, in resources, and in decision making—if the provision of mental health services are to be comprehensive, accessible, and accountable to ethnic minority communities. To effect such change, social activists may either stress task or process goals (Johnson, 1982). Task goals may be perceived as the accomplishment of a definitive objective, and process goals as gradual changes leading to a particular result. Here, a task goal might be the modification of hiring practices so that more ethnic minority persons are hired by mental health centers. Treatment programs for sexual dysfunctions have, for example, been staffed by white practitioners (Wyatt, Strayer & Lobitz, 1976); the failure to hire and train adequate numbers of minority professionals may be in part responsible for low utilization of services. The hiring of bicultural/bilingual workers may increase the accountability and responsiveness of mental health programs to sexual concerns of ethnic minority persons, because of cultural compatibility regarding perceptions of sexual experiences, mental health and mental illness, diagnostic practices, process and outcome measures of treatment.

Another example of a task goal is the development of services structured around providing comprehensive services in ethnic communities. Ethnic authorities suggest that multiple-service agencies located within ethnic communities increase the relevance of services to Black Americans, Hispanic Americans, and Asian and Pacific Islander Americans (LeVine & Padilla, 1980; Atkinson, Morten & Sue, 1979). The barrio service center illustrates the community center staffed by bicultural/bilingual staff who address a variety of client needs ranging from basic economic services (for example, bank loans, unemployment) to all forms of therapy. Possible role responsibilities of the social-actionists may include organizing citizen participation to assess the scope of services needed to meet the community's unique circumstances. Persons interested in advancing the needs and concerns of the sexually oppressed may, for example, participate in community advisory groups. A community advisory group can assure agency goals and operations will coincide with varying community interests and needs through policy formulation, financial planning, treatment specification, and the evaluation of services.

Related to these task goals is a process goal: holding a series of "open forums"

which focus on in-service training of staff in the skills necessary to effectively assess and treat problems of ethnosexual oppression. These open forums serve as educational vehicles on such topics as sexual myths, and the degree these myths permeate the greater community and affect self-concept and intra- and cross-cultural relations.

Task and process goals require that the human service worker take direct action against the prevailing power structure and be involved in labor unions, civil rights groups, welfare rights organizations, minority power groups, and so on. The intention is to organize and mobilize the sexually oppressed so that they may "place demands on the 'system' for better treatment, have more input in decision-making, and an increased sharing of societal resources" (Johnson, 1982, p. 320).

Social planning. Social planning, the second intervention strategy, seeks through the process of rational analysis to bring about planned and controlled change. The tangible improvement of the mental health system in terms of comprehensiveness, accessibility, and accountability may rely on technical fact-finding, needs assessment, program implementation, and program evaluation. Since community-oriented programs emphasize focusing on the particular needs of the populations being served (Baker & Northman, 1981), needs assessment, mentioned above, will be used to illustrate some general points.

The field survey is one way to conduct needs assessments. This is the collection of information through interviews and/or questionnaires from a sample of the population in a specified community. The basic strategy is to encourage fact-finding in areas such as the nature and incidence of the problem, who is affected, financial and social costs, and coping mechanisms/resources used. Given an increasing scarcity of funds for social programs, information from such surveys may be useful as lobbying tools to justify increased funds for ethnic communities from federal and state sources. For example, census statistics reveal that families headed by ethnic females tend to be an increasing component of the American population. Economic and social vulnerability is evident in low employment figures, inadequate housing, public assistance barriers, and educational difficulties. In a survey conducted by Wagner and Schaffer (1980), Hispanic and Black women who were heads of families reported that social networks comprised of family and friends helped them to meet their family's physical, social and emotional needs. The implication is that mental health services directed toward sexual discrimination and ethnic minority women should take into account the importance of resource networks and plan programs accordingly. One possibility may be to allow for greater involvement of family and friends in treatment; another might be more community outreach so that individuals may be treated in familiar systems. Social planners subscribe to the idea that social change may be best pursued through a wide range of participation and people at the community level. A detailed needs assessment can enhance the efficiency of service delivery, particularly if citizens from the community have some form of "delegated power" (Baker & Northman, 1981, p. 139) in the planning and actual implementation of the study.

Intervention strategies such as social action and social planning utilize a variety of practitioner roles, many which were presented in more detail in Chapter 4: activist, trainer/consultant, educator, mobilizer, planner, evaluator, outreach worker. The dearth of literature on ethnosexual oppression and social system strategies is dismaying. There is great need for research focused on attempts to handle problems of sexual oppression for Black Americans, Hispanic Americans, and Asian and Pacific Islander Americans at the social systems level. Until we can educate the public and restructure the major institutions of our society, the sexual freedom of these ethnic minority groups cannot be actualized.

CONCLUSION

This chapter is based on the premise that racism underlies ethnosexual oppression. There is no simple solution for the eradication of racism or the elimination of ethnosexual oppression. But acknowledgement of the complexity and pervasiveness of the problem is no reason for inaction. The beginning for the human service worker is to nurture the sense of commitment and compasion for all peoples, to build the knowledge base of cultural experience, world views, and values, and to cultivate the ability and skills to sensitively translate and implement direct practice and social systems strategies to the sexual problems of ethnic minority peoples. This is our first step.

REFERENCES

ANDRADE, S. J. Family planning practices of Mexican-Americans. In M. B. Melville, ed. *Twice a minority, Mexican-American women.* St. Louis: C. V. Mosby, 1980.

ATKINSON, D. R., MORTEN, G., AND SUE, D. W., EDS. *Counseling American minorities, a cross cultural perspective.* Iowa: Wm. C. Brown Company Publishers, 1979.

BAKER, F., AND NORTHMAN, J. E. *Helping, human services for the 80s.* St. Louis: C. V. Mosby, 1981.

BASS, B. A. The validity of sociocultural factors in the assessment and treatment of Afro-Americans. In B. A. Bass, G. E. Wyatt, and G. J. Powell, eds. *The Afro-American family.* New York: Grune and Stratton, 1982.

BLAUNER, R. *Racial oppression in America.* New York: Harper and Row, 1972.

CARTER, S. H. Some perspectives on black male sexuality. In D. Kunkel, ed. *Sexual issues in social work.* Honolulu: School of Social Work, University of Hawaii, 1979.

CROMWELL, R. E., AND RUIZ, R. A. The myth of macho dominance in decision making within Mexican and Chicano families. *Hispanic Journal of Behavioral Science,* December 1979, 1:355–373.

DANIELS, R., AND KITANO, H. L. *American racism: exploration of the nature of prejudice.* Englewood Cliffs, N.J.: Prentice-Hall, Inc., 1970.

DAVENPORT, W. H. Sex in cross-cultural perspective. In Beach, ed. *Human sexuality in four perspectives.* Baltimore: Johns Hopkins University Press, 1977.

DAVIS, J. F. *Minority-dominant relations.* Chicago: AHM Publishing Corporation, 1978.

DRAGUNS, J. G. Counseling across cultures: Common themes and distinct approaches. In P. Pedersen, W. J. Lonner, and J. G. Draguns, eds. *Counseling across cultures.* Honolulu: University Press of Hawaii, 1976.

GOCHROS, J. S. Sex and race: Some further issues for social work practitioners. In D. Kunkel, ed. *Sexual issues in social work.* Honolulu: School of Social Work, University of Hawaii, 1979.

GREEN, J. W. *Cultural awareness in the human services.* Englewood Cliffs, N.J.: Prentice-Hall, Inc., 1982.

HERNTON, C. *Sex and racism in American Society.* New York: Grove Press, 1965.

IVEY, A., AND AUTHIER, J. Microcounseling. Springfield, Ill.: Charles Thomas Publishers, 1978.

JOHNSON, H. W. *The social services, an introduction.* Illinois: F. E. Peacock Publishers, Inc., 1982.

JOHNSON, L. B. Blacks. In H. L. Gochros and J. S. Gochros, eds. *The sexually oppressed.* New York: Association Press, 1977.

KARDINER, A., AND OVESEY, L. *The mark of oppression.* Cleveland: World, 1951.

KARNO, M., AND MORALES, A. A community mental health service for Mexican-Americans in a metropolis. In N. N. Wagner and M. J. Haug, eds. *Chicanos: Social and psychological perspectives.* St. Louis: C. V. Mosby, 1971.

KITANO, H. L. Race relations. Englewood Cliffs, N.J.: Prentice-Hall, Inc., 1974.

KNOWLES, L., AND PREWITT, K. *Institutional racism in America.* Englewood Cliffs, N.J.: Prentice-Hall, Inc., 1969.

LEVINE, E. S., AND PADILLA, A. M. *Crossing cultures in therapy: Pluralistic counseling for the Hispanics.* Monterey, Calif.: Brooks/Cole Publishing Co., 1980.

MACCOBY, M. On Mexican national character. In N. N. Wagner and M. J. Haug, eds. *Chicanos: Social and psychological perspectives.* St. Louis: C. V. Mosby, 1971.

MACKLIN, J. All the good and the bad in this world. In M. B. Melville, ed. *Twice a minority: Mexican-American women.* St. Louis: C. V. Mosby, 1980.

MANZANEDO, H. G., WALTERS, E. G., AND LORIG, K. R. Health and illness perceptions of the Chicana. In M. B. Melville, ed. *Twice a minority: Mexican-American women.* St. Louis: C. V. Mosby, 1980.

MATSUSHIMA-MOKUAU, N., TASHIMA, N., AND MURASE, K. *Mental Health treatment modalities of Pacific Asian American practitioners.* San Francisco: Pacific Asian Mental Health Research Project, 1982.

MENDES, H. A. The role of religion in psychotherapy with Afro-Americans. In B. A. Bass, G. E. Wyatt, and G. J. Powell, eds. *The Afro-American Family.* New York: Grune and Stratton, 1982.

MIRANDA, M., AND KITANO, H. L. Barriers to mental health: A Japanese and Mexican dilemma. In C. A. Hernandez, M. Haug, and N. Wagner, eds. *Chicanos: Social and psychological perspectives,* 2nd ed. St. Louis: C. V. Mosby, 1976.

MOON, A., TASHIMA, N., AND MURASE, K. Help-seeking behavior and attitudes of Southeast Asian refugees. San Francisco: Pacific Asian Mental Health Research Project, 1982.

MURASE, K. Mental health treatment for Pacific Asian Americans. Pacific Asian Mental Health Research Project Grant #95-171691-A1. Washington, D.C.: National Institute of Mental Health Grant, 1979.

OGAWA, D. Asian Americans. In H. L. Gochros and J. S. Gochros, eds. *The sexually oppressed.* New York: Association Press, 1977.

————. *From Jap to Japanese: the evolution of Japanese-American stereotypes.* Berkeley: McCutchan Publishing Corporation, 1971.

PEDERSEN, P., DRAGUNS, J. G., LONNER, W. J., AND TRIMBLE, J. E. *Counseling across cultures.* Honolulu: University Press of Hawaii, 1981.

PEDERSEN, P. The cultural inclusiveness of counseling. In P. Pedersen, J. G. Draguns, W. J. Lonner, and J. E. Trimble, eds. *Counseling across cultures.* Honolulu: University Press of Hawaii, 1981.

POUSSAINT, A. Cheap thrills that degrade blacks. *Psychology Today.* February 1974, 22–23.

RUIZ, R. A., AND CASAS, M. M. Culturally relevant and behavioristic counseling for Chicano college students. In P. Pedersen, J. G. Draguns, W. J. Lonner, and J. E. Trimble. *Counseling across cultures.* Honolulu: University Press of Hawaii, 1981.

SIMMONS, O. G. The mutual images and expectations of Anglo-Americans and Mexican-Americans. In N. N. Wagner and M. J. Haug, eds. *Chicanos: Social and psychological perspectives*. St. Louis: C. V. Mosby, 1971.

SOLOMON, B. B. The delivery of mental health services to Afro-Americans and their families: Translating theory into practice. In B. A. Bass, G. E. Wyatt, and G. J. Powell, eds. *The Afro-American Family*. New York: Grune and Stratton, 1982.

STAPLES, R. The myth of the impotent black male. *The Black Scholar*, 2(10): June 1971.

SUE, S., AND MCKINNEY, H. Asian-Americans in the community mental health system. *American Journal of Orthopsychiatry*, 1975, 45(1):111–118.

SUZUKI, B. H. Education and the socialization of Asian Americans: A revisionist analysis of the "model minority" thesis. In R. Endo, S. Sue, and N. N. Wagner, eds. *Asian-Americans: Social and psychological perspectives*—vol. II. Palo Alto, Calif.: Science and Behavior Books, Inc., 1980.

UNITED STATES DEPARTMENT OF COMMERCE. Bureau of the Census, 1980.

URDANETA, M. L. Chicana use of abortion: The case of Alcala. In M. B. Melville, ed. *Twice a minority: Mexican-American women*. St. Louis: C. V. Mosby, 1980.

VELEZ-I, C. G. The nonconsenting sterilization of Mexican women in Los Angeles: Issues of psychocultural rupture and legal redress in paternalistic behavioral environments. In M. B. Melville, ed. *Twice a minority: Mexican-American women*. St. Louis: C. V. Mosby, 1980.

VONTRESS, C. E. Racial and ethnic barriers in counseling. In P. Pedersen, J. G. Draguns, W. J. Lonner, and J. E. Trimble, eds. *Counseling across cultures*. Honolulu: University Press of Hawaii, 1981.

WAGNER, N. N. AND HAUG, M. J., EDS. *Chicanos: Social and psychological perspectives*. St. Louis: C. V. Mosby, 1971.

WAGNER, R., AND SCHAFFER, D. Social networks and survival strategies: An exploratory study of Mexican-American, black, and Anglo female heads in San Jose, California. In M. B. Melville, ed. *Twice a minority: Mexican-American women*. St. Louis: C. V. Mosby, 1980.

WEISS, M. S. Selective acculturation and the dating process: the pattern of Chinese-Caucasian inter-racial dating. In S. Sue and N. N. Wagner, eds. *Asian Americans: psychological perspectives*. Palo Alto, Calif.: Science and Behavior Books, Inc., 1973.

WILLIAMS, L. Sex, racism and social work. In H. L. Gochros and L. G. Schultz, eds. *Human sexuality and social work*. New York: Association Press, 1972.

WYATT, G. E. Identifying stereotypes of Afro-American sexuality and their impact upon sexual behavior. In B. A. Bass, G. E. Wyatt, and G. J. Powell, eds. *The Afro-American Family*. New York: Grune and Stratton, 1982.

WYATT, G. E., STRAYER, R., AND LOBITZ, W. Issues in the treatment of sexually dysfunctioning couples of Afro-American descent. *Psychotherapy: Theory, Research, and Practice*, 1976, 13:44–50.

CHAPTER
12

GAY MEN
Raymond M. Berger

"Will all heterosexuals please stand and move into the aisles?" Pandemonium reigned when a social work lecturer recently made this request in a large undergraduate class. This consciousness-raising exercise illustrated three important truths about homosexuality in contemporary society: (1) most people are uncomfortable about homosexuality; (2) there is confusion in the public mind about what it is; and (3) homosexuality, like heterosexuality, is the result of an arbitrary social process. While the majority group determines how normative and deviant behavior will be socially defined, alternative views are available to upset the majority world view. In the 1980s this is the reality facing helping professionals attempting to understand this area.

Although societal rejection was the theme of pre-gay-liberation homosexuality, the flavor of the current era is ambivalence. We can talk about it now, we can recognize that the phenomenon is widespread, that gay people have some rights, perhaps even that we know some gay people who are "all right." But we cannot advocate for it, we cannot abandon some controls over it, and we cannot talk about how uncomfortable it continues to make us. In these respects human service workers are no different from any other group.

Still, the actions of helping professionals touch the lives of gay people every day. It is important that our knowledge be accurate, that it reflect not only the majority perspective but, more importantly, the perspective of gays themselves. Practitioners must be aware of the ways in which other labels— "client," "parent," "alcoholic," "spouse,"— combine with homosexuality. And we must know what the gay community is doing on its own and how we can be a part of it, and that we ponder future avenues for our involvement.

The purpose of this chapter, then, is to define and describe this population, to review areas for possible intervention, to review ways in which gays experience oppression, to propose organizational and policy interventions directed at alleviating this oppression, and to briefly note areas deserving the future attention of professionals.

THE PROBLEM

Demographic Basis

Paraphrasing the title of a popular book, some homosexuals of the early 1960s proclaimed that every "sixth man" was gay (Stearn, 1961). Those conservatives who objected to the sensationalism of this claim would not have been much comforted by the truth.

From the perspective of sexual behavior and fantasies alone—lifestyles were not considered in determining the figures—the survey data collected by the Institute for Sex Research and Alfred Kinsey in the late 1940s remain the best estimates of incidence. The subsequent outcry against the Kinsey studies was partly a reaction to the finding that fully 37 percent of white American males had had at least some overt homosexual experience during adulthood (Kinsey, Pomeroy & Martin, 1948, p. 650). It seemed almost as if most American males had a "touch" of it, reinforcing psychoanalytic theories about polymorphous and latent sexuality. (In fact, Kinsey et al. reported that about half of all males had had some overt or psychic homosexual experience in adulthood).

A reasonable interpretation of the Kinsey data is that about 10 to 13 percent of adult males are predominantly or exclusively homosexual at any given time. In numbers alone, this makes the male homosexual minority nearly as large as the black minority, and certainly larger than other minorities which have achieved a much larger claim of public and governmental attention. Gays are not a group to be ignored.

Social Basis

Kinsey was certainly correct to study human sexual behavior by measuring the incidence of overt same-sex contact and self-reported fantasies. So little was known at the time about *any* aspect of human sexual functioning that it was important to select dependent variables that were simple and subject to rechecking by alternate interviewers. Unfortunately, the Kinsey incidence figures are often used with the implication that the respondents in the "homosexual" categories were self-identified homosexuals. But the truth is that the link between an individual's overt sexual behavior and fantasies, on the one hand, and his self-image as "heterosexual" or "homosexual," on the other, is often incomplete or entirely absent. This was illustrated by Riess's (1967) study of male adolescents who regularly engaged in fellatio with adult males but never thought of themselves as homosexual, and never developed adult homosexual "careers." This phenomenon is in fact widespread (Berger, 1983b). Careful perusal of the Kinsey incidence figures themselves suggests that this must be the case, since the number of self-identified homosexual men is certainly less than the number who have significant homosexual histories as revealed in the Kinsey study.

This incongruence between behaviors/fantasies and self-identification ought to alert us to a central feature of homosexuality in our society: its arbitrariness. In fact, if many (perhaps most) men have some homosexual component but only a few are gay, why are there gay people at all?

Imagine that Dr. Kinsey had studied the eating, rather than the sexual, behavior of American men. It is conceivable that he would have found that a sizeable portion of the male population ate only nonmeat foods during some portion of their adult lives, and that a much smaller but nonetheless significant minority were exclusive vegetarians.

The differences between our hypothetical vegetarians and gay men should be obvious. Vegetarians are not oppressed. They don't harbor a secret that may harm their relations with family, or friends, or may limit or destroy their career opportunities. Their interpersonal relationships are largely unaffected. They are not condemned and subjected to "treatment" by clergy, physicians, psychiatrists, and social workers. Professionals do not seek to explain the causes of their vegetarianism by looking for weak fathers, overly intimate mothers, or poor heredity. Although they may have special organizations, clubs, and support groups, their ability to be who they are without fear and anxiety is uninhibited. Although some groups in society believe that certain eating habits are immoral (for example, Jews who eat pork; formerly, Catholics who ate meat on Fridays), on the whole it isn't considered that important. We tolerate wide diversity in eating without making it a determinant of the eater's *core* identity. Not so with sex. Eating a vegetable doesn't make you a vegetarian. But sleeping with a member of your own sex, even once, in the eyes of some people makes you a "homosexual."

Even though eating has more immediate survival value than sex, our society is less concerned with regulating eating behavior. Why? Smith (1975) suggested that advanced societies are able to progress only by regulating the sexual behavior of their members through laws and customs, in order to ensure survival of the group. An underpopulated society, for example, might prohibit homosexual relations and emphasize heterosexual coitus in order to ensure a high birth rate. In a world of rapid social change many restrictive laws and customs remain, even after they have lost their survival value. For instance, in the overpopulated societies of the twentieth century, homosexuality, once dysfunctional, might actually enhance survival by keeping the birth rate low. But the old prohibitions continue for some time. It is within this context that human service professionals traditionally have sought to eradicate or contain homosexual behavior in the interests of the heterosexual majority.

Old Model

Since the helping professions receive their mandate from society, it is not surprising that until recently helping professionals served as agents of social control. They did so by defining homosexuality as an illness. Just as the priests of earlier eras legitimized the appropriateness of their efforts to control homosexuals by declaring homosexuality to be a sin, modern-day physicians, psychiatrists, psychologists, and social workers brought homosexuality into their purview by declaring it an illness (Szasz, 1970). Most of the helping professions took an antihomosexual position early in their development when they adopted conservative psychoanalytic theories beginning in the 1930s. Although Freud (1951, p. 252) himself did not consider homosexuality an illness, his followers certainly did, and they have been and continue to be the most ardent antihomosexualists (Bayer, 1981).

Despite its position as champion of the underdog, social work has lagged behind psychiatry and psychology in recognizing the legitimacy of homosexuality, as evidenced by the actions of the respective professional organizations. Perhaps it is not surprising then that, in a recent survey of social workers, psychologists, and other mental health practitioners, social workers were found to be the most homophobic (disapproving of and fearful of homosexuality) (De Crescenzo & McGill, 1978, p. 63).

Until recently most clinicians took it for granted that a homosexual client should be treated for his homosexuality, that is, converted to heterosexuality. One must admire the tenacity with which practitioners held to this treatment goal in the complete absence of evidence that any kind of individual or group therapy could affect this change. Wasserman's chapter in a highly regarded text on social casework, published in its second edition in 1976, is a clear example of this traditional approach.

In that chapter, which is a detailed case

study of a troublesome 19-year-old boy, the "illness" model is evident in that the paper identifies the *primary symptom* as "homosexual acting-out behavior." The caseworker's homophobic revulsion of the client, fears of contagion, association of homosexuality with illness, and insistance on conversion, are evident in the case history:

Because of our limited knowledge in the treatment of sexual deviations such as overt homosexual behavior, we caseworkers approach individuals of this symptomology with understandable reluctance and hesitancy. (p. 250)

It is . . . difficult to determine at what point the adolescent is forming a homosexual, pathological adjustment which may become a fixed pattern and perhaps be irreversible, and what is merely the "temporary" acting-out which will gradually be replaced by stronger inner controls and defenses. (p. 251)

On his arrival at the treatment center he made a most promising, appealing, initial impression, but underneath the clean-cut, wholesome look was a deeply angry, damaged, frightened, sensitive, unloved child who had, in a large sense, given up on himself. (p. 252)

. . . he developed a strong homosexual attachment to a 12-year-old-boy. . . .At this time it became necessary to set up extra controls and supervision for A. to protect him as well as the other boys. . . .The group contagion of the problem. . . . can present considerable difficulties. . . .(pp. 252–253)

. . . A. was acting out and showing little concern about his behavior . . . it was decided that I continue to try to stir up his anxiety by pointing up his behavior as unacceptable . . . . (p. 253)

After five years of "treatment" the outcomes are modest but telling. Although the author warns us that "it would be deception to conclude that A. is now 'cured' . . . verbalization of his homosexual feelings lessened," and he was able to "keep these feelings under control." One wonders where the client is today.

This author has identified the major assumptions of the traditional model of practice which was applied with such conviction in the above case history (Berger, 1977):

1. Adult individuals are either exclusively heterosexual or homosexual, and same-sex behavior "interferes" with heterosexual functioning.
2. The homosexual is rarely encountered in typical human service settings.
3. The homosexual individual is readily identifiable; he is generally male and is recognized by a cluster of overt characteristics such as distinctive dress and mannerisms.
4. Homosexual behavior nearly always causes problems.
5. Homosexuality is an individual phenomenon and is the result of a person's psychological disturbance. (pp. 280–283)

None of these assumptions are true:

1. The Kinsey studies and subsequent research have revealed that most individuals have some combination of the homosexual and heterosexual in their histories (defined in terms of overt behavior and feelings). A minority of men function sexually with *both* men and women (Kinsey et al., 1948; Bell & Weinberg, 1978). In any case, male homosexuality does not result from a fear or revulsion of women, but from positive feelings toward men.
2. Homosexuals are a sizeable minority. Homosexuals and homosexual behavior occur with similar frequencies in every social, ethnic, geographic, economic, and religious group and can therefore be expected as a common phenomenon in the practice of most helping professionals (Kinsey et al., 1948).
3. Few male homosexuals can be distinguished on the basis of overt characteristics. Even trained clinicians have been unable to differentiate between heterosexuals and homosexuals using case histories and projective tests (Hooker, 1975).
4. Most homosexuals are well-adjusted (Bell & Weinberg, 1978, pp. 195–216; Berger, 1982, Chapter 10). Difficulties in adjustment are almost always due to a homophobic society.
5. Homosexuality is a socially determined label (Becker, 1963); it is not an illness. Homosexuals are no more likely than heterosexuals to suffer from mental illness (Gonsiorek, 1982).

To determine a more appropriate method for intervention with homosexuals, we need to review some definitions and to present a model showing the formation of the homosexuality identity.

Definitions

In order to understand this group it is useful to distinguish among three components of sexual identity that are sometimes confused (Berger, 1983a).

Gender identity. The term "gender identity" refers to the individual's self-perception as male or female, and is fixed irrevocably by the age of four or five. The unshakable nature of one's feeling of being male or female is illustrated by unsuccessful attempts to change the sex of assignment after this age, with children who have been incorrectly assigned at birth as a result of genital abnormalities (Green, 1975).

Gender role. The term "gender role" denotes a set of behaviors which are believed to be appropriate for a male or female. For example, in traditional western culture men are expected to be strong, unemotional, and aggressive while women are expected to embody opposite characteristics. In advanced industrial societies there is currently much controversy about gender role differences, spurred on by the changing role of women and by the feminist movement. Even so, differences between men and women in gender role behaviors are nearly universal although the specific differences vary within and between cultures.

Sexual orientation. The term "sexual orientation" refers to individual, adult sexual preferences. Individuals who desire sexual and affectional relationships primarily with members of the opposite sex are said to be heterosexual. Same-sex preferences indicate a homosexual orientation. Although in the popular mind sexual orientation is determined solely by one's sexual desires, in fact, whether one prefers a primary emotional relationship with the same or opposite sex is also an important component.

Because many people, including some gay clients, confuse the components of sexual identity—gender identity, gender role, and sexual orientation—it is important for the practitioner to distinguish among them. It is culturally expected that a person of the male gender will perceive of himself as male (gender identity), will act like a male (gender role), and will be heterosexual (sexual orientation). When this image is upset, as in the case of a male who is homosexual, confusion begins. The homosexual male is thought by some to have a female gender identity and a female gender role. Although this is possible, as in the case of the transexual, the vast majority of all males—homosexual and heterosexual—think of themselves as male and act in ways typical of men. Thus, each component of sexual identity must be considered separately.

Helping professionals often confront these issues with a client who has had isolated intimate experiences with the same sex or who is beginning to recognize homosexual feelings. The client may be terrified of "becoming" homosexual, because he believes that homosexual men have female gender identities or gender roles. Since he is not like that, or does not want to be like that, he is left without a reference group and without a label with which to categorize his troublesome feelings and experiences. By clarifying the components of sexual identity, the practitioner can assist the client in his journey to an appropriate self-identity.

But practitioners must know more. They must also know how an individual comes to possess a homosexual identity, in his own eyes and in those of others. How does a homosexual come to be?

Identity Formation

The author has proposed a model to explain homosexual identity formation (Berger, 1983b). The model recognizes that the process by which an individual comes to be homosexual is complex and involves a number of factors within the individual and his environment. Three independent tasks are involved in achieving a homosexual identity: sexual encounter, social reaction, and identity. The tasks are independent in that each may occur without the others, although they often occur simultaneously.

Sexual encounter involves intimate physical contact with a member of the same sex. When the individual is publicly labeled by others (for instance, peers or co-workers) as homosexual, the *social reaction* task has occurred.

Identity actually refers to a series of tasks culminating in the individual's acceptance of himself as homosexual. Almost universally, this series of tasks begins with a period of *identity confusion* in which discrepant self-perceptions, feelings, and experiences collide within the individual's awareness. This is experienced as a subjective feeling of discomfort or distress. For instance, the individual may believe himself to be heterosexual but experience a homosexual love fantasy, or perhaps a sexual experience with a same-sex friend. It is discomfort with this identity confusion that propels the individual toward some resolution.

For the person who will come to have a homosexual identity, *self-labeling* as homosexual is crucial. Labeling oneself as homosexual is one way to resolve the pangs of identity confusion. It may be facilitated by one of the other tasks: sexual encounter or social reaction, by the individual's own feelings and fantasies, and by the availability of information about other homosexual individuals.

Once the individual begins to think of himself as homosexual, he faces the task of *managing* a "new" and usually hidden identity. This is the point at which "coming out" issues are most salient, although identity management is a task which most homosexuals must negotiate in some form throughout their lives. Should the individual come out to friends? to family members? at work? In what form should he reveal his identity, under what circumstances, and to which particular individuals? What are the costs and benefits of keeping a secret versus being open?

Almost all homosexuals use *peer association* with other homosexuals to help them resolve these issues of self-labeling and identity management, and to provide a source of support, companionship, and social validation. The peer group provides tangible and comforting evidence that others have pursued the same solution to the problems of identity confusion, offers models for successful coping with coming out and other life tasks, and provides a reference group which validates a homosexual lifestyle in the face of majority culture disapproval.

Successful resolution of sexual encounter, social reaction, and identity tasks results in *self-acceptance,* and is achieved by the vast majority of homosexuals, as evidenced by the repeated finding that homosexuals as a group cannot be distinguished from others on various measures of mental health (Gonsiorek, 1982). Self-acceptance means that the individual perceives himself to be a homosexual and that this perception is congruent with his other thoughts and feelings about himself.

IMPLICATIONS FOR INTERVENTION

Understanding the process of homosexual identity formation will enable the helping professional to carry out informed and sensitive interventions with clients and families struggling with issues of sexual orientation. A major implication of the model is that practitioners need to focus, more than has been the case in the past, on environmental variables. Although intraindividual factors, such as same-sex fantasies, play a role in individual adjustment, environmental factors like the reactions of others and the availability of a peer group may be equally important. And individual historical factors such as parent-child relationship, which have been a central concern of past interventions, may actually be of little or no importance to current adjustment of the client.

Another implication of the model is that homosexuality is not just something that "happens" to an individual. He is an active participant in determining his own career. So, unlike the traditional image of the homosexual as the victim of an illness caused by forces beyond his control, he is an actor making self-conscious choices. This is not to imply that homosexual feelings are freely chosen but rather that, given certain feelings toward the same sex, the individual can choose how those feelings will shape his life. And since self-acceptance results from the successful completion of consciously chosen tasks, it is possible to learn how to be *competent* in handling those tasks. This is certainly a more optimistic view of homosexuality, one which returns both responsibility and dignity to the individual, and, coincidentally, it also provides a role for helping professionals in assisting gay people to learn competence.

The author's model also reveals that there may be a discrepancy between self-labeling and overt behavior of the individual. The practitioner should not be dismayed by the client who has sexual contact with the same sex but denies being homosexual. Nor should the worker assume that such a client is a sociopathic liar or a "latent" homosexual. Efforts of the worker to label a client as homosexual when he does not label himself as such are misguided and are likely to result in "hidden agendas"—for example, "he really needs to recognize his homosexuality or to change his homosexuality"—and a broken client-practitioner relationship. In carrying out interventions, the key issue will be whether the current situation causes discomfort or negative consequences for the client or his significant others. If avoiding self-labeling as homosexual is functional for the client, then this may not be an appropriate area for intervention.

On the other hand, if the client is uncomfortable about the inconsistency between his self-perception and his behavior—that is, if he is in a state of identity confusion—the worker can facilitate resolution of this task by openly discussing the inconsistency and

helping the client through the tasks of homosexual identity formation, if that is appropriate.

The model also alerts us to the situation of the individual who is convinced he is homosexual in the absence of any overt sexual experience with the same sex. Fueled by an implicit bias in favor of heterosexuality, many practitioners make short shrift of the client's deeply felt homosexual feelings and subtly urge the client to abandon these feelings in favor of heterosexual expression. This sort of inappropriate intervention is most likely to occur with adolescent clients who may have not as yet established a firm sexual identity; but recurrent yet unacted homosexual desires also occur among some adult men, even those with extensive heterosexual histories (Berger, 1983b). Urging the client to dismiss these feelings as "incidental" or "unimportant" impedes the process toward self-acceptance for homosexual clients. The tasks of self-labeling, peer association, identity management, and self-acceptance are made more difficult.

Practitioners must also be sensitive to the role of social reaction in determining the identity of their clients. A client without homosexual feelings may nonetheless be labeled by his peers as homosexual, and may experience much distress as a result. This is particularly likely to happen to male adolescents who are effeminate or different in some way from their peers, since adolescent male culture is notoriously unaccepting of deviations from traditional male gender-role behavior. The labeled adolescent may come to believe that he is indeed homosexual, when he in fact has a strong heterosexual orientation. The role of the practitioner here is to help the adolescent distinguish his own identity apart from the judgments of his peer group.

Of course, many individuals who are self-identified as homosexual also suffer from the hostile reactions of others. Intense social disapproval is still a regular feature of the lives of most homosexuals, as well as a major deterrent to achieving self-acceptance (Paul,

1982). Homosexuals sometimes seek the help of professionals in coping with this problem. One of the author's clients, for example, was a man in his thirties who worked in a blue-collar setting, was separated from his wife, and had custody of their 8-year-old son. His work situation had become unbearable because of constant tormenting from his co-workers, who had publicly labeled him a "queer." He was particularly vulnerable because he also feared the hostile reaction of his parents and of his wife, both of whom were likely to challenge custody of his son if they discovered his homosexuality. Professionals can be helpful in these situations by assisting the client in decision making, suggesting coping strategies, and providing emotional support.

The author's model also suggests that a point of great anxiety for gay men is the period of identity confusion; it is at this point that many clients seek the help of a professional. The most important contribution that can be made by the practitioner at that time is to serve as a nonjudgmental and objective facilitator in the process of the client's own decision making. Is the client gay? If so, what implications does that have for the client's life from here on?

A good practitioner will meet three requirements. First, he or she will be sufficiently comfortable with his or her own sexual feelings so that the client's situation will not threaten the worker. Second, the practitioner will be comfortable in discussing intimate sexual issues. Finally, the practitioner will be truly unbiased: he or she will avoid the all too common tendency of mental health professionals to "push" their clients toward a heterosexual adaptation.

Moses and Hawkins (1982, p. 37) offer guidelines for helping the client to determine his sexual orientation. They suggest that the practitioner explore three areas with the client: sexual activity and relationships, affectional relationships, and the client's fantasies. Each of these should be reviewed historically and currently. To the extent that these components are consistent—for exam-

ple, sexual activity, affectional relationships, and fantasy all involving men—a clear sexual orientation will be apparent. Where incongruities exist—for example, a preference for men in sexual activity and for women in affectional relationships—the practitioner can clarify and validate the client's preferences. Moses and Hawkins also stress the importance of recognizing that sexual orientation exists on a continuum from "exclusive homoerotic" to "exclusive heteroerotic," and that mental health and good adjustment are independent of one's position on this continuum (pp. 39–40).

The author's model also indicates that peer association with other homosexuals is a necessary component in achieving self-acceptance. Professionals often see clients who are beginning to struggle with their perception of themselves as homosexual but who have not yet begun to interact with other homosexuals. These individuals are likely to suffer from poor self-esteem since they are constantly exposed to negative messages about homosexuals, as reflected in our homophobic society, without the benefit of a homosexual reference group to counter the negative messages with positive ones. Indeed, "gay is good," but the message isn't heard until gays seek each other out and form support systems.

Often a client in this position is reluctant to contact a gay organization, go to a gay bar, or involve himself with other gays. He may fear disclosure. He may have inaccurate information about the homosexual community: for instance, he may believe they are out to "seduce" him, even though he is not quite sure what he wants. Or he may simply lack the necessary information or social skills to accomplish this task. An informed practitioner can be useful on all counts.

The practitioner can help the client to plan contacts with other gays without jeopardizing his standing with family, friends, and employers. The practitioner can provide accurate information and debunk myths about gay people. He or she can share up-to-date information on gay community life, including social, political, and religious organizations, support groups and bars. Social skills training with use of coaching, modeling, rehearsal, and feedback is a very appropriate tool for maximizing the client's success in relating to others once he contacts a gay community resource (Duehn & Mayadas, 1976). Most cities have Gay Switchboards or other gay information and referral services that can be used by professionals and their gay clients. In the author's own experience, the most dramatic improvement in the lives of gay clients who are coming out occurs when these clients become involved in the local gay community.

In addition to knowledge about homosexual identity formation, professionals' understanding of gay men will be incomplete unless they are familiar with the various forms of antigay oppression.

Oppression

One of the greatest barriers to a better understanding of homosexuality has been society's refusal to believe that homosexuals are oppressed. Persons distinguished on the basis of race, ethnicity, and religion are at least perceived as members of distinct socially relevant groups. But many people think of homosexuals as troubled individuals rather than as members of a social group. Still, there should be little question that homosexuals constitute a social group, and one which is oppressed. This oppression takes many forms.

Unlike racial, ethnic, and religious minorities, homosexuals are oppressed even within their own families. Gays universally report that the most difficult aspect of "coming out" (revealing their sexual orientation) is worry over its impact on family members. Millions of gays hide their sexual orientation from their families. Hiding creates psychological strain between generations and causes myriad complications that inevitably lead to tension and eventual estrangement. Whether the individual is open or not, family members often create problems by pressuring

him to marry and raise children, rejecting his lover and friends, and being hostile to his lifestyle. Sometimes families reject the child outright. In response gays have learned to cultivate self-reliance and to form close bonds with friends (Berger, 1982b).

Employment is another area of concern for all homosexuals. When the individual's homosexuality is suspected or known, it may be difficult to get a job, to keep it, or to advance within it. In some settings the absence of a wife to serve a social function, and the fact that a single male does not fit easily into the "old boy network" present barriers to advancement. Ironically, this may take place even though the single or gay employee provides an advantage to his employer: in the absence of family responsibilities he is often the worker most able to accept assignments which require evening or weekend work or travel.

In some settings gay workers have the uncomfortable task of enduring antigay humor and other forms of homophobia. Homophobia is institutionalized in some occupations. For instance, law enforcement, blue-collar, and child-centered occupations such as teaching are notoriously homophobic, and even an exemplary gay employee is likely to lose his job if his sexual orientation becomes known. The San Diego County grand jury, for example, recently upheld the county sheriff's stated policy of refusing to hire gays as deputies (Burke, 1984). Most police departments have similar written or unwritten policies. In 1977 the supreme court of the state of Washington ruled that the Tacoma School District was justified in firing an outstanding teacher simply because the teacher admitted he was gay (*Gaylord* v. *Tacoma School District*, 1977); the U.S. Supreme Court has refused to review this case.

Gays also experience discrimination in housing. This is particularly likely to occur to gays who are coupled, and to older singles who are often assumed to be homosexual. Although some municipalities and two states (Pennsylvania and Wisconsin) prohibit such discrimination, in most areas it is legal to refuse to rent to gays. Many landlords prefer to rent to heterosexual couples, and better housing is often reserved for such couples. At many large universities, for instance, only heterosexual, not homosexual, couples are eligible for university subsidized housing.

With the recent epidemic of Acquired Immune Deficiency Syndrome (AIDS) among gay men, attention has focused on the difficulties gays experience in obtaining health care. Federal and state governments have been slow in appropriating funds for research and treatment (*Gay Men's Health Crisis,* 1983). Gay AIDS patients have been fired from their jobs and thrown out of their houses and apartments. Due to the fear of contamination on the part of health care providers, AIDS victims are often shockingly neglected or mistreated in hospitals, and social service agencies have provided few supportive services (Dowd, 1983). There are often barriers to obtaining income support such as Aid to the Disabled under Social Security.

The AIDS epidemic has served merely to highlight a health care system that already treats its gay patients badly. Health care providers are often uninformed about or insensitive to the unique sexually related health problems of gay men, most notably, atypical gonorrhea, hepatitis B, and enteric infections. Each of these requires special screening and treatment procedures which are often not forthcoming because of the patient's reluctance to admit he is gay and to the provider's insensitivity or hostility (Berger, 1983c).

Many religious institutions have actively or passively contributed to the oppression of gays. Religious groups have lobbied against civil rights protections, as in New York City, where the organized opposition of the Catholic Church over the past decade has been a major factor in the continuing defeat of a gay rights bill. Other religious groups spread bigotry and misinformation, prohibit same-sex relations among their members, or force conversion to heterosexuality. Few allow gay persons to become clergy. On the other hand, religious opposition to gays is not universal, and many groups such as the National Council of the Churches of Christ and the Central Conference of American Rabbis have been publicly supportive of gays and gay civil rights laws.

Gay men are often the victims of violent attacks. "Gay bashing" is a popular activity among some male adolescents, and gays are sometimes attacked going to or from gay functions, particularly if they are effeminate. Several local campaigns around gay rights ordinances have been characterized by attacks against gays, and gay neighborhoods are periodically attacked.

Like its closely related counterpart, violence against women, antigay violence is an almost institutionalized feature of our society. A homophobic criminal justice system has implicitly encouraged this violence. Police officers are often openly sympathetic to violent perpetrators and sometimes engage in violence themselves. They provide little support to the gay victim. Attacks are justified by blaming the victim: "What was he doing in a gay bar?" or "He shouldn't have been dressed like that." Police departments have been hostile to the rights of gays within their departments (most will not hire gays and will fire officers who become known as gay). In the few instances when violent perpetrators come to trial, judges often mete out light sentences since violence against gays is "understandable."

Although police are among the most homophobic of occupational groups, gays are getting some recognition even here. Some departments invite representatives of the local gay community to present educational talks to officers or to serve as community liaisons, and gay police officers themselves have begun to organize openly. (One example is Gay Officers Action League in New York City). San Francisco has become the first city to openly recruit gays as police officers.

The gay community has also responded. The National Gay Task Force (NGTF) sponsors an antiviolence project. The project conducts research on antigay violence, encourages better reporting by victims, and teaches preventive antiviolence measures to potential victims. Groups such as NGTF, as well as helping professionals, can also pressure the criminal justice system to be more responsive to the needs of gay victims.

The military has always been a source of oppression for gays. Despite screening procedures to exclude gays from service, millions of gays have served in the military (Bérubé, 1983). Until recently, discovery of homosexuality meant immediate dishonorable discharge. Thousands of gays who performed outstanding service for years, saw active duty, or were wounded, were subsequently removed from the service and stripped of all benefits. In recent times a number of gay servicemen and women have challenged this practice. The result has been that many gays are now able to obtain a general discharge which preserves their benefits, but the military continues to refuse to allow gays in the service. In 1981 the U.S. Court of Appeals for the Ninth Circuit ruled there was no constitutional right for gay people to serve in the military (*Beller* v. *Middendorf*).

Antigay policies have also characterized immigration. In the past, the Immigration and Naturalization Service (INS) refused to allow into the country any person known to be homosexual. This policy was based on the fact that the Public Health Service classified homosexuality as a "psychopathic personality disturbance." Although the Public Health Service has removed homosexuality from this category, the INS continues its exclusionary policy. Unlike married heterosexual couples, the citizenship of one partner does not confer citizenship rights on the other partner.

The legal system embodies much of society's oppressive stance toward homosexuals. Despite progress over the past decade, as some laws and court decisions have protected or extended gay rights, the legal system is most often directly punitive. Often it creates barriers for gays by ignoring their existence and leaving them in legal limbo.

Antisodomy statutes embody the punitive approach. In general, they proscribe specific sexual *acts* rather than *persons*. Nevertheless they are enforced primarily against gays, even though the greatest number of violators are heterosexual. In practice, these laws are seldom enforced, but they have been destructive to the gay community because they are used to justify other antigay laws and policies. For instance, sodomy statutes have been cited in defending the constitutionality of antisolicitation laws which are used to harass gay men. A phone company used the sodomy statute to justify the policy of refusing to list the name of a gay organization in the telephone book. Universities have refused to grant recognition and funding to gay student organizations on this basis. The argument is that a nondiscriminatory policy would encourage gays to come together for the purpose of breaking the antisodomy law. Currently, almost half the states have laws which restrict private adult consensual sex acts.

After the widely publicized campaign in Miami in 1976 over the passage of a gay rights ordinance, the civil rights of gay people became a national issue. The resulting backlash led to the first passage of laws aimed specifically against gays. For instance, Florida passed a law which prohibited gay persons from adopting children, and another law which barred state universities from recognizing gay student organizations. Now that the gay community can no longer be ignored, the gay community will have to deal increasingly with such antigay laws.

Laws governing marriage represent an area in which government and other organizations have not been punitive toward gays so much as they have ignored them. A host of benefits available to married couples are not available to same-sex partners, who cannot marry. (There have been only a few exceptions to the same-sex marriage prohibition.) These benefits relate to areas such as insurance—life, health, auto—eligibility for social services and other government programs, income tax treatment, and family-based pricing in the private sector.

Policies of institutions such as hospitals, nursing homes, and prisons also provide rights to the heterosexual spouse not available to the gay partner. A promising exception to this discrimination against same-sex partners was the enactment by the Berkeley City Council of a "domestic partners" bill, which assigns benefits normally available only to a married spouse to an unmarried domestic partner. (A similar bill was vetoed in San Francisco at about the same time.)

Legal problems of gay partners extend to concerns about inheritance. Again, statutes create problems for gay couples because gay partnerships are ignored and only the legal rights of relatives by blood or marriage are recognized. Many gay couples have been caught in a tragic situation. The couple's property is put in one partner's name to protect the couple's anonymity. When that partner dies, the surviving partner loses his life's investment to the deceased's relatives, even though they may have been estranged from or hostile to the deceased. Even when the gay couple has passed property from one partner to another in a will, that will may be contested by hostile relatives. Nevertheless, gay couples are beginning to take greater care in the drafting of wills and other legal arrangements, and in larger cities lawyers who specialize in this area are increasingly available (Berger, 1982b).

Homosexuals experience oppression in many aspects of their lives. By continuing to oppose misinformation and discriminatory policies, gays will publicly expose their oppression while at the same time they will lessen its effects. The progress of the last decade in achieving greater equality and public understanding is a good indication that further progress is possible.

So far this chapter has reviewed the process of homosexual identity formation and the nature of antigay oppression. It will also

be useful for the helping professional to be familiar with the special needs of gay men who couple, marry heterosexually, or parent.

Gay Couples

Some level of secrecy is necessary for most gay men. Those who are or have been in a relationship with another man—and that is the majority of gays (Bell & Weinberg, 1978, p. 86)—know that concealment places a unique set of pressures on a gay couple. For instance, the couple may need to be cautious in dealing with neighbors and co-workers; they may have to suppress spontaneous feelings of affection in public; they may have to create stories about separate bedrooms, vacations, and the like, and keep track of what they have said and not said. Ultimately the pressures of hiding may be too great a burden, added to all the other pressures which impinge on couple relationships in a complex and mobile society.

Despite these pressures, many gays achieve long-term relationships: about 29 percent of gay men are currently in a couple relationship (Bell & Weinberg, 1978, p. 91). Is it surprising that many gay couples are in need of relationship counseling but that most don't seek the help of professionals? Those professionals who specialize in work with gay couples find a striking similarity in the needs and issues that characterize heterosexual and homosexual relationships, since the core issues are the same: the need for intimacy versus autonomy, assignment of roles and responsibilities, and communication patterns. But some issues are different for the gay couple.

Nonmonogamy is more accepted among gay than among heterosexual couples, and may even be the norm among gay couples (Moses & Hawkins, 1982). As with so many other aspects of the gay relationship, since there are no legal or societal rules to follow, and no relatives to monitor and enforce them, the couple must create its own rules.

Should the relationships be sexually open or closed? Under what circumstances are "outside" relations all right, and what limits should be imposed on them? What about relations with women? How much information about outside activities should be shared between the couple?

Nonmonogamy is workable, but it may create complex situations. A professional can assist gay partners in clarifying and communicating their values about monogamy and resolving some of the difficulties that often result from lack of clarity about rules and expectations.

Relations with relatives is another area that differs for gay couples. As discussed above, if the couple is not open about its homosexuality, all the pressures related to secrecy affect the couple. Holidays are often a stressful time, when the partners cannot be together because each must spend the holiday with his respective parents. Even when parents are aware of a gay son's relationship, they may apply pressure in subtle and overt ways to dissolve the relationship. Parents have been known to bribe their children away from a gay relationship with money or promise of rewards, or they may just refuse to recognize the partner, they may be openly critical of him, or they may continually pressure their son to "settle down" and marry. Caught between the intense attachments of a lover on one hand and parents on the other, the gay man may benefit from the supportive attention of a professional. Ideally, the entire family should be the focus of the worker's intervention, with the goal of restoring mutual respect and tolerance for different lifestyle choices (Silverstein, 1977).

Finally, gay couples may have unique needs related to sexual dysfunction. Helping professionals, like others, have been misled by the stereotype of the gay man as a sexual athlete. Popular culture has so exaggerated the "sexual" in homosexual, that few professionals recognize the agonizing difficulty of gay men who are sexually dysfunctional. The dysfunction may be related to the client's lack of self-acceptance and the revulsion he has acquired toward same-sex relations as a result of societal homophobia. In this case, the practitioner needs to help the client achieve a greater level of self-acceptance. The problem may also be due to a lack of information, deficient opportunities, or specific inabilities such as erectile failure.

Masters and Johnson (1979) at the Reproductive Biology Foundation have developed the first major program to treat sexual dysfunctions in gay men and women, largely through application of a treatment program first developed with heterosexuals. It is all too obvious, perhaps, that professionals cannot help sexually dysfunctional gay clients unless their clients believe they will get an informed and nonjudgmental response to an airing of this problem. Given the sensitive nature of the issue, the practitioner must convey to the client that in his or her view gay love is on a par with heterosexual love, and that fulfillment of one is just as important as the other. Professionals with expertise in treatment of heterosexual dysfunction should be able to carry this expertise over to work with gay sexual dysfunction. Other workers should seek to find or develop referral sources for such treatment.

Married Gays and Gay Parents

Many human service professionals may be surprised to learn that a sizeable minority (anywhere from one-fifth to one-third) of gay man have been heterosexually married (Bell & Weinberg, 1978, pp. 160–162; Ross, 1983). In the past, the most common pattern was for the gay man to keep his homosexuality secret from his wife and family. The man may have had gay experiences early in life but abandoned these in order to have a family, often in response to pressure from parents. Later in the marriage the man often began a double life, pursuing sexual and sometimes affectional relationships with other men. More recently, many gay husbands have decided to openly reveal their interests to their wives. In some instances, this occurs prior to the marriage. It is a myth, outside and within many parts of the gay community, that a gay man cannot maintain a fulfilling heterosexual marriage. Trust and love seem to be more important than sexual orientation to these couples.

Nevertheless, the married couple may find its way into the professional's office when the husband's orientation is suddenly revealed, or when an outside event occurs, such as the appearance of the husband's lover on the scene. The professional may be called upon to assist in the couple's agonizing decision to separate or to try to make a go of it. If the wife is of a traditional or moralistic background and unaccepting of her husband's sexuality, separation or divorce may be the only option considered. But often the practitioner confronts two individuals who share a special bond which is acquired only through long years of companionship, support, and, frequently, the raising of children.

It is important for the practitioner to understand the wife's perspective. Particularly if she did not know of her husband's homosexuality, she may feel deceived. She may feel that she was used by her husband to establish his legitimacy. She may question his affection and his honesty. She may feel that she plays "second best" to her husband's lover or other homosexual relationships. She may feel that her husband has followed a double-standard, pursuing outside relationships for himself, but not allowing them for her.

If the couple decides to remain together the practitioner has the delicate task of fitting the relationship back together. Anxieties and anger must be aired. The wife must be reassured of her own value to her husband, and the gay husband must be clear about his commitment to the relationship. There must be negotiations and clear understanding about rules regarding relationships outside the marriage for both husband and wife, how information will be shared with children, relatives, and friends, and what expectations will be held regarding each partner's sexual, affectional, and economic needs.

What of the homosexual man who conceals his orientation from his wife? The practitioner should not make an *a priori* decision about whether disclosure is appropriate. This is a highly individual decision which can only be made by the husband. Often husbands in this situation achieve a remarkable marital stability and a reasonable adjustment to their own needs. Since there are many levels of "knowing," it is likely that among many of these couples there is a tacit understanding: the wife knows at least the general nature of her husband's situation, but there is a family conspiracy of silence. The equilibrium should be altered only with the utmost of care. The husband may perceive quite correctly that open discussion would merely cause a reasonably good marital situation to disintegrate. He cannot afford to risk the loss. If the husband does wish to open up to his wife, perhaps to lessen his anxiety, affirm himself, or prepare to leave the relationship, the professional can help him to weigh options, consider their likely consequences, and rehearse a variety of approaches.

Many married gay men are also parents. Contrary to popular belief, gay men, just like heterosexual men, cherish the role of fatherhood. In the author's own research older gay fathers, asked to name their most satisfying life experience, generally mentioned parenthood (Berger, 1982). A primary reason why the public, as well as professionals, have rejected the idea of gay parenting is the erroneous belief that a gay parent will raise a gay child. But we could just as easily argue that children should not be raised by heterosexual parents, because almost all gay people were raised by such parents. There is no causal connection. Recent research shows that homosexual parents are no more likely than heterosexual parents to produce homosexual offspring (Maddox, 1982, p. 68).

It is sometimes also believed that revelation of a parent's homosexuality will traumatize a child or that the child will not be able to accept the parent. Despite media propaganda to the contrary, most children, especially younger ones, are more accepting of a parent's homosexuality than are adults. And while some children may be taunted by their peers for having an openly gay parent, children do remarkably well in adjusting to a variety of life circumstances without ill effect. Thus it is not surprising that children of homosexual parents are no more likely to be disturbed than children of heterosexual parents (Maddox, 1982, p. 68). Certainly no one would argue against parenting by other minority groups simply because the child will one day have to face discrimination. In light of these observations, the professional should be prepared to assist gay fathers in being open with their children, and assist children in understanding and accepting this information.

The gay father unfortunately can be severely constrained by a homophobic society. In the event of a marital separation or divorce, the father may find it particularly difficult to obtain custody of the children, even if his custody is in their best interests. He must of course overcome the bias of many judges against custody for the father. In addition he has the burden of establishing that his homosexuality does not diminish his capacity as a parent. At the present time, a gay father involved in a custody dispute is not likely to win. Professionals can help by becoming familiar with the professional literature on gay parenting, and by offering expert testimony in child custody cases based solely on the best interests of the children, rather than the parent's sexuality.

A final development is worth noting. In recent years, social workers within child welfare agencies have placed children with openly gay foster fathers (Maddox, 1982, p. 69; Schultz, 1983). These placements are the result of helping professionals' observations that some children are firmly self-identified as homosexual long before the age of 18. Such children are often poorly accepted in traditional placements, but they are likely to achieve a better adjustment with an openly gay foster parent.

Organizations and Policies

Before 1970 a practitioner seeking community resources for gay clients would have had little to choose from. A large city might have had a few gay bars, and a very few places—San Francisco, Washington, D.C., New York City—had fledgling social and political organizations such as the Mattachine Society. Homosexuality was primarily a private affair.

Today gay community organizations number in the thousands. In fact, there is today an extensive Gay Service Network that represents interests as diverse as gay fathers, interracial gay couples, and gay Catholics, and reaches into every major and minor urban area and into many smaller towns. A gay person can join a hiking club, a Democratic party caucus, a health club, a church or synagogue, an engineering society, an organization for deaf members, or a professional social work caucus—all of them part of the gay community. Gay political organizations influence major election campaigns in San Francisco, Los Angeles, Dallas, and New York City, and in 1984 presidential candidates openly courted the gay vote.

Gay community organizations fall into five major types. Helping professionals—heterosexual and homosexual—can lend their expertise and support to all of these.

Political. Organizations such as the National Gay Task Force, based in New York City, and the Gay Rights National Lobby, based in Washington, D.C., serve as political advocacy groups. They monitor current issues of concern to the gay community, such as inflammatory media presentations, local gay rights ordinances, and state and federal legislation affecting the rights of gays. These groups have also taken an active advocacy role in lobbying the media, representing gay concerns on such local agencies as human rights commissions and on federal boards, and lobbying Congress for passage of federal gay rights protection.

Religious. Among the most successful institutions in the gay community are religious organizations. This movement began with the birth of a nondenominational church for gays and lesbians who were not welcome or comfortable in traditional churches. The Metropolitan Community Church (MCC) was founded by the Reverend Troy Perry in Los Angeles in the late 1960s. MCC spread quickly until it included dozens of chapters in cities and towns all across the country. Other religious groups modeled themselves after MCC: the Metropolitan Community Synagogue for Jews, Dignity for Catholics, and Integrity for Episcopalians.

Social. Every city has at least one social organization and larger cities have groups which address themselves to specific needs such as interracial relationships, the outdoors, or leather attire. Social groups in smaller cities and towns tend to attract a less specialized range of interests and are often affiliated with college campus groups or political organizations.

Professional. Most major professional societies have professional gay caucuses. For example, within social work, separate gay and lesbian task forces have been recognized by the National Association of Social Workers and by the Council on Social Work Education. These task forces are active on both the local and national levels in advocating for the needs of gay/lesbian social workers and gay/lesbian clients.

Volunteer. Finally, there is an extensive network of mostly volunteer social services within the gay community. In many smaller cities the social service organization is part of a university campus group, is run entirely by volunteers, has a small budget, and provides information and referral, a crisis phone line, support groups, and a library. The Gay Community Center in Los Angeles is an ex-ample of a more specialized social service organization typical of larger cities. It is supported in part by grants from local and federal government sources, has a board of directors, is organized into separate departments (youth services, employment counseling, health care, etc.), and is staffed by both professionals and volunteers. It functions much like any large community-based social service.

The gay social service network historically has reflected three trends within the gay community. First, there has been a bias against involvement by professionals and against professional knowledge. For too long, social workers, psychiatrists, and other professionals were seen as representatives of a disapproving and controlling society. The gay community was aware that professionals were trained in a traditional model that sought to restrain, isolate, and eventually eradicate gay people. More recently, with the emergence of affirmative models of intervention, establishment of gay caucuses within professional associations, and the willingness of gay professionals to come out publicly, professionals are assuming a larger role in the service network.

Second, the gay service network has been organized within a separatist framework. This has been due not only to a desire on the part of gays for "their own place," but also to the failure of mainstream social service agencies to address the needs of gay clients. For example, few community mental health centers have any programs targeted for gay clients or provide specialized staff training, and many still employ uninformed or homophobic workers. At the present time this separatist trend appears functional and is likely to continue.

Third, the gay service network reflects a strong self-help trend. This is a result both of gays' antipathy to traditional professionals' antihomosexuality, as well as a lack of interest in gay needs on the part of most social service agencies. Increasingly the gay community is showing itself able and willing to look after its own needs—from supportive counseling and placement of adolescent runaways to home care services for the elderly.

In recent years human service workers have been playing a greater role in the establishment and continued operation of some organizations within the gay social service network. But they could certainly do more. As agencies become larger and more specialized, professional expertise in administration, management, and supervision will be more needed. By creating client groups dependent on their services, these organizations will have a responsibility to seek diversified and regular sources of funds to ensure their survival. Professional expertise in fundraising can be useful here. And hand in hand with funding, experienced program evaluators and organizational analysts will of necessity be involved in documenting process, outcome, and efficiency in order to satisfy the requirements of funders.

Many organizations in the gay social service network have large or expanding volunteer programs that can benefit from the skills of an experienced director of volunteers. There will also be a need for continued training of staff in gay social service agencies as well as staff of other community agencies such as mental health centers, alcohol treatment programs, elderly services, and the police. This training should begin with basic facts and desensitization to homosexuality, but it must also include emerging knowledge areas such as the care of AIDS victims and new legal rights of gays.

Human service professionals do not have to work directly with the gay service network to be helpful to the gay community. They can be part of the fight against discrimination and oppression in many ways in their professional and personal lives. A professional can be an advocate for a gay client— for example, by assisting a gay person in filing a housing discrimination complaint with the local human rights board; or an advocate for a group—for example, by opposing aversion therapy for hospitalized gay psychiatric patients.

On a personal level the practitioner can oppose antigay jokes and other instances of homophobia on the part of colleagues. Heterosexual staff can help their openly gay colleagues to establish a more secure atmosphere for gay professionals and clients within the agency. For example, they can petition that personnel policies be revised to include nondiscrimination on the basis of sexual orientation, sponsor a prominently displayed Bill of Rights for clients that includes the right to freely express one's sexual orientation, and influence funding agencies such as United Way to be more responsive to gay community needs.

Since misinformation perpetuates homophobia, public education is an important avenue by which helping professionals can contribute. Personal contact with gays appears to be the most powerful method for neutralizing homophobic attitudes. The helping professional can organize workshops in which local gay representatives can begin a dialogue within helping agencies and within other community settings. But professionals who are themselves openly gay will have the greatest impact on attitudes, both within their own families and friendship circles, and among co-workers.

On the local level the helping professional can work on issues of concern to gays. For example a worker might organize a liaison between the local gay community and the police department; or a worker might organize a petition for introducing a gay rights ordinance by the city council. One important local effort which is often overlooked is the monitoring of content related to homosexuality in the local media. The worker may encourage the local newspaper or radio station to produce a series on activities of the local gay community.

On a national level workers can support national lobbying groups and can petition their representatives to support increased funding for research on AIDS and passage of a federal gay rights bill. They can also oppose the Family Protection Act and other antigay legislation.

LOOKING FORWARD

Sexual orientation is a complex phenomenon. Becoming homosexual is the result of both personal and social variables, and is determined in part by how one's behavior is labeled by others. By any definition, homosexually-oriented individuals are an integral part of society, yet they have been subjected to harsh societal controls, implemented in part by human service professionals. More recent professional efforts have focused less on control and suppression, and more on assisting gays to adapt *as* gays, within a homophobic society. Where do we go from here?

Certainly more research will help. But future research should focus more on society and less on the homosexual. It is time to turn away from the victim and examine the culprit: What is homophobia? How does a society become homophobic? How are attitudes formed and changed? In what ways is homophobia functional for a society? In what ways is it dysfunctional?

In addressing the mental health needs of gays, no research priority could be greater than the question of *prevention*. How can the problems of individual gays be prevented by minimizing societal oppression? How can programs for public education achieve this effect? Perhaps even more important than the design of these educational efforts is their implementation: how can those who control the media be persuaded and pressured to alter their campaigns of disinformation and omission? What other avenues are there for public influence?

We also need more answers to the nature-versus-nurture controversy on the development of sexual orientation; but we should avoid research that leads toward the "correction" of homosexuality. Rather we need to understand how sexual orientation develops for individuals across the heterosexual-homosexual continuum.

Finally, we need to learn more about the needs of special groups within the gay community: the disabled, the elderly, racial and ethnic minorities, substance abusers, the institutionalized, and the mentally ill. Studying the perspectives of such doubly stigmatized groups will not only guide our interventions, but will enlighten our understanding of human survival, of coping in the face of adversity. This understanding will be universally applicable.

REFERENCES

BAYER, R. *Homosexuality and American psychiatry: The politics of diagnosis.* New York: Basic Books, 1981.

BECKER, H. S. *Outsiders: Studies in the sociology of deviance.* New York: Free Press, 1963.

BELL, A. P., AND WEINBERG, M. S. *Homosexualities: A study of diversity among men and women.* New York: Simon and Schuster, 1978.

Beller v. *Middendorf,* 632 F.2d 788 (Ninth Cir. 1981).

BERGER, R. M. An advocate model for intervention with homosexuals. *Social Work,* 22 (1977):280–283.

_____. *Gay and gray: The older homosexual man.* Champaign, Ill.: University of Illinois Press, 1982a.

_____. The unseen minority: Older gays and lesbians. *Social Work,* 27 (1982b):236–242.

_____. Sexual orientation. *Supplement to the seventeenth edition of the encyclopedia of social work.* Silver Spring, Md.: National Association of Social Workers, 1983a.

_____. What is a homosexual? A definitional model. *Social Work,* 28 (1983b):132–135.

_____. Health care for lesbians and gays: What social workers should know. *Journal of Social Work and Human Sexuality,* 1 (1983c):59–73.

BÉRUBÉ, A. Coming out under fire. *Mother Jones,* Feb.–Mar. 1983, pp. 23–29, 45.

BURKE, P. San Diego, California, grand jury supports sheriff's ban against gay deputies. *Advocate,* June 26, 1984, p. 28.

DECRESCENZO, T. A., AND MCGILL, C. *Homophobia: A study of the attitudes of mental health professionals toward homosexuality.* Unpublished manuscript, University of Southern California School of Social Work, Los Angeles, 1978.

DOWD, M. For victims of AIDS, support in a lonely siege. *The New York Times,* December 5, 1983, p. B1.

DUEHN, W., AND MAYADAS, N. S. The use of stimulus/modeling videotapes in assertive training for homosexuals. *Journal of Homosexuality,* 1 (1976):373–381.

FREUD, S. Letter to an American mother. *American Journal of Psychiatry,* 107 (1951):252 (originally published in 1935).

GAY MEN'S HEALTH CRISIS. *Newsletter Number Two* (January 1983). Available from Gay Men's Health Crisis, Inc., 132 West 24th Street, New York, N.Y. 10011.

Gaylord v. *Tacoma School District No. 10,* 559 P.2d, 1340 (1977).

GONSIOREK, J. C. Results of psychological testing on homosexual populations. In W. Paul, J. D. Weinrich, J. C. Gonsiorek, and M. E. Hotvedt, eds. *Homosexuality: Social, psychological and biological issues.* Beverly Hills, Calif.: Sage Publications, 1982, pp. 71–80.

GREEN, R. *Sexual identity conflict in children and adults.* Baltimore, Md.: Penguin, 1975.

HOOKER, E. The adjustment of the male overt homosexual. *Journal of Personality Assessment,* 21 (1975):18–31.

KINSEY, A. C., POMEROY, W. B., AND MARTIN, C. E. *Sexual behavior in the human male.* Philadelphia: Saunders, 1948.

MADDOX, B. Homosexual parents. *Psychology Today,* February 1982, 62–69.

MASTERS, W. H., AND JOHNSON, V. E. *Homosexuality in perspective.* Boston: Little, Brown, 1979.

MOSES, A. E., AND HAWKINS, R. O. *Counseling lesbian women and gay men: A life-issues approach.* St. Louis, Mo.: C. V. Mosby, 1982.

PAUL, W. Minority status for gay people: Majority reaction and social context. In W. Paul, J. D. Weinrich, J. C. Gonsiorek, and M. E. Hotvedt, eds. *Homosexuality: Social, psychological and biological issues.* Beverly Hills, Calif.: Sage Publications, 1982, pp. 351–370.

REISS, A. J. The social recognition of queers and peers. In J. H. Gagnon and W. Simon, eds. *Sexual deviance.* New York: Harper and Row, 1967, pp. 197–227.

ROSS, M. W. *The married homosexual man.* London: Routledge and Kegan Paul, 1983.

SCHULTZ, M. Expanding the parent pool: Adoption and gay men who wish to father. *Advocate,* 372 (1983):25–26.

SILVERSTEIN, C. *A family matter: A parent's guide to homosexuality.* New York: McGraw-Hill, 1977.

SMITH, R. W. Why are many societies sex negative?: A social-functionalist theory. *Counseling Psychologist,* 5 (1975):84–89.

STERN, J. *The sixth man.* Garden City, New York: Doubleday, 1961.

SZASZ, T. *The manufacture of madness: A comparative study of the inquisition and the mental health movement.* New York: Harper and Row, 1970.

WASSERMAN, S. Casework treatment of a homosexual acting-out adolescent in a treatment center. In F. J. Turner, ed., *Differential diagnosis and treatment in social work,* 2nd ed. New York: Free Press, 1976.

LESBIANS
Janne Dooley

As consumers of mental and physical health care, lesbians must deal with the dual oppression of women and gays. The health care system serves as an agent of social control in reinforcing the sexism and homophobia that exists in all areas of the society. The oppression of gay people is rooted in all institutions of society such as religion, science, law, medicine, and psychiatry. Historically, gays have been considered immoral, deviant, illegal, and sick. Attitudes stemming from these judgments have filtered down to a social and personal level which gays must deal with in their everyday life. Some of the evidences of oppression are the lack of civil rights and protective legislation in terms of housing, employment, education, custody, and visitation rights. Attitudes of homophobia affect the lives of gay people in social support and family systems where they have been rejected on the basis of sexual orientation. In public and work situations, gays must either hide their lifestyle or be subject to a range of negative attitudes and reactions.

The oppression of women in the society has an economic base which also funnels down to a personal level, affecting all areas of women's lives. Traditionally, women have been seen as the weaker sex needing men to support and care for them. Because of this belief, women's growth has been limited in all areas—employment, education, and personal. Feminists have made inroads in many areas of social change for women, but women who go against the traditional norms must still struggle against many obstacles. Protective legislation such as the Equal Rights Amendment and reproductive rights has not been clearly established on a federal level. Legislation for equal opportunity in education, employment, and so forth, has been established, but personal attitudes of people in power still limit the effectiveness of these processes.

In the spheres of mental and physical health care a disease model has been historically employed in dealing with women and homosexuals: "Until the 1960s homoerotic behavior is described in the literature as, among other things a neurotic structure, a mental disease, a behavior symptom of deep seated and unresolved neuroses and a personality disorder. . . . Gays have been characterized as egocentric, satirical, lonely, unhappy, tormented, alienated, sadistic, masochistic, empty, bored, repressed and neurotic" (Moses & Hawkins, 1982). Within this disease model, various and at times extreme attempts at cures have been made. So-called cures have ranged from insight therapy to electric shock, from aversion therapy to clitoridectomies (Katz, 1976).

Lesbian clients of the health care system must also deal with issues of sexism. To quote Ehrenreich and English (1973), "Since Hippocrates bewailed women's 'perpetual infirmities,' medicine has only echoed the prevailing male sentiment": the medical view of women's health has identified all female functions as sick—including puberty, menstruation, and childbirth. Women also are seen as the weaker sex in physical and mental health. In the midnineteenth century most affluent women lived a life of enforced leisure with limitations on meaningful work. "Affluent women were seen as inherently sick, too weak and delicate for anything but the mildest pastimes. . . . The boredom and confinement of affluent women fostered a morbid cult of hypochondria and female invalidism" (Ehrenreich & English, 1973)—supported and reinforced by the medical system. In psychoanalytic theory there is no concept of the healthy female. The mental health field has set up a double bind in its view of women. Women traditionally have been seen as hysterical, weak, and passive, expected to adjust to their role as wife and mother. A woman who is ambitious and assertive is seen as not adjusting to the traditional female role. This framework has created a no-win situation for women as clients in the mental health system.

Today, most health care practitioners are not attempting to cure gays and sexist attitudes are at least being examined on a superficial level. Sexism and homophobia, however, remain deeply ingrained in attitudes of health care providers and policies of the health care system. Homophobic or antilesbian attitudes of health care workers and agencies are a major problem for the lesbian client. Attitudes and policies may prevent or hinder treatment as well as hamper the emotional well-being of clients. Lesbian clients may hesitate or refuse to reveal their identity or facts that may uncover their identity; this may be true even when the facts are important to their treatment. They may fear discrimination or abusive treatment as a result of attitudes of health care workers.

Another issue connected to homophobia is heterosexism, or the inherent assumption of heterosexuality. The health care system not only assumes heterosexuality of its clients but builds a framework or perspective which meets the needs of heterosexuals. By denying their existence the health care system does not have to identify or even deal with the special needs of the lesbian clients.

Lesbians not only have to deal with the issues of homophobia and heterosexism but are also subject to issues that affect all women in this society as well as sexist attitudes of health care workers.

Lesbians as well as heterosexual women are subject to discrimination on the job and in education and housing. They are generally put in the role of caretaker in family situations, a role neither respected nor economically supported by the society. Women tend to be the main consumers of health care services and have the most to lose when jobs or services are cut. Although not always visible as lesbians, they must deal with the same issues and discrimination as heterosexual women.

Lesbians come into contact with the health care system in all areas of practice: physical and mental health, community and social services, education and research. This chapter explores issues of homophobia, heterosexism, and sexism in the entire health care system, and further discusses implications for practice with lesbian clients.

OPPRESSION OF LESBIANS IN THE HEALTH CARE SYSTEM

Lesbians and Physical Health Care

"For a host of reasons connected with [gynecology and] reproduction, women continue to visit doctors and enter hospitals far more frequently than men do" (Ehrenreich & English, 1973). Although lesbians have less incidence of cervical cancer and sexually transmitted disease than heterosexual women, they tend to have most of the same health care needs as heterosexual women. In addition, however, dealing with sexism, heterosexism, and homophobia are constant ongoing problems for the lesbian client as she visits the doctor's office or is admitted to a health care facility. Medical histories or admissions interviews are geared to the heterosexual client. A lesbian may be asked to identify significant others in her life within a framework that does not apply to her. She may be listed as single because she does not have a husband and may only be able to identify her lover as a friend.

In times of emergency or medical crisis, visitation and important decisions may be limited to a legal spouse or blood relative. If a patient is, for some reason, unable to make her own decision in regard to medical treatment, a distant relative may have priority to do so over a lover. This is true even though the lover would have more information in determining how the patient would have made her decision.

Antilesbian attitudes of health care workers can have a direct effect on the medical care given the patient. It has been reported that lesbian or gay patients have had trouble getting nurses to respond to buzzers and have received less supportive care and attention of staff members. Hospitals are gener-

ally less sensitive to the needs of lesbian patients and many receive inferior treatment (Willenbecher, 1981).

A visit to the gynecologist's office can be a stress-provoking experience for a lesbian if she has issues on questions pertaining to her lifestyle. She will also have to decide how to deal with the inevitable questions regarding birth control due to most doctors' presumption of heterosexuality.

An interesting issue for all unmarried women but particularly complicated for lesbians is the one of artificial insemination. Artificial insemination gives a lesbian the right to make choices regarding her own fertility. There are, however, many problems for lesbians in dealing with the health care system. Although artificial insemination is "not against the law in most western countries, its practice has generally remained in the hands of the medical professionals" (Hanscombe & Forster, 1982). Artificial insemination has almost entirely been approached as a therapy for infertile couples rather than for lesbians or single women (Hanscombe & Forster, 1982). A lesbian wanting artificial insemination not only has to deal with doctors' attitudes toward gays in general, but with their attitudes toward lesbians as parents. In essence doctors can control whether artificial insemination is administered according to their personal beliefs.

Sexist attitudes of the health care system have greatly contributed to the mystification of women's bodies and health care needs. According to the Boston Women's Health Collective (1976), "The attitudes of many gynecologists—their condescension, their technical manner, their assumption of women's ignorance and stereotyped view" of women have kept women from gaining knowledge and control of their own health care. Inadequate health care services and lack of training in issues specific to women have also contributed to problems of women's health. Women have been subjected to needless hysterectomies and other extreme surgical procedures. Myths that women's complaints are psychosomatic have led to undiagnosed illnesses and inadequate medical treatment. Economics is also an issue for women dealing with the health care system. Medical fees are exorbitant for all kinds of services, and most medical practices and treatments are based on a disease rather than prevention model. Combined issues of homophobia, heterosexism, and sexism may tend to impede the lesbian client from receiving health care which adequately meets her needs.

Lesbians and Mental Health

The medical psychiatric establishment has had profound and unfortunate effects upon the mental health professions, particularly in the clinical field. The static concepts of "study, diagnosis and treatment" are rooted in pathology and illness (Goodman, 1980). The removal of homosexuality from the list of diagnostic categories in the Diagnostic and Statistical Manual III marked a major victory for supporters of homosexuals, but it is a far too optimistic view to assume that this victory would make an immediate and significant change in the deeply ingrained attitudes of mental health professionals dealing with lesbians and gay people. Some professionals still uphold the illness model and advocate "curing" homosexuals, while others do not recognize the effects of social oppression of lesbians and gays and either deny or do not give support to special issues of homosexual clients. Still other mental health practitioners take a more liberal, although harmful, stance believing that homosexuals are the same as heterosexuals. This denies the richness and diversity of lesbian people as well as the stresses of dealing with a heterosexist and homophobic society.

Mental health workers, agencies, and institutions are also deeply ingrained with sexist attitudes and practices. "In clinical practice across the board, the majority of consumers are female" (Goodman, 1980). Therefore, clinical models of mental health tend to support therapy models of adjustment rather than change, upholding tradi-

tional roles of women and "institutionally undermine their individual and communal growth" (Goodman, 1980).

For lesbians dealing with the mental health system, both aspects of homophobia and sexism combine to form a reinforcement of the dual oppression. For many lesbian clients their homosexuality does not present a problem; for others, coming out or managing a lesbian identity may be the primary issue or may compound other problems. It is important for health care workers not to make assumptions but to help clients to sort out for themselves the effect of their lesbianism on certain situations. Dealing with these issues may be very complicated for the untrained mental health worker.

Denial or lack of support concerning specific issues of lesbian clients by practitioners creates services that are at best inadequate, at worst destructive to the personal growth of the client. Reinforcement of gay and female stereotypes closes down rather than opens up options for the development of individual potential. Assumptions of sickness or weakness support a blaming-the-victim model by seeing the source of the problem within the individual rather than the society.

Special issues of lesbians, such as coming out, isolation from the lesbian or gay community, and alienation from mainstream society, family, and peers can be a major problem for the lesbian client. Diversity of lesbians is also an important issue to be looked at. Lesbians are not only white and middle class, but must deal with the issues of race, class, age, mental and physical disabilities, and a host of other issues that come up for all people.

Although gay men and women do share many similar characteristics as sexually oppressed groups, this is by no means to assume they are basically alike. For example, as Jay and Young (1978) have observed, "Culture is one area in which lesbians have greatly diverged from gay men." Moreover, as women traditionally tend to be the developers of culture through family and parenting roles, lesbian culture is a well developed one. For many lesbians, culture is combined with politics in an attempt to challenge the previous heterosexual, male-dominated institutions and ways of relating. Many lesbians see themselves as pioneers in establishing new ways of thinking and relating, especially in looking at issues of power and equality in all aspects of lesbian life (*Considerations in Therapy with Lesbian Clients*, 1979).

It is important for the mental health practitioner to have an understanding of lesbian culture and feminist values when working with lesbian clients.

Sexism also impacts on the lesbian client. "A number of studies have shown lesbians in general to be more assertive, autonomous, self-actualizing, and inner directed than heterosexual women" (Sang, 1978). Such qualities put the lesbian in direct opposition to mental health practitioners who uphold adjustment models as the only option for mental health.

Attitudes of mental health professionals have begun to be examined and even changed in some areas. But change is slow, and sexist and homophobic attitudes are deeply rooted in the mental health field.

Lesbians and Community and Social Services

Lesbians require many of the same community and social services as heterosexual women, but this is an area where the issue of lesbianism is most hidden. Consider that welfare mothers, battered wives, runaway teenagers, alcoholics, and a host of other clients may be women also dealing with the issue of lesbianism. In these cases, lesbianism may not be the presenting problem and may never be identified by the client (for valid reasons). This, of course, does not mean that the issue of lesbianism is not a contributing factor that needs to be dealt with. Here the lesbian client is in a more tenuous position than if she were a medical patient requiring a concrete service. If a teenager is running away because she is afraid to tell her family about her homosexuality, or because they have found out, she is caught in a bind of now having to decide whether to risk dealing with the worker's attitudes regarding homosexuality or try to hide the issue. If she does not reveal her identity, the problems of running away may never be resolved. A welfare mother who may be having problems regarding her lesbianism may fear losing custody of her children if she reveals her lifestyle to a social worker.

Lesbian clients have suffered greatly from homophobia in the area of community and social services. The disease model of mental health regarding lesbians has been a tool in the hands of the homophobic worker, who may have the power to make major decisions regarding the lives of lesbians and their fitness to function. A prime example is in the area of parenting; adoptive, welfare, and foster parents have been denied or had children removed from their care on the sole basis of their lesbian identity. Housing, employment, and social service benefits can also be negatively affected by homophobic workers.

The absence of community services for lesbian clients is an obvious form of heterosexism. Community centers do not run groups or workshops for lesbian mothers or gay and lesbian youth. Here services are not only inadequate but nonexistent.

Lesbians are also affected by sexist values in the society. Poverty and violence are two prime examples. Poverty is a woman's issue which affects lesbians in jobs, housing, and parenting, and single mothers have been said to be the new poor. Fighting for child support and fair settlement in divorce actions becomes tricky for the lesbian mother who rightfully fears loss of custody if she pushes too hard for her children's and her own rights.

Violence against gays and women is a double threat, for the lesbian is vulnerable to attack as a member of both groups. Violence against women is prevalent in this society, and lesbians are not immune to street violence, rape, battering, and personal attacks. Violence against gays is also a constant threat to lesbians especially if they do not conform to traditional norms of appearance or if they are blatantly affectionate with lovers in public.

Lesbians and Education and Research

Training of health care workers has traditionally disregarded issues specific to women and gays. Although with the advent of the women's movement, feminist issues have begun to be analyzed, most traditional settings of health care education have not yet integrated this analysis. Homosexuality is rarely brought up in training health care professionals. If brought up at all, it is usually included as a small section in a human sexuality course, material that mostly pertains to gay men, deals with sexuality rather than lifestyle, and is not a required course. The absence of training regarding homosexuality and women's issues is in itself homophobic and sexist, but students of health care services are also subject to more blatant forms of sexism and homophobia in classrooms and field training. Many teachers still teach or reinforce disease models of homosexuality or present women as the weaker sex.

Research on women and homosexuality has traditionally been based on homophobic and sexist notions. Using clinical samples for research in mental health has helped to reinforce a disease model for both women and gays. Research on homosexuals has been done primarily with gay men and has been focused on the aspects of cause, with underlying themes of blame and cure. Research on gays has been correlated with gender identity and tends to reinforce stereotypes rather than reflect the diversity of the gay community. Social factors which reinforce oppression of women and gays have rarely been investigated and, when done, many times set up a framework of blaming the victim. Lack of research and funding sources have posed additional problems for gays and women.

Medical research is lacking in areas specific to women's problems, while mental health research reinforces the stereotypes of women and tends to reinforce this stand by advocating adjustment rather than social change.

Although recent trends in research and education regarding sex roles, women's issues, and homosexuality have showed some positive changes, these areas have focused primarily on gay men and heterosexual women and research and education on lesbians has lagged behind.

INTERVENTIONS WITH LESBIAN CLIENTS

Lesbian and gay health services, and the philosophies developed by the women's health movement, can serve as sources of information in dealing with the lesbian client. Many lesbian health care providers work within the lesbian, gay, or women's communities, providing direct health care services, developing theories, and advocating for the rights of lesbians as consumers of health care services. Lesbian services include varied community programs, therapy, and medical treatment. These services have been developed *by* lesbians with the specific needs of lesbians in mind, and may serve as a model for professionals dealing with lesbian clients. Lesbian and gay professional groups encompass all health care professions, and many other professional health care organizations have lesbian and gay task forces. In these organizations, lesbian and gay professionals advocate for the development of quality services for lesbians and serve as a referral source for other health professionals.

The women's health movement advocates for health care geared toward a health rather than a disease model, encouraging women to take control of their bodies and lives—issues important to lesbians as well as heterosexual women. The women's health movement has also established the concept of self-help and explores alternatives to traditional health care when appropriate. It also investigates the issues of women as consumers in order to increase their self-determination and definition of needs (Polansky, 1980).

Health care providers can become active participants in establishing health care services which recognize the needs of lesbian clients. Conscientious health care providers must first become aware of the issues of lesbian clients, they must then examine their own attitudes and practices as well as policies of the agencies and institutions where they work. Only when this awareness is developed can the health care provider become actively involved in combatting homophobia, heterosexism, and sexism.

Combating Homophobia

In all fields, homophobic attitudes of health care workers as well as policies of agencies must be fully examined. An open atmosphere should be created in health care agencies, allowing clients to identify their sexual preference if they wish to. Workers should develop an understanding of the lesbian lifestyle and of lesbian health care issues, so they can provide support and empathy to their clients. Supervisors should monitor the attitudes and practices of workers, assuring that lesbians receive the same quality of services and emotional support as heterosexual clients.

Training programs need to be instituted to help staff examine their personal biases and sensitize them to the special needs of lesbian clients. Best qualified would be a health professional who is also a lesbian; she could provide training approached from a personal as well as a professional point of view. The development of an extensive updated resource file for lesbian clients would also serve to bridge the gap for those seeking services in a nongay agency. Qualified lesbian trainers and updated resources can be found at local universities and colleges, women's, lesbian, and gay centers, and organizations such as the National Gay Task Force.

Mental health workers need an understanding of feminist, as well as gay, values, in order to create a therapeutic model which encourages pride in lesbians. Practitioners should shed the disease model of homosexuality: "Therapists should stop offering therapy to help homosexuals change [their sexual orientation] and should concentrate instead on improving the quality of interpersonal relationships" (Coleman, 1978). They should also be helping clients to develop innovative and satisfying ways to grow as gay people (Hawkins, 1983).

Specifically, clinical issues may include supporting lesbians to develop and build alternative support systems, especially if nongay friends and family reject the lifestyle. Developing self-esteem and techniques to deal effectively with oppressive attitudes are also an important goal for all lesbians. Group work on specific issues—such as coming out, parenting, sexuality—is an effective means of breaking down isolation and encouraging a positive self-image.

The issue of lesbianism should never be used to judge a client. Judgments should be made solely on a basis of eligibility for services and ability to function in certain situations separate from issues of sexual orientation. Community and social services should also be able to help lesbian clients break down their isolation, when necessary, by making referrals to lesbian groups, community functions, and professional services. If counselors or community workers cannot deal fairly and effectively with lesbian clients, they should be conscientious enough to refer these clients to another worker or to specific lesbian or gay workers.

Research and Education

Research on lesbian issues should move away from previous trends of focusing on cause and adjustment. "Present and future research should be built on a new paradigm, one that affirms the rights of people to differ" (Weinrich, 1982). Emphasizing a nonclinical basis, lesbians should be studied separately from gay men. Research should be relevant to the lives of lesbians and reflect a diverse rather than a stereotypic view. Social research, documenting the oppression of lesbians and examining how this oppression influences their lives, should also be a priority.

Combating Heterosexism

Heterosexism within the health care system can be fought by putting an end to inherent assumptions of heterosexuality in attitudes, procedures, and practices. Respecting homosexual values—declaring them to be equally valid to heterosexual ones—and creating an atmosphere of support and acceptance, these are the goals.

This can be done by some simple, concrete methods. A sign in the office or waiting room can announce a nondiscriminating policy in terms of sexual preference. Informational materials on lesbianism should also be available in waiting rooms too. Use forms and open-ended questions in interviews that allow clients the option to identify themselves, if desired; and respect clients who choose anonymity. For example, when interviewing clients, leave out pronouns of gender and terms such as *husband* and *wife;* use *partner* instead.

Don't dismiss unexpected answers either. When a patient tells you she doesn't use birth control and doesn't need it, she may be telling the truth. Ask if she has sexual relations with men. Ask if she is celibate. If the answer to both questions is no, then you can ask if she has sex with women. (Pogoncheff, 1979)

The status of "significant others" should be recognized. This is true in hospitals, nursing homes, and other institutions of health care. A lesbian may request the presence of a lover or friend during certain medical procedures, such as gynecological exams, emergency room treatment, or in delivery rooms. These requests should be respected. Lesbian clients should also have the right to deter-

mine who has access to medical information and decision making in time of crisis. For example, lesbian clients could draw up a contract stating that, if they become incapacitated, medical consent would be passed on to a lover or close friend (Willenbacher, 1981).

One attitude of heterosexism that affects lesbian clients is the notion that heterosexual values are superior to homosexual ones. Many values of the lesbian community are different from the general values of the mainstream society. Don't assume heterosexual values for lesbians on issues such as relationships, sexuality, and dealing with family, friends, and co-workers. Health care workers need to be acquainted with these differences and continually examine their attitudes and practices in order to understand and respect differences rather than judge them inferior.

Combating Sexism

The women's health movement has made tremendous strides in identifying and combating sexism. It has dealt with both traditional health care services and alternative methods of health care. Self-help groups were formed to help women learn about their own bodies and mental well-being and also to gain control of their health and health care needs. Health care workers may do well to follow the work of the women's health movement.

Clients as well as workers need to be involved in the process of demystifying issues of women's health care. Complaints of illness and disease need to be respected and not discounted as psychosomatic. A stop must be put to unnecessary medical procedures. In terms of physical well-being, women should be encouraged to live active lives. Exercise and body development should be seen as healthy and normal. Lesbians like heterosexuals must explore issues of consumerism and take power to choose health care services which are supportive and meet their needs. Within the health care system and women's health movement, lesbians need to have support to deal with their special needs as lesbians and women.

Mental health workers must become acquainted with sexism and issues of women's oppression in dealing with lesbian clients. They must keep informed as "new models [of feminist] therapy emerge that recognize the relationship between the personal and the political and offer new responses to avert and correct victimization and oppression" (Robbins & Siegel, 1983). Nonsexist therapy is especially important. Lesbians often need to be autonomous and self-supporting, since they usually choose not to rely on the economic benefits of traditional heterosexual marriage. Mental health workers need to support such assertive, autonomous behavior. Since women are primarily affected by cuts in social services and community programs, it is also important for human service workers to advocate for the continuation of funding for such services and programs.

Research on women's health issues should reflect issues dealing with lesbians. Research should be based on health and prevention. Mental health research should see women as whole people who need to be autonomous and independent in this society. Social research is very important in the area of women's issues, as it breaks down the blaming-the-victim model and places the responsibility on a sexist society rather than on individual women.

Advocacy and Commitment to Change

Homophobia, heterosexism, and sexism are deeply ingrained in all areas of society, including the health care system. Efforts to effect a change for lesbians must be focused on society as a whole as well as specifically at systems of health care. On a larger scale, people can work toward social and political support for lesbians by working to pass supportive and protective legislation for women and gays. Issues of civil rights and of child custody and visitation rights for lesbians are being worked on within the gay community, for example, in national organizations such as the National Gay Task Force and Gay Rights National Lobby. The Equal Rights Amendment and reproductive rights, as well as specific lesbian rights, are focuses of action by the National Organization for Women. State and local groups are also advocating for these issues and actively supporting politicians who support them.

Changing administrative policies in the health care system can be approached by working with unions or by joining the policy committees of social agencies. Participation in creating change can include all health care workers, heterosexual and homosexual. Many times nongay workers can make stronger advocates than can lesbians, because it is not as threatening to their jobs.

Professionals can advocate for supportive services that are based on homosexuality as a healthy alternative, and that recognize the needs of lesbian clients. Educators and researchers also need to advocate for training programs and research which deal with supportive and positive models of lesbian and gay issues.

Gay doctors, nurses and other health care workers as well as those who need their services can lobby for better treatment of gay patients, insist that hospitals respect the rights of gay patients to receive visits from their lovers and gay friends, and work for the right of a seriously ill patient to transmit medical consent to someone they trust—not just someone they are related to. (Willenbocher, 1981)

"If each one of us at work and in our agencies and schools would agree to change the environment to challenge old ideas and values, and 'come out' as supportive of all differences" (Goodman, 1980), we might begin to see some real changes in mental and physical health care services for lesbian clients.

REFERENCES

Boston Women's Health Collective. *Our bodies ourselves.* New York: Simon and Schuster, 1976.

COLEMAN, E. Toward a new model of treatment of homosexuality: A review. *Journal of Homosexuality.* Summer 1978, 3(4):345–359.

CONSIDERATIONS IN THERAPY WITH LESBIAN CLIENTS. Philadelphia: Women's Resources, 1979.

EHRENREICH, B., AND ENGLISH, D. *Complaints and disorders: The sexual politics of sickness.* New York: The Feminist Press, 1973.

GOODMAN, B. *"Where will you be?" The professional oppression of gay people: A lesbian/feminist perspective.* New York: J & P Distribution, 1980.

HANSCOMBE, G., AND FORSTER, J. *Rocking the cradle, lesbian mothers: A challenge in family living.* Boston: Alyson Publications, 1982.

JAY, K., AND YOUNG, A. *Lavender culture.* New York: Jove Publications, Inc., 1978.

KATZ, J. *Gay American history, lesbians and gay men in the U.S.A.* New York: Avon Books, 1976.

MOSES, A., AND HAWKINS, R. *Counseling lesbian women and gay men: A life issues approach.* Missouri: C. V. Mosby, 1982.

POGONCHEFF, E. The gay patient. *RN,* April 1979, 46–49.

POLANSKY, E. Women and the health care system: Implications for social work practice. In *Women's issues and social work practice.* Itasca: F. E. Peacock Publishers, Inc., 1980.

ROBBINS, J., AND SIEGEL, R. New strategies in feminist therapy. *Women and Therapy,* Summer/Fall 1983, 2(2/3):157–158.

SANG, B. Lesbian research: A critical evaluation. In *Our right to love.* Englewood Cliffs, N.J.: Prentice-Hall, Inc., 1978.

WEINRICH, J. Task force findings, overview, and prospect. In *Homosexuality, social psychological and biological issues.* Beverly Hills: Sage Publications, Inc., 1982.

WILLENBECHER, T. When a loved one dies. *The Advocate,* April 1981, 14–15.

CHAPTER 14

THE INSTITUTIONALIZED MENTALLY ILL

Dianne F. Harrison

This chapter addresses the needs of persons who are either voluntary or involuntary patients of mental hospitals. For mental health professionals who work with the institutionalized mentally ill, an understanding of the relationships between different aspects of sexuality and mental illness is essential. Professionals also need to understand the various forms of sexual oppression which take place in mental health institutions and the role that they as caretakers play in maintaining this oppression. The first section of this chapter briefly describes the current social context of mental illness, including views toward definition, treatment, and setting. The second section examines different ways sexuality and "mental illness" interact and the consequent problems these interactions can produce for institutionalized patients and their significant others. The chapter's third section details a range of interventions which mental health professionals can employ at the institutional and societal levels of change and in direct service work with psychiatric in-patients and their families. The final section identifies future research needs and implications of the prevention of sexual oppression for mental health practice. Although this chapter is directed at the needs of the institutionalized mentally ill, many issues and concerns raised have equal relevance for psychiatric out-patients as well.

SOCIAL CONTEXT OF MENTAL ILLNESS

Before examining ways in which sexuality and so-called "mental illness" interact, it is necessary to briefly address the current social context of mental illness, that is, both societal and professional views toward mental illness and its treatment, including the status of institutional care.

In spite of criticisms by such writers as Goffman (1961), Scheff (1966), and Szasz (1970, 1974), use of the term and concept of "mental illness" remains fairly standard in the literature. Various approaches to defining and determining the etiology of mental illness exist, ranging from a traditional medical model to nonmedical models which emphasize the social and environmental aspects of mental illness. Currently the most widely accepted view is that mental illness is caused by an interaction of genetic predispositions and environmental factors (Vattano, 1980). This approach is illustrated in Mowrer's (1972) conceptualization, which is based on contributions made by heredity, social processes, reeducation, and existential factors in the development and maintenance of mental illness.

In the context of various approaches to defining and identifying the cause(s) of mental illness, different models of treatment also exist. Psychoanalysis, use of psychoactive drugs, psychosurgery, behavior modification, family therapy, meditation, gestalt therapy, transactional analysis, and self-help groups are just a few of the numerous approaches to treating mental illness (or maladaptive behavior or behavior disorders) (Vattano, 1980). It is beyond the scope of this chapter to discuss the relative merits and efficacy of these treatment models. It is sufficient to point out simply that current mental health treatment in the United States is best characterized by diversity and a general lack of agreement as to what constitutes the most efficient, effective, and humane solutions to mental health problems.

The community mental health movement, augmented by President Carter's Commission on Mental Health (1978), has resulted in increased efforts at deinstitutionalization and attempts to create more responsive community-based services for both chronically and acutely ill patients. In spite of (and in some cases because of) the movement away from institutional care, societal views toward the mentally ill are still beset with prejudices, notably fear and lack of understanding. In many communities, including the author's, large numbers of people have reacted with hostile opposition when faced with the prospect of having some type of mental health facility (for example, a center or foster or group home) locate in their residential neighborhoods. Although the Presidential Commission (1978) suggested that at any one time approximately 15 percent of the population is in need of some type of mental health service, both professional and lay attempts to "normalize" mental health problems have not been generally successful. This is particularly true in reference to those persons whose behavior is judged to warrant hospitalization. The stigma associated with institutionalization in this society is still great.

The actual number of people directly affected by this stigma, however, has decreased in the past 30 years. The Bureau of Census reported a population of 167,000 residents in public and private psychiatric hospitals in 1982–83. Although this figure represents a dramatic reduction from the peak figure of 555,000 in 1955, the ratio of admissions per resident has increased. As a result, while long-term residence in mental hospitals has in effect been stopped, deinstitutionalization has "brought about a 'revolving door' pattern, with high admission rates but short periods of retention" (Segal & Baumohl, 1983, p. 20). The implications for practice of these trends in admission and retention rates will be discussed in a later section.

Finally, given the significant decline in the population of mental hospitals, it might be speculated that the problems of the institutionalized mentally ill will eventually cease as more hospitals close and the population of existing hospitals dwindles, thus allowing for improved patient-staff ratios and presumably improved treatment. Unfortunately, a significant proportion of discharged patients who require supportive living arrangements (10 to 30 percent) have been found to reside in alternative institutions or sheltered living facilities (Segal & Aviram, 1978). Many of these community care facilities have been criticized as simply community-based replicas of the hospitals they were meant to replace and represent "transinstitutionalism" or the "lateral movement of individuals from one dominant institutional form to another" (Segal & Baumohl, 1983, p. 23). Consequently, it seems the problems of the institutionalized mentally ill can be found both within and outside of the confines of traditional mental hospital settings.

MENTAL ILLNESS AND SEXUALITY

The relationship historically between mental illness and sexuality in the United States has been a close one (see Alexander and Selesnick, 1966; and Haeberle, 1978). Beginning with the "Age of Enlightenment" in psychiatry in the late 1700s, behaviors which violated sexual norms were labeled as sexually deviant ("sick," "immature"); such deviance was equated with mental illness. Conversely, sexual conformity was viewed as mental health ("healthy," "mature") (Haeberle, 1978). Behaviors which have been considered deviant by society and mental health professionals through the years range from "promiscuity" to masturbation to homosexuality. Currently, although societal and psychiatric notions of what behaviors constitute sexual conformity and sexual deviance have undergone changes, there are still many professional and lay people alike who regard certain types of behavior (for example, homosexuality, transsexualism, bisexuality) as "sick" and in need of "cure" even though the American Psychiatric Association (DSM-III, 1980) does not. The current relationship between sexuality and mental illness is complex, consisting of numerous levels or types of interactions. Before describing these, it is useful to keep in mind that many present professional attitudes about sexuality, rather than based on scientific evidence, are closely tied to religious assumptions concerning sexuality as well as current moral standards (Haeberle, 1978).

Types of Interactions

The kinds of interactions that can occur between mental health problems and human sexuality for persons who are institutionalized can be viewed as either primary, secondary, or environmental.

Primary interactions. Primary interactions are those in which some type of sexual behavior is labeled as a mental disorder and is the major reason for institutionalization. Examples of sexual "disorders" which can lead to hospital (or prison) incarceration include pedophilia, exhibitionism, voyeurism, sexual masochism, and sexual sadism. The vast majority of people who have a paraphilia diagnosis are male (DSM-III, 1980). With the exception of the psychosexual dysfunctions—for example, inhibited sexual desire, inhibited orgasm, premature ejaculation, functional dyspareunia (DSM-III, 1980)—most sexual behavior which is psychiatrically defined as a mental disorder is usually a legal offense as well. Although state laws vary considerably regarding legal definitions of these offenses, a number of states have laws which allow for the commitment and forced psychiatric treatment of sex offenders (Haeberle, 1978). Patients who enter a state hospital via the judicial system as "criminal sex offenders" are typically confined to forensic units for the so-called criminally insane.

Secondary interactions. Secondary interactions occur between non-sex-related mental disorders and sexual functioning. The results of such interactions are often some type of sexual dysfunction. For example, among the affective disorders, depression can impair and even extinguish libido, reduce responsiveness to arousal, and affect the physiological vasocongestive sexual response (Renshaw, 1974; Haslam, 1978a, 1978b). Anxiety and stress states can result in impaired sexual functioning, reduced sexual drive, and decreased testosterone levels (Schumacher & Lloyd, 1981; Allgeier & Allgeier, 1984). In some cases, obsessive-compulsive reactions can produce excessive sexual desire (Kaplan, 1979), or inhibited sexual desire and inhibited sexual excitement (DSM-III, 1980). Severe, acute, and/or chronic schizophrenic behavior can lead to appetitive, excitement, and/or orgasm difficulties and either prevent the formation of sexual relationships or seriously constrict preexisting relationships (Kaplan, 1974; DSM-III, 1980). Chronic substance abuse can result in impaired sexual response by diminishing sexual desire and performance. In the case of long-term alcohol consumption, typical sexual problems are erectile dysfunctions in males and arousal and orgasmic difficulties in females (Briddel & Wilson, 1976; Renshaw, 1978). The relationship between other nonprescription drug abuse (for example, marijuana, LSD, heroin, cocaine, amphetamines) and sexual dysfunction is less clear, although it appears that long-term use of such drugs can have varying effects on sexual response such as to inhibit sexual desire, decrease vaginal secretions, lower testosterone levels in males, and/or inhibit ovulation in females (Jarvik & Brecher, 1977; Allgeier & Allgeier, 1984). As a last example of secondary interactions, patients who have been hospitalized with organic brain disease (from either brain tumors, injuries, infections, or maldevelopment) may display sexual disturbances in the form of hyposexuality or hypersexuality (Andy, 1982). It should be noted that any drug which is prescribed to treat these (and other) mental disorders also has the potential to negatively affect sexual function. The effects of medications on sexual behavior will be discussed later.

Environmental interactions. Environmental interactions are those which result from the institutionalization experience itself, with no direct (primary) or indirect (second-ary) connection with sexual disorders or dysfunctions *per se.* This type of interaction between mental health problems and sexuality stems largely from environmental control issues and results in the denial of sexual rights to institutionalized patients. Ginsberg (1977) has even suggested that this deprivation of sexual rights is rarely due to a particular mental disorder itself but, rather, is due primarily to the total control of sexual behavior exerted by the institution. Haeberle (1978) asserted that "with regard to sexual rights all institutionalized mental patients are equal: They do not have any" (p. 457). Examples of environmental interactions which serve to suppress sexual rights include the lack of patient privacy and the segregation of patients by sex.

Recognition of all of these potential and actual types of interactions between mental illness and sexuality is important because their net effect is the entrenchment of sexual oppression in mental hospitals. If left unattended, because of biases, oversight, ignorance, or intentional control mechanisms, they can result in the extreme curtailment of sexual freedom, or the right of an individual to function as a sexual being within the confines of an institution and later in the community.

Population Characteristics

Because of numerous differences in recordkeeping across institutions and regional differences in hospital admission rates due to uneven availability of alternatives, accurate nationwide demographic profiles of the institutionalized mentally ill are difficult to discern. Some general and sometimes conflicting characteristics, however, have been described. With regard to sex differences, Chesler (1972) asserted that women were more likely to be labeled as mentally ill and subsequently hospitalized than men. Tudor, Tudor, and Gove (1977) argued that males labeled psychotic were channeled into psychiatric treatment quicker and tended to have longer hospitalizations than females labeled psychotic. Longer hospital stays were also found for males labeled neurotic as compared to females labeled neurotic (Tudor et al., 1977). In a Canadian study of psychiatric service utilization, D'Arcy and Schmitz (1979) found that women used almost twice as many private sector services as men, the sexes were about equal in utilization of public services, women had only a slightly greater chance of hospitalization than men, and that men were more likely than women to have organic or addictive diagnoses. As stated earlier, significantly more men than women are likely to carry one of the psychosexual disorder diagnoses (DSM-III, 1980) that result in incarceration. Additional characteristics of "mentally disordered sex offenders" are impossible to describe because as Steadmen and associates (1982) found in a nationwide survey, most states do not keep simple descriptive statistics on the admissions or census rates of such patients.

Concerning race and income, it is widely accepted that a greater proportion of racial minorities and persons of low income are hospitalized, particularly in state institutions, than whites and middle- and upper-class groups. Maas (1967) found that while blacks were more reluctant to seek voluntary treatment, once hospitalized their final release rates were lower than for other patients. She also found that black males had longer hospital stays than females (Maas, 1967). Although whites and higher-income groups are overly represented in private psychiatric facilities, it should be noted that with respect to the sexual rights of such patients, private care is not necessarily "better," and may even exert greater control over the sexual behavior of patients.

To summarize, the socioeconomic characteristics of the institutionalized mentally ill are sketchy, at best. More descriptive research in this area is needed to substantiate existing beliefs regarding such variables as sex, race, income, and the role of labeling processes in diagnoses, admission and discharge rates, and length of hospital stay.

Range of Sex-Related Problems and Sexual Oppression

While some of the sex-related difficulties encountered by the institutionalized mentally ill have been identified in the earlier section titled "Types of Interactions," it is also useful to consider certain problems experienced by this population as related to the different aspects or components of sexuality. Problems connected to *sexual identity* arise in large part from traditional sex role biases. For example, the overrepresentation of women among depressed patients has been attributed to such psychosocial factors (rather than hormones) as the women's movement with the consequent effects on marital and family life; the low status of women and concomitant legal and economic problems; and women's learned helplessness (Langsley, 1982). Effeminant behavior displayed by male children has been suggested by some authors as a precursor to the later development of various types of sexual "disorders" including transvestism and transsexualism (Zuger, 1978). Although certain mental health concepts, including "mother-generated pathology," have been criticized as rooted in sex role stereotypes (Spurlock & Rembold, 1978), it is clear that these stereotypes continue to play a part in the definitions of mental health/illness subscribed to by many professionals.

Until recently any nonheterosexual sexual preference, or *erotic choice*, was considered a mental illness and was grounds for hospitalization (Haeberle, 1978). Even though the American Psychiatric Association in 1974 removed homosexuality *per se* from its classification of mental disorders, a category labeled "Ego-dystonic homosexuality" (homosexual arousal by the individual is unwanted and distressful) does exist (DSM-III, 1980). There is no corresponding disorder for what might be termed "Ego-dystonic heterosexuality," raising doubt as to whether the APA has taken a "truly unbiased position on sexual preference" (Allgeier & Allgeier, 1984, p. 493).

Many factors impinge on the *reproductive ability* of the institutionalized mentally ill (and those who have been discharged into the community). Similar to other groups of the sexually oppressed, the overriding bias concerning the mentally ill and reproduction is the simple message, "don't." This message is carried out by such policies as lack of privacy, segregation of the sexes, compulsory sterilization (legal in Virginia until 1972), and, for patients who manage to be sexually active, compulsory use of birth control. In some states even consensual sexual intercourse with a "mentally defective" female is regarded as rape (Haeberle, 1978). Additionally, the side effects of medications administered to the mentally ill are rarely considered important, even though such drugs can seriously affect not only reproductive capability, but every stage of the sexual response cycle as well (Sacks & Strain, 1982). Antidepressants, for example, can cause decreased libido, erectile failure, menstrual irregularity, and testicular swelling (Ehni, 1982). Antipsychotic agents can produce ejaculatory and erectile disturbances, gynecomastia, menstrual irregularities, and decreased sexual desire, excitement, and orgasm (Karpas, 1982; Graedon, 1983; Allgeier & Allgeier, 1984). A frequently used birth control method in mental hospitals is oral contraceptives. The prescription of such pills is usually accomplished on a "mass" basis, that is, cartons of the same type pill are ordered and used for all female patients who are thought to be sexually active. The possible interactive effects of the oral contraceptives and the other medications being given are not normally taken into account. The risks or problems associated with both the birth control method and psychopharmacological agents are considered much less important than the perceived benefits. Given this state of affairs, even the American Psychiatric Association has criticized the manner in which medications are administered in public mental hospitals (Gerhart & Brooks, 1983).

Lack of privacy, segregation of sexes, and the detrimental effects of medications can also impinge on patients' abilities and desires to achieve *intimacy* and *sensuality*. Kenner and Genevay (1981) have reported that lack of affective touch among the elderly can result in depression. Such touch deprivation also exists in institutions, and patients who violate this norm are often labeled as "homosexual" or "clinging and dependent." With families and friends, patients find intimacy and sensuality sometimes hard to produce, especially when their attempts are met with attitudes of fear or suspicion.

Sexualization (or sex for nonsexual purposes), especially in the form of sexual assault, is thought by many to be a common problem in mental institutions (for staff and patients) (LeGrand, 1982). Evidence to confirm this belief is only recently being collected. As another aspect of sexualization, many professionals subscribe to the notion that the various sexual offenses and disorders are prompted not by sexual reasons but by such factors as schizophrenia, marital and family disturbances, and/or social skill deficits (Barlow & Wincze, 1980).

In summary, all aspects of sexuality can be affected by the patient's institutional experience, the majority of effects being negative. The obstacles to functioning as a nonoppressed sexual being are further compounded when other variables are added to the existing label of "mentally ill." The geriatric, physically disabled, and/or racial minority patient is often burdened with double or triple "whammies" when it comes to sexual functioning.

Effect on Family Members

The effects on the rest of the family of having a relative hospitalized can vary considerably. Part of this variation is dependent upon the patient's diagnosis and status as it relates to sexuality and to the degree of severity of behavioral dysfunction (for example, sex "offense" versus manic-depression). In any case, with respect to attitudes and problems associated with mental illness and sexuality, the family can be perpetrators and victims alike. For example, Schwoon and Angermeyer (1980), in a study comparing relationships between family members in which a son was hospitalized with a diagnosis of schizophrenia versus families with sons hospitalized for surgical treatment, found that fathers whose sons were labeled as schizophrenic had more problematic parent-child interactions. The authors interpreted these troublesome relationships as stemming from the sons' lack of conformity with the fathers' male sex role expectations, and the fathers' subsequent lack of identification with their sons. Further, professionals can view the family as being the "source" of problems, even in cases where the patient has been hospitalized for a considerable number of years. Parents, spouses, and adult children of patients can believe their relative is deviant, sick, and "crazy" solely because of certain sexual behaviors and/or sexual orientation.

An effect that is particularly difficult for some spouses is the fact that their partner's hospitalization, as in the case of prisons or medical facilities, removes the opportunity for a continued sexual relationship. Even when the patient is discharged to home, sexual relations may be impaired due to medications. Families, as do patients themselves, lack information regarding drug side effects and sexual functioning. As a result, sexual problems that may develop can be attributed to "mental illness" or to the relationship itself. Sexual problems that can accompany some of the non-sex-related disorders described earlier (for example, depression) can further exacerbate what may be an already tenuous relationship.

Ginsberg (1977) has identified several civil rights which can be denied patients who are determined incompetent. Many of these rights affect the family. For example, divorces may be granted, marriages prevented or annulled, and child custody removed, all on the basis of a person's institutionalization.

The major point for professional consideration is that families can either add to the sexual oppression of their patient-relatives or can be similarly oppressed themselves. The effect of restrictions imposed by institutions and the experiences of being mentally ill are not necessarily limited to the patients' sexual rights but may include the family's as well.

Summary

The first section of this chapter gave a brief discussion of the social context of mental illness by a review of current attitudes toward mental illness and its treatment. Limited descriptive characteristics of the institutionalized mentally ill were also given. In the second section, the types of problems and oppression which occur in institutions were viewed from the standpoint of primary, secondary, and environmental interactions between mental illness and sexuality. The influences of mental illness on different aspects of sexuality were also illustrated. Finally, attention was given to the effects on families of having a member hospitalized. The next section details a range of interventions related to sexuality which professionals can employ in working with the institutionalized mentally ill.

INTERVENTIONS

Unlike other groups who have been sexually oppressed—such as the physically disabled for whom at least some progress is being made with respect to sexual rights (Montgomery, 1983)—virtually no efforts have been made on behalf of the mentally ill. As stated earlier, although some attitudes toward mental illness and sexuality have changed (for example, the APA's view of homosexuality) the topic of sexuality and mental illness still retains the "double whammy," that is, many attitudes about both areas separately are typically negative and, when combined, the topic approaches being viewed as taboo. Yet the types of interventions for managing sex-related problems and insuring sexual rights for the institutionalized mentally ill are numerous, ranging from broadscale interventions including legislative changes and attempts to reduce the degree of social control exerted by both public and private hospitals, to direct therapeutic treatment of sexual disorders and client advocacy in regard to the administration of antipsychotic medications.

Broadscale Intervention

It is likely that before any major changes are made in the formal and informal policies which govern the sexual rights of the mentally ill, significant changes in attitudes toward both sexuality and mental illness must first occur. Probably the most helpful attitude to actively develop is one which attributes a degree of "normalcy" to sexual behavior *and* to disturbances in living. Other critical attitudes are those which accept individual differences and accept the need for *variation* and *flexibility* in the allowance of sexual rights for the mentally ill (Ginsberg, 1977). Recognizing that there is more to sex than reproduction, not *every* patient and possibly not *any* patient needs total official denial and restriction of his or her sexual rights. Widespread adoption of these kinds of attitudes toward the mentally ill will require simultaneous efforts on many levels, including legislation, state mental health department and institutional level policy changes, community education, and public awareness and resource and staff development.

Techniques. State legal codes and case law that permit blanket limits on the sexual rights of the mentally ill—on the grounds of incompetence to restrict (among other things) marriage, divorce and divorce defense, child custody, consensual sexual behavior between adults, and reproduction—should be altered. Although competency is determined on an individual basis and with periodic review, the effects of being judged incompetent often are not individualized and can be permanent. Laws are needed that mandate a return of lost rights and privileges to an individual who is no longer a danger to him or herself or to others. To effect such legislative changes, some procedural lessons can be learned from the MADD group ("Mothers Against Drunk Drivers"). During the past five years this volunteer organization, in spite of liquor industry lobbyists and numerous influential social drinkers who opposed their efforts, has conducted a nationwide and state-by-state campaign to toughen the laws on drunk drivers and raise the drinking age. The MADD campaign has been based on extensive mailings and media blitz illustrating some of the tragedies which resulted from drunk driving and arousing public sympathy and support. They also provided expert witness testimony at national and state hearings. On a topic as unpopular as limiting the alcohol consumption in the United States, the limited success of the MADD group has been phenomenal. With regard to the equally unpopular notion of sexual rights for the mentally ill, similar media campaigns to educate the public and garner their support (and sympathy) can be used. Lobbying efforts and use of expert witnesses (mostly to dispel myths regarding mental illness and sexuality) can further move the process. Efforts should be made to cooperate with other civil libertarian groups, professional groups (for example, American Psychological Association, National Association of Social Workers), and self-help (National Alliance for the Mentally Ill) lay organizations. These kinds of networks can provide impressive human and even financial resources for "cause" work. As another resource, many states have human rights commissions whose clout can be tapped to advocate for the mentally ill.

Efforts also need to be directed toward state departments of mental health and institutions or hospitals themselves. Numerous formal and informal policies need to be changed; these include: (1) policies which relate to blanket restrictions of sexual behavior (for example, through prohibiting sexual contact with others, segregation by sex, lack of privacy, mandatory sterilization or contraceptive use); (2) policies which allow the use of sexual behavior as a basis for institutionalization in instances where an individual is not incompetent or a danger to him or herself, or others; and (3) policies which often fail to consider sexual functioning as a necessary, normal, and important component in a patient's overall well-being and capacity to function outside the institution. Instead, policies should be established whose purpose is to normalize sexual behavior by permitting variation in rights and privileges depending on individual patient needs. Ginsberg (1977) and Haeberle (1978) suggested the use of conjugal visits in hospitals and that masturbation may be more relaxing and less destructive than tranquilizing drugs. Ginsberg also proposed that patients be granted sexual freedom "so long as they do not infringe upon the rights of others" (Ginsberg, 1977, p. 223). In one of the few available studies on integration of the sexes in psychiatric hospitals, Morgan and Rogers (1971) found no detrimental effects of integration but at the same time did not reach any conclusions regarding possible benefits. This area needs further investigation. With respect to privacy, Bogan (1981) noted a proposal for "privacy rooms" in nursing homes. As mentioned early in this book, this type of room could also be used in mental hospitals for patients whose condition did not specifically contraindicate such activity as hand-holding, petting, or sexual relations. Finally, the benefits of antipsychotic medications especially for the chronically mentally ill have been seriously questioned (Gardos & Cole, 1976; Gerhart & Brooks, 1983). The debilitating side effects of long-term drug therapy, particularly in the form of tardive dyskinesia (Jeste & Wyatt, 1981) would appear to make a strong case against their continued

long-term use, thus greatly assisting in the potential for sexual functioning of the mentally ill.

State and hospital policies that reduce the amount of social control exerted by institutions can be adopted, in part, by the techniques of public awareness, lobbying, and organizational networking identified earlier. Further, staff awareness (from state higher administration level to hospital treatment team) needs to be increased through attitudinal examination (and reshaping) and accurate information on client needs and preferences related to sexuality. This type of awareness and knowledge can be gained via accessible training seminars sponsored by either the state, a public or private hospital, a university, or some professional organization. Depending on the target audience, some sponsors and training settings are more effective than others. It would be important for the trainer/organizer to consider, for example, whether a particular group was more likely to listen to an inside staff member at a regular in-service training session, or to an outside consultant with meetings held away from the normal workplace. It would also be extremely useful if influential staff members who serve as role models for other staff believe that this kind of awareness and information is important or, at least, acceptable.

Based on extensive research surveys of clients and service providers, Cornelius and associates (1982) put together an impressive array of general techniques for enhancing the sexuality services for the physically disabled. These included guidelines for increasing public awareness, assessing "attitudinal accessibility," making policy decisions, training, and community action. The majority of their techniques can be adapted to the area of mental health and sexuality. In the matter of resource development for establishing training programs, for example, Cornelius et al. recommend the use of experienced people in the area of sexuality training, attendance at existing programs, and they provide a partial listing of available printed materials and audiovisual resources, most of which have relevance to the field of mental health and sexuality.

Intervention example. Based on the author's research and clinical experience in inpatient mental health facilities and background as a sex educator, the following program agenda was designed as a two-day inservice training program for professional and paraprofessional staff in psychiatric hospitals. While the content can be modified to fit either shorter or longer training modules, the two-day format seems to be an ideal time frame for *beginning* the process of attitude awareness and knowledge enhancement. Additional follow-up or "booster" programs are advised.

BRIEF PROGRAM AGENDA: *MENTAL ILLNESS AND SEXUALITY*

Purpose: To increase participants' knowledge and comfort levels related to sexuality and mental illness; and to provide at least beginning skills necessary to handle the sexual needs and concerns of mentally ill persons.

Format: Short didactic presentations, participant discussions, slides, films,[1] written attitude assessment tools, and bibliographies.

Topics: Day 1

Attitude Assessment: Sexuality and mental illness

Aspects of Sexuality and Effects of Being a Patient: Mental illness does not mean automatic disinterest and dysfunction

Interactions Between Sexuality and Mental Illness: Primary (sexuality and DSM-III), Secondary (non-sex-related disorders and sexual functioning), Environmental (institutional control of sexual behavior)

Additional Forms of Sexual Oppression in Mental Health Institutions: Effect of sex role biases on treatment outcome, reproductive bias

---

[1]Use of audiovisual resources may vary depending on availability and funding. The author has found the careful and considered use of such materials to be highly effective in promoting learning and facilitating discussion.

Topics: Day 2

Additional Forms of Sexual Oppression (con't): Effects of drugs on sexual functioning; effects on family members

Clinical Interventions: Case illustrations of sexual "disorder," non-sex-related disorder, and relationship distress

Use of Referrals and Other Treatment Team Members

Patient Advocacy

Policy Recommendations: Masturbation as an alternative to sedatives

Attitude Reassessment

Direct Service

Direct work with hospitalized patients and outpatients can involve a range of activities depending on whether the "presenting problem" is a bona fide DSM-III sexual disorder or a minor sexual concern that is unrelated to the reason for hospital admission or retention. As in many instances of sex education and counseling, Annon's (1974) PLISSIT model—introduced in Chapter 3, "Levels of Clinical Intervention"—provides a useful framework for clinical intervention with this population. To briefly reiterate, this model is based on a hierarchy of interventive levels (permission-giving, limited information, specific suggestions, and intensive therapy), each successive level requiring greater amounts of skill and expertise to employ. A basic axiom of the model is to start with the least intrusive intervention (permission giving) and work up to more complex interventions as needed. The following examples will serve as an overview of the types of techniques that can be used for sexual problems in psychiatric hospitals.

1. Permission-giving. The essence of permission giving on the part of mental health professionals frequently involves the message to patients that "it's O.K. to be (or *not* to be) a sexual being." Extensions of this message include permission to masturbate in privacy if desired; permission to use affective touches when appropriate; permission to have a relationship; and/or permission to be, act, think, or feel as feminine or masculine as an individual wants. It may also involve giving permission to a patient to ask the psychiatrist about the effects of medications on sexual response. Permission giving in mental hospitals should always take into account individual patient values and the safety and rights of self and others.

2. Limited information. There are several areas where the provision of limited information by a professional relevant to a patient's concern can be useful, and can, in some instances, even prevent further more complex sexual problems. In addition to the spectrum of usual sexual myths and misinformation that plagues the nonhospital population, hospitalized patients may also have the burden of deliberate attempts on the part of well-intentioned family members to "protect" them from any sexual information whatsoever. For this reason some patients (particularly those with long periods of hospitalization) require very basic sexual facts and education. Patients may also need information regarding the side effects on sexuality of various psychiatric disturbances and effects of psychotropic medications.

3. Specific suggestions. Following a history of sexual problems, Annon recommends this treatment level particularly for heterosexual problems that are related to arousal, erection, ejaculation, orgasm, or painful intercourse (1976). He identifies such sample suggestions as: redirection of attention, graded sexual responses, sensate focus techniques, dating sessions, squeeze technique, and vaginal muscle training; these can be given through the mediums of therapist talk, films, videotapes, audiotapes, and/or pictorial brochures (Annon & Robinson, 1978). Although such suggestions may be relevant at times for individual hospitalized patients, familiarity with additional techniques is important. (Contraindications for sex therapy related to degree of psychopathology will be discussed later.) For example, social skills training may be useful for patients whose

skill deficits preclude meeting or acquiring potential partners. Similarly, anxiety reduction, shaping, and/or modeling techniques can be employed to help patients meet and/or retain partners. In another area, masturbation programs for preorgasmic women have been reported as successful prior to couples treatment (Barbach, 1975; Lobitz & LoPiccolo, 1975), a technique which may, when used with appropriate patients, have useful implications for hospital settings. For patients who are capable of changing their irrational self-talk, the self-talk approach can be used in conjunction with other suggestions to modify a variety of sexual difficulties (Ellis & Harper, 1977; Zastrow, 1979). There is little agreement as to what the most effective suggestions would be for substance abusers (and in particular alcohol abusers) who have sexual difficulties. Lobitz and Lobitz (1978) recommended withholding treatment until patients had controlled their drinking for at least six months. Likewise, Franek and Franek (1981) advised no sex therapy during the first month of recovery and urged patients to refrain from sex during and for several months after detoxification. Edwards (1983) disagreed, however, and reported successful treatment using Kaplan's (1974) model and rational therapy (Ellis & Harper, 1977) techniques for sexual dysfunction of inpatient alcoholics. In summary, while the range of specific suggestions that could be used with psychiatric patients appears limitless, evidence to support their application to this particular population remains lacking. For this reason, caution is urged and the need for systematic evaluation and replication in hospital settings is encouraged.

4. Intensive therapy. The fourth level in Annon's model (1974) is designed to be highly individualized treatment for complex problems that have not responded to the first three levels of treatment. For hospital settings the most appropriate problems fitting this level are the sexual "disorders" or "offenses." The most comprehensive model for the assessment and treatment of sexual "deviations" is that provided by Barlow and Wincze (1980). This model, although using the term "sexual deviation," does not differentiate between normal and abnormal sexual behavior; rather, all aspects of sexual behavior (including arousal patterns) are seen on a continuum. As a result, the decision to treat a sexual problem is made by the client after examining with the therapist results from a detailed assessment and evaluating the patient's motivation for treatment. Although Maletzky (1978) reported no difference in the treatment of court versus self-referred exhibitionist patients, Barlow and Wincze (1980) insist that patients settle any legal consequences of their behavior independent of treatment. Their model conceptualizes problematic behavior as consisting of three components: sexual arousal or behavior (either excess or deficit); social skills and emotional factors (for example, anxiety) associated with sexual interactions; and gender role deviations (conflict between biological and psychological sex). Treatment may focus on one or more of these components; changes in one area may be independent of changes in another. In addition to ongoing, multimethod assessment of each of these components, individual characteristics (for example, intelligence, health, self-image), past experiences (trauma and childhood experiences), and current situation (for example, partner relationship, job stress) are also assessed. Numerous treatment techniques have been used (see reviews by Caird & Wincze, 1977; and Springer, 1981); the most frequent being fading procedures (Barlow & Agras, 1973; Abel & Blanchard, 1976) and orgasmic reconditioning or masturbatory training (Barlow & Wincze, 1980) to increase deficiencies in arousal. The fading procedures, designed to alter stimulus control, have been based on errorless discrimination training using slide projector images and fantasy (Abel & Blanchard, 1976). Masturbatory training (sexual arousal from masturbation is paired with new or different fantasies) is a more widely used procedure but

less evidence exists of its effectiveness with clinical or hospital patients (Barlow & Wincze, 1980). For decreasing unwanted arousal, the evidence is more substantial on the treatment of choice; namely, Cautela's (1967) covert sensitization procedure (Barlow & Wincze, 1980; and Blair & Lanyon, 1981), in which imagined aversive scenes are paired with undesired sexual arousal. On the whole, while recent advancements have been made in the assessment and treatment of sexual disorders (Barlow & Wincze, 1980), empirical support for the procedures used has relied on a relatively small number of subjects, most of whom have been convicted sex offenders in prisons (Allgeier & Allgeier, 1984). Although dangerousness may be predictable (Abel et al., 1977), there is little evidence that either psychodynamic or behavioral techniques will effect dramatic changes in a person's sexual behavior (Walker, 1978).

Whether clinicians are involved in giving permission, information, suggestions, or intensive treatment, consideration must be given not only to a patient's past level of sexual knowledge, early learning, and experience (values, attitudes, and belief system), but also to the patient's current values, knowledge level, and experience. Within this context, the education most relevant to patients and/or to counseling can be provided.

Individual, couple, or group treatment format. The involvement of a patient's partner, although preferred by most sex therapists (Springer, 1981), may or may not be feasible in hospital settings. Moreover an alternative, group treatment, is feasible, efficient, and widely used for inpatients. Several treatment techniques have been found effective with only one partner in a group format. For example, Barbach (1975) reported successful masturbatory training programs with groups of preorgasmic women. Zilbergeld (1975) effectively used group treatment for males experiencing premature ejaculation and erectile failures. Gillan (1980) found group treatment effective for women with low sex interest. None of these studies, however, used hospitalized subjects. In one of the few research studies based on inpatient treatment, Murphy, Coleman, Hoon, and Scott (1980) reported the successful use of a sexual enhancement group with female alcoholics. Finally, clinicians (and researchers) are referred to an excellent article by Barbach (1979), who discusses the ethical issues pertaining to confidentiality, right to privacy, and group coercion in the group treatment of sexual dysfunctions.

Indications and contraindications of clinical treatment of sexual problems in a hospitalized population. It has been mentioned several times earlier that the evidence is not entirely clear on the effectiveness of various techniques for enhancing sexual function as applied to hospitalized mental patients. In fact, many authors caution against the use of sex therapy procedures in the presence of "psychopathology" (see review by Springer, 1981). Perhaps the most important criteria which should be used in selecting appropriate sex education and therapy techniques with inpatients are the particular needs, capabilities, and goals of each individual patient, regardless of specific diagnosis or psychiatric status. In this context, some general guidelines concerning indications and contraindications for treatment (especially sex therapy) can nonetheless be derived from the literature. Meyer and associates (1975), based on data from 52 couples, cautioned that "neurotic" pathology should be evaluated in terms of the degree to which it can be bypassed in short-term, task-oriented treatment. Lansky and Davenport (1975), based on their work with military couples, further cautioned that treatment might be sabotaged if the process interfered with the role the sexual dysfunction played in the "psychic and/or marital economy" (compare Springer, 1981, p. 21). O'Connor (1976) reported an inverse relationship between improvement in sexual function and level of psychopathology among three groups of subjects with mild, moderate, and severe pathology. Perhaps the most practical guidelines for

using sex therapy in the presence of severe psychological problems have been issued by Lobitz and Lobitz (1978). These therapists have reported successful treatment of couples where one or both partners had a chronic major psychosis (apparently outpatients) and who had been accepted for sex therapy under the following conditions: (1) nonacute psychosis; (2) patient seen concurrently by psychiatrist who monitors medications and/or provides individual supportive treatment; and (3) structured treatment so that "patient's defenses were not threatened" (for example, no forced increased intimacy on couple, change steps slower, treatment longer than usual fifteen to twenty sessions, and concrete homework assignments) (Lobitz & Lobitz, 1978, p. 89). Unfortunately, the empirical basis upon which these conditions were formulated was not given. At this point, more systematic data are needed before reaching definitive conclusions and making specific recommendations. This is especially true in regard to answering the question "what particular techniques (including either sex education or sex therapy procedures) are most effective with what particular type of patient with what particular type of problems?"

Patient advocacy. The role of patient advocate is a critical one in mental health settings, particularly mental hospitals where the environment is usually structured to limit and control patients' rights. As Gerhart and Brooks (1983) pointed out, however, advocacy on behalf of mentally ill persons can be especially arduous, partly because of "the irrationality, ambivalence, mood swings, and inarticulateness characteristic of many forms of mental illness" (p. 456). Even reasonable patient requests tend to be discounted by many staff due to the patients' supposed incompetence and pathology and because reasonable requests frequently accompany unreasonable ones (Gerhart & Brooks, 1983). With respect to sexual behavior, the difficulty in advocating for patients is increased. Nonetheless, professionals must assume this type of role if patients' sexual rights are to be preserved. Primarily through the techniques of staff education, use of gradual change, and advocate persistence, such items as privacy rooms and patient sex education programs can be implemented. The role of advocate/consultant has also been described by Gerhart and Brooks (1983) in regard to the administration of antipsychotic medications. Nonmedical professionals undertaking this role must have expert knowledge of medications, their side effects, mental illness, law, and advocacy. Such attention to the problematic consequences of medications will necessarily also involve attention to the effects on sexual functioning.

The following case illustrates how brief techniques of sex education and counseling can be used in a hospital setting.

CASE EXAMPLE: JIM B.

Jim B. was a 44 year old Caucasian, married, father of two teenagers, who lived in a rural area of the state. As a patient in the state hospital, Jim had been diagnosed "manic-depressive" and had been routinely hospitalized for two–three months every six months for the past fourteen years, most often during the depressive periods of his illness. Jim had been prescribed lithium carbonate to reduce his symptoms. After several sessions with the social worker discussing non-sex-related concerns, Jim felt comfortable enough to complain about a "private matter." Up to this point he had reported a satisfactory sexual relationship. Now, it seemed that he was experiencing some erectile impairment when he attempted sexual relations with his wife and/or during masturbation. He reported that his capacity for erection returned to normal during some of his "peak" (manic) phases, when he typically discontinued his medication. Following a sexual problem history, the social worker first explained to Jim that one of the typical side effects of lithium carbonate was some degree of erectile impairment. Stressing the continued need for medication until otherwise informed, the social worker also suggested to Jim some alternative techniques for sexual pleasuring that he and his wife could possibly try when Jim was home. Jim was additionally referred to the psychiatrist for a drug dosage reevaluation. Following the next home visit, Jim reported increased satisfaction in his sexual relationship. He also expressed gratefulness for the information that his erection difficulties were not the result of what he termed his "craziness."

Family involvement. Historically, hospital involvement of a patient's family was a matter of happenstance, usually started by the family or in cases of staff initiative, and the main purposes were to explain to the family their role in the patient's problems or to get the family to take the patient home. Current philosophy seems to be a determined, frequent involvement of available family members, if possible, in all phases of a patient's hospital treatment. In terms of sexuality, whenever feasible, appropriate relatives (spouse, parents, adult children) should be included in all discussions of sexual matters, primarily to enlist their support and to avoid misunderstanding. Given the "revolving door" admission and retention rates described earlier, more opportunities now exist for hospital staff to interact with patient families. Unfortunately, a study of patients' families conducted by Hatfield (1979) found low levels of satisfaction with all forms of treatment they received. Rather than insight therapy, families expressed their desires for clear explanations of the patients' illness, help in learning how to manage the patient, and referrals to appropriate community resources. To meet these kinds of needs and to establish and maintain open channels of communication regarding sex-related issues, mental health professionals need to employ several approaches. First, families need to understand that it is O.K. and normal to have questions or concerns about sexuality; to want to continue or assume the role of sexual partner with their patient-relative if desired; and when necessary, to want to learn alternative ways of sexual expression. Sensitive professionals can give these messages verbally by comfortably inquiring about sex-related issues as a routine part of family interviews and nonverbally by such techniques as insuring the family privacy when interviewing in the hospital setting and having literature displayed related to sexuality. With these kinds of actions, therapists become "askable" both for families and patients (Gordon, Scales & Everly, 1979). Another important approach is the provision of clear, concise information to families about their relative's illness (*and* how it may affect the patient as a sexual being) and about its treatment (*and* how medications may affect the patient as a sexual being). This kind of education can be implemented either to separate families or groups of families. Relatively inexpensive brochures can be made available (as are frequently used in medical settings) outlining common points of information. In a different vein, Mathis and associates (1981) discussed the loneliness problems of psychiatric patients and former patients in communities. To counteract the loneliness, isolation, and feelings of alienation common among such patients frequent visits by relatives who demonstrate continued interest and affection were encouraged. For community patients without friends or relatives, community agencies including churches and service groups were recommended as able to make significant contributions (Mathis et al., 1981). The desire for warm, affectionate relationships on the part of patients *and* families is an important issue in counseling that clinicians and families frequently overlook. Gentle reminders can be useful. When appropriate, professionals can give specific suggestions to families relevant to a myriad of possible sex-related concerns. For example, suggestions might include the same therapeutic techniques which were described earlier for patients (sensate focus, anxiety reduction, masturbatory training). Other suggestions, obviously dependent upon the family or partner's immediate concern, might involve some type of sex education program for either the family or patient, concrete techniques for increasing expressed affection, or communication training for improving information exchange about sexuality. Finally, Hatfield (1981) has identified several types of self-help groups for families of mentally ill persons; these groups have as their primary objectives the provision of emotional support, education, and consumer advocacy. Examples are the National Alliance for the Mentally Ill and the Huxley groups.

The following case briefly illustrates the extent to which families can overreact to sexual events, especially those in the lives of their children (even adult children), and the role professionals can play in "normalizing" sexual behavior in institutions.

CASE EXAMPLE: SARA H.

Mr. and Mrs. H. informed the Treatment Team of their desire to have their 25-year-old daughter, Sara, sterilized. As Sara's guardians, their request was based on recent awareness of their daughter's increased "involvement" with another patient. According to staff, this involvement consisted of handholding and light petting. Sara, diagnosed schizophrenic, had been in and out of institutions since she was 14 years old. She reported that she "really liked" her new boyfriend (27 years old) and probably wanted to marry him. In an interview with Mr. and Mrs. H., the social worker learned that this family never communicated about sex (except to rule that one did not talk about it) and had tried to "protect" Sara from potential harm by leaving her essentially ignorant about sexuality. The social worker reviewed with the parents the present situation, discussed the "normalcy" of Sara's behavior, and the consequences (both current and future) of either sterilization or other forms of contraception. The worker also referred the H.'s to an educational group for parents wanting to talk to their children about sexuality. In the context of a nonjudgmental, supportive environment the worker assisted the H.'s in value clarification and decision making about their daughter's behavior and her future potential. Sara (and her boyfriend) were also referred to a sex education group which operated in the hospital. Within several weeks, the parents decided to postpone their sterilization request and agreed to have birth control pills prescribed for Sara. They also reported increased comfortableness in talking with their daughter about this situation as well as about other less intimate topics. Meanwhile, Sara's boyfriend was discharged and Sara claimed she "did not really like him anyway."

In summary, the kinds of interventions that are both available and necessary for insuring the sexual rights of the institutionalized mentally ill are numerous and entail broadscale interventions aimed at attitudinal and policy change, as well as direct counseling with patients and families. Because we exist in a society that attempts to keep everyone, including the mentally ill, in "sexual straightjackets" (Cassell, 1983), efforts must be focused on both macro- and microlevels.

CONCLUSIONS AND IMPLICATIONS

Haroran, McIlvenna, and Pomeroy (1984) have recently presented a manifesto, "Basic Sexual Rights," which includes the following:

The recognition by society that every person, partnered or unpartnered, has the right to the pursuit of a satisfying consensual sociosexual life free from political, legal or religious interference and that there need to be mechanisms in society where the opportunities of sociosexual activities are available to the following: disabled persons; chronically ill persons; those incarcerated in prisons, hospitals, or institutions; those disadvantaged because of age, lack of physical attractiveness, or lack of social skills; the poor and the lonely. (p. 1)

This chapter has tried to introduce at least some of the available mechanisms for altering the plight of the institutionalized mentally ill related to sexual rights. Lamb (1982) has sensitively reminded mental health professionals that both long-term and young patients are affected by everyday stresses and lifecycle concerns and that we must maintain a service delivery system that provides "human relationships with patients and recognizes them as individuals" (p. 151). This goal is not possible unless sexual rights are also included. Because so little progress has been made to date, the opportunities for professional impact are virtually limitless.

Implications for Research

Knowledge gaps in the area of sexuality and mental illness are plentiful, and thus needs exist for research on many topics. First, more systematic, descriptive information (according to sex, race, income) is needed on the characteristics of persons labeled mentally ill, both for public and for private hospitals. The specific role played by traditional sex role biases in the etiology, diagnosis, and treatment of various mental health disturbances also requires further investigation. Additional study is needed on the differential effects on sexual functioning of various drug treatment regimes and the general uses and abuses of psychotropic medications. Component analyses would be useful of the necessary and sufficient variables in the treatment of sexual disorders. Perhaps more crucial at this point are studies that test the effectiveness of various educational and therapeutic techniques as applied to a hospitalized population. This area is especially deficient as it relates to alcoholics and chronic sex offenders. Finally, investigation is needed into the effects of sexual oppression and sexual freedom (for example, segregation, privacy rooms) on treatment outcome and deinstitutionalization. The area is ripe for data-based decisions and treatment planning as opposed to traditional, morally (nondata) based ones.

Implications for Practice

Several important implications for practice should be noted before concluding. In order to affect one or more of the problems identified in this chapter and to implement the suggested interventions, improved training is needed in sex-related areas both on an in-service institutional basis *and* during formal preparation for mental health careers. Another implication is that clinicians and administrators must constantly question the assumptions that underlie much of the current treatment which takes place in the mental health field, particularly as they relate to the relationship between sexual behavior and mental illness (Ginsberg, 1977). Once professionals have managed their own biases, the need exists to assertively and repeatedly manage the probable resistances from staff, relatives, and others who attempt to maintain the status quo. Partnerships with families and significant others can be formed to work toward improved service delivery, including education and consumer advocacy. This type of collaboration between professionals and families of the mentally ill may serve to strengthen the overall service delivery system in the mental health field. And, as pointed out earlier, former patients who are now in the community have many of the same problems and needs as those described for hospitalized patients.

Finally, caution should be noted about the possible unrealistic expectations held by patients regarding a possible "sexual paradise," because as Johnson (1979) so aptly warned in referring to "special group members": "when they are ushered into the world of normals they are bound to be disappointed" (p. 77).

REFERENCES

ABEL, G. G., BARLOW, D. H., BLANCHARD, E. B., AND GUILD, D. The components of rapists' sexual arousal. *Archives of General Psychiatry*, 34:895–908, 1977.

ABEL, G. G., AND BLANCHARD, E. B. The measurement and generation of sexual arousal. In M. Hersen, R. Eisler, and P. M. Miller, eds. *Progress in behavior modification*, vol. 2. New York: Academic Press, 1976.

ALEXANDER, F. G., AND SELESNICK, S. *The history of psychiatry: An evaluation of psychiatric thought and practice from prehistoric times to the present.* New York: Harper and Row, 1966.

ALLGEIER, E. R., AND ALLGEIER, A. R. *Sexual interactions.* Lexington, Mass.: D. C. Heath, 1984.

AMERICAN PSYCHIATRIC ASSOCIATION. *Diagnostic and statistical manual of mental disorders* (DSM-III), 3rd ed. Washington, D.C.: American Psychiatric Association, 1980.

ANDY, O. J. Sexual symptoms of organic brain disease. *Medical Aspects of Human Sexuality,* 1982, 16(8):137–144.

ANNON, J. S. *The behavioral treatment of sexual problems—vol. 1: Brief therapy; vol. 2: Intensive therapy.* Honolulu: Enabling Systems, Inc., 1974.

————. *The behavioral treatment of sexual problems: Brief therapy.* New York: Harper and Row, 1976.

————, AND ROBINSON, C. H. The use of vicarious learning in the treatment of sexual concerns. In J. LoPiccolo and L. LoPiccolo, eds. *Handbook of sex therapy.* New York: Plenum Press, 1978.

BARBACH, L. *For yourself: The fulfillment of female sexuality.* New York: Doubleday, 1975.

————. Ethical issues in group treatment of sexual dysfunctions. *Journal of Sex Education and Therapy* 1(6):65–67, Winter 1979.

BARLOW, D. H., AND AGRAS, W. S. Fading to increase heterosexual responsiveness in homosexuals. *Journal of Applied Behavior Analysis,* 6:355–367, 1973.

BARLOW, D. H., AND WINCZE, J. P. Treatment of sexual deviations. In S. R. Leiblum and L. A. Pervin, eds. *Principles and practice of sex therapy.* New York: Guilford Press, 1980, pp. 347–375.

BLAIR, C. D., AND LANYON, R. Exhibitionism: Etiology and treatment. *Psychological Bulletin* 89:439–463, 1981.

BOGAN, I. Sexual myths and politics. *Journal of Sex Education and Therapy* 7(1):7–14, Summer 1981.

BRIDDEL, D. W., AND WILSON, G. J., Effects of alcohol and expectancy set on male sexual arousal. *Journal of Abnormal Psychology,* 1976, 85:225–234.

CAIRD, W., AND WINCZE, J. *Sex therapy: A behavioral approach.* Hagerstown, Md.: Harper and Row, 1977.

CASSELL, C. A. Beyond the rose-colored glasses. *Journal of Sex Education and Therapy* 9(1):11–13, Spring/Summer 1983.

CAUTELA, J. R. Covert sensitization. *Psychological Reports* 20:459–468, 1967.

CHESLER, P. *Women and madness.* Garden City, N.Y.: Doubleday, 1972.

CORNELIUS, D. A., CHIPOURAS, S., MAKAS, E., AND DANIELS, S. M. *Who cares? A handbook on sex education and counseling services for disabled people,* 2nd ed. Baltimore: University Park Press, 1982.

D'ARCY, C., AND SCHMITZ, J. A. Sex differences in the utilization of health services for psychiatric problems in Saskatchewan. *Canadian Journal of Psychiatry,* 1979, 24(1):19–27.

EDWARDS, D. W. Treatment of sexual dysfunction in male alcoholics: An experimental study.

Journal of Social Work and Human Sexuality 1(3):75–81, Spring 1983.

EHNI, B. L., AND KLINE, D. G. Hyposexuality caused by neurologic dysfunction. *Medical Aspects of Human Sexuality* 16(7):101–106, July 1982.

ELLIS, A., AND HARPER, R. *A new guide to rational living.* Hollywood, Calif.: Wilshire Book Co., 1977.

FRANEK, B., AND FRANEK, M. Sexual rehabilitation in alcoholism recovery. Paper presented at 27th International Institute on the Prevention and Treatment of Alcoholism. Austria: ICAA Publication, 1981.

GARDOS, G., AND COLE, J. O. Maintenance antipsychotic therapy: Is the cure worse than the disease? *American Journal of Psychiatry* 133:32, January 1976.

GERHART, U. C., AND BROOKS, A. D. The social work practitioner and antipsychotic medications. *Social Work* 28(6):454–460, Nov.–Dec. 1983.

GILLAN, P. Group therapy for sexual dysfunction. *Journal of Sex Education and Therapy* 6(1):27–30, Summer 1980.

GINSBERG, L. H. The institutionalized mentally disabled. Chapter in H. L. Gochros and J. S. Gochros, eds. *The sexually oppressed.* New York: Association Press, 1977.

GOFFMAN, E. *Asylums: Essays on the social situation of mental patients and other inmates.* Garden City, N.Y.: Doubleday Anchor, 1961.

GORDON, S., SCALES, P., AND EVERLY, K. *The sexual adolescent: Communicating with teenagers about sex,* 2nd ed. Belmont, Calif.: Wadsworth, 1979.

GRAEDON, J. Drugs that cause sexual difficulties. *Sexuality Today* 6(24):3–4, April 1983.

HAEBERLE, E. J. *The sex atlas: A new illustrated guide.* New York: Seabury Press, 1978.

HARORAN, L., MCILLVENNA, T., AND POMEROY, W. Sexologists suggest manifesto of basic sexual rights. *Sexuality Today* 7(12):1, 1984.

HASLAM, M. T. Depression and anxiety in relation to psychosexual disorder: Endogenous depression. *British Journal of Sexual Medicine,* 1978a, 5(36):33–34.

———. Depression and anxiety in relation to psychosexual disorder: Endogenous depression—part II. *British Journal of Sexual Medicine,* 1978b, 5(37):33–34.

HATFIELD, A. B. Help-seeking behavior in families of schizophrenics. *American Journal of Community Psychology* 5:563–569, 1979.

———. Self-help groups for families of the mentally ill. *Social Work* 26(5):408–413, 1981.

JARVIK, M. E., AND BRECHER, E. M. Drugs and sex: Inhibition and enhancement effect. In J. Money and H. Musaph, eds. *Handbook of sexology.* Amsterdam: Elsevier North Holland Biomedical Press, 1977.

JESTE, D. V., AND WYATT, R. J. Changing epidemiology of tardive dyskinesia: An overview. *American Journal of Psychiatry* 138:297, March 1981.

JOHNSON, W. R. How people in special groups perceive the sex. *Journal of Sex Education and Therapy* 1(6):77, Winter 1979.

KAPLAN, H. S. *The new sex therapy.* New York: Bruner/Mazel, 1974.

———. *Disorders of desire.* New York: Bruner/Mazel, 1979.

KARPAS, A. Hormonal causes of impotence. *Medical Aspects of Human Sexuality* 16(7):468–480, July 1982.

KENNER, P., AND GENEVAY, B. Lack of touch causes depression in elderly. *Sexuality Today* 4(29):2–3, 1981.

LAMB, H. R. *Treating the long-term mentally ill: Beyond deinstitutionalization.* San Francisco: Jossey-Bass, 1982.

LANGSLEY, P. R. Depression in women tied to psychosocial issues. *Sexuality Today* 4(86):1–2, 1982.

LANSKY, M. R., AND DAVENPORT, A. E. Difficulties in brief conjoint treatment of sexual dysfunction. *American Journal of Psychiatry* 132:177–179, 1975.

LeGRAND, C. Sexual assault a problem in mental institutions? *Sexuality Today* 5(27):1–2, 1982.

LOBITZ, W. C., AND LOBITZ, G. K. Clinical assessment in the treatment of sexual dysfunctions. Chapter in J. LoPiccolo and L. LoPiccolo, eds. *Handbook of sex therapy.* New York: Plenum Press, 1978.

LOBITZ, W. C., AND LoPICCOLO, J. Clinical innovations in the behavioral treatment of sexual dysfunction. Chapter in A. S. Gurman and D. G. Rice, eds. *Couples in conflict.* New York: Jason Aronson, 1975.

MAAS, J. P. Incidence and treatment variations between negroes and caucasians in mental illness. *Community Mental Health Journal* 3(1):61–65, 1967.

MALETZKY, B. M. Assisted covert sensitization in the treatment of exhibitionism. In D. J. Cox and R. Daitzman, eds. *Exhibitionism: Description, assessment and treatment.* New York: Garland, 1978.

MATHIS, J. L., BLOSE, I. L., NELSON, P. G., NENNO, R. P., AND WALKER, W. R. Helping patients cope with loneliness. *Medical Aspects of Human Sexuality* 15(12):67–76, 1981.

MEYER, J. K., SCHMIDT, C. W., LUCAS, M. J., AND SMITH, E. Short-term treatment of sexual problems: Interim report. *American Journal of Psychiatry* 132:172–176, 1975.

MONTGOMERY, D. H. Current perspectives on sexuality and physical handicaps. Invitational paper presented at 1983 National Association of Social Workers' Professional Symposium, Washington, D.C., November.

MORGAN, R., AND ROGERS, J. Some results of the policy of integrating men and women patients in a mental hospital. *Social Psychiatry* 6(3):113–116, 1971.

MURPHY, W. D., COLEMAN, E., HOON, E., AND SCOTT, C. Sexual dysfunction and treatment in alcoholic women. *Sexuality and Disability* 3(4), 1980.

O'CONNOR, J. F. Sexual problems, therapy, and prognostic factors. In J. K. Meyer, ed. *Clinical management of sexual disorders.* New York: Williams and Wilkins, 1976.

PRESIDENT'S COMMISSION ON MENTAL HEALTH, THE, vol. 1. Washington, D.C.: Government Printing Office, 1978.

RENSHAW, D. C. Psychosomatic manifestations of depression: Sexual dysfunctions in depression. *Excerpta Medica,* 1974, 86–105.

RENSHAW, D. C. Impotence in diabetics. Chapter in J. LoPiccolo and L. LoPiccolo, eds. *Handbook of sex therapy.* New York: Plenum Press, 1978.

SACKS, M., AND STRAIN, J. J. Commentary on sexual problems of patients with colostomies. *Medical Aspects of Human Sexuality* 16(6):16GG–16II, June 1982.

SCHEFF, T. J. *Being mentally ill: A sociological theory.* Chicago: Aldine, 1966.

SCHUMACHER, S., AND LLOYD, C. W. Physiological and psychological factors in impotence. *The Journal of Sex Research,* 1981, 17:40–53.

SCHWOON, D. R., AND ANGERMEYER, M. C. Congruence of assessments within families with a schizophrenic son. *British Journal of Medical Psychology* 53(3):255–265, 1980.

SEGAL, S. P., AND BAUMOHL, J. Deinstitutionalization. Chapter in S. Briar, A. Minahan, E. Pinderhughes, and T. Tripodi, eds. *1983–84 Supplement to the Encyclopedia of Social Work, 17th Edition.* Silver Spring, Md.: National Association of Social Workers, 1983, pp. 19–24.

SEGAL, S. P., AND AVIRAM, U. *The mentally ill in community-based sheltered care.* New York: John Wiley & Sons, 1978.

SPRINGER, K. J. Effectiveness of treatment of sexual dysfunction: Review and evaluation. *Journal of Sex Education and Therapy* 7(1):18–22, Summer 1981.

SPURLOCK, G., AND REMBOLD, K. Women at fault: Societal stereotypes and clinical conclusions. *Journal of the American Academy of Child Psychiatry* 17(2):383–386, Spring 1978.

STEADMAN, H. J., MONAHAN, J., HARTSTONE, E., DAVIS, S. K., AND ROBBINS, P. C. Mentally disordered offenders: A national survey of patients and facilities. *Law and Human Behavior,* 1982, 6(1):31–38.

SZASZ, T. S. *The manufacture of madness: A comparative study of the inquisition and the mental health movement.* New York: Harper and Row, 1970.

————. *The myth of mental illness: Foundations of a theory of personal conduct,* rev. ed. New York: Harper and Row, 1974.

TUDOR, W., TUDOR, J. F., AND GOVE, W. R. The effect of sex role differences on the social control of mental illness. *Journal of Health and Social Behavior,* 1977, 18(2):98–112.

U.S. BUREAU OF THE CENSUS, *Statistical Abstract of the United States, 1982–83.*

————. *Statistical Abstract of the United States, 1957.*

VATTANO, A. J. Mental health. In D. Brieland, L. B. Costin, and C. R. Atherton, eds., *Contemporary social work, an introduction to social work and social welfare* 2nd ed. New York: McGraw-Hill, 1980

WALKER, P. A. The role of antiandrogens in the treatment of sex offenders. In C. B. Qualls, J. P. Wincze, and D. H. Barlow eds., *The prevention of sexual disorders: Issues and approaches.* New York: Plenum Press, 1978.

ZASTROW, C. H. Self-talk: A new theory to understanding and treating sexual problems. *Journal of Sex Education and Therapy,* 1(6):51–57, Winter, 1979.

ZILBERGELD, B. Group treatment of sexual dysfunction in men without partners. *Journal of Sex and Marital Therapy.* 1:204–214, 1975.

ZUGER, B. Effeminate behavior present in boys from childhood: Ten additional years of follow-up. *Comprehensive Psychiatry,* 19(4):363–369, July/August, 1978

15

PRISONERS
Charles A. Glisson

Concern for the rights and well-being of prisoners in the United States has waned in the past decade. Beginning with the efforts to reinstate the death penalty and continuing with the enactment of mandatory sentencing and the decrease in funding of prerelease halfway-house programs, both state and federal lawmakers have expressed a growing willingness to toughen what some perceive as an overly soft and liberal criminal justice system. This softness in the system, generally considered to have developed with the emerging social consciousness of the 1960s, is frequently believed to be a primary contributor to the current high levels of violent crime. In light of these trends, the sexual rights of prisoners hardly occupy a high priority for legislators or the public. As will be shown, however, the sexual oppression of prisoners has implications that reach far beyond the mere comfort or discomfort of the individual prisoner and the question of "softness" in the system. For the prisoner, sexual oppression contributes to a sub-culture, one that develops and reinforces individuals' thinking patterns and behaviors that subsequently affect society in geometric proportion to the number of prisoners incarcerated and released. Sexual oppression within prison systems has been directly linked to violence and aggression both within and outside the prison, as well as to the destruction of prisoner's familial relationships and recidivism following release.

THE POPULATION: PRISONERS

At the end of 1982 there were 412,303 inmates in U.S. federal and state prisons (U.S. Bureau of Justice Statistics, 1983). Over 90 percent were male and about half were white. The majority of the nonwhite inmates were black. The most important characteristic of the 1982 statistics was that they showed the highest annual increase in total number of incarcerated individuals (43,000) for any year since data became available

210

(1925). Also, the percentage increase (11.6 percent) from 1981 to 1982 was second only to the 12.2-percent increase from 1980 to 1981. The United States now has one of the highest incarceration rates in the world (170 per 100,000 residents). The increase in incarceration is a fairly uniform phenomenon across the country, occurring in 47 states and the District of Columbia, as well as in the federal prison system, chiefly resulting from mandatory sentencing laws. Clearly, prisoners as a target population for social work intervention promise to be available in increasing numbers for years to come.

All of these nearly one-half million prisoners can be described as sexually oppressed because they are denied the freedom of sexual expression available to nonincarcerated citizens. There are, however, specific subgroups of prisoners who suffer this oppression more acutely than others. An accurate appraisal of sexual oppression must include the special characteristics and problems of these groups. These groups include (1) those who are subjected to sexual assault, (2) those who are not given equal protection or treatment by prison staff because of their sexual preferences (gays and transsexuals), (3) those who have had significant, "preprison" sexual relationships terminated with incarceration, and (4) those who through "prisonization" adopt the self-defeating, stereotyped sex roles perpetuated by the psychosocial subsystem of prisons (Glisson, 1981a, 1981b). The problems and characteristics of each subgroup will be described separately in the following sections.

This chapter concentrates on male prisoners because over 90 percent of prisoners are male. Female institutions differ from male institutions in that the oppression of homosexuals apparently is almost nonexistent (Howarth, 1980) and overtly homosexual women frequently enjoy higher status in female institutions (Propper, 1981; van Wormer & Bates, 1979). Victimization, however, does occur in both types of institutions (Bartollas & Sieverdes, 1981). In addition, the problems with extraprison relationships and prisonization most certainly present similar problems to both sexes. It is likely that most of the suggestions for broadscale and direct service intervention apply to incarcerated females, but because of the limited research on female institutions and the absence of any comparative research we know very little about the actual differences. We can be certain, however, that all correctional facilities have a mortifying effect on the sexuality of inmates and significantly contribute to the attitudes and expectations about sexual relationships that the inmate carries into the outside world.

Victims of Sexual Assault

Although sexual assault in prison has been dramatically and repeatedly depicted on film and in novels and has received consideration attention from social scientists (Lockwood, 1980; Cotton, 1982; Moss, Hosford & Anderson, 1979; Nacci & Kane, 1982; Bowker, 1980; Ellis, Grasmick & Gilmer, 1974; Scacco, 1975; Bartollas & Sieverdes, 1981), this subgroup of prisoners may, in fact, represent one of the smallest groups of sexually oppressed individuals in prisons. The widespread attention probably results as much from the violent and threatening nature of the act as from its actual prevalence.

General violence in prison is prevalent, however, and the threat of violence is an integral part of the informal power structure.

Inmates tend to view aggression as one way of getting something they or their friends want and/or getting rid of something/someone that is "bugging" them or their friends . . . For some inmates the gratifications contingent on behaving aggressively—deference from inmates and/or staff, acquiring a sex partner, recovering a gambling debt—outweigh such costs as bringing "heat" down on the inmate group; getting hurt oneself; losing a desirable job, cell assignment, or "good-time" days; and/or being denied visitors and/or parole. (Ellis, Grasmick & Gilmer, 1974, pp. 30–31)

Important to note here as well is the link between sexual behavior and violence in prison, apart from sexual assault, which has been reported by inmates and staff (Ellis, Grasmick & Gilmer, 1974). A recent report published by the federal prison system concludes that reducing consensual homosexual activity in prisons will reduce violence (Nacci & Kane, 1982). Violence, in this case, is reported to erupt when inmates argue over changing sexual partners or compete for the same partner.

The characteristics of victims of sexual and nonsexual assault and of their aggressors have been a major focus of the numerous studies of prison violence mentioned above. The many studies in this area are in agreement that victims tend to be the smaller, younger, and therefore weaker inmates who demonstrate more feminine body characteristics and a less aggressive manner (Nacci & Kane, 1982; Lockwood, 1980). A number of studies have reported that most victims of assault in prison are white and almost all aggressors are minorities, particularly black (Lockwood, 1980; Scacco, 1975; Moss, Hosford & Anderson, 1979; Bartollas & Sieverdes, 1981). Victims also tend to have a history of problems with mental health (Lockwood, 1980; Nacci & Kane, 1982) and the majority are believed or known to be gay (Nacci & Kane, 1982) (This issue will be discussed in detail in the next section.) Although some disagreement exists among researchers regarding specific characteristics of aggressors and victims, there is consensus that victims display obvious physical and/or emotional vulnerabilities that mark them as "targets" to larger, aggressive, and more violent inmates.

In addition to being a minority, the aggressor is more likely to have a prior history of institutionalization (Lockwood, 1980) and of preinstitutional violence (Poole & Regoli, 1983) and to be younger than the average inmate, although older than his victim (Ellis, Grasmick & Gilmer, 1974; Lockwood, 1980; Nacci & Kane, 1982).

Sexual aggression *per se* seems to be more an expression of power and dominance in the prison subculture than of sexuality (Cotton & Groth, 1982). Lockwood (1980) reports 28 percent of a random sample of prisoners to have been victims of sexual aggression, but it is important to note that Lockwood defines sexual aggression "as a continuum of actions, all perceived as aggressive, ranging from verbal propositions to gang rapes" (p. 8). One third of this 28 percent consisted of propositions only, and only one subject reported that he had actually been raped. This pattern was further substantiated through extensive interviews with 107 "targets" in several New York state prisons. Half reported that no physical aggression occurred in contacts with aggressors and that actual rape hardly occurred at all (Lockwood, 1980). Lockwood (1980) also reports that both staff and inmates agree that the most effective way to stop a sexual aggressor is by a violent reaction and that the best way to avoid becoming a target is to establish a reputation for toughness.

Moss, Hosford, and Anderson (1979) also estimate a relatively low incidence of sexual assault, from 0.5 percent to 3 percent of those incarcerated, and along with Scacco (1975) interpret sexual assault as a part of the prison subculture's power struggle, particularly utilized by minorities.

To sum up the literature on the victims of sexual assault in prison, it seems that the phenomenon of "targeting" in prison subjects a sizeable portion of the inmate population to aggressive and even violent acts, but that actual sexual assault is a small subgroup of those acts. The threat of sexual assault, however, is used as one of many methods to establish dominance in a subculture oriented to violence and physical intimidation.

Gays and Transsexuals as Victims

In addition to the greater likelihood of becoming targets, gays and transsexuals are victims of the prison system in other ways as well. Transsexuals in particular present a unique dilemma to institutions—that is, whether to place them in male or female institutions. In many state institutions they are placed in segregated male units to protect them from sexual assault, but transsexuals are sometimes placed in facilities for women (Gardner, 1981). Most institutions allow them to continue hormone treatment if substantiated by a letter from their physician. With the exception of the Gender Identity Clinic at the California Medical Facility at Vacaville, however, services for transsexuals are largely nonexistant and most institutions simply place them in situations where the possibility of assault is minimized (Gardner, 1981).

Prisoners who are known to be gay are also frequently segregated from the male inmate population. Of course, many gay prisoners are never identified by the institution and an accurate estimate of the total number of gay prisoners is impossible. Akers, Hayner, & Gruninger (1974) state that of a sample of prisoners from 7 U.S. prisons, 33.5 percent reported knowing more than 5 individuals who had participated in homosexual relations in the institution at least once in the previous year. Propper (1981) studied 397 female inmates representatively sampled from 7 adolescent institutions and found that 17 percent reported having a homosexual experience in the institution. In Propper's study, however, homosexual experience could be either (1) going or partnered with another girl, (2) passionate kissing, (3) writing love letters, or (4) sex beyond hugging and kissing. These studies, examples of the few attempts to estimate the extent of homosexual activity in prison, suffer two obvious, inescapable measurement problems: the inability to determine who is telling the truth, and a lack of agreement on how homosexual activity is defined.

The extent of homosexual activity within prisons is an important question because known gays are treated differentially by staff on the basis of beliefs that may be unfounded. Nacci and Kane's (1982) study, conducted under the auspices of the federal prison system, reports that correctional officers overestimate the amount of sexual ac-

tivity that goes on in prison; but Nacci and Kane agree with the sampled correctional officers that a chief cause of violence in prison is consensual homosexual activity. They also recommend a complete plan for reducing homosexual activity to make prisons safe.

Such assumptions contribute to institutional practices involving gays and transsexuals that Howarth (1980) has labeled unconstitutional. She argues that the due process clauses of the Fifth and Fourteenth Amendments, the cruel and unusual punishment prohibition of the Eighth Amendment, and the equal protection clause of the Fourteenth Amendment are widely violated by prisons in the treatment of gay and transsexual prisoners. She charges that official prison policies concerning homosexual inmates frequently reflect a punishment or treatment motive, not merely protection, and that the typical extended duration of "protective" custody, frequently in isolation, suggests abuse of the gay prisoner.

Any inmate, then, who is a transsexual or who is identified as gay is likely to be victimized by both inmates *and* staff. Aggressors mark them as targets for sexual assault and staff identify them as instigators of violence through consensual sexual activity as well as by becoming victims. Nacci and Kane (1982) report that correctional officers are less willing to protect homosexual than heterosexual inmates (when, in fact, homosexual prisoners are more likely to be targeted) and that officers misread the rape of homosexual prisoners to be consensual sex. Moreover, protective measures by staff involving segregation or isolation are frequently punitive or oriented toward "treating" the inmate for his homosexuality.

Inmates with Preprison Relationships

For a very large number of inmates, entering prison means leaving behind either a marriage or a long-term sexual relationship. Freedman and Rice (1977) report that returning to a successful relationship is one of the best predictors of postrelease success, but that "numerous aspects of the prison structure and culture work against maintaining marriages and romantic relationships" (p. 175). Both the inmate and partner experience emotional reactions to the stress of separation that are "characterized by feelings of loneliness, isolation, guilt, blame, anger, sexual frustration, suspicion, and frequently, overwhelming depression and apathy" (p. 176). Also, research on the impact of separation on wives has shown increases in depression and dissatisfaction with the marriage to be a function of that separation (Glisson, Melton & Roggow, 1980).

Communication with an incarcerated spouse or mate is limited to prison visits, phone calls, or letters. Visits may be limited to one hour twice a month and usually take place in a crowded, noisy room with rules against expressing affection. Many times, couples are separated by a physical barrier and communication is through an intercom. Phone calls must be short (frequently no more than five minutes) and infrequent (once a month or less). They are always monitored and "an operator may simply disconnect . . . when the time limit is reached" (Freedman & Rice, 1977, pp. 176–177). Wives are usually allowed to write letters to inmates, but friends and lovers may not be approved as correspondents. In almost all prisons, officials read prisoners' mail and sometimes letters are not delivered either way because of topics mentioned or language used in the letters (Freedman & Rice, 1977).

At a time when communication may be most vital to the sustenance of a relationship that could provide the needed support for postprison success, communication between spouses or lovers is limited to forms that may very well magnify the frustration and anxiety already present and ensure the relationship's failure.

Although conjugal association for prisoners—allowing extended, private visits during which sexual intercourse may occur—is one step toward a remedy to this problem, conjugal visits have little future in the United States at present. Conjugal asso-

ciation is widely practiced in Canada, Mexico, Latin America, and the European countries, and, moreover, the Federal Standards for Prisons and Jails issued by the United States Department of Justice recommended the initiation of private family visits in federal prisons by 1984. The Reagan administration, however, has halted the U.S. move toward conjugal visits, and a recent task force appointed by the director of the federal prison system has rejected any reform in that direction (Goetting, 1982a).

In spite of this seven state prison systems currently have conjugal programs. The two oldest are in Mississippi and South Carolina and have been in existence since the turn of the century (Goetting, 1982b). These state programs offer varying opportunities for conjugal association depending on the prison and prisoner, ranging from one-hour visits in a private room within the prison to Mississippi's program, begun in 1974, which allows the prisoner to visit with his entire family for a weekend in an apartment provided away from the prison grounds. Mississippi extended its program in 1982 to include women inmates as well, but most states do not. In South Carolina, common-law wives are eligible, but other states limit their programs to married couples only.

Although these state programs have reported success with conjugal visitation (as have other countries), the moral, practical, and legal objections raised by legislators and prison officials will likely prevent expansion to other states and to the federal prison system. Only one court case, of many, challenged the denial of conjugal rights through imprisonment and won. The most important case, however, was the 1974 Ohio federal district court decision, in *Lyons* v. *Gilligan*, that *denied* a constitutional basis for conjugal rights (Goetting, 1982b).

Moreover, even states which currently have conjugal visitation programs do not extend the rights to unmarried prisoners, and, except for the Netherlands, no programs anywhere in the world extend conjugal rights to gay prisoners.

Prisonization as Sexual Oppression

Prisonization is the process of a prisoner's socialization into the informal social structures of prison life (Thomas, 1977; Glisson, 1981a). There are three general variables that influence adaptations to and the consequences of confinement: (1) the inmate's preprison socialization and experience, (2) characteristics of the prison as a custodial versus a treatment organization, and (3) extraprison influences associated with the quality of contacts inmates maintain with significant others and their postrelease expectations (Thomas, 1977). These variables determine the extent to which an individual prisoner experiences prisonization.

Prisonization results in more immediate rewards for those who "adapt" well than for those who do not, but ironically the product of extensive prisonization becomes less able to successfully function outside the prison (DeWolfe & DeWolfe, 1979). This is because the social patterns which develop within correctional institutions, and to which the inmate is pressured to adapt, are characterized by (1) physical intimidation and violence, (2) an inmate power structure, and (3) rigid and simplistic role stereotypes that define and label inmate behavior (Glisson, 1981a). The extent to which individual prisoners are socialized into those patterns is the extent to which the characteristics of those patterns continue to affect their thinking and behavior following release. The problem is that what works within the prison subculture spells disaster in the outside world.

The personal lines of adaptation chosen by an individual confronted with the social structures of prison have been described by Goffman (1961) as (1) situation withdrawal, (2) intransigence, (3) colonization, and (4) conversion. These categories represent ways in which inmates choose to adapt to the stresses and demands of the "total," formal and informal, social structures of prison life. Each alternative promises the inmate a strategy for acquiring what the inmate perceives as desirable, given the options available.

Those choosing *situation withdrawal* hope to be left alone by acting as if the surrounding environment does not exist. *Intransigence* is chosen by inmates who hope to bluff the staff and gain the respect of other inmates by refusing to cooperate and sending the message, "Don't mess with me!" *Colonizers* benefit the most from prisonization and acquire goods and services through manipulating the informal power structure to their advantage. *Converts* seek protection, and possibly goods and services from staff by becoming perfect inmates, at the expense of the disdain of their peers.

However, no particular line (or lines) of adaptation chosen by the inmate provides protection from the devastating effects of the informal social structure that governs each facet of the inmate's daily life. An important part of that social structure is the definition of roles and values which guide thinking and behavior, including the inmate's understanding of his sexuality and sexual relationships. All inmates—regardless of whether they have been "targeted," are gay, or have had preprison relationships interrupted by incarceration—are susceptible to these roles and values. Those that experience extensive prisonization allow these roles and values to govern their thinking and behavior following release as well.

The simple dichotomy of strength, aggressiveness, and dominance against weakness, passivity, and submissiveness is entrenched as the behavioral option for the male inmate. In a misguided effort to preserve some small positive vestige of self, the general social stereotypes of the outside world are distilled within the institutional subculture to their most basic characteristics. An ironic embracing of the rejectors' sex role models and the subsequent exaggeration of the differences between those roles represent attempts of the rejected to establish convincingly their sexuality and worth. (Glisson, 1981a, p. 192)

In male prisons, the inmate can prove himself to be a "man" to his peers or show himself to be a "woman." Any hint of the latter and he runs the risk of becoming a target. The disdain and distrust shown women, and womanly men, pervades the language and anecdotes of the inmate subculture, revealing attitudes and values that reject understanding and empathy, suspect generosity, and negate trust. Every inmate fears being labeled a "punk" (a feminine inmate who is easily sodomized), worries about "Jody" (the guy who is having sex with the inmate's lover on the outside), and knows the rule is to "beat [his lover] to the punch" by breaking up with her before she does it to him (Freedman & Rice, 1977).

Prisonization convinces the male inmate that his self-worth depends on his manliness and that manliness means withholding expressions of tenderness, showing no feelings except anger, reacting to conflict with aggression, and dominating relationships. Prisonization also teaches that people cannot be trusted and that a man is a fool to believe his lover will be faithful. Prisonization, in short, ensures that the inmate's sexual relationships will be "immature, superficial, 'fuck-oriented' relationships, which are dissatisfying to the inmate and, more important, continue to guide his sexual behaviors after release" (Glisson, 1981a, p. 194).

THE PROBLEM: DEPRIVATION OR IMPORTATION?

Prisonization and the associated problems experienced by the various groups described above have been repeatedly debated in the literature as a function of either deprivation or importation. The *deprivation thesis* argues that the characteristics of the institution and the imposed stress and deprivations produce the informal power structures, violence, roles, behaviors, and values found among inmate populations. The *importation thesis,* in contrast, argues that the major determinant is *pre*prison socialization and that the informal power structures, violence, roles, behaviors, and values are imported into the prison by the inmate population. The resolution to this debate is not merely academic: the pre-

scriptive implications of the two theses suggest very different methods of intervention.

Poole and Regoli (1983) report support for both theses in explaining violence in juvenile institutions. They found that inmates in institutions with a treatment rather than a custodial philosophy were less receptive to the inmate code supporting violence, but that a history of preinstitutional violence was the best predictor of individual violent behavior.

Propper (1981) claims support for the importation thesis in her study of homosexuality in female, adolescent institutions, because she found that most of the girls who reported participation in homosexual relationships stated that they had homosexual relationships prior to their current incarceration. However, 71 percent had their first homosexual experience during a prior or the present confinement, so it seems she should have rightly concluded deprivation. Interestingly, only 50 percent of the participants and only 10 percent of the nonparticipants in homosexual activity felt it was acceptable behavior. Participants explained homosexual behavior to be a function of the lack of access to men, the desire for money, or a persuasive partner.

Akers, Hayner, and Gruninger (1974) report homosexual activity to be a function of the structure and policies of the prison in their study of 7 male institutions. They found more homosexuality in the more custodial prisons and less in prisons emphasizing rehabilitation, thus supporting the deprivation (or as they label it, "functional") model of inmate behavior.

Bowker (1980) attributes prison victimization to both importation and deprivation variables. Among the importation variables he includes racism, gender role definitions, fears associated with homosexuality, preprison violence, age, and criminal and preprison drug-culture participation; as deprivation variables, the struggle for power, the structure of prisons as organizations, and general prison policies.

Ellis, Grasmick, and Gilmer (1974) examined aggression in 55 prisons, using both the prison and the inmate as units of analysis. Two variables which explained aggression at both levels of analysis were age and number of visits. The younger prisoners and those receiving fewer visits were more aggressive. Likewise, prisons with younger inmates and with fewer visitors reported more aggression. Ellis, Gramick, and Gilman (1974) believe their results support a synthesis of the functionalist (deprivation) and diffusionist (importation) models, but they seemingly have found that the characteristics of the inmate (assuming number of visits represents the quality of preprison relationships) are the chief determinants of aggression.

Thomas (1977) appears to have found support for the deprivation model for explaining prisonization. That researcher found that preprison socialization and experience were unrelated to prisonization while "contextual powerlessness" (that felt by the prisoner) was the best predictor, labeled a prison specific variable by Thomas. However, he collected data from inmates in one prison only, so contextual powerlessness should be interpreted as a function of the characteristics of the individual prisoner (which would support the importation model of prisonization).

Although they did not explicitly address the deprivation versus importation debate, van Wormer and Bates' (1979) study of leadership roles in a female institution found that the "willingness to speak for the group in registering a complaint, and the know-how to get what one wants, for oneself or others" (p. 795) was positively related to the inmate's education and her homosexual involvement. Also, inmates who had committed violent crimes were also more likely to register complaints. These findings support the importation model's assumption that adaptation to prison life is a function of the individual inmate's characteristics and preprison history.

The mixed results of the above studies regarding the determinants of inmate behavior, attitudes, and roles are evidence of the lack of consensus in the current literature regarding the dominance of either the deprivation or importation model. With so little research available, it is premature to assess the validity of the models, but support has been found for both types of variables and it appears that any intervention which focuses only on deprivation (suggesting broadscale intervention) or only on importation (suggesting an emphasis on changing the individual) will likely be inadequate.

BROADSCALE INTERVENTION

Intervention based on the deprivation model assumes that "targeting," the collapse of extraprison relationships, and prisonization are all determined to some extent by the characteristics of the prison system. Intervention at this level, therefore, requires structural, procedural, and policy changes that will impact on such problems. In addition, more research and better education of legislators and other decision makers, through the dissemination of research, is needed for any broadscale intervention to be undertaken.

Organizational Structure

Prisons are classic "Catch 22" situations. The control and constraint deemed necessary for a secure prison prevent the development of an optimum treatment environment which would enhance rehabilitation, and at the same time the less than successful rehabilitative efforts make the control and constraint necessary. However, within the boundaries prescribed by security requirements, there can be found across a sample of prisons a considerable range in the emphasis on treatment versus custody. Numerous studies have established that the organizational structure of a correctional institution has an impact on the extent to which treatment goals can be pursued and on the attitudes and behaviors of both staff and inmates that are related to rehabilitation

(Street, Vinter & Perrow, 1966; Akers, Haynew & Gruninger, 1974; Glisson, 1978; Poole & Regoli, 1983).

Organizational structures that are less centralized (allow line staff more authority and participation in decision making) and less formalized (have less rigid procedural specifications and divisions of labor) promote less routinized interaction between staff and inmates and promote staff recognition of the unique characteristics of individual inmates. Prison systems, however, function more often than not with highly centralized and highly formalized structures, similar to those incorporated in military organizations, and changes in this area toward more participative management will require extensive education of both administrators and staff. Increased education (the majority of Japan's prison guards have college educations) enables staff to have a wider variety of responsibilities and administrators to implement control through consensus among staff rather than through dictate. These are the types of structural variables that determine the extent to which inmates are treated rather than merely contained.

Policy and Procedural Changes

Some policy changes can be implemented with less difficulty than can structural changes. First and foremost is the development of higher security standards for the protection of victimized inmates. This would include the development of an ombudsman system, with particular attention to the dynamics of targeting described previously. As suggested by Howarth (1980), policies concerning homosexual inmates, in particular, must be developed with an emphasis on protection while also safeguarding those inmates from punitive custody.

Second, policies that emphasize the education of security officers in specific areas, such as prisonization and the dynamics of incarceration, are needed to upgrade the quality of inmate/staff interaction. Nacci and Kane (1982) point to the specific need for educating security officers regarding homosexuality within prisons and their responsibility in preventing sexual assault.

Third, improved classification policies should emphasize the determination of prisoner security based upon empirically validated criteria rather than on anecdotal information or traditional criteria. Minimum, medium, and maximum security classifications should be based upon the inmate's potential for violent behavior and not upon other, unrelated variables.

Fourth, one pressing need listed by Bowker (1980) is a data-based monitoring system to keep track of prison victimization. This system should accompany the policy changes suggested above to document location, frequency, and aggressors. Currently, few prisons have such a monitoring system.

Finally, a long-term objective nationwide is for conjugal rights to be extended to all state and federal prison systems. These programs can provide outlets for sexual and emotional frustration, reduce tension and hostility, provide an incentive to prisoners for following rules and regulations, promote a more normal lifestyle for prisoners, and foster stability in relationships that may determine postrelease success (Goetting, 1982b; Freedman & Rice, 1977). Conjugal rights should be extended to all prisoners who qualify under reasonable security restrictions without regard to sex or marital status.

Research and Education

Research and education regarding the prison system are intimately linked. The more we have of the former, the more we can do of the latter. At this point, research on victimization is very limited and that on sexual oppression is almost nonexistent. In fact, this chapter has presented the small amount of research that does exist. Much more information about our prison system must be collected and disseminated to legislators, prison administrators, and the public if any progress is to be made in implementing such broadscale interventions as described in this chapter.

DIRECT SERVICE INTERVENTION

A human service practitioner within a prison system actually has a very narrow array of direct service alternatives. There are several reasons for this: the lives of clients are under observation and control of prison authorities twenty-four hours a day. The time, frequency, and place for meetings between practitioners and clients are not determined solely by practitioner and client. Often the involvement of family and significant others is extremely difficult if not impossible to obtain. And there are few alternatives for clients in terms of how they will spend their time and whom they will spend it with. All these factors adversely affect the development of positive outcomes. Freedman and Rice (1977), however, offer a number of specific and practical strategies that can be implemented, as well as suggestions on pitfalls to be avoided. Their suggestions have been relied upon in developing the following sections.

What To Look For

Inmate victims of sexual abuse, inmate transsexuals whom other inmates and staff believe to be gay and who are "targeted," inmates attempting to maintain shaky extraprison relationships, or inmate victims of prisonization may display one or more of the following emotional or behavioral reactions.

The range of emotional reactions will be limited for most inmates. With the exception of anger, emotions are not sanctioned by the prison subculture; most inmates will resolve to keep a stiff upper lip in the face of their problems. Feelings of frustration and perhaps helplessness may be evident, but the social worker should expect very little outward expression of emotion, other than anger, in conjunction with such problems as victimization, loss, or deteriorating extraprison relationships.

Behavioral reactions frequently take the form of acting out and can include rule breaking, fights, escape attempts, or threatening letters to significant others on the outside. Masculine-proving behavior may be especially evident among inmates who are facing the loss of a relationship, who have been victimized, or who are experiencing the process of prisonization. The inmate may brag about deeds and conquests on the outside, abuse weaker prisoners, or provoke encounters with staff and other inmates. These behaviors fall under the intransigence form of adaptation described earlier (Goffman, 1961).

On the other hand, the prisoner may simply withdraw (Goffman, 1961; Freedman & Rice, 1977). As a result, he may experience insomnia, loss of appetite, of weight, and avoid associating with others. Psychosomatic complaints and loss of interest in either masturbation or sex may be associated with these symptoms as well. A general apathetic and passive demeanor will characterize inmates who withdraw. In more serious forms, withdrawal may culminate in a suicide attempt, especially if the inmate's problem involves a significant extraprison relationship (Freedman & Rice, 1977).

Some inmates choose denial when faced with an aversive situation. For example, the inmate may refuse to believe that a significant relationship is ending or refuse to admit that he has been targeted. With denial, the inmate may demonstrate hypomanic behavior, build a considerable fantasy life, and/or become dependent on drugs. In this case, there is no problem from the inmate's point of view.

Another response frequently observed among inmates is regression. They become more infantile and dependent and resort to various manipulative behaviors in an attempt to convince the human service practitioner or other prison official to take over the problem for them. They may become extremely demanding, engender sympathy, or threaten self-destructive behavior as a means of getting the social worker to solve the problem, while they remain passive.

What To Do

Freedman and Rice (1977) offer a number of suggestions for intervention with inmates, which in this section are developed for intervention with inmates who are members of sexually oppressed groups. Any of the emotional or behavioral symptoms listed in the previous section may follow from the inmate's problems, including lack of emotion, acting out behavior, withdrawal, denial, or regression. While a range of traditional approaches may be applied in prison environments hospitable to therapeutic intervention, the professional does have several practical options that may be implemented in any correctional facility regardless of whether it is "treatment" or "custody" oriented.

An initial objective in any intervention within a prison is to forestall any drastic action by the inmate. If an inmate is angry and seems capable of acting out in a self-destructive way, the inmate should be persuaded to request external control by isolation. In extreme cases, the practitioner may initiate isolation under the following conditions: (1) the inmate refuses to talk about the situation or admit any feelings other than anger, (2) the practitioner fully explains why the inmate is being placed in isolation, and (3) the inmate is able to control the duration of the isolation by stating he is no longer angry.

An equally important objective is to forestall any further harm to the inmate who has been targeted or victimized. It may be necessary for the practitioner to initiate the movement of the prisoner to a protected area even if, in cases of denial, the inmate refuses to admit he or she is in danger. As described earlier, the distinction between protection and punishment must be clearly maintained.

One objective that applies in almost all intervention attempts with inmates is increasing the inmate's feelings of control and potency. This can be accomplished in part by helping the inmate acquire information. The information may concern facts about behavior that concerns the inmate, such as homosexuality or stress-related responses to incarceration. It may, on the other hand, concern information about significant others on the outside, such as what a wife is doing or planning, or information about situations within the prison, such as how to obtain a desired job assignment or cell. It is crucial that the practitioner not promote regression by simply obtaining the desired information and delivering it to the inmate. Instead, the practitioner should help the inmate acquire the information by suggesting methods and sources.

A second component to increasing the inmate's feelings of control and potency is to provide emotional support and encouragement while the inmate is attempting to obtain information or is making any specific effort to resolve an aversive situation within the prison. The practitioner may even serve as ombudsman between the inmate and the institution as long as the inmate initiates the action and accepts the responsibility to follow through with his or her efforts.

A third component to increasing a sense of control and potency, related to the first two points, is the rearrangement of the inmate's lifestyle and relationships within the prison. The practitioner can help the inmate identify those aversive aspects of the inmate's prison life that can be modified and help the inmate formulate a plan for implementation. The information-gathering process and support from the practitioner are key ingredients to the success of the modification.

Interventions which focus on the inmate's interactions with others—staff, other inmates, or significant others on the outside—may be helped by role playing and coaching. Depending on the inmate it is possible that poor social skills, a hostile demeanor, or low self-confidence will hamper any efforts made by the inmate to establish some sense of self-determination and control. The practitioner and inmate can role play potentially volatile or especially crucial encounters before they occur, and spot problems that could hamper success. In addition, social skills training can be used to teach the inmate how to deal with stressful situations (Bellack & Hersen, 1979).

In addition to helping inmates initiate and follow through attempts to modify their prison existence, the practitioner may assume a more active role by providing alternative means within the prison for inmates to act assertively and to make decisions. This is possible to the extent the practitioner has the formal authority to manipulate inmate work assignments or to intervene with the formal procedures governing inmate requests and activities. In some cases the practitioner might have the client work with an inmate peer whom the social worker judges to be empathic and insightful. This should complement other efforts and should not be accomplished in a manner that suggests the practitioner is in control and responsible for the outcomes.

Organizing groups for inmates undergoing similar experiences may be especially useful, providing support and especially evidence that their personal reactions do not indicate weakness or failure. Whether the group is made up of the sexually victimized, transsexuals, self-identified gays, or those whose extraprison relationships are collapsing, coleadership by a male and a female can provide the opportunity for positive modeling. For example, the woman leader can assume a rational, instrumental role and the man can assume a nurturing and expressive role. In addition, the woman can provide the "woman's" perspective on an issue, which inmates may see as valid. Freedman and Rice (1977) also report that the presence of a woman coleader in male inmate groups elicits more raw expressions of emotion that can lead to constructive discussions and insights.

The practitioner may also form groups outside the prison made up of the lovers, spouses, or family of inmates. These groups,

oriented to providing support, may form the basis for training members in peer counseling. They can then become the nucleus of an active support network for the inmates' significant others who must endure long separations and possibly hostile communication from a frustrated, incarcerated spouse or loved one. As described earlier, the practitioner should concentrate on helping the members acquire information and provide needed encouragement, as each adjusts to separation and makes decisions about the relationship they expect to maintain with their incarcerated spouse, lover, child, or parent.

CONCLUSIONS

Although all incarcerated individuals may be considered sexually oppressed because of the constraints placed on all facets of their lives, this chapter has identified four subgroups of prisoners that are especially at risk: prisoners who are "targets," who are transsexuals or whom inmates and staff believe to be gay, who are attempting to maintain extraprison relationships, or who have become "prisonized." Such inmates present problems not experienced by other prisoners. A description of characteristic problems was presented for each group along with a review of the current related research.

This chapter has also reviewed the deprivation versus importation debate, the etiology of the attitudes and behaviors of prisoners that contribute to the above problems. It was concluded that research thus far has found support for both theories. It therefore seems likely that successful intervention on behalf of the four "at risk" groups necessitates broadscale as well as direct service intervention.

Suggestions for intervention through policy and structural changes and through direct services to individual clients were presented. In reality, however, most human service professionals in prison systems have very little authority and few resources for making broadscale changes. Direct intervention can accomplish only limited objectives when the individual must continue to exist within a system that perpetuates attitudes and behaviors which contribute to the problem. Thus a major goal for the practitioner is to help the inmate develop some sense of control and potency through information gathering, and to help the inmate to positively rearrange those elements of prison life that can be modified. Individual and group intervention that provides support, emphasizes the inmate's normality, and encourages emotional expression has been suggested as well.

Widespread problems remain within the U.S. prison system, however, and little impact can be made at the individual level until changes at the broadest level are implemented. Higher educational and training requirements for prison personnel at all levels are needed to ensure a greater understanding of prisoner behavior and attitudes and of the complex phenomenon of prisonization. More emphasis on the safety of individual prisoners and on the control of intimidation and violence is needed. Finally, conjugal association programs that help prisoners maintain extraprison relationships could reduce recidivism by sustaining the valuable social-support systems necessary for postrelease success.

REFERENCES

AKERS, R. L., HAYNER, N., AND GRUNINGER, W. Homosexual and drug behavior in prison: A test of the functional and importation models of the inmate system. *Social Problems* 2:410–422, 1974.

BARTOLLAS, C., AND SIEVERDES, C. M. The victimized white in a juvenile correctional system. *Crime and Delinquency* 27(4):534–543, 1981.

BELLACK, A. S., AND HERSEN, M., EDS. *Research and practice in social skills training.* New York: Plenum, 1979.

BOWKER, L. H. *Prison victimization.* New York: Elsevier, 1980.

COTTON, D. J., AND GROTH, A. N. Inmate rape:

Prevention and intervention. *Journal of Prison and Jail Health* 2(1):47–57, 1982.

DEWOLFE, R., AND DEWOLFE, A. S. Impact of prison conditions on the mental health of inmates. *Southern Illinois University Law Journal* 4:497–533, 1979.

ELLIS, D., GRASMICK, H. G., AND GILMAN, B. Violence in prisons: A sociological analysis. *American Journal of Sociology* 80:16–43, 1974.

FREEDMAN, B. J., AND RICE, D. G. Marital therapy in prison: One-partner "couple therapy." *Psychiatry* 40(2):175–183, 1977.

GARDNER, R. For transsexuals, prison is "ten times as tough." *Corrections Magazine* 7(1):32–36, 1981.

GLISSON, C. Dependence of technological routinization on structural variables in human service organizations. *Administrative Science Quarterly* 23(3):383–395, 1978.

_____. Correctional facilities. In D. A. Shore and H. L. Gochros, eds. *Sexual problems of adolescents in institutions.* Springfield, Ill.: Charles C Thomas, 1981a.

_____. A contingency model of social welfare administration. *Administration in Social Work* 5(1):15–29, 1981b.

_____, AND MARTIN, P. T. Productivity and efficiency in human service organizations as related to structure, size, and age. *Academy of Management Journal* 23(1):21–37, 1980.

GLISSON, C., MELTON, S. C., AND ROGGOW, L. The effect of separation on marital satisfaction, depression, and self-esteem. *Journal of Social Service Research* 4(1):61–76, 1980.

GOETTING, A. Conjugal association: A world view. *Criminal Justice Abstracts* 14(3):406–416, 1982a.

_____. Conjugal association in prison: Issues and perspectives. *Crime and Delinquency* 28(1):52–71, 1982b.

GOFFMAN, E. *Asylums.* Garden City, N.Y.: Doubleday, 1961.

HARTNAGEL, T. F., AND GILLAN, M. E. Female prisoners and the inmate code. *Pacific Sociological Review* 23:85–103, 1980.

HOMER, J. Matsqui Institution, Abbotsford. *Canadian Journal of Criminology* 23(3): 331–342, 1981.

HOWARTH, I. W. The rights of gay prisoners: A challenge to protective custody. *Southern California Law Review* 53(4):1225–1276, 1980.

LOCKWOOD, D. *Prison sexual violence.* New York: Elsevier, 1980.

MORTON, D. R. Strategies in probation: Treating

gay offenders. *Social Casework* 64(1):33–38, 1983.

MOSS, C. S., HOSFORD, R. E., AND ANDERSON, W. Sexual assault in a prison. *Psychological Reports* 44:823–838, 1979.

NACCI, P. L., AND KANE, T. R. *Sex and sexual aggression in federal prisons.* Washington, D.C.: U.S. Federal Prison System, 1982.

POOLE, E., AND REGOLI, R. M. Violence in juvenile institutions. *Criminology* 21(2):213–232, 1983.

PROPPER, A. M. *Prison homosexuality: Myths and reality.* Toronto: Lexington Books (D. S. Heath and Company), 1981.

———. Make-believe families and homosexuality among imprisoned girls. *Criminology* 20(1): 127–138, 1982.

SCACCO, A. *Rape in prison.* Springfield, Ill.: Charles C Thomas, 1975.

STREET, D., VINTER, R. D., AND PERROW, C. Executiveship in juvenile correctional institutions. In *Organizations for treatment.* New York: Free Press, 1966.

THOMAS, C. W. Theoretical perspective on prisonization: A comparison of the importation and deprivation models. *Journal of Criminal Law and Criminology* 68:135–145, 1977.

U.S. BUREAU OF JUSTICE STATISTICS. *Prisoners in 1982.* Washington, D.C.: U.S. Department of Justice, 1983, Bulletin NCJ-87933.

VAN WORMER, K. S. Social functions of prison families: The female solution. *The Journal of Psychiatry and Law* 9(2):181–191, 1981.

———, AND BATES, F. L. A study of leadership roles in an Alabama prison for women. *Human Relations* 32(9):793–801, 1979.

THE DEVELOPMENTALLY DISABLED
Winifred Kempton
Jean S. Gochros

Many groups of people have been oppressed in their efforts to express their sexuality for various reasons such as age, lifestyle, or disability. No group, however, has been more drastically oppressed because of the mere fact that they are *sexual* than those labeled as "retarded." This chapter discusses the problems faced by retarded persons and their caretakers, the factors involved in their sexual oppression, some efforts being made to lift it, and will offer suggestions for professional interventions.

Historically anxiety—parental, professional, and public—that a person who is retarded may also be sexual has often reached a panic state in which reason flies out the window. Society has generally imposed rigid restrictions upon the retarded, often with a kind of hopeful anticipation that such people would become desexed. Prior to 1970 there was almost no mention of their sexuality in professional journals save for a few debates

about whether or not they should be allowed to marry or have children. Only recently has their right to sexual expression been given consideration. Many of their needs and rights continue to be neglected. Even when recognized, they are often subjected to rigid control by parents, professionals, communities, and indeed by the legal system.

FACTORS CONTRIBUTING TO SEXUAL OPPRESSION

Fear of Pregnancies

Several factors have resulted in the oppression, both general and sexual, of retarded persons. Underlying many of these factors is the fact that retardation may be a prime example of how the reproductive bias affects attitudes toward people. Those who are retarded simply do not fit the public's standards for social acceptability, and society has historically been determined that they shall not reproduce. Because of the results of some studies at the turn of the century, for example, fear that their procreation rate would lower the national IQ resulted in most states passing laws requiring the sterilization of retarded individuals.

Parents and the public at large share serious and realistic concerns about reproduction. Already overburdened with the care of a retarded offspring, many parents are deeply concerned that they will be burdened with the care of a handicapped grandchild. In general there are three important concerns voiced by all involved with the retarded: (1) the genetic risk that the handicap would be repeated in the offspring, (2) the inability of retarded parents to provide proper health and home care, and (3) the likelihood that mental stimulation would be insufficient for the child to develop intellectually (Garber, 1973).

Often the only solution was to deprive retarded individuals of all heterosexual relationships in order to keep them from becoming parents. Consequently the professionals frequently worked hand in hand with parents in committing retarded persons to institutions for the main purpose of preventing procreation, especially when an attractive, seductive young retarded girl reached puberty. In fact, the authors know of one institution that bore the subtitle "The Institution for Childbearing Women," as its residents were mainly women of childbearing age who were never permitted to be in the company of men outside their families.

Anxiety over sexuality haunts almost everyone in one form or another. The worry over retarded people's procreation often puts an additional strain on those who care for them (and who already may be unable to deal with their sexuality). In the past not only were attractive girls often institutionalized to prevent childbearing, but parents often kept them as near prisoners in their own home. Sterilizations were frequently arranged by both parents and professionals, most of the

adolescents not knowing what was happening to them. Some staff members in institutions viewed residents' homosexual activity as being more acceptable than heterosexual involvement, because there would be no danger of pregnancy.

For example, a resident might be harshly punished for the slightest attempt to communicate with the opposite sex but be permitted to participate in sexual activity with the same sex uninterrupted; consequently, he or she would deduce that homosexual behavior was more desirable than heterosexual behavior. Currently some rehabilitation counselors preparing former institutionalized men to live in the community face a difficult problem: to help orient them to their true sexual lifestyle. If homosexual activity is all they have ever known because of lack of opportunity for heterosexual pleasures, they need help in sorting out what their true sexual needs are so they can establish their sexual role identity.

Myths about Retardation

Although the prevention of parenthood is perhaps the most obvious and serious single factor in the deprivation of sexual rights of retarded people, other attitudes have also contributed to this oppression. One is the myth, held by most of society, that retarded men are sexually dangerous; that they automatically lack control of their sexual impulses and will assault strangers, especially little girls. Workers in the retardation field currently attempting to establish group homes find communities belligerently opposed to them: "We won't be able to allow our children to play outside if retarded men live in the neighborhood," they worry.

There has been no extensive research to statistically disprove this myth, only the assurances by those who work closely with retarded men that most of them are not sexually threatening but are only seriously lacking in social skills. When retarded men have approached others inappropriately, it has usually been for want of training in social behavior. Since the retarded often are not keenly perceptive of what sexual behavior is or is not acceptable, many do not learn what conduct wins social approval and what makes others uncomfortable. For numerous reasons such as guilt or discomfort over the handicap, caretakers have traditionally been so lax in discipline that many retarded adults lack social skills or awareness of other peoples' feelings. It is not uncommon for a retarded man to be overly friendly, perhaps touching a person who does not know him. Not only does this conduct make him socially unacceptable, but at times there can be an involvement with the law.

For example, when a 250-pound young retarded man tried to thank a woman who had helped him in a grocery store by stroking her arm, the frightened woman screamed for help. Equally frightened and subjected to considerable trauma at the hands of the police, it was some time before he could explain to his social worker that he had simply been making a gesture of appreciation. His father, it seemed, had told him that ladies enjoy having their arms stroked. Unfortunately, his father had not thought to say anything more about it.

According to Myerowitz (1971), one-third of the crimes committed by retarded males are sex related. Closely examining these "crimes" one finds that they consist in careless, ignorant acts, such as not having properly zippered pants, urinating on the sidewalk when a public toilet is not easily accessible, approaching strangers for attention, or a homosexual act with no judgment or finesse. Rape by men who are retarded is practically nonexistent, unless they are emotionally disturbed. Yet the result of such ignorant, unschooled behaviors is often arrest and sometimes imprisonment for "sexual perversion."

Whatever the cause or the situation, society's fear of the sexual behavior of the retarded male sharply reduces his chances for a normal social life in the community. We need community education to dispel the myths, and retarded persons need to be taught to understand what is appropriate and responsible sexual behavior.

Realistic Concerns

Another factor that contributes to oppression is that often retarded people have characteristics that make them more sexually exploitable than their nonhandicapped peers. If a child molester, for example, has a choice between retarded and nonretarded children, he will usually molest retarded children. Why? Because they are more likely to (1) trust strangers, (2) lack the ability to discriminate what is appropriate behavior, (3) not know how to judge the motivation for others' behaviors, (4) do what they are told, (5) show and receive affection more readily, (6) not have the ability to defend themselves, and (7) not communicate about or report the incident effectively. (Moreover, their testimony would not be upheld in court.) Without proper training, an individual often retains these characteristics throughout life, and it is not unusual for retarded women to be sexually exploited by men or for retarded men to be sexually exploited by male homosexuals.

Realistically it is important that retarded persons be protected from this kind of exploitation, and a certain amount of supervision is called for throughout their lives, especially if they are severely retarded. However, in too many cases the anxiety over exploitation results in such overprotection that again they are deprived of their sexual rights and freedom. Instead of receiving training, being supervised only when necessary (at some risk perhaps), retarded individuals have been treated as perennial children who will never learn to fend for themselves.

Recently, however, there has been strong emphasis on protection from such assault for both handicapped and nonhandicapped children. Special materials, training packages, and curriculum have been developed. Seminars are being presented for professionals and parents, and some schools are including training in their programs. Role playing, for instance, has proven a helpful technique for teaching retarded persons to guard against exploitation.

Another sexual oppression of mentally retarded people is the manner in which their masturbatory activities have been handled. In promoting the sexual rights of the retarded, one could hardly expect every retarded person to someday find sexual fulfillment with another human being. For some, masturbation may be the best outlet for their sexual impulses, allowing them some degree of sexual satisfaction. However, most of them are not receiving effective guidance toward this goal.

Historically masturbation was thought to be a causative factor in mental retardation. This belief has been discarded. Nevertheless masturbation has often been dealt with harshly, with beatings or rigid physical restraint. True, because retarded persons have not been given satisfying activities or opportunities for pleasurable social outlets, they may understandably spend more time masturbating than other people. It is also more likely that they will masturbate publicly because they have not been properly taught that it is not appropriate to touch one's genitals in the presence of others. But since they expose their sexual feelings in this manner, people tend to conclude that handicapped people cannot deal with their sexual impulses, and overly stringent methods are used to control their behavior.

Although myths about masturbation have decreased, their vestiges remain and lead to inconsistent and often oppressive approaches. In a living center, for example, one caretaker may punish residents for masturbation, another may joke about it, another may inappropriately encourage it for its tranquilizing effects, another may inappropriately pretend not to notice public masturbation, and yet another may provide both positive attitudes and appropriate behavioral guidelines. For those living at home, similar inconsistencies may occur in familial and school training. The combination of

negative, fuzzy, and inconsistent messages becomes a confusing, guilt-provoking, destructive process.

Another factor creating sexual oppression is the wealth of myths about retardation that lead to either deliberate oppression or simply "benign neglect." Retarded people are often stereotyped as all alike, unteachable, sexually uninhibited, and either innocent young children who will never be interested in sex, or as maniacal male assaultists and uncontrollably promiscuous women. At the other extreme, some people, incensed at such stereotypes, deny any difference between retarded and nonretarded people, insisting that retarded people be treated exactly the same as anyone else.

We ourselves have witnessed examples of both extremes. During a planning session for an upcoming workshop on sex education for retarded citizens, for example, a prominent physician listened to the discussion and then said to the other planners,

I don't understand all this talk about sex education. The retarded can't be educated. All you can do is see that they don't run around flooding the countryside with a bunch of retarded babies. Whenever I see a retarded girl in my office, the first thing I do is sterilize her. Then I don't give a damn what she does!

Often one set of myths sets in motion an endless process of problems. When faced with obvious and immediate difficulties in the care and feeding of retarded children, parents and professionals who believe the myth of lifelong innocence often put off even thinking about or discussing sexuality until adolescence forces the issue. Of course reluctance to provide sex education is not limited to parents of retarded children. Seldom, however, does panic rise as high as it does when a retarded child reaches adolescence. Often a few belated attempts to provide basic information and behavioral rules fail miserably with adolescents who (like other adolescents) want to "be like" everyone else, who may lack the capacity to benefit from crash courses, and who (like their peers) may be too embarrassed to talk about sex.

These anxious parents demand an unnecessary sterilization and are sometimes encouraged by unknowledgeable and equally anxious professionals. Sterilization, however, may not solve the problems. It may increase the adolescent's sense of difference, betrayal, and rebellion. Moreover, parents often remain as worried about their daughter's reputation, safety, and other sexual issues as they had been earlier about pregnancy.

At the other extreme, reluctance to admit and face "differences" also creates problems. One of us was present, for example, when a psychologist tried to tell a distraught mother that she needn't handle her retarded adolescent's sex education any differently than she had with any of her other children. As might be expected, the psychologist's attempts to lower her excessive anxiety failed. A school sex education program that does not take into account such individual problems as concrete thinking, short attention span, visual and hearing impairment, and limited retention, or that may not give adequate help in developing basic social skills, not only misses the mark—it may harm rather than help.

The reality of retardation, which in itself is another oppressive factor, is that there are wide differences between categories or "levels" of impairment, individual differences within categories, and variations over time within each person. The needs, abilities, and helpful interventions may be far different for educable children, who can fit into a public school with relative ease, than for profoundly impaired children who cannot learn basic functioning skills.

There are also wide variations in the residents of the special learning centers now widely replacing institutions. One resident might have well-defined sexual and social needs and abilities, with the intellectual capacity to benefit from simple instruction and to participate in birth control. Another may have multiple physical as well as mental handicaps, poorly defined sexual tension,

and may need instruction or help even to gain the tension relief of masturbation. Even relatively intelligent individuals may vary in capacity from moment to moment, losing fragments of sentences because of anxiety, minor brain seizures, or simply short attention span.

Of course most people vary in their needs and intellectual capacities from time to time and are similarly "handicapped" in certain areas. Anyone who has become blocked when trying to understand statistics has probably suffered from conceptual problems, short attention span, embarrassment about sounding "dumb," and so forth. Retarded people, in short, are perhaps not so different after all. One might suggest, in fact, that many problems lie not so much in difference as in the exaggeration of problems faced by most people.

Most people, however, are able to recognize when they have missed something, are able to fill in gaps in information through their own efforts (reading, listening, seeing movies), and have the conceptual ability to transfer information about one situation to other similar situations. Most people learn basic appropriate behaviors and social skills simply by correctly interpreting often subtle cues from others.

Retarded persons, to varying degrees, are severely hampered by lacking such skills. Unless given repeated concrete, specific behavioral rules, for example, they may not know when or where masturbation is appropriate. Affectionate and eager to please, they may be unable to tell when or with whom it is appropriate to bestow kisses and hugs. Such problems are compounded by the fact that retarded individuals are often given double messages. It is not uncommon for them to be reinforced for "cute" behavior or for adults to engage in inappropriate sexual joking with retarded adolescents. Such educators as Sol Gordon frequently comment that people reward behaviors with the retarded that they would not tolerate with anyone else.

Retarded people are often unable to even recognize or defend against disregard for their rights by authorities who presumably are there to help them. In the now famous Relf case (USDC, 1974), a federally funded agency was sued by the parents of two adolescent, retarded black girls for sterilizing them allegedly without informed consent. The nation was alerted to the plight of people who undergo such a procedure without being told, or without understanding what it means, or who consent to "birth control" without being told specifically what will happen to them. (In this case, there was warranted suspicion that the girls were victims of "quadruple whammy" oppression—that is, aimed not only at the retarded, but at women, blacks, and the poor.) The governmental response seems typical of the unplanned, panicky solutions so often seen in attempts to solve social problems. Stringent restrictions were placed on the use of sterilization for minors and legally incompetent adults, and new regulations were drawn for such sterilizations as were allowed. Although this remedy does protect the rights of some people, its new blanket restrictions interfere with the rights of those adults who wish sterilization and are capable of participating in the decisions that affect their lives. Similarly, guardians of those who are incapable of decision making may be deprived of their right to act for the good of their charges.

Writing legislation that protects everyone is certainly a difficult process. No matter how well one tries to explain to a retarded person, for example, and no matter how well that person thinks he or she has understood, one cannot be sure that consent to sterilization is truly informed or that there has not been unintended coercion. Yet one cannot be sure that other birth control procedures have been truly understood, and unplanned pregnancies or forced abortions are equally oppressive. Perhaps there is no completely satisfactory solution. Blanket restrictions, however, have seriously complicated the issue. Despite lack of adequate research, there is experiential evidence that given adequate training and information, many retarded persons can participate in both the decision

making and carrying out of their own birth control programs. Moreover, there is no reason to assume that prevention of pregnancy is required for all retarded persons, either for genetic or child-care reasons.

Ironically, recent efforts to recognize the rights of some retarded persons to marry and have children may themselves contain the seeds of oppression. Often there seems to be an "either-or" philosophy on the part of those authorized to make decisions for retarded people. The decision is often based on whether or not a retarded couple can independently manage traditional nuclear family roles and responsibilities. It has been observed that few retarded couples can fulfill such obligations without help. Yet other more intelligent segments of society have also begun to express the strain imposed on them by traditional marriages and have found nontraditional ways to share the burden of housekeeping, finances, and child-rearing. To magnanimously "allow" a few of the retarded population to enter the same kind of marriage that has already been labeled oppressive to others sounds suspiciously like the magnanimity with which one ethnic group "allows" a new one into the ghetto it is beginning to leave.

The interweaving and reciprocal factors of the reproductive bias, myths about retardation, lack of adequate training, and both the nature of the handicap and its variations have resulted in confusing, haphazard, often conflicting approaches, even in recent attempts to attend to the needs of retarded persons. Despite great gains in the past two decades, people who are retarded continue to be oppressed both deliberately and inadvertently. They are in the triple bind of being the people who need the greatest amount of basic planned sex education, who receive the least, and who are then punished by society for not knowing what others know. Their caretakers, particularly their parents, are often in the double bind of being both victims and oppressors at the same time. Contrary to many people's beliefs, retardation does not make people immune to the same needs, worries, joys, and woes of others, nor does it make them "blissfully ignorant" of their place on society's totem pole. We ourselves have frequently heard our retarded clients make such comments as, "I *want* to be sterilized. I don't want to bring a baby into the world to go through what I've gone through," or "I don't want a baby. It would be too hard for me to care for it right."

INTERVENTIONS

In the past decade the concept of "normalization" (Nirje, 1969), started in Scandinavia and utilized in this country as "mainstreaming," has led to great progress in treatment of retarded people. This concept essentially tries to help retarded people live as normal a life as possible, by giving access to the patterns and conditions of everyday life, as closely as possible, that are part of the mainstream of society. This process includes access to the rythms of work, recreation, interpersonal relationships, developmental experiences of childhood, adolescence and adulthood, education, and so forth, that other people enjoy. It includes making one's own life decisions and seeking sexual fulfillment according to one's own needs and abilities, as part of a heterogeneous society, mixed in culture, gender, and intellectual ability. In short, it is a principle that tries to integrate retarded individuals into society as fully as possible, rather than to separate them as fully as possible.

This philosophy has already given rise to changes in education, legislatively mandating education in special settings as needed and in regular schools and classes as appropriate. It has helped to radically deinstitutionalize retarded people, relocating them in half-way houses, hostels, and private apartments. Moreover, it has recognized the need for residential settings to approximate "normal" mixed-sex life.

It is important, however, that we see the new civil rights movement of retarded people as being unique. It is the one such movement that cannot be planned and carried out by those who benefit from it. Even though with assistance many such people are beginning to recognize and enunciate their needs and rights, they must depend mainly on others—parents, guardians, such groups as the Association for Retarded Citizens, and the helping professions—to verbalize their needs for them, to organize and fight their battles for them, and to improve the counseling and other social services already offered to them. Some creative approaches that have already been initiated in a few areas must receive more widespread implementation. More thoughtful and creative approaches must be found. Interventions, then, need to take place in several spheres and at both macro- and microlevels.

Direct Services

Interventions for people who are retarded differ from those for other oppressed groups in that there are few other clients whose coping abilities are so dependent on other people. Even individual or small-group counseling, then, must almost always include work with or service to others. That work may include individual, family, or group counseling; consultation, advocacy, and mediation; referral services, education, policy making, or all of the above.

For example a couple, in which one or both partners are retarded, may want to marry. The content of their premarital counseling may be similar to what might be offered any other couple, including information and guidance about sex and family planning. It might, however, also require genetic counseling. It might entail not only referral to a doctor, but help in coping with the doctor-patient relationship, helping medical personnel to be more responsive and sensitive to the couple's needs, and assistance in making sure that both partners understand medical instructions.

Similarly, such a couple might need legal and financial assistance, help in finding housing and employment, and assistance in finding friends. Helping professionals may need to be not only referral sources and counselors, but liason agents, "interpreters," trouble shooters. They might need to take an advocacy role simply to enable parents, guardians, or legal authorities to permit such a marriage. In short, helping professionals may need to help all concerned—the couple, the family, neighbors, other community agencies—to create and utilize a support system that allows the couple to maintain as much independence and privacy as possible, while using appropriate help as needed.

One such couple might need to live in or near a residential treatment center, to avoid pregnancy, to be supported financially, and to be supervised closely. The marriage may need to be simply a looseknit arrangement that allows a limited amount of intimacy, closeness, sexuality and responsibility, without imposing the emotional and intellectual demands of a traditional nuclear family.

Another couple may be able to live in a traditional marriage, simply needing someone to help with housework or child care, with little or no financial help. Yet a supportive educational, social, counseling network may be needed to help with minor problems, fill social/recreational needs, and provide trusted resources readily available at times of crisis.

At the other extreme, sexuality-centered services for individuals who are more profoundly retarded may be largely confined to helping them obtain some sort of sexual satisfaction, to defend themselves against or to report sex abuse, to cope with such developmental changes as menstruation, and to generally obey rules for appropriate social behavior. Even with low-functioning clients, there may be considerable variation in their abilities, and hence in interventions. One person may simply need to be reassured about masturbation and to be given the rules for appropriate behavior. Another may be so grossly impaired that masturbation may be the only potential outlet for general tension as well as sexual tension, and help may be

needed for the resident to even achieve that gratification. For example, in a certain institution a resident who was hurting himself by constant head banging was taught how to masturbate. Not only did his head banging decrease, his general tension also decreased, and his general functioning improved.

While the deinstitutionalization process during the past fifteen years has emptied many institutions of their higher-functioning residents, some institutions still have residents capable of participating in group counseling and education, making requests for staff help, participating in organized social activities, and engaging in satisfying sexual relationships with other people. For such capable functioning to occur, however, the professional helper may need to serve in many roles—as advocate, consultant, educator, in-service trainer, and program planner—in order to fulfill many differing goals—to initiate programs, change institutional policies, coordinate services and educate general staff, advise and counsel parents, or act as liason between the institution and the community.

Sex Education

Perhaps with no other sexually oppressed group is "help" so closely tied to "sex education," that the two terms become almost synonymous. All of the interventions discussed above involve sex education. Yet in many settings sex education still tends to be regarded as frivolous, to lag behind other programs, and to receive inconsistent attention.

It is understandable that parents would be more concerned about immediate physical care problems following birth of a retarded child. It is the responsibility of the helping professions to help them look ahead and to take responsibility for providing planned sex education from infancy on. It is also the helping professions' responsibility to share that burden with them, and to ease the sense of guilt that may prevent them from accepting such help.

To do so starts with realizing (1) that the

basic ingredients and skills of sex education are the same for all people, regardless of age or intelligence, (2) that those basics must be (and can be) modified to fit the needs of individuals in such special groups as the mentally or physically handicapped, and (3) that depending on the degree of retardation, the needed modification may be less a problem of difference than of needing to do *more* of what one would do for anyone else. We are not suggesting here that the task is simple. We *are* suggesting, however, that the tendency to view sex education for different populations as completely separate and different processes discourages parents or other caretakers from taking the steps they need to take, and hence compounds the difficulties they will face. It is essential, then, for the helping professionals to themselves recognize some realities of all sex education, to distinguish between "planned" and "unplanned" sex education (Gochros, 1980), and to organize specific techniques for providing helpful sex education. Utilizing that conceptual framework in planning the modifications needed for retarded "students" can make the task of "modification" a far simpler process than many realize is possible.

Part of that process will be the need to redefine "sex" and "sex education," and to examine basic values about individual rights. For example, if "sex" is defined broadly to include love, intimacy and a sense of masculinity or femininity apart from child-bearing ability, and if the emphasis is on sensuality rather than on sexual intercourse, the right and ability to give and receive some form of sexual gratification (masturbation, thumb sucking, hugging, being cuddled, etc.) extends even to infants and small children and, hence, includes intellectually limited children and adults. If even infants and small children can be taught some form of responsibility (holding on to one's spoon or toy, not running into the street, not masturbating in public, not hitting, or not going away with strangers, etc.) then even adults

with severe retardation can learn some degree of responsible behavior.

Professionals need to realize, and help their clients realize, that sex education is an unavoidable and lifelong socialization process in which *everybody continually* gives and receives information and values about sexuality both verbally and nonverbally. That education comes from many sources. It is often given unintentionally, through body language, tones of voice, through newspapers and movies, through spontaneous reactions to some incident, and so forth, with neither the giver nor the receiver realizing what messages have been transmitted. Hence most sex education (even some in formal courses) is unplanned; whether it is helpful, harmful, or useless thus is strictly up to chance.

Neither parents nor professionals, then, can "choose" whether or not to provide sex education to a specific group, individual, or age. They can only choose to take the initiative in making the sex education they *do* provide as clear, helpful, and effective as possible—that is, to provide as much planned sex education as possible. *Planned sex education* stems from advance planning, in which one (1) clarifies one's own values, (2) thinks about the information *adults* may need, (3) plans both verbal and nonverbal ways to build such information and values into daily relationships and conversations, and (4) devises specific techniques for specific situations, people, or ages. Planned sex education, then, does not necessarily mean formal education. It simply provides a more thoughtful approach, increasing the possibility that spontaneous and unplanned "education" will be consistent with what one would truly wish to provide.

The specific technique of "door opening" (discussed in Chapter 3) gives parents and professionals alike greater ability to create opportunities for education. Sadly enough, because professionals have given the impression that it is the "right" way to provide sex education, too often parents wait for questions to come from the child and professionals wait for questions to come from the parents. The result is that such questions sometimes never come or, when they do, the parent or professional is unprepared and cannot cope. Moreover, too often it has taken some drastic situation to force the issue, and the lack of foundation for communication plus the panic of a crisis situation has made the discussion far more difficult than it would have been earlier.

Parents for example, often fail to mention birth control until adolescence, when the discussion is more necessary but far more complicated. Moreover, adolescents who are sexually active are notoriously fearful of asking a partner to use protection and will hardly be apt to do so if values about birth control have not been ingrained. The same problems exist and are perhaps accentuated with retarded adolescents, who may be even more afraid to alienate others. And if the first discussion of birth control or sterilization is seen as an attempt to deny the retarded teenager the pleasures and rights that others seem to have, heightening feelings of difference and lowering self-esteem, it is not apt to be received with much enthusiasm. Parents need to be helped to start talking about birth control when their children are little, and to think through ahead of time what to say and how they might talk to a six year old, how to provide occasional "reminders" as the child gets older, and how they might initiate the fuller discussion that an adolescent will need. A three year old, for instance, may need no more than the information that *many* people do not wish babies, or can't care for them, and take steps to prevent them. A retarded child may need such simple information repeated many times over the years in order to eventually participate in a family planning program or to accept sterilization without feeling betrayed and resentful.

If planned sex education is necessary for average children, it is even more important for retarded children. It is especially unfortunate that the parents whose planning tasks will be the most difficult are often given too little direction too late. Professionals, then, must become role models themselves by opening doors to discussion and advance thinking about sexuality, using the same ground rules that they help others to use:

1. "Door openers" are a tool of initiative. Practitioners need not wait for people to ask, nor need they force people to "walk through." They need only utilize any opportunity to stimulate thinking and discussion, increasing the chances to be helpful.

2. It is never too early or too late to use them, but they are more effective when started early and continued. It is the responsibility of the most knowledgeable (the professional or the parent) to not only open doors once, but to be willing to reopen the same doors periodically, and to open wider the doors that a "student" has opened a crack.

3. Door openers can provide specific information or values, answer questions, or stimulate thinking and questions. They can be verbal or nonverbal, and range from simple facial expressions or one-liners to full-blown discussions. (Example: "I was just thinking, soon your body is going to start changing. Want to know how?")

4. Common sense and empathy must be used to fit the specific "education" to the specific person and situation. Generally, however, the basic idea applies to all ages and intellects. Only the specifics need be changed. For example, all young children need their education in simple, concrete terms, often with simple pictures or games, and with very specific behavioral rules. They need information repeated often, and more complex discussion needs to be added bit by bit. Retarded youngsters and adults need *more* simplicity, *more* aids, *more* repetition, *more* specificity, and far more initiative on the part of the educator.

For example, an occupational therapist in a special education school helped children develop general body image by having their body outlines traced on large sheets of paper and then asking them to write in the names of the neck, legs, arms, ears, and so forth. Watching this, the social worker in charge of sex education simply asked the occupational therapist to include genitalia and breasts in the body parts. For the youngest children, that "sex education" was simply part of the basic knowledge they needed. For older children, it became a door opener to slightly more complicated discussion.

Creativity and planning are needed for fitting adult subjects to children's levels of understanding. This is true for all students. It is even more true for retarded students, who may need to grapple with complex adult issues in ways that a child can understand. Many interesting materials have been developed to fit sex education to the needs of retarded students. Slides, pictures, books, dolls with genitalia, and life-size models all help to get points across. Special materials still need to be made more accessible. But until they are, parents, teachers, and other professionals can create their own materials and use such techniques as work with clay, story telling, and so on, to overcome such problems as short attention span and lack of conceptual ability.

Sex education must include the teaching of social skills and coping with the handicap. Role playing, for instance, has proved helpful in teaching the art of conversation, teaching appropriate behavior, learning how to judge and avoid danger, and how to cope with stigma and face retardation without losing self-esteem (Gochros, 1980; Kempton, 1980; Johnson & Kempton, 1981).

Again, sex education of the retarded almost always involves service to, work with, and/or education of others. Parents and appropriate colleagues must be engaged in a team problem-sharing effort, with every possible technique used to ensure that the retarded student has understood what he or she has been told. Parents and colleagues must be encouraged to ask students what they have learned, to give feedback to each other, plan and coordinate strategies, work out areas of disagreement, and join in mutual problem solving. This can be done through workshops, parent groups, personal contacts, staff meetings, and letters. Role playing can be helpful to parents and staff

alike. Often a videotape of a professional discussing sex with a group of retarded children or adults, with the professional comfortable about discussing his or her errors as well as successes, can be both reassuring and encouraging. In viewing such films, parents often realize for the first time that their children are interested in and capable of learning about sex. Nervous parents or staff members can also be helped to gain comfort by including them in a professionally led demonstration group gradually drawing them into the discussion.

Levels of Education

Since retarded students have limited and sometimes no capacity to evaluate information and apply it appropriately to their own individual situation, and since there is such a wide variety of abilities and levels of functioning, the specific content of sex education cannot be generalized to fit the total population. What is appropriate for a mildly impaired person might be inappropriate for a severely handicapped one. The following guidelines, however, can be used.

Generally, the more impaired the student, the simpler the education can be. The content and approach should be based on (1) the level of understanding the student can reach, (2) the purpose or goals for teaching, and (3) how the material can be most effectively presented.

For example, how would one help a young woman prepare for her first menstrual period? At the lowest functioning level, the *purpose* would be mainly to prevent her from being frightened at the sight of menstrual blood emerging from her body. A slightly higher goal, but one which should be attempted even for seriously retarded young women, would be to teach proper social behavior while menstruating (that is, not to flaunt the fact that she is menstruating before others) and to teach the self-care of cleanliness, changing and disposal of soiled pads, and so forth. Achievable objectives might end right there with assurance that proper steps had been taken for the young woman's needs.

At a higher level, teaching why one menstruates should be possible, with some effort to explain the monthly time factor. At this level young men should also receive information about menstruation. At an even higher level one could explain the reproductive process still further and attempt to find out what more the student is interested in and capable of learning. Finally, at the highest level, the same information and discussion used in any sex education program could be included, such as psychological and social factors, implications of menstruation in the entire reproductive process, menopause, hormonal body changes, and so on.

Methods of instruction must again be geared to the level of functioning. At the lowest level, the young woman might have to see or experience to learn: for instance, she might need to see someone else's soiled pad in order to be reassured that menstruation is not dangerous. At a higher level she would need explicit pictures, much repetition, very simple terms, very short sessions, and possibly dramatic play such as pantomime to rehearse behaviors. At the next level pictures would still be needed, but with more complicated explanation and a slightly higher language level. At the highest level of functioning, a verbal exchange of ideas can take place and may not be too different from discussion with any other student. Still, the special problems of each individual must be kept in mind.

There are, of course, situations which present unique problems and require unusual creativity. In an example used earlier, teaching a head banger to handle his sexual needs through masturbation, the psychologist working with the young man was faced with both an ethical issue (how does one teach someone to masturbate?) and a communication problem (the young man was deaf and mute). Her solution was ingenious. Searching a local "sex shop" for potential models, she found an inflatable man with a huge penis, and using the model she pantomimed

her instructions. With the rest of her staff cooperating she was also able to pantomime social ground rules.

It is important to remember that guidelines must be used flexibly. A seriously impaired person may at times be able to use limited discussion and may be able to conceptualize. A mildly impaired person, like anyone else, may be able to manage very complicated material at one time and fail to comprehend the simplest material at another.

Mid- and/or Macrolevel Interventions

Many services such as advocacy, parent counseling and education, and in-service training have already been mentioned. These, of course, have been aimed at people who play some direct role in the life of a particular client. Just as important, however, is the need for broader interventions serving to effect institutional changes and social and legislative reform, to increase public awareness and understanding of retardation and its victims, to find better methods of caring for and teaching retarded persons, and to prevent and cure retardation.

For example, social-political action is needed to design and secure fair abortion laws that allow voluntary termination of pregnancies apt to result in a retarded child and that do not discriminate between those who can use private facilities and those who must use state or federally funded facilities. Similarly, we need to obtain sterilization laws that neither interfere with the rights to obtain sterilization when needed and to use less permanent measures when possible, nor the right of the retarded individual to be involved in the decision making to the fullest extent possible.

Other social-political action might focus on obtaining and maintaining programs aimed at retarded citizens or indirectly benefiting them. For example, there must be protections against mainstreaming being misused as a way of closing facilities or programs without providing adequate substitutes. Although legislation now mandates the right to general education, planned sex education needs to be explicitly made part of the curriculum. Right now the approach to both sexuality and retardation is very uneven: we have seen schools in which retarded children are the only ones not to receive planned sex education, and others in which the special-education sexuality program is better than that taught to the rest of the school.

"Paper" rights are only a beginning: beyond rights must be ways to translate those rights into actual living. For example, it does little good to prepare retarded people for social-sexual relationships if they have no place to conduct activities and nobody with whom to associate. It does little good to teach them that sexual behavior should be conducted in private if they have no private space. It does no good to grant the right to marriage or children and then deny them even the same supports available to others, to say nothing of the added supports that will compensate for their handicap. Social-political action has been making progress in establishing smaller residential institutions, daycare centers, and community centers to supervise retarded persons living in the community. This must continue and increase.

Welfare programs, including child-care facilities and services, must be made more responsive to the needs of retarded adults not only in providing financial assistance but in helping to cope with daily living. Innovative ways can be sought to help retarded persons share the joys of family life and having children. For example, in a controlled setting, mildly and even moderately retarded women are often excellent with children, since they become less bored than most adults with childrens' games. Special adoptive or foster care contracts or group-parenting programs could be developed to allow retarded and nonretarded adults to share the parenting of a child. Such a program would have its problems, to be sure. But there have been many recent examples to suggest that creative thinkers can find creative solutions to seemingly insurmountable problems.

The Nipon Society, a Philadelphia socialization agency, for instance, is an example of creative progress in enhancing social activities. Its retarded clients take busses to and from the agency for counseling, education, and social events. The "Guided Tour" program, an offshoot of this agency, takes groups of retarded adults on trips across not only the nation but also the world. Under the guidance of excellent counselors, they encounter much fewer social-sexual problems than the average tour group often has. The "Guided Tour" clientele consists of both single and married people, and there are many among them who feel that its programs have changed their lives. A strong advantage of these tours is that the mentally retarded tourists are mingling with the general public as peers. Many a tourist has admitted that his or her entire conception of retarded people was changed after conversing with them as fellow travelers on the plane or bus. Retarded people *can* be their own advocates, given opportunity and training.

One of us was recently involved in a special seminar that exemplified the possibility for creative approaches. Attended by 300 professionals, it was devoted entirely to sharing ways and means of helping handicapped persons carry on successful marriages. Special programs are being offered married couples in some areas, with group meetings, sex therapy, and counseling on all aspects of dating and marriage. The Crafts, a professional couple in North Wales, have proved that even severely mentally and physically handicapped couples can be happily married if they are provided a sheltering home on the premises of their institution, and constant, vigilant supervision. In their book *Handicapped Married Couples* (1979), the Crafts describe 35 of these marriages. Unfortunately, the above programs are not universally available. Helping professionals would do well to work toward creating such programs in the United States and other countries.

Education and Research

To truly effect change, the public must become more informed about retardation. Thus much of the needed intervention is education aimed, not at changing retarded citizens or their families, but at changing public perceptions and attitudes. To a large extent this has been and must continue to be done *for* rather than by the retarded population itself. Yet with help many retarded citizens have proved more effective myth-dispellers than their more eloquent champions, not only in such programs as "Guided Tours," but as speechmakers and as actors in TV programs and movies that focus on their special problems.

Finally more research is needed to prevent, diagnose, and treat retardation, to evaluate teaching and counseling effectiveness, and to provide the information on which both policy and attitudinal changes are based.

CONCLUSION

Actions that can be taken to end sexual oppression of the retarded are much the same whether it be a professional, a parent, or an outside member of the community who undertakes the task. There will be differences in time and energy spent and in the amount of ground that can be covered, but in order to succeed the same essential process must be followed by all.

We must (1) take inventory of our own personal feelings and accept our own sexuality as being a positive part of ourselves; (2) believe that this can also be the case for people who are retarded; (3) give retarded people as much knowledge as they can integrate, including special training in preventing exploitation; (4) give them the opportunity to marry, with much supportive help; (5) if they wish to extend a social relationship into a sexual relationship, see that they have the same opportunity to do so as anyone else; (6) concentrate on training them to be socially acceptable and helping them develop social skills so that they can enjoy the company of both sexes; (7) help them have fun, travel, enjoy all the adult activities that anyone else can enjoy, within their limitations.

We could mention many more possibilities; it should be unnecessary to do so. Sexual oppression of retarded people will have to end if the overall goals of normalization, deinstitutionalization, and mainstreaming are to be realized in the not too distant future. Progress may be erratic, but, now that it has begun, it is our conviction that we can't turn back. The sexual revolution—whatever we believe that means—just won't allow it.

REFERENCES

CRAFT, M., AND CRAFT, A. *Handicapped married couples.* Boston: Routledge and Kegan Paul, 1979.

GARBER, H. The Milwaukee Project: An experiment in the prevention of cultural-familial mental retardation—intervention at birth. In M. Bass and M. Gelof, eds. *Sexual rights and responsibilities of the mentally retarded.* Santa Barbara, Calif.: Channel Lithograph, 1973.

GOCHROS, J. *What to say after you clear your throat: A parent's guide to sex education.* Kailua, Hawaii: Press Pacifica, 1980.

JOHNSON, W., AND KEMPTON, W. *Sex education and counseling of special groups.* Springfield, Ill.: Charles Thomas, 1981.

KEMPTON, W. *Sex education for persons with disabilities that hinder learning: A teacher's guide.* Philadelphia: Planned Parenthood of Southeastern Pennsylvania, 1980.

MYEROWITZ, J. Sex and the mentally retarded. *Medical aspects of sexuality,* November 1971.

NIRJE, B. The normalization principle and its human management implications. In R. Kugel and W. Wolfensberger, eds. *Changing patterns in residential services for the mentally retarded.* Washington, D.C.: President's Committee on Mental Retardation, 1969.

RELF ET AL. V. *WEINBERGER ET AL.,* Civil Action Number 73-1557; and *National Welfare Rights Organization* v. *Weinberger et al.,* Civil Action Number 74-243, USDC, DC. 1974.

17

THE PHYSICALLY DISABLED
Susan E. Knight

It is common for professionals and lay people alike to view persons with disabilities as asexual. The media say that sexual activity is acceptable only for the young, the rich and powerful, the physically attractive and/or agile. Although most able-bodied persons come to the self-awareness that "while I'm not perfect, neither is anyone else," the person with a disability is seen as too far from physical perfection to be attractive.

Societal expectations of people with disabilities include celibacy, poor body image, and physical and emotional dependency. As with all stereotypes, there is a grain of truth. People will always be able to point to someone with a disability who seems sexually unattractive and/or disinterested, ill at ease with his or her body, and very dependent on others to meet all personal needs. It is, however, the acceptance of these stereotypes as the "norm" that is erroneous. Persons with disabilities are as varied as the able-bodied.

Such myths can hold individuals back from reaching their full sexual and social potential, because it labels the person before he or she has an opportunity to construct a self-definition.

Because people with disabilities struggle with such negative expectations, it is not uncommon for many of them to need sexual education and counseling services in order to gain sexual pleasure and self-esteem. Helping professionals, once aware of the need, are in a position to assist the individual and couple in gaining the services that will enrich this very important part of each person's life.

THE PROBLEM

Understanding the process of sex therapy for persons having a physical disability is a very difficult task. People with physical disabilities, and their partners, are men and women first and disabled second. Their experience of the sexual effect of the disability varies dramatically from person to person, and from couple to couple. Because of this diversity of personal sexual experience, it has been difficult if not impossible to develop step-by-step interventions to remediate the sexual concerns of this very diverse population. Limitations aside, there are specific issues that most people who are personally dealing with disabilities report as concerns. For example, sexual discrimination and negative body image can be dealt with, if not systematically, at least in an empathetic and focused manner. This chapter will discuss these and other common issues of persons with disabilities as well as give examples as to how these concerns can be addressed therapeutically.

One reason that persons with disabilities form such a heterogeneous and diverse grouping has to do with the impact of the person's age and prior life and sexual experience on their adjustment to the disability. The person born with a disability will have a much different initial self-awareness sexually than a person disabled as an adult. Although the exact degree and type of disability is important to the person's self-image, as is family and peer support or lack thereof, the age of onset of disability does appear to be a highly significant factor in sexual development.

A decade ago the disabled lived in a society that basically saw them as radically different from others, unattractive, and as people who do not experience sexual feelings. For example, during the early work at the Sex and Disability Unit of the University of California Human Sexuality Program (San Francisco), it was not uncommon to counsel persons with disabilities who wanted to know why they *were* feeling sexual. Then, not only were stereotypes of sexuality held by the society at large, but often by the individual with the personal experience of disability as well. The civil and social rights movement of the disabled in the 1970s did much to erode such myths so that, today, most persons with disabilities know that they are sexual. The universality of sexual feeling is also acknowledged increasingly by health and human services personnel and, to a lesser degree, by the society at large due to such popular movies as *Coming Home*. However, acknowledgment of one's sexuality by oneself and others does not erase the problems of social and sexual skill development, partner selection, and the impact of sexual discrimination that still exists, embodied in the phrase: "Yes, I know they're sexual, but I'm not sure I'd want my (son or daughter) to marry one."

The feelings of the actual or potential partner, whether disabled or able-bodied, are also extremely important. If I have a disability how do I feel about other persons with disabilities as potential partners, and if I'm able-bodied what attitudes about disability do I bring to this relationship? If the person I'm in a relationship with has significant mobility restrictions, what role do I play in their life? Am I a lover, personal care attendant, or both? What do I feel about restrictions, if any, on our social and sexual lives? If I am either disabled or able-bodied, what do I say and feel when my family and friends question why I've picked a person with a disability as a partner? These issues are central to the therapeutic process when dealing with the individual and couple and need to be addressed along with concerns of sexual enjoyment and pleasure.

BROADSCALE INTERVENTIONS

It is both impossible and undesirable to provide direct sexual therapy to all disabled and their partners. Many people can be helped to a very significant degree by educational programs that address sexual myths about disability and which provide appropriate information on the impact of various disabilities on sexuality.

Seminars on sex and disability have been conducted throughout the country for the last 15 years. At the Human Sexuality Program just mentioned, lay persons, many of whom themselves had disabilities, were trained to provide community education. In researching this effort, it was found by this author (Knight, 1981) that:

Disabled persons with sexual and social concerns do not, for the most part, need psychotherapy to deal with these issues. Instead, education and information sharing in an empathetic manner, either individually or in a group, often supplies the support many of us need to make our lives more fulfilling.

Thus sexual counseling can be reserved for those people who either do not have access to educational seminars or who are still struggling with sexual issues after obtaining correct information.

COUNSELING ISSUES

Lifelong Disability

For most able-bodied parents and siblings, the birth of a child with a disability is often their first personal exposure to society's view of disability and what it feels like to be seen as different from peers. When parents or siblings show the child to family and friends or walk down the street with the child, they are often confronted by reactions of pity, repulsion, inappropriate curiosity, sadness, and even anger from both strangers and those people closest to them. Since the child is an extension of themselves and because others, in fact, do see them as different because they are related to the child, the family experiences firsthand the isolation and sometimes shame that comes from being "not normal" or "disabled."

When a child is born with a disability, the parents experience the loss of the able-bodied child they had hoped for. Because the child with a disability is not dead but rather is alive and "imperfect," the child reminds the parents daily of the loss they have suffered (Solvit & Stark, 1961). If the parents see these feelings as a healthy response

to having a child with a disability, they will be able to accept the feelings and go on with their life tasks. Positive expression of sexuality signifies one's sense of aliveness and joy in living. If I experience my life and that of my child as mainly tragic, I will not experience my own sexuality or the child's as a positive and natural part of life. Certainly one way to ensure positive sexual growth of these children is to encourage the sexual rights of their parents. Counseling and helping parents to find time for themselves and their relationship(s), and providing sex education and counseling for them as indicated, will go far in preparing them to see their children as having sexual rights.

Establishing mature sexual relationships demands that one achieve a significant degree of independence from parental figures. A complicating factor in the emotional development of people born with a disability is that they often remain physically dependent much longer than able-bodied individuals. The parents of the adolescent or young adult with a disability must not only condone the independence of their child but, because of mobility and sometimes speech problems, must encourage the child's individuation and actively participate in the means by which this can be accomplished. The parents of the able-bodied child know that the child will most likely "take" its independence. Unfortunately, parents of the child with a disability such as cerebral palsy must actually give and encourage independence to the degree that the child is able to manage. Parents are often put in conflict with an often unspoken social norm: that is, that a person can be sexual when they become independent of their parents or parental figures. Given this value in society, it is not surprising that many parents, wanting the best for the child, often have great difficulty helping their child obtain access to the social and sexual information and experience they need to mature. Thus it is common for people with congenital disabilities to seek out sexual counseling *after* they become physically independent of their parents.

A 40-year-old man with moderate cerebral palsy came to see this author, and when asked why he came for counseling said, "I think I'm old enough to learn about sex." He was college-educated, fully employed, and had been living by himself away from his parents for three years. In questioning him further, the author found that the full extent of his sexual knowledge was that he knew he had a penis, but knew nothing about male or female sexual response or female anatomy. When asked if any "white sticky stuff" ever came out of his penis, he replied: "Yes, and doesn't that have something to do with my cerebral palsy?"

This man had obviously gotten the message early in life that sexuality was something that only able-bodied people experienced, that since he wasn't "normal" all the sexual messages and information that surround us didn't apply to him. Two things in this man's experience stand out as common to the sexual awareness of congenitally disabled persons:

1. Independence from parental figures usually allows the individual to ask questions about sexuality for the first time, no matter what the person's biological age is.
2. Prior to adequate sex education, the individual often links sexual feelings and experiences with the disability rather than as pleasures shared by all people. At this stage of awareness, a person often sees him or herself *as* a disability, rather than a person *with* a disability.

Initial therapy sessions with this man consisted of having him purchase a book on sexuality and discussing the information with this author. He became very excited to learn that his feelings and sensations were normal and soon began to acknowledge that he masturbated to orgasm, an experience which he had had no label for previously. Once he had information about female anatomy and sexual expression, he became very interested in what a sexual experience with a woman would be like, as well as how he might meet women as either friends or lovers. He was very isolated, and time in counseling was spent on developing social skills and on discussing ways he might gradually increase contact with women through coffee dates, attending church and social functions, and taking classes where interesting people might be. He was also encouraged to begin attending meetings and social events within the disabled community. Not only was he unaware that his sexual responses were normal, but this man also did not realize that his sense of being "different" was shared by many of his disabled peers. Developing a sense of group identity with other disabled persons is often a necessary step in the individual realizing that he or she is a person first and seeing the disability as secondary to their self-concept.

The next step was for this man to gain some sexual experience so that he could know what partner sex felt like, as well as what part his disability played, if any, in his sexual expression. A significant number of virgins with disabilities have difficulty in developing early sexual relationships due to fears that they will not know how to perform sexually or that they cannot function sexually at all. Initial sexual experience in a supportive environment, such as sessions with a sexual surrogate, can answer such questions, freeing the person to then initiate contact with potential sexual partners. This man was seen by a sexual surrogate for five two-hour sessions. During these meetings, he was able to learn what sexual experiences he enjoyed with a partner, what female genitals looked and felt like, as well as how to touch, kiss, and ask a partner how she would like to be pleasured. Supportive, therapeutic sexual experience with surrogate partners does not necessarily erase or mediate performance fears in future "nonclinical" sexual encounters. However, this kind of body-work therapy can answer the question, "How can I do it?"—which is critical to the sexual development of persons with disabilities who have limited access to initial sexual experience.

Some therapists, especially those outside large metropolitan areas, may not have access to the services of trained sexual surrogates and may wonder if this learning might not be gotten through experience with prostitutes. The answer most often is no. One man, with mild cerebral palsy, came for counseling because he could not develop close social or sexual relationships with women. He had been sexually active with prostitutes for five years. He felt that he could not develop a relationship because he did not make "enough" money (he was fully employed and lower-middle class), and because he felt he came too quickly for a woman to accept him sexually. He had been given the feedback from a number of women, including the therapist, that he approached them as sexual objects and in a very aggressive manner. He left therapy early on, admitting that it was too anxiety provoking for him to talk about his feelings, especially when in the presence of a woman he felt was attractive. He had been used to dealing with this anxiety by "getting off and getting out." By paying for sex, with the expectation that he was there to ejaculate rather than to relate interpersonally and experience pleasure, the stage was set for him to feel that he needed to be wealthy and last a long time to be attractive to a "real" (nonprostitute) woman. This client's experience points out both the limitations and, more importantly, the potential destructiveness of sustained sexual experience with prostitutes. A business where sexual response is timed, paid for, and feelings are ignored and/or repressed is not a place where sexual or personal growth can occur. It is not surprising that this man equated paying for therapy with prostitution, so that paying this author for therapy meant in his mind that the therapist couldn't possibly care about him. Given his image of how a man acts toward a woman he pays, he continually made sexual approaches and expressed in many ways that, to prove the therapist saw him as a person rather than a "customer," she had to drop the therapeutic relationship and date him socially and sexually. This man's experience is truly tragic, because he has been conditioned through his own na-

iveté and low self-esteem to be continually frustrated and sexually limited in his relationships with women. Society might say, "Well, at least he can get off with a prostitute," but this is damning the disabled man to a very restricted and unfulfilled sexual and social life. "You get what you pay for" is not an attitude of life experience conducive to the development of intimacy and sexual growth.

It is not surprising that this discussion about gaining sexual experience has focused on men. Culturally, we have expected men to gain sexual experience before developing an intimate relationship. Although "sowing wild oats" today is less an expectation for men than it once was, it still exists in our social and sexual repertory for American men. Likewise, the idea that a woman, able-bodied or disabled, would seek out a therapeutic relationship for the purpose of exploring her sexual response with a partner is seen by most people as very strange, indeed. Surrogates who work with women do exist and their services are equally valuable; however, they are used much less frequently than are the equivalent services for men. Most women with disabilities rely on either the development of a committed relationship or, more commonly, the approach by a willing but casual partner for initial experience. Although casual can mean caring, pleasing, and even educational, more often it is experienced as a "sympathy fuck" or "he is only doing this because he doesn't think anyone else will." Women who feel that "I'd better take what he is offering, even if I don't particularly like him," are experiencing a not too dissimilar experience as do men with prostitutes, mainly that, "I'm not worth anything more."

Persons disabled from birth may never have experienced making choices in relationships. Like many of their able-bodied peers, they may need counseling in assertiveness (which can mean learning to say "no, thank you" as well as "I'd like to"), in making choices, and in sexual exploration through masturbation. Such experiences allow the individual to learn about his or her own sexual responses and to be able to see partner sex as an option, rather than the only way to be sexual.

Acquired Disability

The person who has spent his or her childhood and adolescence as an able-bodied person and then becomes disabled grieves over the loss of a body part, a lost degree of mobility, or other handicap. Acquired disability covers a vast range of disabilities and experiences, from surgery and traumatic injury and disease all the way to, for some people, the aging process itself. A man this author knows, who uses a wheelchair, once told of an experience where a woman approached him and said, "I know just how you feel; I lost a finger in a work accident two years ago and my life hasn't been the same since." Although we both laughed at the extreme nature of this woman's identification with him as disabled, this is a very good example of how the loss associated with an acquired disability is as great as the person, him or herself, experiences it and is not necessarily tied to the specific degree of physical impairment or disfigurement. Not surprisingly, persons who have had positive relationships with disabled people before their own experience often can put the disability in a more productive perspective than can someone with no positive history. Sexually, the same holds true. The person who experiences sexual difficulties and/or great sexual anxiety before their injury will most likely see a disability (whether or not it actually affects sexual mobility or response) as a major hurdle or the "death blow" to their sexual experience. Likewise, an individual who in the past felt satisfied sexually only within a narrow range of sexual expression (for example, only in the missionary position) and who now, with an amputated leg, could have sex more comfortably in the side-to-side or woman-on-top position, may similarly feel that, sexually, "I'm no good anymore."

Sex therapy for the person and/or couple experiencing acquired disability needs to focus on an exploration of how the person(s) experience the impact of the disability. This examination needs to address what has and has not changed physically and emotionally, and specifically how this change relates to their sexual activity. In the case of a change in physical mobility and/or sexual response (that is, in spinal cord injury), increasing the number of sexual activities is often necessary for satisfactory sexual expression. The spinal cord-injured individual can often have coitus as well as be able to stimulate the partner through oral and manual means. However, the unimpaired partner may feel frustrated, not being able to sexually satisfy the person with the injury. The impact of spinal cord injury on the sexual response cycle is described elsewhere (Geiger, 1981). The often more important aspect of how a person with limited sensation can gain sexual satisfaction is much less explored in the literature. Through clinical data developed at the Sex and Disability Unit (University of California, San Francisco) and elsewhere, it is known that through self and partner sensate focus exercises, a number of persons with spinal cord injuries have found areas of their bodies—the breasts, ears, and neck, for example—that when stimulated lead to successful completion of the sexual response cycle. The Masters & Johnson Institute provides a very explicit example of this physiological phenomenon in this description of a paraplegic woman without genital sensation during masturbation in the laboratory (Kolodney, Masters & Johnson, 1979):

When this subject was monitored . . . during breast stimulation, it was noted that cardiopulmonary responses to sexual excitation and orgasm were normal and changes observed in the breasts and nipples were normal, but there was no significant degree of pelvic vasocongestion or vagina lubrication. However, in the late portion of the plateau phase of the response cycle (identified by the breast changes that occurred), the lips of the woman's mouth became engorged to twice their normal size. At the moment of orgasm, a pulsating wave was observed in her lips and the swelling then dissipated rapidly in a manner almost identical of the pattern seen with the dissipation of the orgasmic platform formed at the outer portion of the vagina in non-cord-injured women.

To date, no systematic treatment plan of sensate exercises has been published for persons with limited or no genital sensation. However, the model of group or individual treatment of a nonorgasmic woman using self and partner sensate focus exercises described by Barbach gives good guidelines for development of treatment exercises for cord-injured men and women (Barbach, 1980). Although these individuals are not anorgasmic in the classic sense, the need to develop sexual response in a previously understimulated area can be seen as analogous to the treatment of women who have not experienced full genital arousal and response.

A note of caution is warranted here for the clinician not familiar with the range of disabilities that cause limitations of movement. It is assumed by many that anyone who uses a wheelchair must have limited genital sensation. Although a number of persons with spinal cord injury, spinal bifida, and, in some cases, multiple sclerosis, do experience changes in genital responsiveness, the majority of persons with other disabilities who use wheelchairs have complete genital sensation and unchanged genital sexual response. Even among persons with "changes" in genital sensation, many have some degree of genital sensitivity and awareness remaining which they may or may not know of themselves and which may possibly be incorporated into their sexual repertoire. Sensation and response can be separate phenomena in this population. Up to 85 percent of spinal-cord-injured women lubricate vaginally when stimulated directly and the same percentage of men get erections whether the individual is aware of it or not (Geiger, 1981). Therapy should include assignments to the individual and couple which explore these responses, finding what degree of sensation and/or response exists and how it can

be incorporated into the sexual repertoire if desired.

Issues of Partners

The partner of the disabled person has often been neglected in the therapeutic relationship. When persons acquire a disability, their partners will often face many of the same feelings and social reactions that the parent of the child born with a disability does. Partners, who most likely have no previous experience with disability, now find themselves flooded by their own negative stereotypes of what a disabled person is, including feeling their loved ones must now be asexual, dependent, and emotionally inadequate. At the same time, if they are successfully able to label these messages as untrue, they will still meet pity and/or morbid curiosity from family, friends, or strangers who speak about how noble, crazy, or unaware they must be to be with this person after the injury. They may also be receiving these messages from their partners, who, especially in the early stages of dealing with the disability, may feel they can no longer fulfill their social, intimate, and sexual roles. The sexual and relationship needs of the partner are often disregarded by helping professionals; they should be dealt with in counseling, both in individual and couples formats (Hartman, MacIntosh & Engelhart, 1983).

Whether or not the couple was in the relationship when the disability occurred, the issue of what physical roles the able-bodied or less disabled partner will take on can have great impact on the sexual relationship of the couple. If one person has to do all the physical tasks around the house, it is important for the other to take on activities such as managing financial or social-recreational activities, so that both partners feel an equality of effort. Of course hiring others to take on some of the household duties of one or both partners is certainly an attractive alternative for partners with resources. Yet surprisingly, these issues often need to be negotiated in couple counseling. There may be an injunction in the relationship that the able-bodied or less disabled person should do all physical tasks . . . "if they really love the other person." This attitude needs to be challenged: inequality does not help to sustain love, and besides, many "normal" couples would be delighted to hire someone else to do these chores. An associated issue has to do with how much personal care (dressing and toileting) one partner should do for another who has severe mobility impairment. Some couples feel that being both an attendant and a lover has a negative effect on the sexual relationship, finding that one or both people have difficulty switching from a clinical perspective to a more intimate touching relationship. Still other people find that this kind of interaction and the physical ramifications of disability enhance their sexual expression. Such an example is described in the following candid vignette written by a woman with a spinal cord injury whose lover served as her attendant:

A sense of humor is so very necessary in our relationship; we goof about everything that goes on. You can't get too serious about incontinence. We allude to it in our lovemaking; we talk about "golden showers." Even though we empty my bladder before intercourse, there's no guarantee that I won't be incontinent while we're having intercourse because of the stimulation of pushing on the bladder. If I should get wet, well, that's a normal and exciting part of our relationship. (Finkle et al.,1981)

Couples need to be reassured that the issue of attendant care is not one of love but of personal and couple preference. They need to realize that barbershops and laundries exist for couples who choose not to do each other's hair or shirts, and the same goes for the hiring of outside attendants when available and affordable. There are enough issues, such as the limits on shared physical activities, that cannot be changed; the ability to hire outside help should at least be explored with a couple. Such inquiry is impor-

tant; it could increase equality and decrease real or potential frustration and unresolved anger in the relationship.

In closing, we should emphasize the need to utilize current sex and communication techniques in working with individuals and couples affected by physical disabilities. Persons with physical disabilities and their partners can and do experience sexual and communication difficulties not related to the disability. Such concerns, and those which are specifically related to the disability, need to be dealt with in as supportive, educative, behavioral, and efficient a fashion as possible, just like they are with able-bodied individuals and couples.

Other issues such as sexual preference, religious attitudes, sexual and physical abuse, and problems with alcohol and drug abuse can impact greatly on one's sexual experience and adjustment. This is as true for the individual with a disability as it is for the able-bodied. These factors need to be assessed and dealt with in the counseling process, along with the topics already discussed.

Social Skills Issues of the Disabled

Problems with social skills are common for the disabled individual and may make obtaining social and/or sexual relationships difficult. Fear of rejection, questions of how to present the disability to people one is interested in getting to know, and what to look for in a potential partner are all issues that are shared by single persons with disabilities.

Many persons with disabilities anticipate more rejection than they actually face. The person born with a disability may have experienced rejection by able-bodied peers during the school years, and such early programming can cause the individual to overanticipate rejection in the adult world. Likewise, people who later acquire a disability, depending on their own attitudes about disability before their injury, may paint a very isolated and bleak mental picture of their social future. Practitioners need to acknowledge to clients that sexual and social discrimination toward people with disabilities exists. However, the individual's stereotypes about how others view and treat them need to be explored to make sure that he or she is not acting inappropriately and thereby fostering rejection for nondisability-related reasons. Likewise, clients need to be questioned to see if they are avoiding being socially assertive, thus avoiding any chance of either rejection or *acceptance*. Asking a question such as "Tell me about the last time you remember being rejected?" will give valuable information on how much the person interacts with others or whether the person is interacting in a rejecting or overly aggressive manner. Some people appear to be a carbon copy of the rejection they fear; rejecting others through conscious and unconscious means. Another indication of a person's social development can be measured by their nonsexual relationships. Although it is true that a person with a disability may not at any given time have a potential or real sexual partner available to them, most persons can be partners for successful and close friendships with disabled and able-bodied peers. Individuals who portray themselves as someone no one likes need to develop friendships before they can progress into greater degrees of intimacy and interpersonal vulnerability. Books on social skills development, such as Zimbardo's *Shyness* (1977), are as applicable to a person with a disability as they are for the able-bodied. Assigning a shy individual to speak to three people each day, or to ask someone out for a coffee date, are good steps to allow the person to begin to interact appropriately with others. Two common social mistakes are made by disabled and other shy people: (1) they assume no discretion and will spend time with anyone of the appropriate sex and age range who will spend time with them ("I don't have any personal preference and certainly would not reject another person's interest in me"); and (2) they ask people out for too long a period of time. Most people will spend fifteen minutes at coffee with a friendly acquaintance but, unless very attracted to that person, will turn down an entire evening or day interaction. Social skills exercises need to maintain the comfort level of both persons, or the person with a disability will invariably face rejection because of his or her style of relating. The individual needs to learn enough patience to allow him or herself to interact with another individual slowly enough so that each positive interaction builds on the one previous.

Another reason that disabled people experience rejection is due to others' discomfort with disability itself. People who are socially skillful learn ways to speak about their disability in a way that decreases others' anxiety and shows their sense of positive self-esteem. One client with a prominent speech problem was assigned to answer others' questions about his speech, not by describing what his disability is or by talking about its negative impact on him, but rather by stating, "I have a speech disability that affects how I pronounce certain words." This exercise allowed him to contain the effects of the disability and its specific ramifications in the particular situation. The statement implied that, while he had a difficulty, it was only with "certain" words. This man needed to speak further about his disability when he made longer and more intimate social contact. However, he began to fit the explanation of the disability to the particular situation rather than the other way around. Such containment of disability also allows people to present themselves first, rather than their physical limitations. When one woman was approached by strangers who told her they were sorry she had a disability, she had an effective standard reply: "I looked them in the eye and, smiling in a friendly way, said 'Thank you, but it has added more to my life than it's been a problem.' I usually excused myself at that time saying, 'Sorry, I can't talk now, I have to get back to work.'" Such polite but purposely brief responses indicate a solid sense of self and also reflect a personal sense of priority (I'm a busy, productive person, not the "victim" you might imagine me to be). Such positive nonstereotypical responses serve two purposes: (1) they provide a paradoxical situation for the stranger, causing the stranger to question his or her own assumptions; and (2) talking positively and nondefensively about oneself does much to actually increase self-esteem. Each individual client needs to role play ways to answer public questions, both to insulate them from others' negative attitudes and to increase their own sense of well-being.

People often ask: "Given the terrible social attitudes about disability, how do I let people know I am a sexual person?" The way *not* to do this is to sit with a person you're sexually interested in and mention the word "sex" to the person for the first time by saying: "I'm really nervous about saying this, because you probably won't like this, but I want to have sex with you." Although painfully honest, this approach is asking for rejection. To interact successfully, sexually or otherwise, we must project those qualities we want to share with others. By this, we mean that to let others know we are sexual we need to communicate that to people in general, not just to those few people we are specifically interested in. Through dressing and carrying ourselves (as best as our disability will allow) in a sensual way, and—as appropriate—discussing our sensual and sexual preferences (types of touching we like, people we find particularly attractive) we let others know that we express and see ourselves sexually. Increasing our amount of personal and sexual sharing with a person we are attracted to sets the stage for possible sexual interactions. The question, "Will you be sexual with me?" still often needs to be asked. If it's brought up following increased intimate communication, however, it will increase the possibility of the other person agreeing to the request. As part of the agreement to be sexual together, it is important for the individual with a disability to share with the new partner any information not previously voiced about the sexual ramifications of the disability, if any. Also, it is important to ask the partner if they have any questions or concerns, as well as finding out about their sexual response and preferred activities. Although this amount of communication seems cumbersome and certainly not spontaneous, persons with disabilities do not have the luxury of being "swept away" by passion without communication. It sounds mechanical, but this kind of honest communication of preferences and physical limitations sets the groundwork for good sexual communication on an ongoing basis.

Unfortunately, most persons with disabilities encounter times when a potential partner cares deeply about them but can't get past their negative feelings about disability to be involved sexually. This can happen during the couple's first sexual encounter, when the partner enters the sexual relationship hoping to overcome their feelings about disability. Therapists can encourage clients to role play such possibilities (as well as other highly charged sexual situations, such as incontinence during lovemaking for some people with limited sensation) so that a disappointment does not have to be something that "I never even thought could happen." The sense of helplessness and anger that a person with a disability experiences, associated with not being able to change the negative attitudes of someone they care about, is very common and should be accepted by the therapist with empathy. It is important not to say phrases such as "none of us are acceptable to everyone," or "it's like racial discrimination." Sexual discrimination is not racial discrimination. People with disabilities (except the deaf) do not have a subculture where they are openly accepted. Even among people who are disabled, there is much individual and subgroup discrimination.[1] The person's sadness needs to be accepted and expressed. Once the pain of the

---

[1]In many organizations run by the disabled, the executive positions are usually held by persons with acquired disability (once "normal") while lower-eschelon positions are held by congenitally disabled persons. Relationships formed by persons with disabilities usually follow this matching by types of disability as well.

specific event has lost some of its power, the therapist needs to discourage continued attempts to convince the desired person to have sex with the client, or to spend more time with the client than the desired person wants to, given the fact that it is to be a nonsexual friendship. Although one certainly does not need to throw away a good friendship if a loved one doesn't want sex, spending a great deal of social time with that person, and thus not meeting other potential partners, is self-defeating. Many people in these situations settle for the attention of the loved one at the cost of their own desires and wants. This compromise needs to be continually challenged by the therapist, and plans to meet other potential partners explored.

Clients need to know that their particular social-sexual concerns are human issues shared by many others, both able-bodied and disabled. Persons with disabilities need encouragement to develop social skills in the mainstream of society, rather than in "special" programs for the disabled, unless individuals desire this themselves. For example, people who have concerns about their body image (that is, Will people feel I'm repulsive?) and their ability to give sensual pleasure can be encouraged to attend a workshop or class on massage with either able-bodied people or a combination of able-bodied and disabled individuals. Concerns about one's acceptance by others, physical accessibility of facilities, and so forth, will be voiced by many clients. The therapist will need to assist the client in finding a way to accomplish the task of gaining access to these activities and experiences.

In speaking of dating skills, it is important to ask, who are the partners of the disabled? Clinical and personal evidence points to the theory that potential partners are often individuals who have had a positive relationship with a person with a disability in the past, usually during childhood. Therefore, siblings, children, nieces, nephews, cousins, and next-door-neighbors of persons with disabilities are all potential partners. The exact nature of the significant person's disability seems not to be important; however, the fact that this was an attractive person in the individual's life who happened to have a disability seems very important. Such individuals with previous positive experience seem to easily integrate the idea that a desirable person can have a disability. It is appropriate for persons who are seeking relationships to casually inquire into the past disability experience of potential partners. Although this should certainly not be used to totally exclude any individual, it can give an indication of a person's initial comfort with the issue of disability. Client's can also be encouraged to stop or limit the development of a relationship they do not really desire or where they feel the other person's attitudes about disability are counter to their own self-esteem. Clients need to know that they do not have to accept another's feelings or attitudes if they disregard themselves in the process.

CONCLUSIONS

Human service practitioners interested in providing sex counseling to people with disabilities have some specific work to do before they begin. First, they need to examine their own attitudes about both sex and disability and to gain some degree of comfort in discussing the issues involved. Working with centers serving the disabled (especially if they are consumer run) can do much to help one face personal attitudes about the social and sexual lives of these people.

Second, it is important to recognize and use individual client's knowledge of themselves and their particular situation to come up with creative and workable solutions. Each person's disability affects him or her differently, and there is no standard of "normal" disabled behavior. Individuals should be encouraged to problem-solve for themselves with the support of the practitioner. In the same regard, it is important not to apply too strenuously specific information gathered from reading about sex and disability. It is important to share such information openly with the client and dialogue on its applicability to this particular person's experience.

Lastly, the nondisabled professional needs to find resource people with disabilities who can provide peer counseling and information and referral to clients. Interaction with other persons experiencing disability can be very important to the client's sense of self-respect. Although counseling by a therapist with a disability should not be pushed on clients, it needs to be brought up as a possibility, especially at times when clients express feelings that they are the only ones having a particular experience. Peer counseling at such times can be very valuable.

This is certainly not an exhaustive discussion of the social and sexual concerns of those people who are labeled "disabled." It can be used, however, as a guide in the development and refinement of therapeutic techniques valuable in this very important clinical area. Unfortunately, there is no Mecca for clinicians to go to for answers. Answers must be developed with, and by, the disabled individuals and couples themselves as they work with the practitioner toward reaching full social and sexual satisfaction.

REFERENCES

BARBACH, L. Group treatment of anorgasmic women. In S. Leiblum and L. Pervin, eds. *Principles and practice of sex therapy.* New York: Guilford Press, 1980, pp. 107–146.

FINKLE, P., FISHWICK, K., NESSEL, K., AND SOLIZ, D. Sexuality and attendant care. In D. G. Bullard and S. E. Knight, eds. *Sexuality and physical disability: Personal perspectives.* St. Louis: C. V. Mosby, 1981, p. 122.

GEIGER, R. Neurophysiology of sexual response in spinal cord injury. In D. G. Bullard and S. E. Knight, eds. *Sexuality and physical disability: Personal perspectives.* St. Louis: C. V. Mosby, 1981, pp. 147–154.

HARTMAN, C., MACINTOSH, B., AND ENGELHART, B. The neglected and forgotten sexual partner of the physically disabled. *Social Work* 28(5):370–374,1983.

KNIGHT, S. E. Consumer-based sex education. In D. G. Bullard and S. E. Knight, eds. *Sexuality and physical disability: Personal perspectives.* St. Louis: C. V. Mosby, 1981, p. 272.

KOLODNEY, R., MASTERS, W., AND JOHNSON, V. *Textbook of sexual medicine.* Boston: Little, Brown, 1979, p. 368.

SOLVIT, A., AND STARK, M. Mourning the birth of a defective child. *The Psychoanalytic Study of the tive child. The Psychoanalytic Study of the Child* 16:533,1961.

ZIMBARDO, P. K. *Shyness.* Menlo Park, Calif.: Addison-Wesley Publishing Co., 1977.

CHAPTER
18

THE UNATTRACTIVE
Elaine Hatfield

Once research on the impact of physical attractiveness on love, sex, and intimacy was virtually taboo. A decade ago, when Dr. Ellen Berscheid and this author (1974) reviewed research done by psychologists, we could ferret out only a few such articles. This year in a second review (Hatfield & Sprecher, 1986), we easily retrieved more than a thousand relevant articles. Let us review what social psychologists have discovered in the last decade about the importance of appearance in people's most intimate of relationships.

THE PROBLEM

Definition

Webster's New World Dictionary (Guralnik, 1982) defines beauty this way:

Beauty: (1) the quality attributed to whatever pleases or satisfies the senses or mind, as by line, color, form, texture, proportion, rhythmic motion, tone, etc., or by behavior, attitude, etc.; (2) a thing having this quality; (3) good looks; (4) a very good-looking woman; (5) any very attractive feature. (p. 124)

Scientists' conceptual definition is much the same:

Physical Attractiveness: That which represents one's conception of the ideal in appearance; that which gives the greatest degree of pleasure to the senses. (Hatfield, in press)

Existing Research

Good looking men and women have an advantage in life; the unattractive encounter enormous obstacles. People assume that

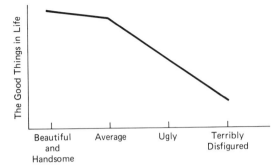

FIGURE 18-1. The relationship between physical attractiveness and assumed success in school, work, relationships, and in life.

good looking men and women are special, they treat them that way and the reverse is often true for the "unattractive." As a consequence the attractive/unattractive may well develop very different personalities.

There is considerable evidence that people do assume that "what is beautiful is good; what is ugly is bad." For example, Dion, Berscheid, and Walster (1972) asked men and women to examine photographs of good looking, average, or homely men and women. Most people assumed that the good looking must possess nearly all the good traits known to humanity. The good looking were assumed to be more sexually responsive, warmer, more sensitive, kind, interesting, strong, poised, sociable, and outgoing . . . to be more "exciting dates," more "nurturant," and have better characters than were the unattractive. A multitude of studies document the fact that people do assume "What is ugly is bad" (See Cash, 1984; or Hatfield & Sprecher, 1986.)

Not only do people *think* that the attractive are special, they treat them that way. Some examples: teachers take it for granted that beauty and brains go together—and they grade accordingly (Clifford & Walster, 1973). In the job market, too, beauty pays. Good-looking people are more likely to be hired, get paid more, and are more likely to be promoted. Psychiatrists try harder . . . and are more successful with good-looking clients. The handsome and the beautiful have a friend in court. Good-looking

defendants are rarely found guilty; and even if they are, they are likely to be given unusually lenient sentences.

Once again, as a consequence of their different experiences, the good looking and the ugly may develop different personalities and characters.

An observation: the evidence then makes it clear that two basic societal suppositions are at work here—that what is beautiful is good; and that *what is ugly is bad*. Both phrases are true. *But* a more careful analysis of the data we have cited, as well as other research (Dermer & Thiel, 1975), makes it clear that the emphasis should be on the latter. If we look carefully at the relationship between appearance and a host of other variables—self-esteem, job opportunities, dating popularity, happiness—we soon discover that things look like Figure 18-1. The data made it clear that only a small advantage is offered in being beautiful or handsome rather than average. Stunningly good-looking people have only a slight advantage over their more ordinary peers. What is really important is to be *at least average*. The average-looking have a real advantage over the homely or the disfigured.

Appearance: Its Impact on Love, Sex, and Intimacy

Society's biases ensure that good-looking men and women have a marked advantage at every stage of an intimate relationship:

1. The attractive have an easier time meeting potential dates and mates.
2. They have an advantage in trying to sustain a relationship.
3. They find it easier to attract the kind of dates and mates in which they are interested.
4. If things go wrong, they find it easier to start anew.

Let us review some of the research documenting these four contentions.

Romantic beginnings. Appearances are extraordinarily important in romantic beginnings. In the 1960s, this author and colleagues (Walster [Hatfield] et al., 1966) organized a dance for University of Minnesota freshmen. Men and women were led to believe that a computer would match them up with a blind date. In truth, couples were randomly matched with their partners. Then we set out to find out all that we could about the couples. We assessed their physical attractiveness, intelligence, personalities, and social skills.

At the dance, the 400 couples talked, danced, and got to know one another. Then, during the 10:30 P.M. intermission, we swept through the buildings, rounding up couples from the dance floor, lavatories, fire escapes—even adjoining buildings. We asked them to tell us frankly what they thought of their dates. This study was the first to discover the inordinate importance of good looks in romantic beginnings. (See also Brislin & Lewis, 1968; Brodie, 1971.) We found that:

Everyone (including the homeliest men and women) insisted on being matched-up with a good-looking blind date.

Everyone, good-looking or not, insisted that their dates be exceptionally charming, bright, and socially skilled.

If fate paired up men or women with a good-looking date, they tried hard to see their matches again. When we contacted couples six months after the dance, we found that daters—regardless of what *they* looked like

themselves—had asked out the good-looking men and women; they'd not given the unattractive a second chance.

Every effort to find any other characteristics that mattered failed. Men and women with exceptional IQ's and social skills, for example, were *not* liked any better than those who were less endowed.

Finally, both men and women cared equally about their dates' looks. (See also Curran & Lippold, 1975.)

A variety of studies document that attractive men and women are more popular and have more dates than do their homely peers (Berscheid & Walster [Hatfield], 1974; Cash, 1983). Moreover, when it comes to the relationship between appearance and sexual activity, handsome men and beautiful women do seem to get more "offers they can't refuse." Kaats and Davis (1970) were the first to investigate whether attractive people are more sexually permissive than others.

Traditionally it was assumed that most men would be inclined to press their dates for sex, but only the most appealing men would be successful; handsome men were expected to have far more sexual success than homely ones—the "James Bond v. Woody Allen" phenomenon. Traditionally women were supposed to be coy—to engage in sex was seen as evidence, not of desire, but of desperation (Symons, 1979). Thus, early researchers were uncertain whether to predict that beautiful women would be unusually sexually experienced (because they had an unusual number of enticing opportunities) or unusually chaste (because they didn't have to "put out" in order to get dates). When push came to shove—when researchers were forced to settle on a hypothesis—they predicted that beautiful women would be more sexually experienced than their less attractive counterparts. And that's just what they found.

In a study at the University of Colorado, Kaats and Davis (1970) found that 56 percent of the attractive women were non-virgins. Only 31 percent of the average and 37 percent of the homely women were sexually experienced. Attractive women were experienced, but they were not "promiscuous." Attractive versus homely women (who had had sexual intercourse) did not differ on the number of times they had tried sex, or on the number of men they'd experimented with. Kaats and Davis concluded that attractive women were more likely to have premarital intercourse because they had more opportunities and more pressure to experiment. The attractive women had been in love more often, dated more often, and had petted more often.

Other studies support the contention that attractive men and women have unusually permissive sexual attitudes and behaviors. Kelley (1978) interviewed a sample of 668 students at the University of California. They found attractive men and women to be more permissive in their premarital sexual attitudes. For example, attractive men and women did not want to be virgins, nor did they want to marry inexperienced mates. Good-looking men and women were more liberal in their activities as well. For example, they were more likely to be having intercourse regularly with a steady date, and occasionally with other partners, than were their peers.

Finally, Curran (1975) found that attractive men and women had more sexual experience than anyone else on every item of the Heterosexual Behavior Scale: they were more likely to have kissed, french kissed, engaged in oral sex, and had intercourse, than their peers.

So, overall, the results are clear. Attractive men and women tend to have more social and sexual experience.

Maintaining an intimate relationship: attractiveness and social skills. People expect the good-looking to be socially appealing, and treat them that way. But what are the good-looking/homely *really* like? The evidence suggests that a sort of "self-fulfilling"

prophecy generally operates. People expect the good-looking to be charming, treat them that way, and as a consequence, they *do* become more skilled.

That there is a self-fulfilling nature to the physical attractiveness stereotype was demonstrated in an intriguing study by Snyder, Tanke, and Berscheid (1977). Men and women at the University of Minnesota were scheduled to participate in a study on the processes by which men and women get to know each other. When a couple arrived they were directed to different rooms. They had to use the telephone to become acquainted. Before the telephone conversation began, men were given a snapshot of their partner, along with some biographical information. In truth, the snapshot was not of their actual partner, but of a (fictitious) beautiful or homely woman. The man was asked his initial impressions of his partner. Men who thought they would soon be talking to a beautiful woman, expected her to be sociable, poised, humorous, and socially skilled. Those who thought she would be homely, expected her to be unsociable, awkward, serious, and socially inept. Those were the men's expectations, but they really aren't so surprising—we already know that good-looking people receive more positive first impressions than homely ones.

What is startling is that men's expectations had a dramatic impact on the women's *behavior* in the short space of the telephone call. Men thought their partners were either beautiful or homely, with no midground. In fact, of course, the women on the other end of the line varied greatly in appearance—some were attractive, some average, some homely. Nonetheless, within the space of a telephone conversation women became what men expected them to be. The psychologists recorded (separately) the men's and the women's portions of the telephone conversation. Then they asked judges to listen to the women's voices and say what they seemed to be like. If men thought they were talking to a beauty, the woman unconsciously began to sound like one. If men thought she was homely, she soon sensed that too, and began acting that way. Women who had been depicted as attractive, became more animated, confident, and adept; women who had been depicted as homely acted just the opposite way. As the authors put it, "What had initially been reality in the minds of the men had now become reality in the behavior of the women with whom they had interacted." The men expected certain women (those who had been randomly assigned to be attractive) to be more sociable, and indeed they became so.

What happened to transfer the reality in the minds of the men into the reality in the behavior of the women? When the men's sides of the conversations were analyzed, it was found that the men who thought they were talking to a beautiful woman were more sociable, sexually warm, interesting, independent, sexually permissive, bold, outgoing, humorous, obvious, and socially adept then were men who thought they were talking to a homely woman. The men assigned to an "attractive woman" were also judged to be more comfortable, to enjoy themselves more, and to use their voices more effectively. In a nutshell, the men who thought they had an attractive partner tried harder.

If the stereotypes held by the men formed their own social reality within only ten minutes of a telephone conversation, one can imagine what happens over several years. If year after year, attractive people are given more opportunities and encouragement in social interaction than unattractive people, undoubtedly attractive and unattractive people become different social beings.

What would happen if a study similar to the above one were conducted, only this time men were not biased? This time they hadn't a clue as to what their partners looked like? This time would the women's real appearance shine through? In reality, do attractive men and women display more social skill over the phone? Such a study was conducted (Goldman & Lewis, 1977), and it was found that attractive men and women were judged by their telephone partners to be more socially skilled than unattractive men and women. Apparently, the physical attractiveness stereotype does contain a kernel of truth.

In general, researchers have concluded that attractive people have different everyday social interactions from homely people. In one study, for example, (Reis, Nezlek & Wheeler, 1980), freshmen men and women at the University of Rochester kept records of their social experiences for 40 days. Researchers found that handsome men had *more* interactions, *longer* interactions, and with more women, than did homely men. Attractive people tended to spend more of their interaction time conversing or partying, while less attractive people spent more time at work. Attractive men and women were more satisfied with their encounters with the opposite sex than were less appealing people. Over time, physically attractive people became more and more satisfied with their relationships.

Other researchers (Reis et al., 1982) support the contention that attractive men and women have the most satisfying social interactions. They found that attractive men and women report that their relationships are more intimate and disclosing than do ugly men and women.

In the end, attractive people end up with better dating and marital relationships. There is considerable evidence that people do generally end up with mates who are about as attractive and who have as much to offer *overall* as they do. (See Walster [Hatfield] et al., 1966.) Studies in the United States, Canada, Germany, and Japan find that people generally end up dating and marrying someone who is similar to themselves in appearance (Cavior & Boblette, 1972; White, 1980; Brislin & Lewis, 1968; Tessler & Brodie, 1971; Berscheid, Dion, Walster [Hatfield] & Walster, 1971.)

In a typical study (Silverman, 1971; Murstein, 1972), couples were observed in several natural settings—in movie theater lines, in singles bars, and at assorted social events. A team of researchers rated the daters' looks. Most couples turned out to be remarkably similar in attractiveness. A handsome man was most likely to have a beautiful woman on his arm. A homely man was likely to be spotted buying a drink for a homely woman.

It was also found in this study that "similarity breeds content." The more similar the couples were in physical appeal, the more delighted they seemed to be with one another, as reflected in intimate touching. Sixty percent of the couples who were similar in attractiveness were engaged in some type of touching. Only 22 percent of those couples who were mismatched were touching.

Matching: More Complex Cases

Of course couples can be "well matched" in a variety of ways. For example, the beautiful Jacqueline Kennedy chose Aristotle Onassis, who was not particularly good-looking but who was unusually bright, charming . . . and rich. We probably all know of similar cases closer to home.

Murstein et al. (1974) provide a description of the way such complex matching operates: A handsome man is seen with a woman of mediocre attractiveness. "I wonder what he sees in her?" may be the quizzical question of a bystander. Quite possibly she possesses compensating qualities, such as greater intelligence, interpersonal competence, and wealth than he possesses, of which the bystander knows nothing.

Another case of compensatory exchange might be indicated if an aged statesman proposed marriage to a young beautiful woman. He would probably be trading his prestige and power for her physical attractiveness and youth (pp. 3–4).

The evidence supports the contention that people do engage in such complicated balancing and counterbalancing in selecting mates. The better looking the man or woman, the more loving, kinder, richer, more socially powerful partners he or she is likely to attract (Elder, 1969; Holmes & Hatch, 1938; Udry & Eckland, 1972; Taylor & Glenn, 1976; Udry, 1977).

In sum the evidence makes it clear that the good looking have a real advantage and the unattractive, a real hardship in life. Once again, two basic factors operate: (1) People assume that "What is beautiful is good; what is ugly is bad." The good looking are assumed to possess nearly all the good traits known to humanity. (2) Not only do people *think* that the attractive are special, they *treat* them that way. Teachers give good-looking students better grades; the good looking are the first hired, the last fired; the handsome and beautiful "have a friend in court." And (3) as a consequence the good looking and ugly develop different personalities and characters. The good looking are more socially poised as a result of the opportunities they have for just the sort of intimate relationship they wish.

INTERVENTIONS

We have seen that the unattractive are at a real disadvantage in intimate encounters. What can they and we do about this? Since the author is a family therapist (at King Kalakaua Clinic in Honolulu) and an experimental social psychologist (at the University of Hawaii at Manoa), the suggestions offered here will necessarily be drawn from her experience with individuals having trouble initiating, maintaining, or dealing with broken relationships. Social workers may well have other suggestions as to how society, in general, could be restructured so that such problems could be minimized.

In any case, in this chapter, we will review what advice professionals can give to the unattractive—*who* should they look for, for a mate? *Where* should they look? Once they are involved in a relationship, how can they move it toward ever increasing intimacy?

Looking for a Mate

Who. One would think that the best way to find a romantic partner would be to focus all of one's energies on just that. The author and a colleague, Dr. Richard Rapson, are therapists in private practice in Honolulu. Many of our clients are desperately eager to find mates. They are extraordinarily calculating; they simply can't "waste their time" on someone who's not a real possibility. Such a single-minded strategy rarely works. If they finally do find Mr./Ms. Right (and they rarely do) things go badly. They have so much riding on a single encounter that everyone freezes.

What does work then? Men and women should assume that they will have to meet and date 50 serious contenders before they find a relationship that "works." These 50 encounters give them an invaluable chance to practice; a chance to allow them and their partners to get to know one another. Thinking of these dates as practice gives people an advantage—they don't care too much. They can perfect their social skills without worrying that they may do something wrong.

What if they can't find *any* dates . . . much less 50? Research indicates that if one is looking for a lover, one should search for a friend (Peplau & Perlman, 1982; Cutrona, 1982). Scientists set out to learn which of two alternative strategies worked best: (1) looking single-mindedly for a mate—most lonely people automatically follow this strategy; (2) concentrating for six months on meeting people—without worrying about whether or not they are just right. Scientists find that the people who follow strategy 1 end up worse off than those who follow strategy 2, taking time off to make a few good friends along the way. In fact, the most effective strategy for finding a lover appears to be to concentrate, at first, on finding good friends. They are easier to find . . . and *they* are likely to introduce the person to someone who's just right for him or her (Cutrona, 1978; Rubenstein & Shaver, 1982).

Where. The evidence is clear (Festinger, 1951; Hatfield & Walster, 1982). Men and women generally meet their romantic partners by bumping into them in the normal course of events. They are most likely to meet their future mates in their neighborhood, in classes, at work.

We should probably *not* encourage clients to attend mixers, singles bars, and so on, in the hope of meeting eligible partners. Looks may be too much of a handicap in such places (Murstein, 1971). Instead, we should encourage them to look in other locations such as museums, supermarkets, and so on (see Novak, 1983; Hatfield & Walster, 1982; Hatfield & Sprecher, 1985).

Enhancing Appearance

At the same time that people are keeping an eye out for potential lovers and friends, people who are looking for a relationship can begin the never ending process of making themselves a "more appealing package"—improving their appearance and their intimacy skills.

We advise clients to spend *some* time improving their appearance. There are an unlimited number of guides which tell people how to do just that—how to fix their hair, use cosmetics, dress well, even alter their appearance via plastic surgery. The data make it clear that such efforts do work. People can alter their appearance, and such efforts do improve their social interactions (see Berscheid & Walster [Hatfield], 1974; Kurtzburg, Safar & Cavior, 1968; Graham, 1984; Roberts, 1984; Pertschuk, 1984; Orentreich, 1984).

So clients may want to spend *some* time on such self-improvement efforts—but, only some time. They don't want to spend enormous efforts. Conceivably, some people do spend all their time improving themselves and becoming more appealing, but such all-out effort is probably counterproductive. A variety of factors—self-esteem, intelligence, an exciting personality, energy level, compassion—as well as physical characteristics, all have an impact on how good looking a person appears to be. If we focus too much on basic appearance, we are likely to neglect other critically important things and end up impoverished, not just in appearance—but spiritually, personally, and socially.

Working Toward Intimacy

The word intimacy is derived from the Latin *intimus,* meaning "inner" or "innermost." We would define *intimacy* as:

A *process* in which we attempt to get close to another; to explore similarities (and differences) in the ways we both think, feel, and behave.

Everyone needs a warm intimate relationship. Yet many people have great trouble pushing steadily forward into one.

A basic theoretical assumption provides the framework we use in teaching people how to be intimate with others. People must be capable of independence in order to be intimate with others, and, likewise, capable of intimacy if they are to be independent. Independence and intimacy are not opposite personality traits but interlocking skills. People who lack the ability to be independent *or* intimate can never really be either. They are never really with one another; never really separate.

What we set out to do, then, is to make people comfortable with the notion that they and the person with whom they are intimate are separate people, with separate ideas and feelings . . . who can sometimes come deeply together with one another.

According to theorists, one of the most primitive tasks people face is to learn how to maintain their own identity and integrity, while yet engaging in deeply intimate relationships with others. (For a fuller discussion of this point, see Erikson, 1968; Fisher & Stricker, 1982; Freud, 1922; Hatfield, in press; Kantor & Lehr, 1975; Kaplan, 1978; Maslow, 1954; Pope et al., 1980.)

The unattractive often lack skills in intimate encounters. Once they attract romantic partners, they have trouble keeping them.

Thus, at the same time we help clients find intimate partners, we have to teach them skills at pushing along an intimate encounter.

In therapy, we try to teach clients five sets of skills in a sort of "intimacy skills" training program.

1. Encouraging people to accept themselves as they are. It is a great temptation to dwell in the realm of absolutes. Many people are determined to be perfect; they can't settle for less. They see themselves as saints or sinners. Yet saintliness/evil are the least interesting of human conditions. Real life is lived in the middle zone. Real people inevitably have some strengths; yet everybody possesses small quirks.

The first step in learning to be independent/intimate then is to come to accept the fact that you are entitled to be what you are: to have the ideas you have, the feelings you feel, to do the best that you can do. And that is good enough.

In therapy, we try to move people from the notion that one should come into the world perfect and continue that way, to a realization that one can only gain wisdom in small steps. People must pick one small goal and work to accomplish that. When that's accomplished, they can move on to another. That way, change is manageable . . . possible. One can never attain perfection, only work toward it. (For guides to developing such skills, see Watson & Tharp, 1981; Argyle, 1984; Zimbardo, 1977.)

2. Encouraging people to accept their intimates as they are. People may be hard on themselves, but they are generally even harder on their mates. Most people have the idea that everyone is entitled to a perfect partner, or at least one a little bit better than the one that's available (Hatfield et al., in press). If people are going to have an intimate relationship, they have to learn to enjoy others as they are, without hoping to fix them up.

It is extraordinarily difficult for people to accept that their friends are entitled to be the people they are. From our own point of view, it seems so clear that things would be far better if our mate were only the people we want them to be. It would take so little for him or her to change their whole character structure. Why are they so stubborn?

Once we realize that our lover is the person who exists right now—not the person we *wish* she was, not the person he *could* be, but what he or she *is*—once that realization occurs, intimacy becomes possible.

3. Encouraging people to express themselves. Next, intimates have to learn to be more comfortable about expressing their ideas and feelings. This is harder than one might think.

People's intimate relations are usually their most important relationships. When passions are so intense, consequences so momentous, people are often hesitant to speak the truth. From moment to moment, they are tempted to present a consistent picture. If they're in love, they are hesitant to admit to their niggling doubts. (What if the person they love is hurt? What if their revelations destroy the relationship?) When they are angry, they don't want to speak about their love or their self-doubts, they want to lash out.

To be intimate, people have to push toward a more honest, graceful, complete, and patient communication—to understand that a person's ideas and feelings are necessarily complex, with many nuances, shadings, and inconsistencies. In love, there's time to clear things up.

One interesting thing that people often discover is that their affection increases when they begin to admit their irritations. People are often surprised to discover that sometimes—when they think they have fallen out of love; that they are "bored" with their affair—as they begin to express their anger and ambivalence, they feel their love come back in a rush.

In *The Family Crucible*, Napier and Whitaker (1978) describe just such a confrontation.

What followed was a classic confrontation. If John's affair was a kind of reawakening, so now was this marital encounter, though of a very different sort. Eleanor was enraged, hurt, confused, and racked with a sense of failure. John was guilty, also confused, but not apologetic. The two partners fought and cried, talked and searched for an entire night. The next evening, more exhausting encounters. Feelings that had been hidden for years emerged; doubts and accusations that they had never expected to admit articulated.

Eleanor had to find out everything, and the more she discovered, the more insatiable her curiosity became. The more she heard, the guiltier her husband became and the angrier she grew, until he finally cried for a halt. It was his cry for mercy that finally led to a temporary reconciliation of the couple. They cried together for the first time either of them could remember.

For a while they were elated; they had achieved a breakthrough in their silent and dreary marriage. They felt alive together for the first time in years. Somewhat mysteriously, they found themselves going to bed together in the midst of a great tangle of emotions—continuing anger, and hurt, and guilt, and this new quality: abandon. The love-making was, they were to admit to each other, "the best it had ever been." How could they have moved through hatred into caring so quickly? (p. 153)

(A variety of guides describe how to clarify your feelings and to communicate them to your dates/mates. See Argyle, 1984; Gendlin, 1981; Rubenstein & Shaver, 1982; Derlega & Chaikin, 1975; Gottman, Notarius, Gonso, & Markman, 1976; Egan, 1977; or Zilbergeld, 1978.)

4. Encouraging people to listen to their intimates. It is hard to express yourself; it is even harder to listen to others. In therapy, we often try a trick designed to get couples to listen to their partners. We wait until a small issue comes up and then, in "slow motion," try to untangle the threads of the conversation. As we ask "What did you mean by that? What did you think she was really saying? What were you feeling?" clients begin to learn a great deal about one another. Major issues, deep feelings, quickly emerge. We are always surprised to discover how, a few minutes before, in superficial conversation, we *thought* we knew what was being said. Further analysis often reveals that we missed the point altogether.

By careful listening, it is possible to discover what our intimates are really thinking, feeling, doing. (For guides on how to improve your listening skills, see Argyle, 1984; or Gottman, Notarius, Gonso, & Markman, 1976.)

5. Teaching people to deal with their intimate's reactions. To say that you *should* communicate your ideas and feelings, *must* communicate if you are to have an intimate affair, does not mean your partner is going to like it. You can expect that sometimes when you try to express your deepest feeling it will hurt. Your lovers and friends may tell you frankly how deeply you have hurt them and that will make you feel extremely guilty. Or they may react with intense anger.

Intimates have to learn to stop responding in automatic fashion to such emotional outbursts—to quit backing up, apologizing for what they said, measuring their words. They have to learn to stay calm, remind themselves that they are entitled to say what they think, feel what they feel, listen to what their partner's think and feel, and keep on trying. Only then is there a chance of an intimate encounter. (For guides to developing such skills, see Watson & Tharp, 1981; Bach & Wyden, 1968; Tavris, 1982).

CONCLUSION

This chapter has reviewed a number of the social and sexual problems of people whom we have termed "unattractive." There has been a considerable increase in the literature on the unattractive in recent years, resulting in greater understanding of the problems this rather amorphously defined group of people face. However, increasing attention in the literature has resulted in an "opening up" of the legitimacy of this topic, which in turn has produced a broad variety of strategies for dealing with problems faced by the unattractive. It is likely that the near future will see an even greater loosening of some of the social stigma and personal discomfort suffered by people who define themselves or are defined by others as unattractive.

REFERENCES

ARGYLE, M. *The psychology of interpersonal behavior.* New York: Penguin Books, 1984.

BACH, G. R., AND WYDEN, P. *The intimate enemy.* New York: Avon, 1968.

BERSCHEID, E., DION, K., WALSTER (HATFIELD), E., AND WALSTER, G. W. Physical attractiveness and dating choice: A test of matching hypothesis. *Journal of Experimental Social Psychology* 7:173–189, 1971.

BERSCHEID, E., AND WALSTER (HATFIELD), E. Physical attractiveness. In L. Berkowitz, ed. *Advances in experimental social psychology,* 7. New York: Academic Press, 1974, pp. 157–215.

BRISLIN, R. W., AND LEWIS, S. A. Dating and physical attractiveness: A replication. *Psychological Reports* 22:976, 1968.

CASH, T. F. *Physical attractiveness: An annotated bibliography of theory and research in the behavioral sciences.* Unpublished manuscript.

_____. Physical appearance and mental health. In J. Graham and A. M. Kligman, eds. *The psychology of cosmetic treatments.* New York: Praeger, 1984.

CAVIOR, N., AND BOBLETT, P. J. Physical attractiveness of dating versus married couples. *Proceedings of the 80th Annual Convention of the American Psychological Association* 7:175–176, 1972.

CLIFFORD, M. M., AND WALSTER (HATFIELD), E. Research note: The effects of physical attractiveness on teaching expectations. *Sociology of Education* 46:248–258, 1973.

CURRAN, J. P. Convergence toward a single sexual standard? *Social Behavior and Personality* 3:189–195, 1975.

_____, AND LIPPOLD, S. The effects of physical attractiveness and attitude similarity on attraction in dating dyads. *Journal of Personality* 43:528–539, 1975.

CUTRONA, C. E. Transition to college: Loneliness and the process of social adjustment. In L. A. Peplau and D. Perlman, eds. *Loneliness*. New York: Wiley-Interscience, 1982.

DERLEGA, V. J., AND CHAIKIN, A. L. *Sharing intimacy: What we reveal to others and why.* Englewood Cliffs, N.J.: Prentice-Hall, Inc., 1975.

DERMER, J., AND THIEL, D. L. When beauty may fail. *Journal of Personality and Social Psychology* 31:1168–1176, 1975.

DION, K., BERSCHEID, E., AND WALSTER (HATFIELD), E. What is beautiful is good. *Journal of Personality and Social Psychology* 24:285–290, 1972.

EGAN, G. *You and me: The skills of communicating and relating to others.* Monterey, Calif.: Brooks Cole, 1977.

ELDER, G. H., JR. Appearance and education in marriage mobility. *American Sociological Review* 34:519–533, 1969.

ERIKSON, E. H. *Childhood and society,* rev. ed. New York: W. W. Norton, 1968.

FESTINGER, L. Architecture and group membership. *Journal of Social Issues* 1:152–163, 1951.

FISHER, M., AND STRICKER, G., EDS. *Intimacy*. New York: Plenum Press, 1982.

FREUD, S. Certain neurotic mechanisms in jealousy, paranoia, and homosexuality. In *Collected Papers*, vol. 2. London: Hogarth, 1922, pp. 235–323.

GENDLIN, E. T. *Focusing.* New York: Bantam, 1981.

GOLDMAN, W., AND LEWIS, P. Beautiful is good: Evidence that the physically attractive are more socially skillful. *Journal of Experimental Social Psychology* 13:125–130, 1977.

GOTTMAN, J., NOTARIUS, C., GONSO, J., AND MARKMAN, H. *A couple's guide to communication.* Champaign, Illinois: Research Press, 1976.

GRAHAM, J. A. Overview of psychology of cosmetics. In J. Graham and A. M. Kligman, eds. *The psychology of cosmetic treatments.* New York: Praeger, 1984.

GURALNIK, D. B., ED. *Webster's new world dictionary,* 2nd ed. New York: Simon and Schuster, 1982.

HATFIELD, E. The dangers of intimacy. In V. Derlega, ed. *Communication, intimacy, and close relationships.* New York: Praeger, 1984, 207–220.

———. Physical attractiveness in social interactions. In J. Graham and A. M. Kligman, eds. *The psychology of cosmetic treatments.* New York: Praeger, 1984.

——— , AND SPRECHER, S. *Mirror, mirror: The importance of looks in everyday life.* New York: State University of New York Press, 1986.

HATFIELD, E., TRAUPMANN, J., SPRECHER, S., UTNE, M., AND HAY, J. Equity and intimate relations: Recent research. In W. Ickes, ed. *Compatible and incompatible relationships.* New York: Springer-Verlag, 1984, 1–27.

HATFIELD, E., AND WALSTER, G. W. *A new look at love.* Lantham, Md.: University Press of America, 1982.

HOLMES, S. J., AND HATCH, C. E. Personal appearance as related to scholastic records and marriage selection in college women. *Human Biology* 10:65–76, 1938.

KAATS, G. R., AND DAVIS, K. E. The dynamics of sexual behavior of college students. *Journal of Marriage and the Family* 22:390–399, 1970.

KANTOR, D., AND LEHR, W. *Inside the family.* San Francisco: Jossey-Bass, 1975.

KAPLAN, H. S. *The new sex therapy.* New York: Brunner/Mozel, 1974.

KAPLAN, L. J. *Oneness and separateness: From infant to individual.* New York: Simon and Schuster, 1978.

KELLEY, J. Sexual permissiveness: Evidence for a theory. *Journal of Marriage and the Family* 40:455–468, 1978.

KURTZBURG, R. L., SAFAR, H., AND CAVIOR, N. Surgical and social rehabilitation of adult offenders. *Proceedings from the Annual Convention of the American Psychological Association* 3:649–650, 1968.

MASLOW, A. H. *Motivation and personality.* New York: Harper, 1954.

MURSTEIN, B. I., ED. *Theories of attraction and love.* New York: Springer, 1971.

———. Physical attractiveness and marital choice. *Journal of Personality and Social Psychology* 22:8–12, 1972.

———, GOYETTE, M., AND CERRETO, M. *A theory of the effect of exchange orientation on marriage and friendship.* Unpublished manuscript, 1974.

NAPIER, A., AND WHITAKER, C. *The family crucible.* New York: Harper and Row, 1978.

NOVAK, W. *The great American man shortage and other roadblocks to romance.* New York: Rawaon Associates, 1983.

ORENTREICH, N. Dermatologic treatments. In J. Graham and A. M. Kligman, eds. *The psychology of cosmetic treatments.* New York: Praeger, 1984.

PEPLAU, L. A., AND PERLMAN, D. *Loneliness.* New York: Wiley-Interscience, 1982.

PERTSCHUK, M. Cosmetic therapy for psychiatric disorders. In J. Graham and A. M. Kligman, eds. *The psychology of cosmetic treatments.* New York: Praeger, 1984.

POPE, K. S., AND ASSOCIATES. *On love and loving.* San Francisco: Jossey-Bass Publishing, 1980.

REIS, H. T., NEZLEK, J., AND WHEELER, L. Physical attractiveness in social interaction. *Journal of Personality and Social Psychology* 38:604–617, 1980.

REIS, H. T., WHEELER, L., SPIEGEL, N., KERNIS, M. H., NEZLEK, J., AND PERRI, M. Physical attractiveness in social interaction: I. Why does appearance affect social experience? *Journal of Personality and Social Psychology* 43:979–996, 1982.

ROBERTS, R. Beauty care and cosmetic camouflage service. In J. Graham and A. M. Kligman, eds. *The psychology of cosmetic treatments.* New York: Praeger, 1984.

RUBENSTEIN, C., AND SHAVER, P. *In search of intimacy.* New York: Delacorte Press, 1982.

SILVERMAN, I. Physical attractiveness and courtship. *Sexual Behavior,* Sept. 1971, 22–25.

SNYDER, M., TANKE, E. D., AND BERSCHEID, E. Social perception and interpersonal behavior: On the self-fulfilling nature of social stereotypes. *Journal of Personality and Social Psychology* 35:656–666, 1977.

SYMONS, D. *The evolution of human sexuality.* New York: Oxford University Press, 1979.

TAVRIS, C. *Anger: The misunderstood emotion.* New York: Simon and Schuster, 1982.

TAYLOR, P. A., AND GLENN, N. D. The utility of education and attractiveness for females: Status attainment through marriage. *American Sociological Review* 41:484–498, 1976.

TESSER, A., AND BRODIE, M. A note on the evaluation of a "computer date." *Psychonomic Science* 23:300, 1971.

UDRY, J. R. The importance of being beautiful: A reexamination and racial comparison. *American Journal of Sociology* 83:154–160, 1977.

————, AND ECKLAND, B. K. The benefits of being attractive: Differential payoffs for men and women. Paper presented at American Sociological Association, Sept. 1982.

WALSTER (HATFIELD), E., WALSTER, G. W., ABRAHAMS, D., AND BROWN, Z. The effect on liking of underrating or overrating another. *Journal of Experimental Social Psychology* 2:70–84, 1966.

WATERS, J. Cosmetics and the job market. In J. Graham and A. M. Kligman, eds. *The psychology of cosmetic treatments.* New York: Praeger, 1984

WATSON, D. L., AND THARP, R. G. *Self-directed behavior,* 3rd ed. Monterey, Calif.: Brooks-Cole, 1981.

WHITE, G. L. Physical attractiveness and courtship progress. *Journal of Personality and Social Psychology* 39:660–668, 1980.

ZILBERGELD, B. *Male sexuality: A guide to sexual fulfillment.* Boston: Little, Brown, 1978.

ZIMBARDO, P. G. *Shyness: What it is, what to do about it.* Reading, Mass.: Addison-Wesley Publishing Co., 1977.

19

THE TERMINALLY ILL
Lois Jaffe

Our relationship now is more that of strangers because of hospital separation. His sexual desires have diminished because our thoughts are dominated by the cancer and his impending death. The disease, however, is not repulsive to me. I've had no urge to escape from his touch as other wives have talked about. We still enjoyed sex until he was unable to perform. This was a major frustration to him and made him feel less a man and more the invalid. The frustrations in our lives caused by his illness I'm sure would be eased if we were still sexually bound and still "one." Knowing I could ease his tensions of the day at the office by loving him sexually is such a contrast with knowing I can do nothing now to ease his frustrations when he is dying. He now feels we are on opposite sides of the fence. I'm sure it's because I cannot convince him by words or actions here in the hospital. He feels his masculinity is gone and our "one-ness" is gone. For thirty-three years I took our loving for granted and assumed it would always be there. . . . It may sound like we were forever in bed, but sex is so much more than physical. Even talking on the phone, sitting across from

each other reading, being in a crowd, even being hundreds of miles apart, we felt the union.

These are the words of a wife of a long-term patient hospitalized with brain cancer. She is a member of the group I conduct weekly at a local oncology unit for cancer and leukemia patients and their families. These encounters provide an opportunity for sharing feelings of anger, sadness, frustration and fear, and for learning from one another how better to cope with facing death. Her description captures the essence of the sexual problems facing the terminally ill and their loved ones.

I myself have been an acute leukemia patient for the last twenty-eight months of my forty-seven years of life. In my work as death educator and family therapist, as well as in my role as patient, I have become convinced that the area of sexual problems with regard to the terminally ill constitutes a "double whammy," and thus has been enveloped in silence. There is little discussion in the literature about the fact that sexual expression is generally denied or severely compromised in situations involving terminal illness and impending interpersonal loss (Barton, 1972; Davis, 1974).

Death arouses the basic underlying anxiety that every human being must face. The fear of the unknown is paralleled only by the fear of being cut off from life before fulfilling one's potential. Death anxiety is exacerbated by the invisibility of personal dying in our society. Eighty percent of us die in institutions, and thus we are unrehearsed in ways of interacting with those facing death or with those who are left behind. Confronting death generates more anguish and fear than in any other area of human behavior. Care-givers are no different from anyone else; facing a dying person means facing one's own mortality—a realization which can make even the hardiest of souls begin to twitch. Sexuality is the only other area to engender a comparable degree of discomfort, confusion, and resistance, particularly when it must be handled by clinicians. This combination of sexuality with terminality constitutes a double-barreled taboo.

Since sexuality and death represent the beginning and end points of life itself, anxiety is understandably heightened by their interface. For the dying patient and his loved ones, aspects of confronting death can be a classical "double-bind." In a double-bind situation, a person is faced with contradictory messages which are often concealed or transmitted on different levels. As a result of this invisibility, the individual cannot escape or effectively comment on the paradoxes which confront him (Erickson & Hyerstay, 1974). Preparing for impending death by either partner in the relationship involves accommodation to an ending, a "deadline." Sexuality, on the other hand, represents a moving forward, a perpetuation of vitality, the quintessence of the life force. Yet, despite this contrast, both experiences share a kind of "letting go." As Keleman (1974) has written:

"Dying generates excitement, unformedness, unconnectedness, unknowingness. . . . Excitement is the force that connects sex and dying" (p. 27).

For the healthy spouse, the vitality of sexuality is often experienced as a direct contradiction to the finality of death. As the spouse struggles to stop thinking of the relationship as having a future, he is confronted with the dissonance between sex (a moving forward into the future) and death (an end in the present). Rather than face this clash, the healthy partner may choose not to interact sexually with the patient, and may possibly seek sexual activity with a new partner as an antidote to loss and death. Either way, there is a tendency to move away sexually and emotionally from the dying patient.

For the terminally ill patient, there is the reverse of the double-bind to confront. While the healthy partner may be avoiding sex with the patient, the patient may now desire increased sexual activity with the spouse to counter death anxiety. Sexuality, as Keleman (1974) points out, is almost a training for dying—an intensification of the dying process and a rehearsal for the dying event.

The orgastic state that produces feelings of ecstasy is a surrendering to the involuntary and to the unknown. Orgasm requires giving ourselves over to what is occurring in us. . . . The orgastic state also produces feelings of dying, raises fears of dying, because the social awareness may be threatened by the involuntary. (p. 119)

The terminally ill patient holds in his possession a double-edged sword. He can either become revitalized by the intensity that comes with confronting death, thus making him more sexually aware and responsive, or he can become so frightened by the prospect of death that any stirring up of that anxiety, as in an orgasmic "letting go," may move him into an "asexual" state. It is my belief that the direction a patient chooses is largely determined by (1) his previous experiences with sex and death, (2) the presence or absence of pain, (3) his treatment as "one of the living" rather than as a dying patient, and (4) his perception of hope for being able to live a full and meaningful life in whatever time he has left.

Given this conceptual framework for viewing the sexual problems of the terminally ill patient and his significant others, let us now examine the predisposing, precipitating and perpetuating factors which make this content area so necessary and vital for intervention. By using this primary prevention approach, recommendations can then be made for therapeutic strategies.

PREDISPOSING FACTORS

If one looks at the meaning of death developmentally, it is easy to understand why people are predisposed to inordinate anxiety when handling the interface between sex and death. Psychologist Maria Nagy, studying Hungarian children in the late 1940s, described three phases in the child's awareness of personal mortality as reflected in drawings and words. In Stage One, the preschool child usually does not recognize the irreversibility of death, and regards it as sleep or departure. In Stage Two, between the ages of about five and nine, he tends to personify death as a separate figure, such as an angel or a frightening skeleton, who usually makes his rounds at night. In this second stage, death seems to be understood as final. However, an important protective feature remains: personal death can be avoided if you run faster than the Death Man, lock the door, hide from him, or trick him. Death is still external, and not general. In Stage Three, beginning around age nine or ten, death is recognized not only as final but also as inevitable for all (Nagy, 1959).

Given a child's concept of avoiding death by running away from the death figure, it is no wonder that many adults harbor a primitive fear that they can "catch death" from being too close to their terminally ill partner. Preconsciously, people associate death with night. Consequently, whether to sleep with a terminally ill spouse often arises as an initial conflict for the healthy partner. Case histories point to the number of spouses, who, "out of the blue," pick up and leave home after a long-term hospitalized patient finally goes into remission and/or returns home.

Reinforcing this psychological fear is the well-publicized medical research pointing to viral infection as a probable causal factor in some leukemias and other malignancies. Fear of physical transmission of the disease then compounds the spouse's anxiety. Indeed, patients with many types of malignancies, with unusually low resistance, or who are being treated with steroids, are prone to secondary infections which ordinarily would not affect them. These infections can be potential hazards to people in close contact with the patient (Beeson & McDermott, 1975). Thus, the primitive fear of "catching death" is concretized by publicity regarding possible viral etiology of malignancies, as well as the reality factor of transmissible secondary infections.

Another predisposing factor to inordinate anxiety regarding sex and death is the manner in which parents have handled these topics during the patient's childhood. When parents have been dishonest or evasive in dealing with sex and/or death, "closed communication" around the issue results. When terminal illness occurs—a time when openness is so necessary to avoid isolation and abandonment—the preestablished "conspiracy of silence" is only exacerbated (Zeligs, 1967). Also, if a woman is socialized to believe that sexuality is unimportant, "wrong," useful only for procreation, then she may experience relief at being "exempted" from this felt burden. Obviously, the quality of one's sexuality prior to terminality determines the quality as well as the quantity of sex after diagnosis.

PRECIPITATING FACTORS

Even if a patient has not been predisposed by noxious developmental experiences related to sex and death, the triggering event of the terminal illness and its concomitants invariably precipitate sexual adjustments. These associated factors include numerous drugs, including severe chemotherapy, radiation, body changes and body disability. Yet, when it comes to treating the whole person, the medical team has devoted little or no attention to how a patient's sexuality may be altered or denied during the acute or chronic phase of terminal illness. Drugs, procedures and conditions that can modify the physical or emotional aspects of sexuality are seldom, if ever, discussed with patients, their spouses, or families (Jacobson, 1974).

Medical Aspects

Sexual dysfunction can result from many types of physical disorders along with the emotional reactions associated with illness (Masters & Johnson, 1970). It is important to distinguish anatomic and physiological changes from the related psychosocial effects.

Certain hematologic diseases, such as acute and chronic leukemia and Hodgkin's disease, or their treatment, can in and of themselves cause sexual impotence. Other organic conditions associated with malignancies may decrease sexual function. These include diseases of the nervous system, surgery of the pelvic region and endocrine disorders. None of these conditions, however, regularly destroys all sexual function.

Nervous system malignancies. With regard to brain and spinal cord tumors, sexual function is more vulnerable than are the other autonomic functions of urination and defecation. In the male, orgasm and ejaculation are almost always destroyed by a complete upper motor neuron lesion, although erection is preserved. With a complete lower motor neuron lesion, erections are less frequent, but ejaculation and orgasm may occur. With incomplete lesions, whether upper or lower, erection occurs in over 90 percent, and ejaculation and orgasm may be preserved in 32 to 70 percent of patients (Bors & Comarr, 1960). Bors and Comarr conclude that interest in the other sex and desire for intercourse (or regret of impotence) are present in all male patients with spinal cord lesions. There has been much less research on the sexual behavior of women with neurologic disorders. In these cases, women's libido seems to depend on various psychodynamic factors, as well as their age, and appears to be less constant than in males (Ford & Orfirer, 1967).

Diseases that mutilate. Diseases such as cancer of the rectum and colon not only cause deterioration in bodily processes, but also result in the mutilation and deformation of the body. Consequently, the usual forms of sexual functioning may be diminished or destroyed. Radical surgery employed to prolong life may cause sexual impotence in the male, because the nerves of erection are particularly vulnerable to trauma in the dissection of the rectum and the prostate. The average incidence of this dysfunction is 76 percent (Jacobson, 1974). Regardless of age, men scheduled to undergo such surgery should be apprised of the possibility of impotence afterwards. The availability of a willing and able sexual partner is the most important consideration in continuing sexual activity before and after surgery. Amputation of the penis as treatment for carcinoma is also sexually disabling; yet patients have reported satisfactory sexual lives following plastic surgical reconstruction of the penis (Barton, 1972).

The female cancer patient also presents special needs. An operation on her genitals, breasts or reproductive organs can be an emotionally traumatic experience. Surgery in these areas often threatens a woman's self-image, making her feel a less-than-complete female, and symbolically signifying the end of all sexual sensation. Sexual dysfunction in these cases appears to be primarily psychologically based. Women who had radical vulvectomies performed, with total removal of the clitoris, were repeatedly orgastic in coitus, and felt that their sexual responsiveness was existent to the same degree as before surgery (Daly, 1971).

Endocrine disorders. The main endocrine disorder associated with sexual dysfunction is diabetes mellitus. The incidence of erectile impotence in men of all ages with this disorder is two to five times higher than in the general population (Ford & Orfirer, 1967). Retrograde ejaculation is also not uncommon in diabetes. Diabetes is sometimes a secondary reaction to severe physiological stress that is often a concomitant of various malignancies, and to prolonged steroid treatment sometimes used in cancer therapy. It is interesting to note that in a textbook on diabetes, the authors state: "Libido usually persists. . . . Effective therapy includes a sympathetic understanding on the part of the physician and a highly individualized approach to each patient" (Ellenberg & Rifkin, 1962, p. 337).

Effects of drugs. The effects of drugs on sexuality are generally better documented and understood for males than for females. This is partly due to the fact that the male response of erection and ejaculation is more visible and quantifiable than the lubrication and swelling in the female.

Central nervous system depressants, including alcohol, barbiturates, and sedatives do not have a specific effect on the sex centers. However, small doses of sedatives may temporarily remove sexual inhibitions, while larger doses depress all behavior, including sex. Chronic abuse of sedatives seems to generally diminish sexual functioning. Narcotics, used to control pain, seem to reduce the sex drive specifically. However, this finding is based more upon anecdotal report than on systematically controlled study (Kaplan, 1974).

Firmer evidence supports the finding that androgens, often used in treating breast cancer, stimulate sex centers in both males and females. When phenothiazines are used to control nausea induced by chemotherapy,

they can cause "dry" ejaculation to occur. This phenomenon is due to the peripheral autonomic action on the internal vesical sphincter which causes semen to empty into the bladder instead of the urethra. Antianxiety drugs which are also muscle relaxants probably have no direct sexual effects, but sexual interest may increase as a reflection of diminished anxiety. Muscle-relaxing effects may account for the rare orgasm disturbances which are reported (Kaplan, 1974).

Effects of body changes. Body changes which alter appearance and functioning will influence feelings of self-worth, and consequently exert a profound effect on sexual behavior. Extreme weight loss is generally a concomitant of malignancy. Chemotherapy frequently causes hair loss, a devastating blow to the patient's self-image, as well as a traumatizing symbol of pervasive impending losses. Such changes in the patient's appearance can be repugnant to the spouse, causing a further spiraling downward of sexual interest. Patients may use sex to deny their illness. In order to ward off feelings of loss and "asexuality," they may make sexual demands on the spouse which are quite inconsistent with former patterns in their relationship. This attempted overcompensation often meets with failure, which then triggers even more frantic efforts at denial.

Loss of sexual function due to medical factors in terminal illness is less extensive than is often assumed (Ford & Orfirer, 1967). Nonetheless, a self-fulfilling prophecy persists on the part of the patient, spouse and care-giver: a terminally ill individual will neither be interested nor able to function effectively in sex. This assumption may have evolved from people's association of cancer with pain, such that significant others try to spare their loved ones any additional discomfort. Yet this belief is not necessarily valid, for severe pain occurs in less than 15 percent of cancer patients (Exton-Smith, 1961). Thus, emotional reactions of the patient, family, and care-giver are as important in precipitating sexual dysfunction as is the illness itself (Ford & Orfirer, 1967).

Anticipatory Grief

An important aspect of terminal illness is designated "anticipatory grief"—any grief occurring prior to rather than at the time of or following the loss (Aldrich, 1974; Schoenberg, Carr, Peretz, Kutscher & Goldberg, 1974). One might expect a natural disengagement to occur at the same pace on the part of both the patient and spouse. As the former readies himself to "let go," the latter not only is preparing to "let go" of the patient, but may also be seeking new attachments and investments for the future. While this parallel disengagement generally occurs, the patient and his mate are frequently "out of sync" with regard to their individual experiencing of the stages of dying (Kubler-Ross, 1969). Continual confrontation in his hospital environment with the reality of impending death facilitates the patient's move toward acceptance, a part of anticipatory grief. Meanwhile, the healthy spouse may insist on denying reality, and consequently feel betrayed and resentful when the patient does not embrace his own hope for a miracle. This reaction often occurs when couples have been fused in their relationship, continually presenting a "united front" and unable to tolerate any differences between them. Being "out of sync" in the dying process can then cause an irreparable rift between them.

Clinical observations indicate that overt anticipatory grief does not consistently accelerate in degree as the loss approaches. As a matter of fact, the longer a patient is in remission, leading a normal life, the harder it is for the patient and spouse to "keep in touch" with the reality of impending death. The constant balance and flow between denial (forestalling anticipatory grief work) and acceptance (facilitating anticipatory grief work) may prevent a linear acceleration of anticipatory grief over time (Aldrich, 1974).

Long-term hospitalization, generally accompanied by sexual deprivation, may precipitate problems for either partner. The terminally ill patient generally believes that his mate is understanding and accepting of the imposed abstinence. To the contrary, however, the spouse often experiences lowered self-esteem and depression. Anger may be engendered, and expressed directly as chronic irritability or indirectly in the form of seductive behavior toward others. Forced resignation and hopelessness may characterize some situations (Barton, 1972). Ill health may also be a concomitant of separation for the spouse. A study by Chester (1973) indicates that continuing absence of a husband, as well as loss of a husband, appears to precipitate ill health in 85 percent of women who were studied in a state of psychosocial transition. Other researchers (Murray-Parkes, 1964, 1971; Marsden, 1969; Berkman, 1969) confirm this proneness to ill health during periods of anticipatory grief and bereavement. These findings point to the need for society to furnish such individuals with social support systems.

Severe relationship problems may occur if a patient who has been considered terminally ill does not die as predicted. Paradoxically, both partners may experience a sense of letdown with the shift in prognosis. As Peretz (1970) has pointed out: "Even the loss of an old, familiar symptom as a result of medical intervention can result in unpleasant feeling states when the symptom has provided degrees of secondary gain and control over aspects of the environment" (p. 5). In particular, the healthy spouse may be angry. Having worked through his anticipatory grief, and emotionally buried the person, he lacks the reserves to begin the relationship again. Or he may fear getting close because of the threat of having to endure pain of anticipated loss once again. The former patient must shift his role identity from that of a terminally ill to a healthy individual. Whatever sexual estrangement may have occurred in the course of the illness may now be compounded by these major adjustments (Fellner, 1973).

Double-Bind Communication

As well as the dissonance between sexuality and death, the terminally ill patient is confronted by double-bind communication patterns regarding his impending death. All too often, people significant to the patient emit incongruent verbal and nonverbal messages in their attempts to conceal the patient's terminal status from him. These efforts are futile and misguided: managing a host of contradictory cues is virtually impossible, especially since most dying patients suspect and/or want to know the truth (Avorn, 1973; Feifel, 1963; Glaser & Strauss, 1965; Kelley & Frieson, 1950; Kubler-Ross, 1969). The double-bind process triggers a brutal set of social interactions which can be destructive to the patient in all areas of his life, including sexual function (Erickson & Hyerstay, 1974).

Going along with the charade will cost the patient as much psychological energy as it does his significant others. The dissonance between what the patient hears and what he senses leads him to question his own perception of reality. Cut off from access to valid information concerning his condition, he fills in the gaps with his own fantasies and fears. As a result of his own helplessness and frustration in the double-bind situation, the patient may respond to others with misinterpretations, and exhibit little empathy for them. His constricted and inappropriate emotional behavior serves to estrange him even further from his partner.

This "death dishonesty" is often an overlay of the sexual dishonesty which comprises many couples' *modus vivendi*. When communication patterns have been closed in general, and have been deceptive with regard to sexuality, then dishonesty about death will compound the emotional estrangement. Regardless of the quality of communication before the illness, a patient will withdraw into apathy if he realizes that trusted family members have contributed to the deception concerning his impending death (Glaser & Strauss, 1965).

PERPETUATING FACTORS

The hospital environment is pivotal in perpetuating the sexual problems of the terminally ill. At a time when intimate human relationships are most necessary, the typical hospital design deters any nurturing of bonds between mates. Rarely is there a private room for patients to share intimacies with loved ones. The demand for conjugal visits for prisoners has been voiced more strongly than the same rights for long-term hospitalized individuals. As a human being with basic needs, the patient is certainly entitled to private, tranquil conditions for lovemaking when he is able and desirous.

Diminished sexuality can be considered as a category of loss, with the potential concomitants of depression, grief and process of adaptation which may include suicide. Clinical impressions indicate that as one's sexuality is perceived to decline, the incidence of suicidal ideation, suicide attempt and suicide itself increases (Leviton, 1973). A study found that as suicidal ideation shifted to an actual attempt, body-image and sexual self-concept worsened. Case histories of suicidal patients indicated no sexual expression for months prior to their attempt (Henderson, 1971). These findings accord with Farber's (1968) theory of suicide as a "disease of failed hope." In his conceptualization, suicide is a function of vulnerability of the personality (low state of competence) and a deprivation (threat to acceptable life condition).

Emotional withdrawal is a facet of anticipatory grief. Its manifestation by the patient reinforces the commonly held expectation of patient, spouse and care-giver that the sexual life of the terminal patient ends with illness. Furthermore, the patient and spouse may consider it indulgent or inappropriate to seek pleasure during this period, and both will often refrain from making sexual overtures. The healthy spouse in particular may experience guilt over having sexual desires at this time, and the lack of gratification of these needs can lead to depression. An absence of sexual feelings then derives from the grief and depression, resulting in a decreased sense of femininity or masculinity, in turn a threat to self-esteem. A vicious circle culminates in sexual dysfunction. It is not surprising that mates who become intensely depressed during the stage of anticipatory grief, and lack the comfort of a fulfilling sexual relationship are among those who commonly commit suicide. Ironically, the availability of sedatives and tranquilizers from the patient's doctor, prescribed to assuage grief, often adds to the suicide potential (Danto, 1974).

A patient's sexual fantasies and feelings of sexual attachment often transfer to his primary care-giver, in many ways replacing the spouse as love object. The patient's feeling of dependency leads him to perceive the doctor as an all-powerful soother of ills. This emotional investment is reinforced by the fact that during hospitalization, a patient's body is constantly touched and tended by doctors and nurses. Touching in this framework is exempt from the usual boundaries and taboos: even children carry out sexual exploration under the guise of "playing doctor" (Frankfort, 1972). If a woman has been taught that access to her body is only permitted if love is involved, she may reduce dissonance by developing a romantic attachment to her doctor. The same process may apply to men in relation to female doctors and nurses. Thus, the care-giver's use of tactile comfort to minimize the patient's fear and isolation strengthens that attachment. In contrast, the common fear of a spouse to touch a terminally ill patient leads to a weakening of their bond. The efforts of the care-giver are experienced in juxtaposition with the reluctance of the spouse, and thus the parallel disengagement process is reinforced.

RECOMMENDATIONS FOR THERAPEUTIC INTERVENTION

I will now offer recommendations for intervention, based upon the aforementioned factors which can predispose, precipitate, and perpetuate sexual problems for the terminally ill and their significant others.

1. Honest and open communication regarding sex and death must begin in early childhood in order to change dysfunctional societal attitudes around both issues. In terms of death experience, small losses and griefs can prepare a child for facing larger ones. For example, instead of immediately replacing a pet that has died, parents should encourage a child's expressions of grief and his reminiscences, including a burial ritual. When a death occurs in the family, its cause should be explained to the child, and its finality differentiated from the temporary nature of sleep. The open sharing of sorrow can include funeral attendance for the child should he so desire. A similar candor should characterize the topic of sexuality. Hopefully, honest communication in the home could transfer to a hospital setting, obviating the need for people to maintain an often unwanted charade, ultimately so destructive to intimate relationships. If double-bind communication is considered to be causal in precipitating schizophrenia (Weakland, 1966), then it would certainly appear to trigger fear, rage, and withdrawal in the terminally ill.

2. Sexual interest and activity continue to be important in the lives of a great many long-term patients. In one study of 55 male and female patients, over half indicated that they would have liked to discuss sexual problems prior to discharge, preferably with a like-sexed physician (Sadoughi, Leshner & Fine, 1971). Most helping-profession schools give only cursory attention to the areas of

sexuality and terminality. As a result, caregivers are poorly prepared to undertake frank discussions with patients and spouses about sexual problems and practices, much less about facing death. Until these anxiety-laden subjects can be comfortably handled as part of one's ongoing education, it would seem crucial to provide separate courses on sexuality and terminality at this point in curriculum development. The courses should be offered early in the curriculum, and not as a mere afterthought for in-service training. This early exposure would facilitate students' specialization and competence in the areas. Furthermore, a combined didactic-experiential approach would enable individuals to work through their own discomfort, confusion, resistance, and biases. A combined course on sexuality and terminality could synthesize these phenomena as integral parts of the natural life cycle, rather than as subjects ridden with pathology and taboos.

3. The hospital environment must be arranged to encourage ongoing intimacy for patient and spouse at a time when abandonment is so feared. It is an ironic juxtaposition that there is isolation in hospitalization, but virtually no privacy. In any case, the privacy of a regular hospital room could be self-defeating, since it is associated with so much pain and anxiety. A "Quiet Room" furnished with couch, carpet, soft lights, and music is needed to counteract the usual cold hardware of hospital rooms. Such a room could replicate the home ambience which patients miss so badly, and might be used for family and conjugal visits, as well as for group counseling sessions. To further create "home connectedness" as an antidote to disengagement, patients could bring objects from home reminiscent of shared joys, including their own bed linens. A reclining lounge chair should be available in the room of every terminally ill patient, so that a loved one can rest comfortably near a critically ill mate who needs the reassurance of a continued loving presence. Whenever possible, live-in arrangements for spouses should be

made which are not contingent on wealth as is generally the case. The therapeutic effects of maintaining one's personal appearance are well-known. The accessibility of a hairdresser in a hospital setting would do much to refurbish the patient's sense of looking as well as possible. Recreation also provides a means of breaking the monotony, as well as furnishing a valuable mode for social interaction. Play, like sex, is intimately related to health and life, and should be encouraged by having a recreation facility for the terminally ill patient and others who are meaningful to him.

4. Individual and group counseling related to sexual issues must be an ongoing part of total patient care. Any medical workup should include an evaluation of sexual functioning, determined by a sexual history as developed by Wahl (1967). Because the spouse is so often ignored in the treatment process, yet is so vital in giving support to the patient, total care should embrace the patient, spouse, and family from the beginning. Consequently, in the early stages of the illness, sexual problems may be touched upon briefly, in the form of anticipatory guidance, by indicating how sexual drive or performance may be temporarily reduced by drugs, fatigue, or other factors.

Once the patient is over the acute stage of the illness and able to return home, if only for short visits, the clinician should include sexuality in the list of other topics (such as return to work, living arrangements, and so on) to be discussed with the patient. Later, he may ease the way for the patient and/or spouse to disclose any concerns by making some such comment as, "Now that you're home, I expect that you are finding your relationship somewhat different." This statement also reduces threat by implying that the problem is not unique. A most important task for the practitioner is to ascertain the meaning of sexuality in both personal and interpersonal terms for the patient and spouse. If sexuality has played a major role in the person's overall identity, more difficulties can be anticipated, especially if impairment or deprivation of sexual function is involved. Loss of a sexual outlet often precipitates a reactive depression, which is then exacerbated by avoidance of the topic. A further area of avoidance is that of counseling the elderly about sexuality. An individual over sixty-five years of age, terminally ill, and having sexual concerns, is a victim of a "triple whammy." Age is no barrier to a continued sexual life, and when all intimacy is denied the elderly, inappropriate sexual expression may occur (Weinberg, 1971).

As I have implied throughout this chapter, a team approach to handling the issues of sexuality and terminality is almost mandatory. Much loneliness is engendered by hospitalization, particularly at night. Thus, care-givers, whether they be doctors, nurses, clergy, or social workers, should be interchangeably available to the patient and spouse as anxiety rises. Also, instead of becoming surrogates for the spouse, practitioners should encourage mates to touch the patient frequently.

Group counseling is particularly effective in eliciting patient-spouse concerns. It should be a regular, ongoing group, where feelings can be ventilated, information shared and clarified, and coping behavior modeled. The gamut of behavioral approaches to sexual counseling that have been researched and documented could be utilized. These include the therapeutic use of masturbation ("self-exploration"), fantasies, and the regenerating use of the vibrator for women (Annon, 1973). Counseling can also focus on techniques to remediate sexual dysfunction (Masters & Johnson, 1970; Kaplan, 1974), and coital positions which are more comfortable for the disabled (Goldberg, 1960; Romano, 1973). Groups are settings conducive for discussing sex, since most people have had some experience in peer-group disclosure on the topic (Romano, 1973). Thus, groups can be enabling and educational, providing an opportunity for the modeling of desirable behaviors within a nonthreatening context. The support of other individuals facing similar problems engenders hope for being able to live a full, meaningful life in whatever time is left.

CONCLUSION

Terminal illness and impending loss can lead to an intensification of life and serve as a stimulus for a new and richer phase of development. Certainly the common assumption that the sexual life of the terminally ill patient ends with the diagnosis is not borne out by research or clinical observation. Although this attitude is rarely verbalized, its existence is reflected in care-givers' avoidance of the subject. The available literature, however, indicates that sexuality continues as an important part of many patients' lives, although their drive and rate of performance may be reduced. Today, such patients survive longer and with better functional capacity than ever before. Once past the acute stage of illness, they begin to search for a new equilibrium not centered on sickness or disability. It seems both appropriate and necessary therefore to facilitate life-promoting sexual relationships as a factor in any treatment program. As Arnold Toynbee has so poignantly written: "Love cannot save life from death, but it can fulfil life's purpose."

REFERENCES

ALDRICH, C. Some dynamics of anticipatory grief. In Schoenberg et al., *Anticipatory grief*, 1974.

ANNON, J. The therapeutic use of masturbation in the treatment of sexual disorders. In R. Rubin, J. Brody, and J. Henderson, eds. *Advances in behavior therapy*. New York: Academic Press, 1973.

AVORN, J. Beyond dying. *Harper's*, March 1973, 56–64.

BARTON, D. Sexually deprived individuals. *Medical Aspects of Human Sexuality*, February 1972, 88–97.

BEESON, P., AND McDERMOTT, W. *Textbook of medicine*. Philadelphia: W. B. Saunders, 1975.

BERKMAN, P. Spouseless motherhood, psychological stress and physical morbidity. *Journal of Health and Social Behavior*, 1969, 10.

BORS, E., AND COMARR, A. Neurological disturbances of sexual function with special reference to 529 patients with spinal-cord injury. *Urol. Survey*, 10 (1960):191–222.

CHESTER, R. Health and marital breakdown: Some implications for doctors. *Journal of Psychosomatic Research*, 1973, 317–321.

DALY, M. The clitoris as related to human sexuality. *Medical Aspects of Human Sexuality*, 5 (1971):80.

DANTO, B. Drug ingestion and suicide during anticipatory grief. In Schoenberg et al., eds. *Anticipatory grief*, New York: Columbia University Press, 1974.

DAVIS, E. Eros and thanatos: The not so benign neglect. *Texas Report on Biology and Medicine*, 1974, pp. 32, 43–48.

ELLENBERG, M., AND RIFKIN, H. *Clinical Diabetes Mellitus*. New York: McGraw-Hill, 1962.

ERICKSON, R., AND HYERSTAY, M. The dying patient and the double-bind hypothesis. *Omega*, 5 (1974):287–298.

EXTON-SMITH, A. Terminal illness in the aged. *Lancet*, 2(1961):305.

FARBER, M. *Theory of suicide*. New York: Funk and Wagnalls, 1968.

FEIFEL, H. Death. In N. Faberow, ed. *Taboo topics*. New York: Atherton Press, 1963.

FELLNER, C. Family disruption after cancer cure. *American Family Physician*, 8(1973):169–172.

FORD, A., AND ORFIRER, A. Sexual behavior and the chronically ill patient. *Medical Aspects of Human Sexuality*, 1967, 51–61.

FRANKFORT, E. *Vaginal politics*. New York: Bantam Books, 1972.

GLASER, B., AND STRAUSS, A. *Awareness of dying*. Chicago: Aldine, 1965.

GOLDBERG, M. What do you tell patients who ask about coital positions? *Medical Aspects of Human Sexuality*, 1960, 43–48.

HENDERSON, J. Competence, threat, hope and self-destructive behavior: Suicide. Unpublished dissertation. College Park: University of Maryland, 1971.

JACOBSON, L. Illness and human sexuality. *Nursing Outlook*, 22(1974):1, 50–53.

KAPLAN, H. *The new sex therapy*. New York: Brunner/Mazel, 1974.

KELEMAN, S. *Living your dying*. New York: Random House, 1974.

KELLY, W., AND FRIESEN, J. Do cancer patients want to be told? *Surgery* 27(1950):822–826.

KUBLER-ROSS, E. *On death and dying*. New York: Macmillan, 1969.

LEVITON, D. The significance of sexuality as a deterrent to suicide among the aged. *Omega*, 4, No. 2 (1973):163–174.

MARSDEN, D. *Mothers alone*. London: Allen Lane, 1969.

MASTERS, W., AND JOHNSON, V. *Human sexual inadequacy*. Boston: Little, Brown, 1970.

MURRAY-PARKES, C. Psycho-social transitions: A field for study. *Social Science and Medicine*, 1971, 5.

———. Effects of bereavement on physical and mental health—A study of the medical records of widows. *British Medical Journal*, 1964, pp. 2, 274.

NAGY, M. The child's view of death. In H. Feifel, ed. *The meaning of death*. New York: McGraw-Hill, 1959.

PERETZ, D. Development, object-relationships and loss. In Schoenberg et al., eds. *Loss and grief*, New York: Columbia University Press, 1974.

ROMANO, M. Sexual counseling in groups. *The Journal of Sex Research*, 9, No. 1 (1973):69–78.

———. Sexuality and the disabled female. *Accent on Living*, 1973, 27–35.

SADOUGHI, W., LESHNER, M., AND FINE, H. Sexual adjustment in a chronically ill and physically disabled population: A pilot study. *Arch of Phys. Med. and Rehab.*, 1971, 311–317.

SCHOENBERG, B., CARR, A., KUTSCHER, A., PERETZ, D., AND GOLDBERG, I., EDS. *Anticipatory grief*. New York: Columbia University Press, 1974.

SCHOENBERG, B., CARR, A., PERETZ, D., AND KUTSCHER, A. *Loss and grief*. New York: Columbia University Press, 1970.

WAHL, C. Psychiatric techniques in the taking of a sexual history. In C. Wahl, ed. *Sexual problems: Diagnosis and treatment in medical practice*. New York: Free Press, 1967.

WEAKLAND, J. The double-bind hypothesis of schizophrenia and three-party interaction. In D. Jackson, ed. *The etiology of schizophrenia*. New York: Basic Books, 1960.

WEINBERG, J. Sexuality in later life. *Medical Aspects of Human Sexuality*. 1971, 216–227.

ZELIGS, R. Children's attitudes toward death. *Mental Hygiene*, 51 (1967):393–396.

THE FABLE OF THE RESTORED LEFT ARM
Virginia M. Satir

Once upon a time thousands of years ago, a man was standing on a cliff, high above some jagged rocks below. It happened, as he was standing there, that another man passed by very close to him and accidentally bumped him.

Automatically, the first man's left arm swung out, knocking over the cliff the second man, who somersaulted and made loud and discordant symphonylike sounds as he went over. This had never been heard or seen before.

Some other people, who happened to be near enough to see, became excited with the movement and the sound and began emulating the first man. The rocks below were soon covered with the broken bodies of the people thrown over.

Other people saw this and said there was something wrong with what was going on, so a big investigation was held. All the experts came. It was a very short investigation because *it* was so obvious what the trouble was—THE LEFT ARM.

This required immediate action. A law was soon passed, forbidding anyone to expose his or her Left Arm, or to use it if necessary on any occasion except one hour on his or her birthday, and then only completely in private. Anyone caught exposing or using the Left Arm could be deported, beheaded, or imprisoned. The fact that there were millions of people whose Left Arms had never gotten them into any trouble made no difference. LEFT ARMS WERE DANGEROUS. Every care must be taken to avoid this danger.

This was going to be very hard because Left Arms are very handy to have around, especially if you want to lift anything. But people tried hard. After all, who wants to be deported, imprisoned, or beheaded? They covered their Left Arms very carefully. Only right arms could show. The fact that every left side of a person now had a peculiar hump was obvious to everyone, which, indeed, made them look very ugly. However, no one mentioned the hump or the ugliness except in very low whispers here and there; mostly it was indicated only in looks.

People did try. They walked sideways past each other, so the hump would not show so much. This helped a little.

They got busy building elaborate structures in their homes to hide from one another. After all, it was important to keep the Left Arm clean.

Of course, all of this was extremely difficult, especially at the beginning. People were always having the urge to straighten out their arms. It was very uncomfortable. Many, many persons lost their lives in these early days because they would not control themselves. Some few did manage. They used various means, one of which was to go about only when there were no other people. This was worrisome and not very reliable because one never knew who was going to be popping out of some doorway. People said that people were not friendly any more. They seemed suspicious of one another.

Things eased a little in the succeeding generation. They bound babies' Left Arms tightly to their bodies as soon as they were born. This way maybe babies would not know what they were missing, but they heard about it anyway from the whispers in the alleys from adults who did know.

What adults really wanted to do was to cut off the offending Left Arm, at birth, but they could not quite bring themselves to do this. It seemed so inhuman. However, with some children, by the time they were twelve, the binding had worked so well that the Left Arm just fell off naturally. That was good. It left the hump, but it removed the temptation.

Most of the Left Arms, however, remained very small and shrivelled. (It takes a long time for the body to mutate such a big change.) No one knew for sure but there were stories that fingernails were growing on the Left Arms, and "they" said some would measure twenty feet if uncurled. "They" said that the weight of the fingernails was what made the hand so heavy, which was why the body was off balance. There were many other stories about the ugliness of the Left Arm. It was scary to think about. All the worst dreams were about Left Arms. Children were constantly warned about Left Arms from the cradle on up.

Of course, the backs of all people did become very crooked. One of their arms was used so much more. Everything one did had to be done by one hand. When the people played the game of "Catch the Greased Pig," which was *the* national game, it truly was a great accomplishment. There were very few winners. In fact, there was only one. They made a statue for him. This kept hope alive.

Back pains became very frequent, and of course there were many operations, but somehow that did not seem to help much. (The hump was considered normal, so no one ever thought of connecting that to back trouble.) Backs just kept getting more and more crooked, left arms smaller and smaller, and left sides humpier and humpier.

The research of that day, of course, corroborated what was going on.

One day, an especially daring man in his late 50s, who had had many questions, decided to take *a horrible risk*. He could see that society was falling apart. Something had to be done. He worked out a very secret plan to bring together a few trusted friends in a cave he had found far below the earth's surface, where he was sure to be safe.

After much humiliation, embarrassment, and anxiety, they opened up the dreaded subject of Left Arms. Then they began to look at them, and then TOUCH them. As this happened, the Left Arms had the experience of moving. Then the people noticed that they had strange reactions in the rest of their body which made them think that maybe there was a connection between their Left

Arms and the rest of their body. Later on they even wondered about their Left Arms and friendliness.

Through many trials and tribulations, the small group met and experimented. They came up with the unmistakable conclusion that they *must* for survival's sake, change the law on Left Arms and restore the Left Arm to its rightful place. It was clear now that not only survival, but health and progress of the world depended upon making this change. This would be a big and dangerous job. Many feared that they would not live long enough to see it accomplished.

There were little breakthroughs here and there—enough to keep up hope. Now only a few of their number had found their way to jails.

Gradually new people who were considered trustworthy were added to the group. The news of what was going on leaked out and traveled swiftly through the underground. The movement had begun.

Many years later, one of "them" was elected governor, and to everyone's surprise, another was elected president. Lots of people thought that fraud was involved, but luckily, they lived in a democracy and people had voted by secret ballot.

After the elections, bigger and bigger changes came until one day it was possible for everyone to show their Left Arms openly, talk about them, and even admire them. There were even contests about who had the loveliest one.

People found out how easy it was to lift things with two arms, rather than one. Back troubles began disappearing. Eyesight got better because people did not have to walk sidewards anymore. You see, from so much sideways moving, the eyes had become very narrow and vision had become very distorted.

When people could see openly, the human body without the hump and the crooked back was truly beautiful.

People would often be heard to say afterwards, "Can you imagine that a long time ago in the dark ages, people thought Left Arms were dangerous!"

I don't think we are yet as far along as our fable, but we are going in that direction.

INDEX

NAMES

SUBJECTS